Psychotherapy in Everyday Life

Psychotherapy in Everyday Life details how clients make therapy work in their everyday lives by using what they learned in private sessions. Therapy cannot fulfill its purpose until clients can make it work outside the therapy room in relation to the concerns, people, and places of their everyday lives. Research on therapy has largely ignored these efforts. Based on session transcripts and interviews with a family of four about their everyday lives, this book shows the extensive and varied work that clients do to make their therapy work across places. Processes of change and learning are seen in a new perspective, and it is shown that expert practices depend on how persons conduct their everyday lives. To grasp this, Ole Dreier developed a theory of persons that is based on how people conduct their lives in social practice. This theory is grounded in critical psychology and social practice theory and is also relevant for understanding other expert practices such as education.

Ole Dreier is a professor in the department of psychology at the University of Copenhagen, where he received both his M.A. and Ph.D. He is a leading scholar in activity theory and critical psychology in Europe and combines work on the development of theory with research directed at developing practices in the fields of psychotherapy, health care, and education. He is a member of the Danish interdisciplinary Center for Health, Humanity, and Culture and an approved specialist in psychotherapy and supervision. Dreier has held the Wilhelm-Wundt chair in Leipzig, and he has been affiliated with universities in Mexico, Germany, and the United States. He is a member of the International Society for Theoretical Psychology and the International Society for Cultural and Activity Research.

Learning in Doing: Social, Cognitive, and Computational Perspectives

SERIES EDITOR *EMERITUS*

John Seely Brown, *Xerox Palo Alto Research Center*

GENERAL EDITORS

Roy Pea, *Professor of Education and the Learning Sciences and Director, Stanford Center for Innovations in Learning, Stanford University*

Christian Heath, *The Management Centre, King's College, London*

Lucy A. Suchman, *Centre for Science Studies and Department of Sociology, Lancaster University, UK*

(*Series list continued after Index*)

Psychotherapy in Everyday Life

OLE DREIER
University of Copenhagen

CAMBRIDGE
UNIVERSITY PRESS

CAMBRIDGE UNIVERSITY PRESS
Cambridge, New York, Melbourne, Madrid, Cape Town, Singapore, São Paulo, Delhi

Cambridge University Press
32 Avenue of the Americas, New York, NY 10013-2473, USA

www.cambridge.org
Information on this title: www.cambridge.org/9780521880176

First published 2008

Printed in the United States of America

A catalog record for this publication is available from the British Library.

Library of Congress Cataloging in Publication Data

Dreier, Ole.
Psychotherapy in everyday life / Ole Dreier.
   p. ; cm. – (Learning in doing)
Includes bibliographical references and index.
ISBN 978-0-521-88017-6 (hardback) – ISBN 978-0-521-70613-1 (pbk.)
1. Psychotherapy.   I. Title.   II. Series.
[DNLM: 1. Psychotherapy.   2. Family Relations.   3. Patient Compliance.
4. Patients – psychology.   5. Social Adjustment.   WM 420 D7705p 2008]
RC480.5.D74   2008
616.89′14–dc22   2007013206

ISBN   978-0-521-88017-6 hardback
ISBN   978-0-521-70613-1 paperback

Contents

Series Foreword

This series for Cambridge University Press is widely known as an international forum for studies of situated learning and cognition.

Innovative contributions are being made by anthropology; by cognitive, developmental, and cultural psychology; by computer science; by education; and by social theory. These contributions are providing the basis for new ways of understanding the social, historical, and contextual nature of learning, thinking, and practice that emerges from human activity. The empirical settings of these research inquiries range from the classroom to the workplace, to the high-technology office, and to learning in the streets and in other communities of practice. The situated nature of learning and remembering through activity is a central fact. It may appear obvious that human minds develop in social situations and extend their sphere of activity and communicative competencies. But cognitive theories of knowledge representation and learning alone have not provided sufficient insight into these relationships.

This series was born of the conviction that new and exciting interdisciplinary syntheses are underway as scholars and practitioners from diverse fields seek to develop theory and empirical investigations adequate for characterizing the complex relations of social and mental life, and for understanding successful learning wherever it occurs. The series invites contributions that advance our understanding of these seminal issues.

Roy Pea
Christian Heath
Lucy Suchman

Preface

The project I present in this book grew out of a series of "Theory–Practice–Conferences" in which researchers and practitioners, coming from the tradition of critical psychology, met twice a year, mostly in Berlin, for a period of more than ten years to study psychological practices. These conferences pursued two related goals. The first objective was to study the conduct of psychological practice, broadly taken, in order to become able to describe and understand it better and thereby find better ways to conduct it. As a means to that end, we developed a guideline, the so-called practice-portrait (Markard and Holzkamp 1989), for the analysis of professional psychological practices. The second aim was to work out a better understanding of how to base the conduct of psychological practice on a theoretical conception, that is, of how to use concepts as a basis for analysis and conduct and, at the same time, to utilize the analyses of issues in practice to foster the development of concepts and theories. My project was presented and discussed several times at these conferences.

It was also inspired by my involvement for many years in collaborations between university-based researchers and psychology practitioners in Denmark, many of whom had a strong interest in critical psychology. Thus, I had collaborated for some time with members of the staff at the outpatient unit of child psychiatry where this project took place. It also grew out of my activities as a therapist, supervisor, trainer, and teacher. For thirty years I have used these activities as vehicles for research in my position as a faculty member at a university department. Much of this research has been aimed at developing a critique of problematic aspects of current psychological practice and current understandings of it. This critique was not an end in itself but a means to reach better understandings and identify possibilities for improving practice. Still, critique is necessary because particular assumptions stand in the way of changing our approach to and conduct of practice.

Many colleagues and institutions have contributed to the development of my project. The key figure in critical psychology, Klaus Holzkamp, has been the major theoretical and personal inspiration for my work, and he contributed many important ideas to this project – in the Theory–Practice–Conferences and on many other occasions. I discussed the project with colleagues during my stay as Wundt professor in Leipzig, as well as with fellow members of the Center for Health, Humanity, and Culture in Denmark, headed by Uffe Juul Jensen. Jean Lave has been a source of profound inspiration and strong support throughout, and during my stays at UC Berkeley and hers in Copenhagen. The University of California Humanities Center provided a chance for presentation and discussion during my stay there in 2001, as did the Danish research network on nonscholastic learning, which I co-led with Steinar Kvale and Steen Wackerhausen. Responses from colleagues at other conferences and from my students in Copenhagen spurred the project along. Initially, the Danish Research Council for the Humanities provided funding for a research assistant to do the interviews and part of my later work through its support of the first four years of my work in the Center for Health, Humanity, and Culture. Finally, the Spencer Foundation provided support through a collaborative Small Grant 2000000053 obtained by Jean Lave. My research assistant, Lisbeth Moltzen, and I developed and updated the interview guide together, and Lisbeth played a very constructive role in conducting and developing the interviews. My cotherapist in the chosen case, Ingrid Gehl, graciously contributed her time and expertise in the field to the project. And over the years my wife, Dorte Bukh, lent her ears and important advice, as a practitioner in the field, to my musings and questions.

Introduction

This book is about psychotherapy. But it does not share the perspective normally adopted in the specialist research literature in clinical psychology. Instead, it sheds light on therapy from a perspective that plays a minor role in that literature. Rather than looking at therapist interventions in sessions, I look at the key role of the clients' experiences and activities in bringing about the outcomes of their therapy. What is more, since therapy is meant to work on the clients' troubles in their everyday lives outside sessions, I study the interplay between sessions and the clients' ongoing everyday lives between and after sessions in other places. I did so by following what goes on in the therapy sessions as well as in other social contexts of clients' ordinary lives outside sessions throughout a small number of family therapy cases. Indeed, in order to reach a more complete understanding of the workings of therapy, we need materials that cover what goes on in sessions as well as in other contexts of the clients' lives.

But the book is even more about persons in social practice. I use therapy as a case in point to study clients as persons changing in their ongoing everyday lives, among other things, in response to the deliberate change efforts of their therapy. However, as soon as we stop believing that personal change in relation to therapy occurs only within sessions, we need a theory that takes appropriate account of the fact that persons change and learn in the course of moving through a set of diverse social contexts: their sessions, home, school, workplace, and so forth. It should allow us to grasp how personal changes and learning are accomplished in a complex personal, social practice. Such a conception is also necessary for understanding the workings of other specialist, professional practices on their clientele. What we see in relation to specialist practices, in fact, reflects a much more general and basic feature of what it means and takes to be a person in social structures of practice. Persons live their lives participating in diverse social contexts with diverse purposes, scopes, and coparticipants. They link these parts of their lives in particular ways and pursue their personal concerns across them. We need a theory of persons built on recognizing these basic facts. Such an approach to personhood is of general value for understanding persons living their lives in social practice. In this book I present my work on developing such a conception of personhood. The most crucial theoretical background in psychology for my study and the conception I develop is critical psychology (see, first of all, Holzkamp 1983;

Tolman 1994; Tolman and Maiers. 1991), which is a variant of the activity theory of the Russian sociohistorical school developed by Leont'ev (1978; 1979) and others.

I approach therapy as a social practice and persons as participants in social practice. Researching and theorizing about both in new ways based on a theory of social practice has led me to crucial new insights. This new approach has also contributed to the study of social practice by expanding our understanding of persons in social practice and by studying a field of social practice, psychotherapy, that has barely been studied from the point of view of a theory of social practice and may seem particularly intractable to such an approach. Additionally, I combine a situated approach with a new emphasis on the contextual and structural arrangements of social practice, which adds to our conception of social practice.

My approach to the study of therapy and persons should also be relevant for researchers in other fields of social practice. In fact, its development was deeply inspired by comparisons with studies of other fields of practice. Uncovering similarities and differences between fields provoked, stimulated, and consolidated my viewpoint. Of primary importance is the inspiration offered by Jean Lave's research on learning and education, which encouraged me to launch a similar approach to the study of persons learning in social practice (Dreier 1999a; 1999c; 2001; 2003). Likewise, my project inspired other related projects on various topics, such as child development (Højholt 1999; 2001), genetic counseling of lives at risk (Huniche 2002; 2003), rehabilitation following brain injuries (Borg 2002) and the use of facilities at home after the injury (Forchhammer 2006), educational trajectories of young immigrants (Mørck 2006), and training interventions in the Nigerian prison system (Jefferson 2004).

The book falls into four parts. Chapters 1–3 make up the first part. In chapter 1 I establish the need for my approach and this study in relation to the existing research on psychotherapy. In chapter 2 I introduce my theoretical framework on social practice and persons in social practice, and in chapter 3 I introduce the design and conduct of my study. The next two parts of the book focus on a detailed analysis of a case from my study: a family of four undergoing a prolonged outpatient family therapy. Chapters 4–7 make up the second part of the book. Chapters 4 and 5 address how clients link their participation in sessions and in other social contexts of their ordinary lives. Building on this understanding, chapters 6 and 7 analyze changes of clients and their problems. Chapters 8–11 make up the third part of the book. It begins with a theoretical chapter. Chapter 8 introduces the concepts of personal conduct of everyday life and the personal life trajectory. These concepts provide a broader understanding of the persons in the case. I use these concepts to analyze the two daughters in chapter 9 and the two parents in chapter 10. In chapter 11 I round off the third part by analyzing the conduct of their everyday family life and the unfolding of their family trajectory. Chapter 12 makes up the fourth part of the book. Here I characterize the theoretical and empirical outcomes of my case study and the possible uses of such outcomes.

1 Re-Searching Psychotherapy as a Social Practice

In this chapter I ground the need for my approach and study of the social practice of clients in relation to representatives of characteristic positions in the existing research on psychotherapy.

1.1. The Received View in Research on Psychotherapy

The following framework about the practice of therapy dominates research on psychotherapy: In therapy sessions a professional expert acts on a client with a particular diagnosis (or problem) by means of a particular technique and thereby causes a particular outcome in his client. Many studies include other subordinate factors too. One such factor is about the client and the relationship between therapist and client (Hougaard 2004). But it is seen as the obligation of the therapist, and as a crucial part of his technique and expertise, to account for, call forth, and control those other factors. Studies of them should ultimately add to the prevailing understanding of a publicly accountable practice of therapy as caused by what the therapist does in sessions. Some basic canons of this framework are crucial for grounding my critical arguments in this book.

Technical Rationality

The therapist's expertise consists in a general knowledge from which a set of techniques are derived as professional know-how. The therapist is to effect his client's treatment by applying this knowledge and set of techniques on her. So the concrete conduct of therapy is ultimately derived from a general knowledge. The vast literature about the conduct of therapy addresses therapists with the following message: as an expert you should know and consider all this; you are the sole knower and the ultimately responsible agent and cause of this practice; in your practice you should follow and apply this body of knowledge; if you do so properly, you will cause in your client the general effect that we found. Schön (1983) calls this point of view the technical rationality of modern professionalism. It presupposes a firmly bounded and specialized general knowledge, well-defined general problems and means, and agreement about predefined and fixed ends. Professional practice then simply consists in the application of this general expertise. However, "uncertainty, complexity, instability, uniqueness and value conflict" abound in professional practice (17).

3

Technical rationality, therefore, falls short of offering an appropriate basis for professional practice.

According to technical rationality, a theory offers practitioners direct answers to their questions about what to do in concrete cases and situations. In fact, the argument that a theory offers a general means for practitioners to find out what to do by observing and analyzing in concrete cases and situations is often met with disappointment and frustration. Therapeutic practice is also believed to follow from what the expert does. Yet, the conduct and outcome of therapy is not up to him alone. Other persons are involved in creating them. Good therapists acknowledge and consider this – whether things go as they intended or not. The conduct and outcome of therapy are a distributed effect of what everyone who is somehow involved does and thinks (Dreier 1998b, 627). So it is a mistake to assume that a therapist merely needs a good theory and techniques to succeed and, when he does not succeed, to blame the theory and techniques he adopted for the failure. No theory and techniques can fulfill such demands. If the relation between theory and practice is understood this way, problems of self-evaluation arise for practitioners and between practitioners and researchers (Dreier 1983; 1993b). We need a different conception of this relation. I argue that we need a theory of the social practice of therapy in structures of social practice with multiple participating parties.

Medical Model

The dominating framework is an application of the medical model on psychotherapy (e.g., Bohart and Tallman 1999, 5–14). Its abstract concepts of diagnosis, technique, outcome, session, therapist, and client stem from this model as does the claim that standard procedures of treatment applied to standard diseases and problems produce standard outcomes (Jensen 1987).

Institutional Epistemology

The diagnosis and treatment of diseases and problems are understood from the position and perspective of medical institutions, that is, the institutionalized diagnosis and treatment of mental illness. Practice in these institutions gradually leads to an understanding marked by the special institutional arrangement it emerged from. More specifically, the outlook is affected by the position, perspective, and stakes of therapeutic experts in relation to patients in these institutions. This includes how therapists cope with diagnosing and treating their patients in the special situations of these institutions and the behaviors and mental states they may observe their patients exhibiting here (Prior 1993). Following Foucault, Gordon (1980) calls it an institutional epistemology (see also Rose 1996b, 60–62).

Guild Innovationism

The framework advocates that the decisive condition for improving the lives of patients is to subject them to professional treatment. Accordingly, professionals should be given means to develop their practice. Lewis et al. call this belief guild innovationism (1991, 6) arguing that

> When the mentally ill were treated in large state institutions, both psychi-
> atric and sociological theories viewed patients as if they were a homogenous
> group.... Regardless of disease or label, patients were seen as victims. If their
> situation was to be made better, the system of care had to be changed. Because
> they were victims, the key to improvement lay in changing what others did to
> them. (3)

Decontextualization

The prevalent assumptions about the relation between theory/techni-
que and practice imply a particular definition of the practice of therapy and
delineation of what to study in the wider social practice of therapy. The practice of therapy is seen as occurring exclusively inside an isolated situation: the
session. Although sessions actually are particular parts of clients' lives elsewhere and of therapists' institutional work practices, the conduct of sessions
is assumed to be independent thereof and the mode of working of therapy
to consist in an immediate link between cause and effect in sessions. This is
where the powers of expertise are exerted and consumed and the expert may
witness how the client is reacting. Therapy researchers look for the factors
that bring about the treatment effect in the session, though they do not yet
agree on which factors and details of these sessions really are the effective
mechanisms of therapy. Even so, they are convinced that they must be found
exclusively in the session. This belief also serves the professional interest in
documenting that the therapist is the cause of his client's cure and fits with the
methodological credo of a science of variables (Holzkamp 1983), which must
be isolated and analyzed as immediate links between cause and effect. All the
same, abstracting the session from its links with its participants' practices in
other places amounts to a decontextualized understanding of the very same
therapy (Dreier 1993a; 1993b) that promotes a naturalized notion of diseases,
diagnosis, treatment, and outcome (Smith 1990). The actual contextuality of
the social practice of therapy then goes unnoticed. Neither the institutional
practice of therapists nor the lives of clients in other places surface in the
account of how treatment works. We are left with an institutional epistemology that denies the institutional nature of its understanding and expertise and
dissolves the particular contextuality of the session into a seemingly unobtru-
sive and insignificant container – a privileged nowhere of mental change.

1.2. Process Studies in Sessions

The understanding of the workings of therapy in isolated sessions is carried over from outcome studies to process studies about the unfolding of therapy across time to bring about treatment outcomes. Effective processes in sessions are here construed as immediate causal links across a sequence of isolated
sessions. Though much else goes on between sessions, the process of therapy

is re-construed as a sequence of sessions linked with each other and nothing else in a causal chain across time. The arrangement of a sequence of sessions, of course, links these really separate events with each other, but these links are not immediate and exclusive. Process studies re-construe the course of therapy as a continuous process across discontinuous occasions. Interpretations by therapists and researchers are the means by which this continuity is construed. Thus, in their interpretation, narrative accounts of therapy (e.g., Mattingly 1998; McLeod 1997; Polkinghorne 1988; Rennie 1994b) construe a continuity and wholeness of process and meaning across time (Dreier 2000). We find a similar framing of studies and interpretations in other fields of professional, institutional practice. The social practice of education is an obvious example. Here a student's learning of a school subject is construed as the effect of teaching in isolated lessons. At the end of a school year, the student's level in the subject is assessed as the sum effect of immediate causal links between lessons in that subject, which are scattered across the timetables of days and weeks among many other school subjects and much else in the life of the student.

Process studies of therapy increasingly argue for an eclectic or integrative understanding of therapy. The argument is directed against deriving practice from one theory but not against the idea of deriving practice from theory with the accruing problems mentioned previously, as long as several theories are included and the practitioner himself decides the mix. The argument also goes against the formation of theories as competing schools of therapy and private, professional societies occupying particular specialties, populations, or domains of therapeutic practice (Dreier 1989; 1993b; Markard and Holzkamp 1989).

In line with this trend, nonspecific or common factors are claimed to lie behind therapeutic change regardless of theoretical orientation (e.g., Hougaard 2004; Lambert 1992). These factors are (a) the extratherapeutic factors; (b) the therapy relationship; (c) the therapeutic techniques used; and (d) expectancy, hope, and placebo. Attention has moved away from deriving therapy from a theory and its associated technology, and numerous process studies (e.g., Siegfried 1995) seek new ways of understanding the process and dynamics of therapy.

Greenberg's (1999) programmatic proposal for the study of psychotherapy represents a strong empiricist trend in this research. He claims that the field has been too closely tied to psychological theories and hopes that it is now "mature enough to develop a 'basic science' of psychotherapy. . . . Science proceeds by observation, measurement, explanation, and prediction. Limited attention, however, has been paid to the initial steps. In fact, intensive, rigorous observation of how change takes place probably has been the most sorely neglected" (1467). He advocates

> the intensive analysis of in-therapy performance. One of the major difficulties inherent in the current use of clinical trials or comparative outcome studies is the assumption of direct and linear cause–effect relations between independent

variable (treatment) and dependent variables (outcomes) without taking into account the complex performances that occur between treatment delivery and outcome effects. Rather than treating therapy as a black box, looking only at input and output variables, we need to study and track the complex performance patterns and interaction sequences that constitute psychotherapy. (1467–1468)

Evidently, such process studies also address what happens in isolated therapy sessions, where the effective ingredients of therapy are sought in its particular detailed features. Greenberg has a later phase of research in mind. Once solid, general empirical findings are established, it will be time to construct other theories. But he seems to see them as related to practice in a way similar to what I argue is problematic.

A distinction is often made between two strategies of process studies (Hougaard 2004; 1996). The first strategy uses direct methods of observation considered to be more objective, while the second uses indirect methods of asking participants about the sessions afterwards via questionnaires or interviews. While the first rests on a third-person perspective on clients and therapists, the latter builds to some degree on their first-person perspectives and thus introduces a plurality of perspectives to the same process. Greenberg proposes using both strategies, first closely observing actual behavior in sessions and afterward asking "participants about their subjective experience at particular moments to further illuminate what is occurring in these moments using tape-assisted Interpersonal Process Recall" (1999, 1468).

1.3. Professional Centeredness and Desubjectification of Clients and Therapists

All the same, "the majority of writing and research has been and continues to be on the therapeutic technique, intra-session therapist activity, and the development of treatment models – factors that make a much smaller (15%) contribution to overall psychotherapy outcome" (Miller, Duncan, and Hubble 1997, 37). So we may add a sixth characteristic of the received framework. It is professional centered, that is, it understands therapy from the position and perspective of the professional practitioner – or his ally, the researcher – and highlights what he should know and do in the session (Dreier 1993a; 1993b).

Upon closer inspection, we here see a seventh characteristic. Much writing on therapy is quite desubjectified (Dreier 1993a; 1993b). This is a paradox since psychotherapy deals with eminently subjective matters. Nonetheless, most writing is couched in a third-person perspective, as seen from the position and perspective of someone other than the person whom the statement is about. The ensuing confusion of perspectives reduces our chances of a fuller understanding of the participating persons. Thus, most writing about the therapist sees him as a vehicle for the treatment of his client, thinking, feeling, and doing what he does for his client's sake (Osterkamp 2003), as if his reasons for acting the way he does really could be derived from somebody else. This leads to a skewed and reduced understanding of the therapist as a subject in his own right conducting his work in particular structures of social practice. These and other aspects of therapist subjectivity are relegated from the session into another special setting: the supervision. So, while the majority of the literature in a sense centers on the therapist, it offers a poor understanding of him as an acting and experiencing person. Conversely, most writing about clients is seen from the position and perspective of the therapist or an associated researcher. Clients are described as they are interpreted in a professional centered, third-person perspective and not from their own position and perspective. Much has been written about clients, but they are understood too abstractly from the positioned perspective of professionals and researchers. Even in studies giving voice to clients, they are primarily asked about their perspectives on the workings of their therapy, that is, the sessions, the techniques used, and the therapist, again making them talk about someone else (the therapist) rather than about themselves as acting and experiencing persons in a broad sense. So, we cannot trust the understanding of clients such a framework offers. Miller, Duncan, and Hubble give a vivid account of the professional centeredness and third-person understanding reminding us that when clients enter therapy, they are perceived to be less than competent, to have an understanding of themselves that cannot be trusted, to be bearers of pathology rather than full persons, to be resistant, and to be targets of intervention. Therapists, on the other hand, are seen as masters of coping with this and of curing their clients. "There are hundreds of books about great therapists but few, if any, books about great clients" (1997, 24–25). At professional workshops and conferences, clients are turned into live demonstrations of therapist mastery.

We can now add an eighth characteristic of the framework. A professional privilege or monopoly of interpretation dominates the field and inhibits the articulation of the perspective of clients in a social practice supposed to exist for their sake (Dreier 1991). Because of the therapists' involvement in this practice, they focus on particular features of client subjectivity but gloss over and conceal others by their interpretations. The therapists' desires to do well as therapists for their clients affect their understanding of clients. As time passes, a professional culture of interpretation about their clientele unfolds as part of the existing institutional epistemology (Dreier et al. 1988). It comprises a core blindness (Lave and Wenger 1991) because therapists take for granted, ignore, or reinterpret particular features of their practice.

1.4. Client Perspectives in Sessions

With no comprehensive research on client perspectives, therapists have to create a culture of therapeutic interpretation of clients in their practice. This professional-centered culture of interpretation easily sidetracks the study of client perspectives. Scholars proposing studies of client perspectives assign a different status to client perspectives than to those of therapists and researchers. Therapist perspectives are claimed to represent "expert clinicians' cognitive maps," whereas client perspectives merely represent "clients' internal experience" (Greenberg 1999, 1468). Or, researchers and clinicians possess scientific knowledge about diseases, whereas patients possess experiences of illness characterized by the cultural, social, and personal meaning of symptoms and suffering for the sick persons, members of their family, and wider social network (Kleinman 1988). Still, studies of client and therapist perspectives on their shared session show that they experience even this shared context differently. Therapists and clients tell different stories about the same therapy (Yalom and Elkin 1974), and retrospective accounts by clients offer perspectives significantly different from practitioners (Sands 2000).

The growing trend to study client perspectives indicates a change in research, as seen in *From the Mental Patient to the Person* (Barham and Hayward 1991); that is, investigators are going beyond studying homogenized categories of diseases and treatment in the medical model. Yet, almost all studies of client perspectives focus on their experiences of sessions, techniques and therapists, so they are studies about being a client, as in *On Being a Client* (Howe 1993), rather than about persons living troubled lives. After all, attending therapy is only a part of clients' lives. In their book *User-friendly Family Therapy*, Reimers and Treacher (1995) thus report studies of client perspectives on the therapeutic arrangements, the therapists, and their interventions in the interest of using these perspectives to evaluate traditions of therapy and to develop professional technologies. By zooming in on clients' perspectives on the interventions and their therapists, Reimers and Treacher inadvertently turn away from studying clients as persons in the full sense of the term and toward studying the professional therapeutic practice and therapists from the third-person perspective of their clients. In doing so, they partly desubjectify the interviewed clients and give in to the pull of professional centeredness. Such studies tell us little about what clients learn and do apart from experiencing and consuming these professional services.

A few studies of clients' relations to their ongoing therapy report findings their therapists would normally not come to know about. This indicates a need for separate studies of client perspectives. In deference to their therapists, clients do not report all they are thinking to their therapists (Rennie 1994a). Clients appraise their therapists' plans and strategies, contrast them with their own preferences, and sometimes feel critical of limitations in their therapy and therapists. Nor do clients always find the therapists' responses most helpful, and they sometimes "creatively reinterpret the response so they could use it to stay on their own track" (Tallman and Bohart 1999, 48–49). Such findings question the widely held assumption that good therapy presupposes a good understanding between the therapist and the client, which is taken to mean that they basically share the same understanding. Above all, the therapist's expertise is seen in his ability to understand his client and to do so even better than the client herself does. The attributed lack of self-understanding is seen as an indication of the client's need for treatment, and client progress is seen as the client coming to share the same understanding as her therapist. If clients and therapists hold on to different understandings, that is believed to counteract the workings of therapy and taken as a sign that something is problematic and not going well. Conflicts between them may, of course, become prominent, but therapeutic traditions contain concepts to deal with such conflicts by treating them as expressions of resistance, and so forth; in other words, they are regarded in ways that support therapists' control over their practice.

One study of the relation between client and therapist perspectives on their shared sessions played a crucial role for my project. In a small number of cases Eliasson and Nygren (1983) confronted therapists and clients separately after sessions with video recordings of the past session and interviewed them about their experiences thereof. In all cases studied, therapist and client experiences were strikingly diverse. Asked to identify important episodes in the session, therapists and clients pointed to different episodes. The clients had understandings of their therapists' goals, plans, and intentions that differed from their therapists. The same was true for the therapists' understandings of their clients' experiences and reactions. Still, therapists rarely find out that their clients' perspectives may differ so much from their own. They are highly surprised upon seeing glimpses of contrasting perspectives and normally justify the differences by referring to their clients' lack of background in the therapeutic traditions. Besides demonstrating the need to capture the perspectives of clients as well as therapists, Eliasson and Nygren's study raises other nagging questions: If therapy is experienced so differently by clients, how then are we to account for its phenomena, dynamics, and effects? It seems doubtful to make do with accounting for therapy from the perspective of the therapist – or the researcher. Do therapists and researchers instead need a better understanding of the diverse perspectives of their clients if they are to produce valid accounts of therapy? And do we not need a different understanding of the practice of therapy that allows us to comprehend the existence of different client and therapist perspectives?

1.5. Clients as Agents, Consumers, and Users

Most studies of clients only look at how they experience their therapy in sessions. They capture client experiences as a reaction to what somebody else, the therapist, does. In that sense they see clients as reactive and passive. A few studies also consider clients as agents of their therapy and as instrumental in bringing it about. For instance, Bohart and Tallman view the client as "a creative, active being, capable of generating his or her own solutions to personal problems if given the proper learning climate . . . no matter how emotionally troubled they may be. They can be used as the therapist's creative collaborator" (1999, xi–xii). There are different notions of client agency in these studies. Rennie (1990; 1994a; 1994b) sees clients as exhibiting reflexivity, while Bohart and Tallman assume "a strong, proactive self-healing capacity" in a Rogerian sense (1999, xii). In an overview Bergin and Garfield state:

> It is the client more than the therapist who implements the change process. If the client does not absorb, utilize, and follow through on the facilitative efforts of the therapist, then nothing happens. Rather than argue over whether or not "therapy works", we could address ourselves to the question of whether or not "the client works"! In this regard, there needs to be a reform in our thinking about the efficacy of psychotherapy. Clients are not inert objects upon whom techniques are administered. They are not dependent variables upon whom independent variables operate. (1994, 825–826)

Miller, Duncan, and Hubble state that

> the research literature makes clear that the client is actually the single, most potent contributor to outcome in psychotherapy. The quality of clients' participation, their perception of the therapist and what the therapist is doing, determine whether any treatment will work. . . . Clients, the research makes abundantly clear, are the true masters of change in psychotherapy; they are always more powerful than their therapists. (1997, 25–26)

I emphasize that the effect therapy is meant to produce is essentially a change in client agency, that is, in client activities and experiences, which it therefore takes client agency to bring about (Dreier 1991; 1998a; 2000). But I add a key argument. Therapy is first of all meant to bring about a change of client agency in their everyday lives. We need a broader consideration of client agency within and beyond sessions in the contexts of the clients' everyday lives.

Still, most studies of client agency consider clients as consumers of therapeutic services (Dreier 1998a; Hogg 1999). Examples of such studies of family therapy are Howe (1990), Mallucio (1979), and Reimers and Treacher (1995). To study clients as consumers means that we must look into how they experience and evaluate the therapeutic arrangement, their therapists, and their interventions as well as what all this triggers them to do. Such a point of view lies behind Bergin and Garfield suggesting to look into how clients "absorb, utilize, and follow through on the facilitative efforts of the therapist" and Miller, Duncan, and Hubble stating that "The quality of clients' participation, their perception of the therapist and what the therapist is doing, determine whether any treatment will work." The received framework of therapy distorts the attention paid to clients. What clients experience and do is seen as being triggered by what their therapists have done. Client agency may then be construed as an instrument in the therapist's technological powers in sessions and as merely consisting in consuming what somebody else, their therapist, produced. Accordingly, client agency is only studied in (relation to) sessions where their therapists are present.

The limited views on client agency and experience in consumer studies may lead to findings that make therapists re-consider their practice. Thus, Howe (1990) and Reimers and Treacher (1995) find that the clients studied react against directive and technical forms of intervention, while Sands (2000) is critical of not being believed by her therapist but instead suspected and re-interpreted. Such studies may encourage therapists to explore other therapeutic procedures and adapt their procedure to what particular clients are able and inclined to take part in. In that sense, therapists' conduct of practice may become more collaborative. But these studies may just as well give therapists new ideas about how to maintain their expert powers in sessions. Therapists may, in fact, take consumer studies as a threat. After all, these client perspectives are directly about what the therapists do, and therapists may react defensively when studies report client perspectives on their conduct of practice that differ from their own. Therapists subjected to consumer studies have even filed complaints to the ethics committee of their psychological association claiming that such a study damages a client's treatment by undermining her belief in her therapy and therapist. The problem with these studies is the unmediated way in which they confront two opposed perspectives both captured abstractly as perspectives on sessions in isolation from other parts of the therapists' everyday work and the clients' everyday lives. This leaves little room to ground their different statements in their different practices. We have no alternative other than to choose which of two contrasting perspectives on the same subject matter to believe. In choosing, we may then take rescue in educational, status, and mental health differences between them or in whether we relate a study to our own practice as a therapist or to our experience as a client. Still, if we see this as a choice between two alternatives and as merely being about evaluating isolated sessions, we will not learn enough about those differences and how we may address them constructively.

Since consumer studies often show that clients react against forms of intervention controlled by their therapists, they may be taken to advocate client influence and suitable forms of joint influence between therapists and clients on sessions. But this important and justified consideration is merely directed at what takes place in sessions. It is of little help for clients to have influence in sessions if what takes place there is not suitable and useful for them in dealing with their troubles in their everyday lives elsewhere. In that sense, I distinguish between influence in sessions and usability of sessions and between considering clients as consumers of therapy and as users of therapy. The terms "usability of sessions" and "clients as users" capture the ways in which sessions may be helpful for clients in dealing with their troubles in their everyday lives (Dreier 1998a).

1.6. How Does Therapy Work across Places?

It should be of great concern how clients include their therapy into their lives in other places in order to deal with their everyday troubles (Dreier 1991; 1997; 2000). That is what therapy is there for. So it should be decisive in studying, conceptualizing, and conducting therapy. If the client is to make her therapy work, as Bohart and Tallman put it, the question really is how she makes it work across places. Therapy does not make much sense if it does not work across places. As seen from sessions, it is meant to work on troubles in the everyday lives of its clients elsewhere and later. However, in general the social practice of therapy is structurally arranged as a sequence of sessions that are separated and secluded from other parts of the clients' everyday lives. Based on this arrangement, some believe that therapy works in itself rather than as a (separated and secluded) part of a more comprehensive social practice, and so they study only what goes on in sessions and search for the secrets of why and how therapy works in the details of their conduct (Dreier 1991; 1993b; 1997).

The separation and seclusion of sessions makes it harder to understand more precisely how what goes on in sessions is linked to what goes on else-where and later. It creates particular difficulties for therapists and clients alike with linking sessions and clients' lives elsewhere. In fact, therapy may go wrong if we do not understand how it works across places and conduct it accordingly. I re-interpreted Eliasson and Nygren's findings (Dreier 1984) of deep differ-ences between client and therapist perspectives on their joint sessions in light of the fact that sessions matter to the participants for different reasons. To the clients, sessions matter because of their troubles in their everyday lives in other places and their hopes that these sessions may be linked to dealing with them. But to the therapists, sessions matter because they desire to do well at work; their understanding of the relation between sessions and their clients' lives elsewhere is more abstract and speculative. This raises the key issue of the interaction between sessions, clients' ordinary lives in other places, and ther-apists' working lives outside sessions. Indeed, therapists and clients come to sessions from different places, and hence with different perspectives and con-cerns, and they move out of sessions again in different directions. What is more, the other places of the other party and the links into them are more unknown.

Terminological paradoxes stand in the way of clarifying these links across places in the social practice of therapy. There is even confusion in the research literature over what counts as internal and external to therapy. Lambert's (1992) influential work posits that the outcome of therapy is due to four factors of which the extratherapeutic factor is most important since it accounts for 40 percent of the outcome. But Lambert defines the extratherapeutic factor as "Those factors that are part of the client (such as ego strength and other home-ostatic mechanisms) and part of the environment (such as fortuitous events, social support) that aid in recovery regardless of participation in therapy" (97). Astonishingly, personality properties of the client are called extratherapeutic, though they certainly play a part in sessions. Categorizing them as external boils what the therapeutic refers to down to the therapist and what he does in sessions. This rests on the peculiar idea that the client as a personality func-tions as an external factor in producing a therapeutic effect on herself. So client changes cannot rest on internal causal powers of client agency. In this construal of the causes of therapy outcome, client agency cannot really make a difference in itself. It is wiped out. There are methodological reasons for construing causal factors as external to what they have an effect on. The externalization of cause and effect is a key feature of the psychology of variables in a science of control

(Holzkamp 1983) as opposed to a science of subjective agency. Another terminological paradox in the construct of extratherapeutic factors is that the
occurrence of events in clients' everyday lives is seen as fortuitous. The notion
that clients may cause, influence, or bring about extratherapeutic events is
missing – though this is precisely where we should look for client agency
in the bringing about of therapy outcomes. Client agency should, precisely,
mean that extratherapeutic events need not be fortuitous, since the client may
bring about events. In a more recent review, Asay and Lambert (1999) distinguish between client factors and extratherapeutic events as together making
up 40 percent of the therapy outcome. But both factors are still categorized as
external causes for effects in the client.

1.7. Assuming Identical Client Functioning in Sessions and Elsewhere

A particular assumption about client functioning also works against
studying therapy across places. Clients are essentially believed to feel the same
and do the same, to have the same symptoms, problems, and properties in sessions as elsewhere in their everyday lives. Were that true, it would be unnecessary to look into what clients do, how they feel, and so forth in other places
because therapists can experience and assess all that directly and reliably in
sessions. Although this has been assumed from the earliest forms of therapy,
say, in Freud's (1975) notion of transference, it has not been studied and documented directly in any detail. Likewise, it is generally assumed that clients
transfer insights, advice, and so forth from sessions into their everyday lives
where they act accordingly (Dreier 1998a; 2000). But the comprehensive literature on patient compliance in health care shows this far from always to be the
case (Donovan and Blake 1992; Hogg 1999; Roberson 1992). It is also mostly
assumed that if clients do not do the same elsewhere as in sessions, they have
not yet fully incorporated their treatment, and further treatment is in order
until they do. Finally, it is normally assumed that in documenting the effects
of a treatment we should look for the same mental states, behaviors, feelings,
and insights elsewhere as those believed to be brought about in sessions. If, on
the other hand, clients' mental states and so forth differ in other places, that
indicates an insufficient effect of treatment or complicates its documentation.
Conversely, it is generally not believed that different mental states and so forth
elsewhere and later may, among other things, be an effect of therapy.

These assumptions are built into the institutional arrangement of therapy
and its traditions as an evolved institutional epistemology. They comprise the
assumption that change takes place in sessions, the assumption of identical
functioning across places, and the assumption of transfer as the link between
these places that ascertain the effect of the secluded therapy in clients' everyday
lives (Dreier 1998a; 2000; Lave 1988). The arrangement of secluded sessions
makes identifying and documenting the workings of therapy across sessions
and clients' lives elsewhere more complicated. It may even strengthen the

belief that sessions are an autonomous, if not the only, effect on clients. Other features of the conduct of therapy do the same. Thus, the traditional rule that therapists should not interfere in clients' everyday lives rests on an assumption of therapist neutrality and of therapists respecting and promoting individual autonomy in their clients (Dreier 1998b; Miller and Rose 1994; Rose 1996a). But it also makes therapists refrain from clarifying the effects of therapy more directly in the clients' lives elsewhere. After all, it is up to the clients – to the point that they may feel left alone with it – as autonomous individuals to decide what to make of their therapy elsewhere.

My main point is that it belongs to the institutional arrangement and epistemology of therapy that clients are supposed to do the same in other places as in sessions, but it is doubtful whether that holds as a general assumption. Of course, clients may act in identical ways elsewhere and later, but it is unlikely that they do so in general. In view of the lack of studies of the links between clients' everyday lives elsewhere and their sessions, this general claim is too strong and definitive. Actually, in conversations with colleagues and researchers, therapists express varying degrees of uncertainty about how what they do in sessions works more precisely elsewhere. They are uncertain about exactly which traces their interventions leave on their clients' lives elsewhere. After all, they are not there to see for themselves, and they only hear something about it in sessions as long as the therapy lasts. Therapists' hopes to govern this interface may fuel the research on patient compliance. But it reveals that patient compliance is difficult to obtain and that they may fail.

It may be objected that the session is merely the place to look for the decisive influence and crucial events of change. This objection must rest on the argument that the professional intervention, or the interaction between the therapist and client in sessions, is the decisive part in bringing about client change. A basically identical argument is found concerning the workings of other fields of social practice with a similar institutional and professional arrangement, for instance, in the social practice of education. In arguing for the importance of client agency in therapy, Bohart and Tallman in fact suggest adopting "an educational metaphor for what happens in therapy" taking inspiration from "theory and research on learning in education" (1999, vii). But some educational research has questioned the assumption that learning takes place in the classroom and is merely transferred into other places (Dreier 1999a; 1999c; 2003; Lave 1988; 1993; unpublished manuscript). The problem is that research in both fields normally assumes a particular model about the relation between the sessions/classrooms and other contexts. These contexts are, of course, not unrelated, but they may be related in other, and probably varying, ways than the prevailing model prescribes. Yet, we know little about such other ways since we just assumed the prevailing model to be correct. In both fields, only a few studies have looked at length and in detail into those relations in practice. Literature that seems to promise such studies is rare. What I have found turns out not to do so, and that strengthens my critique. Thus, a book with the promising title, *How People Change: Inside and Outside Therapy* (Curtis and Stricker 1991), does not deal with how clients change across places as they take part in therapy and their lives elsewhere. Rather, the authors study change believed to take place either in therapy or in another place, construe models of change in one context, and compare models from different contexts.

1.8. Looking beyond Sessions

My arguments so far have led to three questions: How are we to decide whether changes, insights, and so forth really are accomplished within sessions when we do not look closely into what happens elsewhere? How can we identify the precise relations between what happens in those places if we do not look into it carefully? And how have studies of therapy looked beyond sessions and related them to clients' lives elsewhere? The term extratherapeutic reveals ambivalence about studying factors outside sessions more directly and thoroughly. Even in the literature on clients as agents in therapy extratherapeutic factors are mentioned only in passing, acknowledging that, of course, they play a major role, but the authors do not go into them and report studies of them. Miller, Duncan, and Hubble interpret this as follows: "As conscientious professionals, most therapists look forward to the time when their clients begin to improve as a result of being in treatment. However, when that improvement results from factors that bear no relationship to events or processes occurring within the therapy – as is always the case with extratherapeutic factors – the changes may be either discounted or overlooked altogether." (1997, 25)

Therapists' knowledge about the relation between sessions and clients' lives elsewhere is marked by considerable uncertainty about how their interventions work elsewhere and later. Follow-up studies are rarely carried out and offer a rather discomforting picture. A given therapeutic procedure may have various impacts, and it is not clear precisely how it interacts with clients' activities and experiences in other places. What is more, if psychotherapy is taken to promote a purely mental change, many see no need to look closely beyond sessions. Mental phenomena are mostly believed to be general characteristics and states that basically remain the same as persons move around in their social practice. But if therapeutic change is understood in a less mentalist manner as linked to what clients do and to the situations in which they live, the need to look beyond sessions increases dramatically.

Extratherapeutic factors, which are believed to account for 40 percent of therapeutic change, consist of personality factors, such as dispositions and motives, and situation factors, such as fortuitous events and social support. But there is widespread conceptual confusion about how to distinguish between personality and situational factors and to relate them systematically to each other. This conceptual confusion mirrors the unresolved person–situation debate in personality psychology (e.g., Funder 2001). Thus, Miller, Duncan, and Hubble define extratherapeutic factors as "factors that bear no relationship to events or processes occurring within therapy," but they offer no precise conception of the relationship between those factors: "In fact, the total matrix of who they are – their strengths and resources, the duration of their complaints, their social supports, the circumstances in which they live, and the fortuitous events that weave in and out of their lives – matters more than anything therapists might do" (1997, 25–26). They link personality and situational factors in a total matrix but offer no help in defining it systematically. Even in the uniquely comprehensive study of psychotherapy summed up by Wallerstein (1986), the researchers could not agree about the relative importance and links between therapy factors and situational factors in the processes of personal change that were followed, in some of the cases studied, for as long as thirty years.

The point rather is that therapeutic factors cannot be separated from situational factors. Their interaction must be studied in order to get beyond Wallerstein's tame conclusion of an unresolved either–or, and this interaction takes place where these factors coexist, namely in the clients' ongoing social practice. We need a conception of clients as agents that recognizes that, in bringing about therapeutic change, client agency reaches beyond sessions. Miller, Duncan, and Hubble (1997, 50) argue in the same direction: "Clients do a good deal of work on their own. For instance, it has been found that when clients return to therapy after a week, 70% of them report changes that have occurred to them outside of therapy during that week" (Reuterlov et al., 2000). Bohart and Tallman agree: "Therapy happens outside the therapist's office. Clients creatively incorporate the material from therapy into their lives. This is a dialogic process whereby they try out what they have learned, modify it, try it out and so on until they have creatively synthesized it with their lives" (1999, 19). Yet, they see what happens outside as a continuation of what happened inside, that is, as triggered by the session as the decisive place and event. In that sense, they hold on to an institutional epistemology and a professional centeredness. I follow a different line of argument (Dreier 1991; 1998a): Of course, clients do much of the work of change outside sessions. After all, that is where they live most of their lives and spend most of their time. In outpatient therapy they normally only visit their therapist for at most an hour a week. How then can sessions be so decisive as to trigger everything else?

1.9. Taking Professional Charge of the Everyday

But if the relation between clients' everyday lives and ongoing therapy is studied at all, it is seen as something therapists must understand and take into consideration in their professional conduct or even control from their location in sessions. So the relation between clients' everyday lives and ongoing therapy is viewed from the third-person perspective of their therapists and researchers and not from the clients' perspective on it and on how they link what goes on in these different contexts. Having emphasized that "Clients do a good deal of work on their own," Miller, Duncan, and Hubble do not proceed to look closely into clients' work on their own or how they link that with their ongoing therapy. Instead, they recommend that therapists become "change-oriented" in sessions, taking advantage in sessions of changes, regardless of their sources, "tapping the client's world outside therapy . . . by incorporating resources from the client's world outside of therapy into the treatment process" (1997, 76). While Bohart and Tallman (1999), Miller, Duncan, and Hubble (1997) and Hubble, Duncan, and Miller (1999) stress client agency in extratherapeutic circumstances, they do not study them directly and intensively. Instead, they suggest that therapists can do this in sessions by noticing what their clients tell them about it and by asking them about it. That is, of course, in part a possible and a constructive suggestion. But everything and everybody from the clients' everyday lives cannot be incorporated into sessions, and this cannot make up for the lack of comprehensive studies of those important activities and relations.

Other scholars propose to study the ongoing interplay between sessions and extratherapeutic events as an interaction between variables rather than directly in clients' activities, experiences, and self-understandings. They recommend gathering more extensive data on extratherapeutic factors for therapists to use as they see fit in sessions. An example is DeVries's (1997) programmatic paper about "Recontextualizing Psychiatry: Toward Ecologically Valid Mental Health Research." Like many authors mentioned earlier, he argues, "The core argument in this paper is that mental health science needs to include the voice of the patient more intimately in its research . . . so that diagnoses and mental health problems may be recontextualized to include the whole person, their development and socio-cultural environment" (186). To accomplish this, we need to study clients in the contexts of their everyday lives. Yet, DeVries does not want to study clients' everyday lives as such but merely occurrences of their mental illness in their everyday lives and how these occurrences change during their treatment. He advocates gathering time-budget data on the changing frequencies and locations of patient symptoms, functioning, and activities in everyday contexts, arguing that "Profiles of symptom experience in context over time allow treatment and rehabilitation to be tailored to the real needs of the patient. . . . The construction of contextualized patient profiles includes variables that counteract the historical trend in medicine toward operationalized, a-historical and a-contextualized diagnoses" (190). DeVries's remedy against shortcomings of a science of variables is a more comprehensive science of variables measuring a broader variety of experiences and activities to capture their distribution and frequency. Behind this lies an interest in improving the diagnosis, planning, and conduct of treatment by feeding these results back to the therapists to use in a professional-centered way. It is certainly relevant to know what he proposes. But when seen as variables from a third-person perspective, we come to know little about how those changing distributions and frequencies are part of the clients' everyday lives in various contexts and about why those changes occur as part of their changing lives. That is discarded for methodological reasons along with the clients' subjective reasons to comply or not to comply with the advice of the professional regimen concerning these "external" changes.

The most common response to the challenge of recognizing the complexity of clients' lives beyond the session is to try to make the session incorporate everything. Gathering comprehensive knowledge about clients' lives in other places is meant to make it possible to mirror their lives in these other places in sessions. Especially, it should become possible for therapists to incorporate this knowledge in their conduct of therapy in sessions. All this knowledge is to be functionalized as causal means for experts in sessions. This interest in clients' everyday lives is professional centered and institutional. But it never becomes clear how therapists may conduct sessions so that they really encompass and incorporate clients' everyday lives as a whole – or at least everything of relevance to their therapy. Demanding that therapists possess such comprehensive knowledge in sessions and conduct sessions with such comprehensive reach echoes unrealistic understandings of therapeutic omnipotence.

Such proposals reflect an urge to make sessions and clients' everyday lives identical by bringing them closer to each other and eliminating differences between them. Sessions are to become ecologically valid by becoming identical in terms of knowledge and overall functionality. But is that a realistic goal? In the social practice of education, parallel attempts have been made. Some believe that the validity of classroom teaching may be secured by incorporating models, representations, or simulated enactments of so-called real-world problems (cf. Haug 1976). In a discipline believed to allow this in much more precise terms than therapy, namely mathematics, the construction of word problems is adopted as a technology to create identical practices of mathematics in the classroom and in everyday math practices, but do they really become identical (Lave 1992)? Drawing on the parallel between education and therapy Bohart and Tallman (1999, xv) claim that the essential learning takes place in sessions. But on top of a basically identical functioning across places, clients will elsewhere and later develop their own idiosyncratic uses and understandings of what they learned in therapy. The use of home assignments as a technology in therapy sessions is a further example of drawing on a parallel between the practices of education and therapy to deal with the relations between sessions and clients' everyday lives while sustaining sessions as the crucial place and locus of control (Tompkins 2004). This goes all the way to working out detailed plans for client behavior in everyday problem situations in cognitive therapy in an attempt to take the contingencies of everyday situations in other places into account and to control their impact on client behavior from within sessions.

1.10. Re-Searching Changing Therapeutic and Everyday Practices

My arguments point toward new ways of studying the links between clients' everyday lives and therapies. A few studies focus on the everyday lives of persons repeatedly admitted to mental hospitals without looking closely into the treatment they receive from time to time (e.g., Barham and Hayward 1991;

Estroff 1985). So these studies cannot illuminate the links between clients' therapies and everyday lives elsewhere directly. A study by Lewis et al. (1991) of a stratified sample of 313 patients in Chicago-area psychiatric state hospitals comes closer. They interviewed them while in hospital and then again six and twelve months later, in whatever settings they were now located, and they gathered questionnaire data on their treatment, social networks, living situations, definitions of their mental illness, functioning level, diagnosis, and experiences with mental health services. In addition, they looked at those who were re-admitted to the state hospital during the study and interviewed a subgroup of them, their families, and clinicians. In the deinstitutionalized psychiatry of our time, they argue that "clinical innovations that involve client and professional are only a small part of the patient's life. Time in treatment is short. . . . Reliance upon the mental health professionals to solve the problems of the mentally ill is a strategy that made sense when the mentally ill were a passive group" (6). Yet, "While the patient and the mental health system have been deinstitutionalized, theories used to understand this new situation have not" (2). So they argue for a deinstitutionalized methodology of research focusing on the everyday lives of former patients outside the state hospital and for a corresponding need for a change in theorizing since "we need approaches to studying mental illness that allow us to see how patients, their families, and professionals interact with, care for, and control the mentally ill. We need approaches that highlight the choices these patients make in the context of their lives. Family, income, job, and housing opportunities all set the stage for action by these people as they cope with mental illness" (9). Compared to the study by Lewis et al. the project I present in this book focuses closely on the relation between clients' everyday lives and ongoing therapy using a method of intensive case analysis.

2　Theorizing Persons in Structures of Social Practice

I shall now introduce a theoretical framework in which to analyze my study. This framework must allow us to grasp how specific structural arrangements of social practice let practices in a social context work beyond their boundaries and affect how they do so. It must also enable us to understand persons moving across diverse social contexts in their ongoing social practice. For that we need a theory of persons in social practice – a term preferred over the clumsier "societal practice," which refers to a practice with intertwined material and social qualities. The framework is of much more general relevance than my study. Its most important backgrounds are in the theory of individual subjectivity from the standpoint and perspective of the subject in critical psychology (e.g., Holzkamp 1983; Tolman 1994; Tolman and Maiers 1991) – which is a variant of activity theory developed by Leont'ev (1978; 1979) and others in the Russian sociohistorical school – and Lave's situated approach to social practice (e.g., Lave and Wenger 1991). As introduced, the framework holds several concepts that were developed in the analysis of the study I present in this book. The challenges I faced in my earlier attempts to analyze these, and other, materials triggered its development. As a result of these experiences, I modified and added some basic theoretical concepts as well as some more specific and local concepts. Some of the additions were due to surprising discoveries that went against my preconception and/or against popular theories in the study of therapy. All in all, the framework I developed is not only the foundation for the analysis of my materials but also an outcome thereof. In section 2.1 I introduce the features of my theory of social practice, which are needed to unfold a theory of persons in social practice emphasizing the practical and structural relations between local social contexts. In section 2.2 I present a theory of persons as situated participants in social practice, which I expand in section 2.3 highlighting that persons live their lives by participating in diverse contexts of social practice. Sections 2.2 and 2.3, the two sections about persons in social practice, are more detailed than section 2.1 because of the field of practice I study and my background as a psychologist and because an increasing number of scholars working on theories of social practice pass over or misconstrue the study of persons. In chapters 4–11 the introduced concepts will be grounded and elaborated in relation to the materials of my study and further concepts will be added as necessary.

2.1. Theorizing Social Practice

Conceptualizing Structures of Social Practice

One of the basic contentions of a theory of social practice is that a social world exists because of participants' unending and diverse work of re-producing and changing it. If they cease doing so, the existing social practice will fall apart and wither away. The existence of a social world presupposes human social activity – even if that activity is only to re-produce a social practice that does not change much. When a social practice stays the same, it is because – intentionally or not – it is re-produced as the same. Continuity really implies continuation – by the same or other means. Older conditions which were part in bringing the present practice about are re-produced, changed or abandoned as parts of the present practice.

A second basic contention holds that human activity is the dynamic middle in which the subject and the social world are connected in such a way that both are re-produced and changed (Holzkamp 1983, chapter 6; Leont'ev 1978; 1979). In practice, the subject and the social world are perceived to be connected; they are not thought to be separate. The fact that individual subjects participate unequally – some perhaps not at all – in the re-production of social practice does not affect this basic property of the relation between human subjectivity and the social world.

A third basic contention is that social structure does not exist independently of social practice. The structure of social practice is re-produced and changed through human social activity. Though social structure is far from always at its participants' command, it is not external to social practice but a structural ordering of ongoing social practice. While we can distinguish analytically between structure and activity, they cannot be separated in practice. Because social practice theorists have been more engaged in studying ongoing activities than in working out a conception of structure in line with a theory of social practice, the social sciences have suffered from a theoretical abstraction of social structure from the ordering of ongoing social practices. The inattention to working out the infrastructures of ongoing social practice stands in the way of unfolding such a conception of social structure. I cannot develop it fully here but I will introduce some key features needed to analyze my topic.

We participate in social practice. It is the fabric that connects us (Crossley 1996, 74). We belong to it – whether we like it or not. Our participation is embodied and therefore always situated in particular locations. This has deep implications for the conception of social practice and social structure. Social structure matters for participants in situated ways in their ongoing practice in moving into and across places. Yet, social theory is dominated by a notion of an overall social structure that is too far away and abstract in relation to concrete, situated practices. As Calhoun puts it, "By and large social theory . . . played down the concrete locatedness of social practice. . . . Especially under the influence of nationalist ideas [social theorists] developed notions of societies as singular, bounded, and internally integrated, and as realms in which people were more or less the same" (1995, 44; cf. Urry 2000). But social practice is not homogenous. It consists of diverse local contexts linked in a social structure. Rather than theorizing persons as participants in local contexts, the prevailing notion of social structure makes social theorists see persons as inhabiting "only a single world or culture at a time" (Calhoun 1995, 44). They see society as a container and individual members and *the* social structure (with *its* culture) as uniformly present everywhere in individual lives.

We need a conception of a structure of ongoing social practice in a set of linked and diverse, local social contexts (Dreier 1994; 1999b). Social theorists did not do much to develop such a conception and, if they tried, found it hard not to fall back into the old conception of a fixed structure of a territorially bounded, autonomous nation-state. Nonetheless, the spatialization of social contexts offers a situated approach to the social formation (Liggett and Perry 1995, 3). It allows us to grasp social structure as translocal and not (just) as an overall or global structure and as reaching across definite – and indefinite – places rather than as unsituated and abstract. We may then address the circulation of things and persons, meaning and references, resources, power, and capital in and across places (cf. Middleton 2003). Social structure becomes anchored in a social landscape where social practice is characterized by movement into and across places. This conception differs from regarding social practice as a duality between an overall system and an everyday life world (e.g., Habermas 1987; Holzkamp 1983) or social world (Strauss 1993). The everyday is certainly no longer, if it ever was, one homogenous world in which immovable persons are located. Such a conception overlooks the particular structures in diverse local arrangements of ongoing social practice. Instead, it must place its bets on a cognitive and linguistic mediation of the overall structure into the immediate life world, thus turning the impacts of structure into cognitive and linguistic matters rather than practical ones so that in practice we focus on a cultural theory of mediation instead of a social theory of structure.

Social Contexts and the Structure of Social Practice

Holzkamp (1983, 383 ff) used the term "overall societal context of action" to denote that a society is re-produced and changed by the activities of its members and that their lives are re-produced and changed by taking part in it. The term is tied to his conception of a duality between an overall system and an immediate life world. Modifying the term, I define a social context of action as a delineated, local place in social practice that is re-produced and changed by the linked activities of its participants and through its links with other places in a structure of social practice (Dreier 1993b; 1994). "Context" means a joining or weaving together (Webster's New World College Dictionary 1997, 301). A social context, then, is a place in which persons, activities, and objects are linked with other, and this place is linked with other such places in a structure of social practice. The actions and possibilities of its members, the meaning of participating in it, and the lives persons live in a social context hang together. Some scholars use the term "setting" to denote what I mean by social context, highlighting the sociomaterial organization of such places (e.g., Lave 1988; Middleton 2003; Schatzki 1996).

Social contexts may be more or less passing or stable. They may be set up and institutionalized in various, more or less specified ways, as we see in schools, homes, workplaces, and so forth, and a set of more or less definite positions may exist in them. Their purposes, projects, and tasks are realized in the plural by interacting participants. So we must consider the practical interrelatedness of participants' actions. Several constellations of participant actions are possible in any context, and the realization of a specific constellation of actions leads to a particular re-production and change of the context and to particular outcomes for (some) participants.

Social contexts are not fully determined by their links with a structure of social practice; nevertheless, they, and their activities, are affected by these links. Contexts are connected by means of "continuous physical structures, avenues of access, and technological connections" (Schatzki 1996, 191) and by means of chains of action. These chains of action may be carried out by the same person moving across contexts, by several participants moving from the present context into the same or a different context, or by other persons in other contexts picking up what participants in the present one did. At any given time, "there must inevitably exist some junctures" between social contexts "where action might make particularly consequential bridges by making or breaking links"; indeed, "some parts are arranged in such a fashion as to be very difficult to disconnect, to prevent from reproducing" (Abbott 2001, 256). The links and separations between contexts thus constitute particular infrastructures of ongoing social practice. Contexts are separated from each other in particular ways, and barriers of access may be erected between them. Particular persons or groups of participants may have access to particular contexts or be excluded from them in particular ways; in other words, they may count as legitimate or illegitimate participants or members (Lave and Wenger 1991). The setting off of one context from the surrounding social practice may be an act of power and/or an arrangement of privacy, seclusion, and intimacy.

Social contexts are often set up as sites for a definite practice and structured for particular primary purposes, projects, and concerns for a particular society, groups, members and participants. In this respect, Holland et al. (1998) talk about figured worlds associated with a culturally preshaped meaning of their purpose, which guides the personal orientation of (potential) participants, and Lee and Gaonkar (2002) call the identity of social spaces half real and half imagined because participants must be able to imagine what they are about if they are to participate properly in them. Some contexts also have a secondary status for the re-production of social practice and for particular participants, and their status may not be the same in these two respects. It follows that the meaning for participants of being in a particular context differs from that of being in any other context, and this affects what they may do locally.

While some social practices are carried out within one context, other social practices stretch across several contexts in a way that may be structurally arranged. In this sense Schatzki talks about an "intersetting layout" between a set of contexts "that coordinates and facilitates the performance in those settings of different constituent actions of a given practice" (1996, 190).

At any given time there are several, alternative possibilities for what may be done in a context; together, they make up a scope of possibilities. Different contexts offer different scopes of possibilities, which may be more or less restricted or far-reaching, and afford participants a context that is more or less at their disposal (Holzkamp 1983, 367–376). What is more, participants in a context may have more or less restricted possibilities for expanding the given scope and for utilizing it to affect events and possibilities in other contexts through the links between them. Power relations imply unequal scopes of participation for persons in a context as well as unequal scopes of the capacity to affect the practice of other contexts from the present one. Persons on different positions in a context have different scopes and relations to coparticipants; different authorities, rights, and obligations; and different links to other contexts. Finally, there may be conflicts (Dreier 1993b) and enduring struggles (Holland and Lave 2000) over what a context is there for, what should be done in it and with it, its links to and separation from other contexts, and the access to it and exclusion from it. These conflicts and struggles are in and about the structure of social practice and testify to the dynamic nature of structure in practice.

Arrangements of Contextual Practices and of the Links between Them

Structure is more than an ordering of conditions and resources. Structural arrangements are important features of structural ordering and essential for a theory of social practice. A structural arrangement is the setup of contexts – such as a classroom (Sørensen 2005) or a kitchen (de Léon 2006) – and of links between contexts for particular practices and purposes and perhaps groups of people (cf. Schatzki 2002, 18–25). The scopes of possibilities for participating in social contexts and linking practices across them are thus arranged in particular ways that incorporate the purpose of the contexts and how the practices should be carried out. In this respect "social structure is itself the memory of the social process. In the arrangements that we call social structure lie all the influences of the past" (Abbott 2001, 258). It incorporates objective forms of thinking, that is, what needs to be thought about to carry out the practices properly (Holzkamp 1983, chap. 7). Arrangements may be more or less definite or loose leaving more or less room for different ways of doing things so that participants must add further specifications and personal reasons to direct their activities in relation to them. They order the functionalities in and across places and affect the unfolding and linking of activities and the lives of persons in them. Arrangements are regulated and maintained by more or less distinct and detailed standards and rules of appropriate participation. Participants may change existing arrangements depending on their scopes and powers, their understanding of the significance of these arrangements, and their negotiating, fighting, and joining to bring about other arrangements. There may also be conflicts and enduring struggles over the arrangements. Finally, some arrangements set up divisions and stations in a context for the trajectory of participation in it, through it, and beyond it into an array of social contexts.

The structure of social practice I outlined enables us to address a complex social practice without merely counterposing a part and the whole, an individual and the societal structure, a family and the society, a life world and the system, and so forth. Instead, social practice is characterized as hanging together. This rests on a crucial idea about structure as *Zusammenhang*, literally, a hanging together. Following Schatzki (2002, 18) I speak of the hanging together of social practice, or of this hanging togetherness as a nexus. Instead of referring to a well-bounded, all-encompassing totality, I consider contexts as parts hanging together in complex constellations of parts in relation to other, more or less definite parts. Structures of social practice then reach across contexts and link contexts in particular ways. So no context can be understood by itself as if it were an isolated island, even though contextual practices are mostly studied one at a time, in isolation. Contexts must be understood through their links and separations with other contexts in a structure of social practice. They depend on each other in particular ways for their re-production and change, and they refer to each other, sometimes in problematic ways.

The idea of an overall structural whole is associated with the belief in an overall point of view, as a privileged nowhere, in the construction of knowledge. Such an unsituated, extralocal view on knowledge reflects and serves an institutional epistemology in the study of concrete contexts and persons (cf. Gardner 2000; Smith 1990; 2005). By subsuming everything under abstract, general categories in isolation, we bracket the particular arrangements, events, and links to particular contexts and silence the particular perspectives and concerns of particular persons to them. To enable studies such as mine of clients' everyday lives in relation to their ongoing therapies, we must re-conceptualize the structure of social practice. This review is also necessary in order to comprehend existing theories, such as theories of therapy, as unreflective expressions of certain arrangements of social practice and to establish the need to re-conceptualize and change these arrangements.

The Local Presence of Cross-Cutting Issues

In studying a social context, we must consider how it is involved in the structure of social practice compared to how other contexts are structurally involved. We must also ask in which ways persons may encounter and address various encompassing social issues through their participation in that context as compared to how they may encounter and address those issues from other contexts. These questions are asked from the perspective of the particular links from and into local contexts.

Compared to earlier historical times, present social practices are less confined to particular places and areas, and local places and practices are more densely and extensively linked. Many theorists celebrate this historical shift as an abstraction from place (e.g., Giddens 1991, 146). What we really see, though, are that local practices partake in more comprehensive structures of practice and that resources, information, power, and people move around in them and across them (Urry 2000), creating direct and indirect links between these practices for those people and others. Here local practices are linked into comprehensive structures in various ways depending on the particular comprehensive reach, and comprehensive influences appear in them in yet other ways. Yet, many theorists argue that local places and our embodied and hence necessarily local practice do not matter much any more. I grant that increased linking and movement affect the significance of local places and our embodied practice so that we must conceptualize them differently – and certainly not as immediate, autonomous life worlds in relation to an immense systemic structure. But local places are not altogether insignificant. The problem is that influential theorists confuse being situated with being situation-bound. Thus, Giddens (e.g., 1991) argues for the rise of a disembedding from place, which he sees as an abstraction. But this notion turns into a detachment from any particular place into an ideational nowhere. So he loses sight of the fact that individual persons always act in a situated, embodied way from definite locations as participants in local social contexts – even when their actions reach across translocal or global, definite or indefinite time–space distances. Whatever we may think of the process of globalization, which many of these theorists have in mind, and regardless of how much some persons travel around the globe, personal social practices are not global. They keep on being situated in and across particular locations, that is, translocal, no matter how scattered the locations are in which persons occupy themselves.

The forms and significance of power may also be conceptualized in a situated way that recognizes how power cuts across places. Power over practices in contexts and over links between contexts may be exercised by arranging the contexts and links in particular ways. Such arrangements restrict influence over contextual practices to particular parties and ends while closing them off to other potential participants or constraining their access to them and the ends they are able to pursue in them. Participation in contexts and the optional uses thereof in the pursuit of one's interests are thus unevenly distributed and controlled. On the other hand, influence over contexts may be democratized by expanding the links between them, the common access to them, the common scopes in them, and the joint command over them in the pursuit of common good. Participants may pursue a democratic perspective on social practices and their development along these lines. This contextual approach recognizes that power and influence may be characterized by different qualities and relations in different social contexts. There are two main differences between this approach to power and the Foucauldian approach. First, I distinguish between power and influence and reserve power to refer to the increase of one party's power at the cost of others. Second, while Foucault, and those who follow his line of thought (e.g., Hook 2003; Rose 1996b), emphasize the historical specificity of forms of power and the omnipresence of power, they find essentially the same logic of power in every local context. Power seems to be historically specific but contextually unspecific. It is an epochal theory of power. Governing through the conduct of conduct of autonomous individuals is a general logic of power that is all over and nowhere in particular in neoliberal societies.

2.2. Persons as Situated Participants in Social Practice

In presenting my framework, I focus on persons in social practice. Cognitive and emotional processes are seen as functional means in and for the activities of individual persons in relation to their world (Holzkamp 1983, chap. 7). In these activities and relations, and through their development, these functional means acquire particular qualities and shifting, functional links. They must be studied as the means of individual persons for their activities in social practice.

In order to study persons as living creatures, we must study them in activity (Leont'ev 1978). So the concept of activity – or action (Holzkamp 1983) – must be a key concept in a theory of persons. Activity is the dynamic link through which the subject and the world are always combined in practice and both are re-produced and develop. Several attempts have been made to give action a crucial role in psychology. They should imply, so one hopes, that psychology moves from considering mental structure as primary to the primacy of practical, situated contents in the lives of persons. But the prevailing psychological approach to human action has been unable to accomplish this change (for a current example see Smith 2000). It conceptualizes the actions of an individual in an immediate environment that is, in general, not precisely characterized. Focus is only on the individual in the individual–environment relationship (Holzkamp 1983). The object of study thus turns into an isolated individual's actions, goals, intentions, plans, motives, thoughts, and emotions. Laws are proposed about this, but such laws refer only to a ghost. Nobody lives and functions like that. Individuals are parts of social practices.

To move beyond the anonymity of psychological theories into a personal psychology, we must build our theory of persons from the standpoint and perspective of local agents in social practice. This involves adopting a first-person perspective on the social context in which that person is located and on her actions, thoughts, and emotions in it. Indeed, for every person in the world, there is a "my first-person perspective." Our theories must generalize about such a first-person standpoint so that we may develop concepts suitable for each of us to make sense of our practices from our perspectives in the world. Critical psychology espouses such a general science of the subject from a first-person standpoint (Holzkamp 1983).

Personal Locations and Perspectives

A personal perspective invariably occurs from a concrete location in social practice. It is embodied and reaches into the world from the place where I am now (Bruner 1996; Harré 1997; Holzkamp 1983; Taylor 1985a). Locations are sociomaterial, mark the concrete situatedness of personal practice, and are incorporated in social contexts. To approach human subjectivity in social practice then requires more than studying persons as beings in time as, say, constructionist and narrative theories do (Dreier 2000; Rogers 2003). Time does not exist by itself but in time–space. And so action and experience, which take place on location in social space and time, do not exist in a vacuum. In talk, thought, and imagination, we may, of course, transpose our perspective into other times and places, but we do so from the perspective of our present location. "We cannot imagine being nowhere. We can visualize ourselves being lost, but that is to be somewhere unfamiliar to us. Being nowhere is quite simply a contradiction in terms." (Benson 2001, 3) Even feeling out of place is a special way of being in a place.

To include a personal perspective does not lead to methodological individualism if we combine it with the structure of social practice in which persons are located and take part. Indeed, we can only really combine the study of psychic processes and social practice from a first-person standpoint and perspective in social practice since that is how they are combined in practice by persons. Psychic processes are aspects of the activities of located persons in ongoing social practices. Purely general psychological conceptions about *the* individual, *the* cognition, *the* emotion, and *the* functional mechanism of this or that are dislocated and decontextualized abstractions.

Persons as Participants

Human action cannot be characterized by purely individual properties, such as purely individual goals and intentions. Individuals have a personal relation to the sociality of their actions, and human actions really exist in the plural as parts of a social practice that is primary to the individual actions involved and gives them their identity. "[A]n action is the action it is as part of a practice. Action, consequently, is essentially social" (Schatzki 1996, 97). This reflects the basic social character of human existence. No individual lives only by his own powers and (except occasionally) in situations with no other participants. Whether acting on their own or not, individuals are participants (Dreier 1999b; Lave and Wenger 1991) in structures of social practice. They re-produce, unfold, and change their lives by taking part in social practice, and sometimes critiques and changes of it. The scope of possibilities in their present situation, and the possibilities for changing it, are not up to one person only but depend on what others do or may become interested in doing. We cannot understand individual possibilities and change processes on the basis of a purely individual conception of subjectivity and action. When we theorize persons as participants, we are propelled to consider personal modes of functioning and the meaning of personal participation as particular parts of social practices. Let me spell out some dimensions of this crucial conceptual move.

First, to adopt participation as a key concept in a theory of persons means that we think of human subjects as already involved in social practice. Human activity is meaningful by virtue of being a part of a common social practice of which we have a more or less common understanding (Taylor 1995b). This participatory dimension of personal activities is crucial to the quality of personal relationships, understandings, feelings, and thoughts. Individual persons must also recognize and pursue this communality. To give direction to their activities they must think beyond themselves into the social practice they are a part of. So, in order to understand the actions, thoughts, and emotions of persons, we must study the ways in which they participate in social practice.

Second, with the concept of participation, we think of persons as being situated in local contexts of social practice and involved from there in primarily practical relations with structures of social practice. The embodied nature of personal being implies that persons always participate locally in social practice.

Third, in contrast to other options for a key concept in a theory of persons, the concept of participation urges us to understand persons by asking what they are a part of and how they involve themselves in it.

Fourth, the concept of participation implies grasping personal participation as a partial aspect of a social practice. In so doing, we comprehend the actions and psychological processes of individual persons as partial in relation to a more comprehensive social practice. Individuals have only a partial grip on and influence over a social practice and a partial ability and knowledge about it. No individual is an omnipotent agent. Individual subjectivity is a partial, personal aspect of a social practice. This concept also follows from the located character of personal participation.

Fifth, the concept of participation urges us to notice that individuals play different parts in a social practice. In other words, participants are particular individuals; that is, they are diverse and not uniform members. They configure their participation in social practice in a partial *and* particular personal way. Persons orient themselves and develop their particular abilities and qualities by being particular parts of social practices.

Sixth, the fundamental human duality between acting within the existing limits of a social practice and expanding its scope of possibilities (Holzkamp 1983) is reflected in a similar duality of modes of participation. Persons may participate in the re-production of the current state of affairs in a (local) social practice or change it by expanding its scope and the degree to which it and its links with other social practices are at their disposal. By the same token, being critical of a social practice is a particular way to take part in its re-production and change. At least implicitly, critique involves an appeal to coparticipants to unite in changing a social practice in accordance with the critique or in leaving it to join or found other practices. Critics do not stand outside social practice; instead, they participate in a particular, critical way. Even a critic fighting alone is not located outside social practice; he operates in isolation and powerlessness in a social practice.

The conception of persons as participants in social practice entails that we neither consider persons to be well-bounded, autonomous units nor diffuse them into mere nodes in relations (Gergen 1995; 1997), dialogue "between people" (Shotter 1997, 5), or positions in discourses. Rather, we maintain that relations and dialogues are grounded in the participating persons. Relations between persons, which are in fact also involved in social relations, are affected by being the social relations of particular social practices. Schatzki puts it as follows: "practices are the medium in which lives interrelate. . . . A Zusammenhang of lives is not interrelated lives simpliciter, but individuals interrelated within and through practices. . . . Participation in such hanging-togetherness is thus what it is for a person to exist in a condition of sociality" (1996, 14–15).

In summing up, there are important reasons to choose the concept of participation as a key concept in a theory about persons in social practice. Choosing the concept of action or interaction would suggest that human activities are mere interchanges with an environment or other people. It would also suggest that action and interaction are free-floating and dislocated in relation to social practice and are only immediate processes instead of being part of more encompassing structures of social practice. Choosing the concept of relation has the same shortcomings and implies that we overlook the fact that persons are related within social practices. Choosing the concepts of dialogue and discourse has similar drawbacks, in addition to turning our attention toward talk and away from social practice in a broader sense. Human actions, interactions, relations, dialogues, and discourses really are parts of particular, local social practices, but these concepts do not ground our understanding of persons in the social context in which they obviously are located and allow us to theorize about them from there. Taken by themselves these concepts grasp the local practice they actually study as a free-floating interchange between people or with an environment. The concept of participation implies that we see activities and persons as a quality that is absent in the other concepts, namely as particular parts of social practices.

Personal Participation in Context

To participants a context presents a scope of possibilities that are more or less restricted or wide-ranging. Persons encounter, realize, and change their possibilities as aspects of social contexts in which they take part, sometimes in restricted and problematic ways. Possibilities are given contextually, and they are contextually arranged. Their realization is involved in the re-production or change of the context, and participant choices between these alternatives depend on the degree to which their context is at their disposal. For a contextual practice to be successfully re-produced or changed, it must be arranged in such a way that participants may come to understand the arrangement of possibilities and relations and then be able to use them. In configuring their participation in a context, persons must take its structural arrangement into account and, somehow or other, use it appropriately. They must come to understand and consider for which purposes and concerns – for a society, groups, members, and persons – it is arranged. Its arrangement for certain practices makes particular possibilities, activities, purposes, and concerns significant, while other activities, purposes, and concerns are left out or made difficult to pursue. Some of these other activities, purposes, and concerns may then be neglected. This selection process has various implications for the activities of persons who are regular participants in a context, potential participants, or individuals who are just passing through.

Personal Positions and Concerns in Context

A social context holds a set of more or less definitely predefined and linked social positions. To varying degrees, persons may select different positions, carry out the positions they adopt in different ways, discard and change them. The opportunities for doing so are contextually constrained and afforded in practice and must be negotiated with coparticipants. Some positions, or sets of positions, belong to only one local context, whereas others belong to a particular kind of context or are adopted in more than one kind of context. Those positions are played out in different ways in different contexts.

In a context, participants occupy different positions. From their different positions, they have different scopes of possibilities, perspectives, and concerns in relation to the context – about its re-production and change as well as about their own lives and the lives of some or all coparticipants in it. So, participants' concerns and contributions in relation to a context depend on their particular, positioned part in it. Positions introduce difference and particularity between the participation and perspectives of individual persons in a context, and they make participants unfold different personal concerns in relation to it. A context is hence not associated with only one world of interpretation, discourse, or figured world. It is experienced in positioned ways; that is, each uniquely positioned participant experiences it differently. What a person notices and takes into account in a context is highlighted from the vantage point of her positioned participation and concerns in it. In short, the significance of a context to a participant depends on the personal concerns she wants to pursue by taking part in it. The arrangements of a context should also be appropriate for participants' pursuits of their concerns.

We need the concepts of position and location because they refer to different but related features in a practice. Locations refer to a quasi-physical definition of space and time, while positions are specified at the level of a structured, institutionalized, and contextualized social landscape. Locations rest on a tightly combined duality of the material and the social, while positions are more socially defined but still associated with locations. If we do not insist on relating locations and positions, positions turn into free-floating entities of a culture or discourse, completely eliminating their practical situatedness and what is at stake locally in relation to them. If we give up the concept of location, we lose the situated, embodied, practical grounding of personal perspectives and participation.

Personal Abilities in Context

Personal abilities are the personal preconditions that enable a person to participate in a social practice (Holzkamp 1983). They are the powers of personal agency (Harré 1997) in social practice. A person develops the powers of her abilities through prior participation in social practice. They are developed through activity in the world and cannot be conceptualized as purely internal properties or determinants as opposed to other purely external determinants like, say, personality traits as opposed to situational factors. Such dualist conceptions suffer from a common difficulty and deficit: How are we to grasp the ways in which persons develop their properties, modify and change them, and, in so doing, change themselves and their world?

The variety of possibilities available in the world only become personal possibilities – that is, conditions a person is able to use – as personal abilities are developed. Indeed, personal abilities are only abilities in relation to possibilities in contexts. Because the possibilities available in the world are contextually distributed and arranged, personal abilities cannot be defined as free-floating entities. What counts as personal abilities presupposes a particular kind of context in relation to which they make up necessary and sufficient personal preconditions of participation. Personal abilities are practical and contextual and, therefore, also more or less definitely positioned, based on particular ways of distributing and coordinating activities among participants. They are defined locally in relation to what is required of a person to be able to participate in a context from her position and in relation to what coparticipants are able to do in their shared constellation of actions. Contextual forms of practice, arrangements, technologies, and artifacts define which personal possibilities are available and which personal abilities are required to pursue particular concerns and purposes. Indeed, contextual arrangements and forms of practice presuppose that participants possess particular, necessary personal abilities. Arrangements and forms of practice define abilities as well as disabilities, such as what it means to be able-bodied (Breckenridge and Vogler, eds. 2001). Both ability and disability are matters of social practice.

Abilities are developed, so they are modifiable. They hold a duality between actuality and potentiality, that is, between what it is already possible to do and what it has now become possible to develop into (Holzkamp 1983; Maiers 1996). A person may develop her abilities in order to expand her participation in a context and exert command over it, to follow changing demands and possibilities in it, and to take part in developing it. In that sense, a person's abilities are characterized by a particular potential for participating within existing contextual scopes and taking part in expanding them (Holzkamp 1983). The range, personal relevance, and quality of a person's scope of possibilities are reflected in her subjective state of mind (Holzkamp 1983).

Personal Reasons and Understandings in Context

Many social theories regard persons as being subjected to and taking over social, cultural, and discursive meanings. They bypass the subjective reasons persons have which make them act in one way rather than another in relation to the personal possibilities that such social, cultural, and discursive meanings reflect (Holzkamp 1996). In the terminology of critical psychology, persons develop particular subjective reasons for action (Holzkamp 1987; 1993) by relating the meanings of social possibilities and their personal concerns. These reasons ground their personal readiness to act in this way rather than that or to abstain from doing anything in an ongoing practice. Participants thus select a personally relevant aspect of a contextual practice for realization.

As mentioned earlier, participants' lives hang together by virtue of their joint context, its arrangements, their participation in it, and the contextually mediated relationships they thereby develop with others. What happens in a context is not up to just one person, and its purposes are realized by a plurality of participants in particular, located, and positioned relations with each other. Even the consequences of what a person does do not depend directly and exclusively on her actions and intentions. All this entails a fundamental critique of any purely individual conception of human action, goals, plans, intentions, and so forth. As a participant, a person must direct her actions and ground her intentions according to the scope of her particular, anticipated part in the practice of the context and to the consequences she wants or fears to come true. A person's reasons to participate in one way rather than another are based on a personal relation to the joint contextual practices, arrangements, and relationships. In the unfolding activities, persons must relate their actions to those of others in particular ways, with and against each other in emerging constellations of actions. If they are to succeed in realizing possibilities and changing their situation without creating major problems and conflicts, they must consider the relations between their own and their coparticipants' concerns and reasons. In short, each participant must develop a personal relation to his or her participation in a context.

Participants have a contextual and intersubjective dimension to their understandings of themselves and each other. They must recognize each other as persons whose lives hang together in a particular, contextually arranged way. Understanding others draws on the basic human potential of putting oneself in somebody else's place, that is, transposing one's perspective onto another's location and position, thereby understanding that person's state of mind, reasons, and participation. By exchanging perspectives with each other, participants may recognize each other as persons with these different, positioned perspectives on their linked lives. This exercise entails all participants recognizing each other as different persons sharing the basic characteristics of being a person with perspectives, understandings, concerns, and reasons. The understanding of each other may be guided by considering the impacts of these different positions and the links between their positions and with the joint context. All this rests on a conception of human experience as being situated. Experiences are my experiences in a first-person perspective from my location in a context and my exchange with others' perspectives in it. Indeed, it is also my relation to others' experiences from my location as a particular part thereof. In understanding the experiences of others from my perspective, I am aware that, just like mine, they are having experiences from their locations in our context. The experiences we exchange share this basic quality.

Individual awareness and action are particular and partial phenomena and not all-encompassing and omnipotent. The particularity of personal understandings and reasons emerges from particular contextual positions. To comprehend the understandings and reasons persons bring to bear, we ask in which partial ways they configure their perspectives and actions from their positions in the context. Human awareness and activity is selective. Some features are configured and addressed, while others fade into the background. Important features may be highlighted or overlooked. This choice is problematic for persons must find out whether they highlight and address "what really matters" or they run into unexpected or unwanted consequences of their activities because they neglected important features. The contents of awareness and activity are selected from a wider background of linked features that affords dealing with what is highlighted and holds resources for other forms of awareness and activity (cf. Searle 1995). Social practices rest on backgrounds that allow them and provide understanding.

Personal Change and Conflicts in Context

The forms, dynamics, and range of personal changes in social practice are varied. I do not discuss all facets of personal change in the study in this book so I shall introduce some basic features. Promoting change is a key characteristic of therapy as is the concept of conflict, and change and conflicts are linked features of personal social practice.

In general, personal change is selective and transformative. One kind of personal change proceeds by discovering and using existing possibilities in other ways, by addressing other existing possibilities or the same possibilities in other ways. This kind of personal change may occur when a social practice does not change. It makes a person participate differently in an unchanging social practice. In a second kind of personal change, a person changes her participation in a social practice that has changed or is changing due to forces other than this person. Personal change is then a process of catching up or following along with ongoing social changes, allowing her to continue participating in social practice and implying a changed personal practice in a changed social practice. In a third kind of personal change, a person changes by contributing to bring about changes in a social practice. In general, a person aspires to bring about changes in a social situation so that expanded, improved, and new possibilities are opened for her. In so doing, she adopts an expanding mode of action (Holzkamp 1983), anticipating a possible, future situation with other, expanded possibilities. She anticipates that possibilities for bringing about this future situation and expanding her personal abilities to do so exist or can be developed. She may then become motivated to do so (Osterkamp 1975; 1976; 1991). Changing by bringing about changes in her social situation requires a realistic and comprehensive understanding of its relations and possibilities and of how they may affect her quality of life. Because persons live in social contexts with others, it also requires an understanding of how particular changes of a shared context may affect the possibilities of other participants and of whether they may be motivated to take part in bringing these changes about – or be against them. In other words, making a change involves an understanding of the possibilities, abilities, concerns, and reasons of other participants in relation to the present and changed situation and of how the change process may be organized among them.

The personal reasons for choosing one of these three kinds of change depend on the possibilities and relations of the existing situation. But all three kinds of change alter personal abilities and possibilities and imply changes in personal understandings. A person becomes aware of other aspects of her situation and highlights other possibilities and relations in her understanding. The change in personal awareness and understanding create a changed orientation toward the possibilities of the situation. It incorporates a changing appreciation of the situation and its possibilities as affording a changed personal practice. A person's state of mind and well-being also change, reflecting the changed scope and quality of possibilities and the changed degree to which she has relevant possibilities at her disposal (Holzkamp 1983, 239–247, 332–342). Finally, personal changes imply a changed awareness and understanding of her power to change her situation and abilities.

However, personal change is not always triggered when a person sees possibilities for improving her life and is motivated to realize them. It is often initiated when the person is driven by tensions and contradictions in the present social practice that get in the way of unfolding the qualities of life she appreciates and aspires to realize. Some tensions and contradictions in contexts are mediated by contradictions and conflicts in social practice across contexts. Other tensions and contradictions occur because participants who have diverse positions in a shared context therefore also have diverse possibilities, concerns, and stakes in it, which may give rise to conflicts between them. Due to such differences and conflicts, participants may disagree on what they appreciate about their present social practice and on what should be done to resolve some of its tensions and improve it. That is, they may disagree about whether and in which respects and directions it should or should not change (Dreier 1993b). They may take part in hindering what one or some participants consider relevant changes or join in identifying and enabling what they all consider to be improvements. Changes may benefit everybody equally or be to the advantage of some participants on particular positions in the shared practice rather than, or at the cost of, other participants who have other positions. Individual persons' reasons for participating in a particular way may, thus, point toward the realization of possibilities that divide and oppose or join and combine participants in re-producing or changing their shared context.

Conflicts between participants in a context catch persons in individual dilemmas and conflicts about how to take part in these conflicting relations and what to do about them. Still, even though conflicts between persons and for persons play an important role in everyday social practice, they play a minor role in those personality theories that consider personality development merely as a task to be accomplished by an individual person. Instead, personality development must be conceptualized as conflict-ridden. It takes place in contexts marked by different and contrary concerns between and for participants, and its direction and course are contested and zigzagging rather than straight. Conflicts turn subjective reasons and concerns into conflicting ones and create numerous forms of personal ambiguity and alternating stances that may sometimes only be disentangled with great difficulty. These conflicts make predetermining the consequences of intended actions, including attempts at change, difficult. Relations between persons then become instrumental ones, filled with compromises, compensations, unequal benefits, and sacrifices. Shared contextual practices and particular persons' positions in them become contested and are turned into objects of struggle. All this affects the goals of the context, participants' reasons for taking part in it, and the concerns they unfold in relating to it. Discords and conflicts of interpretation about a shared social practice and particular persons' roles in it emerge from conflicts in practice and turn events and personal reasons and properties into objects of conflict. Conflicts of interpretation complicate participants' understandings of their shared context, and coparticipants set their stamp on others' self-understandings. Indeed, in conflicts, participants use interpretations as a means for gaining power over the context. Persons' understandings of their own actions, reasons, goals, properties, thoughts, and emotions may also become complicated and entangled. When conflicts abound, social practices are often interpreted from particular positions that are not made explicit and are easily amenable to common reflection. Particular parties may dominate or monopolize interpretations and use them as instruments to pursue their particular concerns. Confounded perspectives of interpretation may also spread among participants.

On the other hand, being engaged in conflicts may encourage better and richer personal understandings of the context and of individual participants' part in it and, thus, help identify other possibilities. To overcome conflicts, participants must find, pursue, and strengthen common concerns. Ordinarily, social contexts are characterized by a mixture of common, different, and conflicting concerns, and this mixture may be changed in connection with changing the shared context and its practices. Involved in these changes is a shared recognition of which differences participants find necessary and treasure as opposed to which other differences they want to overcome and put behind them.

2.3. Personal Trajectories in a Complex Social Practice

In the previous section, I argued that we must develop a theory about persons as participants in a local context with particular arrangements, positions, scopes of possibilities, and social relations. In this section, I introduce an important addition to that conception: Present-day social structures of practice are arranged in such ways that persons take part in more than one social context. They participate for longer or shorter stretches of time, on a regular or occasional basis and for various reasons in several contexts. Indeed, they live their lives by moving across and participating in diverse contexts. Personal social practice is translocal, and persons are involved in personal trajectories of participation across contexts (Dreier 1999b).

The prefix "trans" in "trajectory" indicates the movement across. Even though many social theorists (e.g., Giddens 1991; Strauss 1993, 53–54) view trajectories as unfolding over time, personal trajectories of participation take place across local contexts. They are part of the historical structures of social practice where contexts and some links and modes of access between them are arranged so that they make up societal and institutional trajectories for participation. These societal and institutional trajectories for participation order, channel, and regulate the trajectories persons carry out in and through them. Societal and institutional trajectories may be elaborate and detailed structural arrangements, and persons must somehow shape and unfold their personal trajectories in relation to them (Dreier 1999a; 2003). Persons also take part in changing or creating new societal and institutional trajectories for participation (Mørck 2003).

The trajectory a person chooses to take across particular contexts has meanings for her and for her various coparticipants and social practices. In delimiting and relating to it in a particular way, a person links her possibilities and concerns to those of others and to the re-production or change of the contexts involved. She also promotes concerns that are shared with, different from, or contrary to other participants. So, personal trajectories may be combined with those of other persons and become a matter of conflict.

In their trajectories, persons move around in a situated way in social practice. In configuring their trajectories, they must take into account the structuring of social practice into particular contexts with particular links and use these links in directing their trajectories across them. In fact, the meaning of a context for them depends on its links with other contexts in the structure of social practice as well as in their personal trajectory. The frequency, range, and speed of personal movement in social practice also depends on having at one's disposal particular technologies that have created "the mass-transit dependent" person (Langan 2001, 469) where walking has become a disability in a society of car-driving and "Capital-intensive technologies – not only of speech, but also of mobility – have so altered social being that even the unimpaired (but also unassisted) body has a character of a disabled object" (468).

Complexity and Diversity in Personal Social Practice

The social practice of persons is very complex and diverse. A theory about persons must then include how they become able to take part in diverse social contexts. But research on the person, identity, and self show a remarkable neglect of the significance of this everyday fact about the lives persons live. Personality, identity, and self are not conceived from the perspective of persons involved in such a practice and as a means of orienting them in it, managing it, and reflecting on it. Persons are studied as creatures seemingly immobile in social space moving in time through their life histories (Dreier 1999b; Rogers 2003). They are normally only studied in one context (or situation) and assumed to function in a basically identical way in other contexts. Personality theorists generally insist that individual integration or coherence is the basic hallmark and accomplishment of personality, selfhood, and identity (e.g., McAdams 1996), thereby presuming a basically identical functioning across places. But they do not ground the practical necessity, possibility, and reasons for this basic need and accomplishment in relation to the complex social practice in which persons live their lives (Dreier 1993b). They just stipulate it. Persons need to relate their various practices and concerns for primarily practical, personal reasons, but that does not necessarily entail that they reach a complete personal integration or coherence. This stipulation underestimates the complexity of personal social practice and the robustness of those social diversities that give persons good reasons to participate in diverse ways. Besides, a state of personal integration is easier to imagine in others whom we admire, blame, or do not know so well and harder to recognize in ourselves. The belief in personal integration as the hallmark of good personal functioning also leads us to view a complex and varied personal social practice as a burden. It is not recognized as enriching and indispensable (Dreier 1993b).

When a person moves into another context, she faces other contextual purposes, arrangements, scopes of possibilities, and coparticipants. Her position and influence are also different. Being in this context therefore has a different meaning for her. That also affects the meaning of its possibilities for her including how what may be done here may be linked to social practices in other contexts in which she and/or others take part. A person's concerns and reasons to participate in contexts differ accordingly. Indeed, persons participate in different ways in different contexts for good reasons. They must act, think, and feel in flexible ways, and their conduct can be no mere execution of general schemata and procedures. This calls for theorizing about the changing modes of participation and diverse abilities of persons. We need to conceptualize a complexly changing and flexible personal functioning in structures of social practice in contrast to the theories of personality that primarily operate with notions about a fixed internal structure of traits, goals, life plans, needs, or the like.

Notions about an abstract, individual agency must be replaced by a contextual conception of personal modes of participation rendering personal abilities many-sided and variable. We may then ask how personal stability and change are allowed and inhibited by a person's trajectory of participation in structures of social practice. A theory of structures of social practice with institutional arrangements and trajectories may guide our analysis of how the social world lends order, direction, and significance to ongoing personal activities. Still, theories recognizing that we must grasp the person in a social world see the person as a relatively free-floating agent. For instance, if a person's life is grounded in social practice as seen by social constructionists, she will seem to fall apart into multiple, fragmented selves (e.g., Rowan and Cooper 1999). Much current theorizing about the person is straying from the reality of social practice. Being grounded in social practice – and certainly in one's participation in structures of social practice – seems insignificant in terms of what it means and takes to be and develop as a person. This must somehow reinstate remnants of the dualism and mentalism which these theories seek to move beyond and turn practical matters into mere trivialities for psychology. Oddly enough, precisely theories of the person, self, and identity stop short of theorizing about the eminently subjective aspects of personal social practice that one would expect to find in concepts of the self and identity. If we do not ground a person's life in structures of social practice, we lose track of what that life as a whole is about: what it is a part of, involved in, and concerned with; the full significance of its real possibilities, challenges, dilemmas, problems, and contradictions. Instead of theories about the rich content of personal lives, we develop theories about representations of oneself or about abstract structures of personality. Thus, being a many-sided person is not just having different streaks, sides, or patches to oneself (Griffiths 1995); instead, it is a reflection of living a many-sided life in which we pursue diverse concerns by participating in different ways in diverse contexts. Nonetheless, most theories are preoccupied with the question of unity versus fragmentation in the structure of one's own, or others', representation of self. To gain a richer, more concrete, and lively theoretical conception of the person, we must, paradoxically, not look directly into the person but into the world and grasp the person as a participant in that world. Then we may reach a theoretical understanding of the lives of persons resting on, "a recognition of everyday life as commitments to specific others in rich, concrete social relationships, to specific places and senses of place, to specific activities and organizations of rhythms of life." (Calhoun 1995, 183, in reference to Smith 1987)

Due to their complex social practice, persons come to understand diverse practices and the links between them and become able to unfold and manage complex personal trajectories of participation in which their lives are part of diverse, contextual social practices that call for developing diverse abilities. Socially arranged contrasts between practices in different contexts then make persons realize a partly discontinuous and divided, partly composed and combined personal social practice. Their personal trajectory of participation becomes characterized by a structure of contrasts and similarities, discontinuities and continuations, transitions and combinations.

Distributing, Linking, and Balancing Participation and Stakes in Social Practices

In their trajectories of participation, persons distribute their engagements across contexts in relation to the existing structural arrangements of contexts and trajectories. They preferably or exclusively pursue some concerns in one or some particular contexts but not in others. In doing so they consider what particular contexts are there for and how they may be linked with and separated from practices in other places. Their distribution of concerns is also affected by the influence they have or may gain on the social practices of particular contexts and by the fact that their coparticipants in different contexts vary. Persons share different parts of their lives with different others. They may appreciate this diversity of contextual, interpersonal relations, want parts of their lives to be separate and particular other parts to be linked and overlap.

Still, persons pursue many concerns across contexts, that is, beyond the context in which they presently address them into other contexts. In doing so, the manner in which they pursue a concern in the present context depends on what it is arranged for; on their position, scope, and coparticipants; and on those links to other contexts that allow them to pursue a concern by means of and beyond the present context. Persons then pursue that concern differently in varied contexts and, more or less deliberately, in the present context so that this will enable them to pursue it further elsewhere and later. In that sense, a person's participation in the present context is mediated by its links with other contexts in which she takes part at other times. Her reasons for participating in a special way here are also mediated by the way she distributes and pursues concerns across contexts. Finally, a person's distribution and pursuit of concerns across particular contexts may give rise to conflicts, just like a person may distribute and link her pursuit of conflicts across contexts in particular ways.

On the one hand, then, participant actions, concerns, and reasons are local phenomena. Persons always are on a local position with its perspective on their current relations and events, including their own part in them, and their activities unfold in particular ways in particular contexts. On the other hand, persons distribute, configure and pursue their concerns in and across contexts based on particular links between them. The personal meaning of participating in a particular way in a context, and the personal reasons for doing so, do not stem from that context alone. To sum up, a person's activity in a context is particular in three senses. First, it is a particular, positioned part in the social practice of that context. Second, it is a particular part of that person's trajectory of participation across contexts. Just as we cannot understand the social practice of a context by looking at that context alone, we cannot understand a person's participation in a context by looking only in that context because it is a particular part in her trajectory across contexts. Third, the same context is a different part in participants' different trajectories of participation with different other contexts in which they participate in different ways. There is a distinct configuration to the trajectories of particular persons, which gives the present context a particular status and meaning in their lives. Persons identify and balance off the relative significance of practices in particular contexts for the life they sustain and develop through their trajectory of participation. In some contexts, persons even participate in ways that primarily depend on other contexts in which they participate. Such contexts have a secondary status for them just as some contexts have a secondary status for the re-production of social practice. There is a structure of personal relevance at play, based on the meaning of a particular context for the way a person sustains, unfolds, and develops her life across places. Participants' personal engagements and stakes in a context depend on its status in relation to other contexts in their trajectories of participation.

Gathering, Adopting, and Pursuing Personal Stances

Persons gather, adopt, and pursue stances on what they take part in, do, and find important. They do so in order to be able to compose and manage their complex practice with specific commitments to specific places and specific others in structures of social practice (Dreier 1994; 1999b). These stances assist persons in assuring that their engagements in diverse contexts hang together suitably. Stances thus guide persons in configuring and pursuing their concerns and in balancing off, linking, separating, and preventing various activities and events.

Personal stances are gathered and composed from various experiences and concerns about courses of interaction and conflicts between participants in attempting to find what one stands for in relation to them. Persons may deliberately and coherently elaborate and revise their stances, drawing on the encompassing practical background for those stances. So, stances may be more or less clarified or confused, and persons may modify and develop the stances they adopt. Persons may hold on to what they made up their minds to stand for over a shorter or longer period of time and over a narrower or broader range of situations and contexts. Sometimes a stance is merely adopted in passing. The reach of stances into other times and places, with other participants and parties, differs, and stances are never final and complete. Additionally, persons do not always stick to a stance adopted in one context when dealing with a similar issue in another context.

Stances emerge when persons evaluate, link, and generalize premises of their local, contextual participations in social practice. Persons identify premises that reach across and may make their participations in different times and places hang together. Stances are first of all necessary because of the complexly heterogeneous character of social practice and persons' participations in it. They guide a person's multiple involvements in multiple practices with cross-cutting concerns and issues of an often conflicting and contested nature. This accentuates a person's need not to act at cross purposes in the pursuit of her various concerns. Persons must make up their minds about what they stand for so as not to trip up themselves, and each other, in their diverse participations and in relation to their varied concerns so that they get stuck or important ends cannot be accomplished. Since personal stances are grounded in the complex, heterogeneous, and contradictory character of personal social practice, they are gathered by contrasting and comparing premises from diverse local participations and concerns. These premises are re-considered and re-combined so that a person may develop stances that will guide her participation in a complex social practice. Making up one's mind and taking a stance occurs by relating and comparing a shifting set of premises. Stances are generalized, but since they rest on considering and incorporating multiple participations with diverse and sometimes conflicting concerns, there are limits to how completely they hang together and can be articulated. It is not possible to integrate existing diversities of social practice completely in personal stances. Since diversities and contradictions in the structure of social practice persist, persons must take them into consideration in their personal social practice and stances.

Stances mediate and regulate the personal pursuit of concerns across times and places. They specify what matters about various concerns, and what persons may want to do or not to do about them. Because stances are pursued in personal trajectories of participation in structures of social practice, they are pursued in different ways in diverse contexts. They are realized in ways that fit into the present context, its links with other contexts, and coparticipants' modes of participation. It is no contradiction in terms that stances reach across places not only to ensure that persons' lives hang together but also to give them good reasons to act, think, and feel differently across places. On the contrary, in a complex life, a stance must be pursued differently in different places in order to succeed. Stances allow persons to be flexible without turning into chameleons.

Persons adopt many stances that hang together more or less completely and deliberately, and they balance off and link their stances in accordance with what is relevant in their complex practice and in coordination and contest with other participants. Personal stances have a social dimension in that they relate a person's concerns to those of others in the structure of social practice. A person's stances may be more or less opposed, particular, or general depending on whether their premises are contrary to those of others, encompass only particular others, or encompass everybody. Persons engage in conflict, make alliances, and join with others over their stances. Their stances are dynamic and take sides because they relate to contradictions in social practice.

As defined here, stances come close to Taylor's definition of identity since he stresses the significance of what we stand for. "To know who I am is a species of knowing where I stand. My identity is defined by the commitments and identifications which provide the frame or horizon within which I can try to determine from case to case what is good, or valuable, or what ought to be done, or what I endorse or oppose. In other words, it is a horizon within which I am capable of taking a stand" (Taylor 1985b, 27).

Personal stances are not worked out independently of social discourses and cultural forms, but personal stances are more limited, with areas left more or less unaddressed or indistinct. They are not purely cognitive processes either but rather features of a person's ongoing activities that remain attached to and are pursued, articulated, and elaborated in a person's participation across times and places. In that sense, personal stances anchor discourses in the practice of concrete, experiencing persons by drawing on the links and diversities between contexts in the structure of personal social practice.

In addition to the concepts of location and position, we need the concept of stance. If we operate only with location and position, we lose the theoretical grounds to address how persons relate to their locations and positions, prioritize and balance them, make up their minds and take sides on issues concerning them, affirm and critique them, and contribute to reproduce and change them. Our theory of persons in social practice would then be too impersonal and deterministic. Stances are personal, not generalized theoretical standpoints, and they cannot be categorically ascribed to particular social groups (Calhoun 1995, 171–172). Not distinguishing between position and stance would mean that all persons sharing a similar position, that is, all members of a particular social category of persons are believed to adopt the same stance on social practice and their participation in it. But diverse stances can be drawn from a similar position, among other things because everybody occupies multiple, diverse, and intersecting positions in their trajectories of participation in structures of social practice. We should not gloss over how persons come to terms with intersecting diversities by elaborating stances on their lives in structures of social practice.

The concept of personal stances places my theoretical framework between two theoretical extremes. On the one hand, it differs from the view that the complexity of personal social practice turns persons into multiple, fragmented selves, functioning like a chameleon (Dreier 1993b; 1999b). It is a basic necessity for persons to sustain a sufficient measure of personal hanging togetherness to keep a grip on the ways in which they take part in diverse contexts in their trajectories. On the other hand, most theories of personality oversimplify matters by presuming the individual personality to be fully integrated with a fixed, internal, structural unity of traits, goals, or whatever its structural elements are called. These theories do not consider personal integration a primarily practical matter; instead, they turn it into nothing more than a cognitive, mental, or even spiritual matter. To presume that a purely cognitive or mental integration can be accomplished and sustained oversimplifies the diversity of personal social practice. The issues of personal integration are abstracted from the relations of social practice in which persons live their lives. In reality, though, no person is a perfect and stable unity with no loose ends, ruptures, contradictions, and conflicts. Persons are more complex, incomplete, and varied, and they cannot entirely transcend the diversities and contradictions of their lives into a complete coherence of cognitive beliefs, traits, goals, and so forth. Stances establish a hanging togetherness of more general premises through which persons guide their social practice rather than create a fixed, complete structure. Persons cannot turn into complete wholes detached from their participation in diverse practices.

The Mediation and Reach of Personal Activities across Contexts

Since persons take part in several contexts that are linked in the structure of social practice, these links and their personal concerns in other contexts matter to them. In local ways, they let affairs in other contexts gain a mediated impact on their immediate participation. Persons may do what they do in the present context in order to achieve – or avoid – certain ends or changes in another context. They often are concerned about something in the present context that they need and want to pursue across contexts. In doing so, they include, re-interpret, and modify features from their participation in other contexts into their participation in the present one. The inclusion of indirect relations is crucial to the way persons, more or less deliberately, bring about indirect effects in another time and place. They let indirect relations affect their immediate action in a way they hold necessary and suitable to bring about the indirect effects they seek to propel. The other contexts from which persons include concerns or into which they seek to bring about effects need not even be ones in which they participate. In short, human activity has a potential and varying cross-contextual scope and reach – a feature often neglected in theories about the social practice of persons and institutions.

Persons encounter and address encompassing social issues, for instance, about class, gender, and ethnicity in different local ways. These issues affect the composition and reach of their trajectories of participation and their use of social space in various ways (e.g. Eckert 1989; Stack 1999). But comprehensive issues do not have the same impact in diverse contexts, and these contexts are not implicated in them in the same way. Because persons always encounter and address comprehensive issues from their location in a particular context, their involvement in them and the reach of their activity in relation to them is a particular and partial one. In locating and configuring their involvement in comprehensive issues, persons, hence, need to consider the particular reach of their involvement if they address them from the present context as compared to other contexts, and they need to consider whether and how others may be addressing similar issues from other contexts in common, different, or contrary ways. But the fact that comprehensive issues have different meanings and that persons encounter them in different ways in different contexts not only complicates their engagement in them. Because aspects of these issues appear and are addressed in numerous other ways with varying other dimensions of meaning in different contexts, their covariations may challenge and guide persons in grasping their complex hanging togetherness. It offers the personal comprehension of the complexity of encompassing issues in social practice, and that is relevant for finding out from where to address them and how to gain impact on them in other times and places.

3 A Study – Its Design and Conduct

My project studied persons in social practice by re-searching psychotherapy as a social practice. In a small number of family therapy cases, I looked into the links between the clients' perspectives and activities in their ordinary everyday lives and their sessions. This study throws new light on the way therapy works and on the dynamics of change as clients see it and act on it. It also contributes to a more complete and grounded understanding of client problems and therapy that may be used to develop current practice.

3.1. The Unit of Outpatient Child Psychiatry and the Project

The project took place in an outpatient child psychiatry unit at a hospital in Copenhagen. Other divisions in the hospital, general practitioners, school psychologists, consultant psychologists in kindergartens, and agencies in the social sector refer children, and often their families, to the unit. It is not a frontline unit but one that offers treatment in particular cases which the frontline units cannot handle. So, mostly other professionals have already worked on the problems that led to the referral. Headed by a psychiatrist, the staff also includes a chief psychologist, training positions for a psychiatrist and a psychologist, two social workers, a specially trained pedagogue, and secretaries. The project builds on my prior collaboration with the unit. While it is carried out, it is an extra activity that is given a particular place and integrated into the ongoing practice of the unit (Dreier 1996). That is a condition for carrying it out and for the project gaining an impact on the practice of the unit. My research assistant and I therefore took part in the unit's weekly intake conferences and other meetings, and I worked with different staff members as cotherapists in the project cases. The study is a variant of practice research as developed by the Theory–Practice–Conference of critical psychology, which aims at a better description of the dynamic links that participants may use to develop it (Dreier 1989; 1996; Markard and Holzkamp 1989; Nissen 1994). The Danish Research Council for the Humanities funded the part-time employment of a research assistant, the psychologist Lisbeth Moltzen, for two years and a reduction of my teaching duties for a semester. Combining the agendas and rhythms of my university department and the unit, which was located at a considerable distance from the university, was difficult. During the project, the unit's resources to engage in the project were limited by pressures from a rising caseload and plans to close down the unit. The project comprises four family therapy cases of between fifteen and twenty-six sessions lasting from one year to eighteen months.

To study the links between therapy sessions and clients' everyday lives, we need materials from sessions plus materials gathered outside sessions about their everyday lives. In studies of therapy, researchers normally only have materials from sessions plus, perhaps, symptom descriptions and diagnostic assessments or other test results about the clients that do not address the clients' ordinary lives in other places directly and at length. The materials in my study are twofold. First, all therapy sessions in the project cases were audio-taped and transcribed. Second, the research assistant interviewed the client families in their homes every three or four sessions throughout the period of their therapy and until about half a year after it ended. The interviews lasted between three-quarters of an hour and an hour and a half and were audio-taped and transcribed. The interviewer knew the preceding session tapes and met with the therapists to plan and accommodate each interview to follow the course of the case. We did so because conducting interviews alongside an ongoing therapy is a sensitive issue and because there are almost no reports about doing it in the research literature. In designing a study with materials from sessions plus interviews at home, we took advantage of the fact that participants configure phenomena differently and reflect differently on them in different social contexts with different functions for them and different interlocutors.

The study was presented to the clients after their intake session. We told them we wanted to interview them periodically at home to find out whether we could improve our work. We assured them they would get the same treatment if they chose not to participate, and that they could withdraw from the project any time without consequences for their future treatment. We also told them that their therapists would see the interview transcripts, and that they, and we, were free to bring up any topic from the interviews in the sessions.

3.2. The Interviews

The interviews reflect a decentered understanding of how therapy works (Dreier 1993a; 1997) couched as follows in the brief written presen-tation of the interviews to the clients we asked to participate in the project:

> The sessions are only a small part of your everyday lives. So we are interested in knowing more about how your everyday lives outside sessions unfold and which changes might be taking place there. This concerns changes with no links to the sessions as well as which links there might be between the sessions and your everyday lives. We would like to know more about whether the sessions

are useful or not or whether they should be different or you have other needs than the ones the sessions cover or may cover. In that way we want to learn to improve our work.

The guide for the interviews had the following threefold structure.

In the first part of the interview, the clients were asked about events and changes in their everyday lives since the previous interview. If particular events and changes had occurred, they were asked how these came about, what role the clients played in that, and what the changes meant to the clients. The clients were asked whether they act differently now than they did earlier; how and why those changes came about; whether they think other family members act differently now, and, if so, how and why they do so and what that means to them. Only then were the clients asked whether these events and their participation in them were linked with their sessions in any way. This order of topics in the interviews is an antidote against clients crediting their therapy and therapists with too much in an effort to please the therapists, to express gratitude for their help, or for other reasons. The second part of the interview was about the clients' relations to their previous sessions. They were asked about what they primarily remember from those sessions; about the relevance of their topics and how these topics came up and were decided; about their relation to the sessions when they are at home; about their ideas about their therapists' understandings and plans; about the help they get or do not get; and about talking with these therapists compared to talking with other people and with each other. The final part of the interview dealt with how they now see their situation and problems, and what they now consider necessary to change them, with or without help from their therapists. It also dealt with their perspectives on planning and deciding future sessions. The first interview in each case also took up the history of their problems and referral. Likewise, in the final interview about their lives after their therapy ended, they were also asked to look back from their present perspective at their problems and the course of their therapy as a whole. But, basically, the same questions were asked in all interviews in order to be able to chronicle new responses, understandings, and practices and to ask how they came about.

The interview topics were introduced in broad, open-ended questions followed up in probing, differentiating, exemplifying, and concretizing ways (Kvale 1996). This allows the clients to select and accentuate what they consider relevant and to mention which links they see between various aspects, events, feelings, and so forth. From this information, we can capture how clients as human subjects focus selectively on particular phenomena, taken to be especially relevant, and consider and act on particular links. The clients' points of view are exposed in responses to questions from the interviewer and the ongoing talk between all participants in the interview; they are not elicited in the shape of unfolding, uninterrupted stories. They emerge from exchanges between different points of view where the clients react to each other, making objections and comments, recalling one thing when someone else remarks about something else, and so forth.

3.3. Relations between the Interviews and the Ongoing Therapy

Many therapists fear that if clients are interviewed alongside their ongoing therapy, their treatment will be disturbed. The unit of child psychiatry and I agreed to take measures against such risks. First of all, somebody other than their therapists conducted the interviews, which took place in the family home rather than in the unit. Issues of power are at stake in therapy, and the clients are not interviewed about, among other things, their therapy by the very persons whom they depend on for good therapy.

The clients in this study did not express reservations against the therapists having access to the interview transcripts and meeting with the interviewer to plan and evaluate the interviews. The interviewer was instructed to tell the clients at the beginning of the interviews that "You may, of course, refuse to respond to questions and raise other questions. You may also always raise questions or other matters about the interviews in sessions. There is no guarantee that I raise the questions you find important. And there is no guarantee that your therapists pick up what you find important." To emphasize that we knew what was said in the interviews and that it is up to them to decide whether they want to bring up anything from the interviews in sessions, my cotherapist or I asked them in sessions at the beginning of their therapy and occasionally later: "Is there anything we should take up from the interviews?" Besides, when previous sessions had been divided for a child or parent, the next round of interviews was divided accordingly.

We took great pains to construct and conduct the interviews in accordance with the overall purpose of therapy: to promote changes in relation to troubling symptoms. Because an impact of the interviews on the ongoing therapy cannot be ruled out, we must take care that the interviews are beneficial. After all, an influence that promotes the overall goal of the ongoing therapy cannot be a disturbance – neither of the therapy nor of the research as a piece of practice research (Dreier 1996). In the regular meetings between my cotherapist, the interviewer, and I, we considered possible problems between the ongoing therapy and the interviews, in each case noting those topics that might be especially problematic to go into deeply in the interviews. We took measures to keep the clients from seeing the interviewer as a messenger to their therapists. In order to leave the responsibility for taking up issues about their therapy and therapists with the clients, the interviewer was instructed to ask: "Have you considered doing something about this? Why, or why not? Have you thought about taking it up with your therapists? Why, or why not?" The interviewer was then instructed to move on to other questions. These measures were used in some instances and proved sufficient. Furthermore, even though it is well-known that clients may spring secrets about each other when seen in separate sessions, we registered no instances of this in the interviews. The clients seemed to prefer to spring secrets directly to their therapists rather than indirectly to the interviewer. On the whole, the therapists and researchers registered no disturbing influences from the interviews on the ongoing therapies. The clients were of the same opinion, in spite of the fact that some of the cases contained quite controversial materials and that some of the clients had very bad prior experiences with therapists.

In the final interview after the therapy ended, the clients are again asked about their experiences with these interviews. They report that they enjoyed the interviews and took them as a relief. At best, the interviews were an extra chance for them to talk something over and to get help from the interviewer to configure and focus their reflections. To get this chance together with the other family members allows them to exchange points of view, have thoughts triggered by hearing what the others say, and so forth. Besides, being interviewed means that somebody from the world outside their family is interested in what they experience and what matters to them as persons and as a family and asks them to tell about it. In that sense, they feel recognized as persons and believe that their voices count in a special way. They say that the extra chance to re-consider influences the course of their therapy and their use of it. Of course, we cannot assess or measure the importance of these fora separately because they are linked parts of their ongoing lives. But in spite of these links, and contrary to what many therapists expect, the clients perceived the interviews as clearly different from their sessions and declared having no difficulty distinguishing between them.

A few comments on our experiences with these interviews are in order. First, we did not ask families in very difficult situations to participate in the study. Second, the interviews are a particular situation in the clients' homes arranged for the purpose of our study. Unlike sessions, it was not the purpose of the interviews to concentrate on and affect certain problems but to learn more about their everyday lives and their experiences with the therapy they attended. So, the interviews had a different meaning for them. Something else was at stake for them in the interviews compared to in sessions. For that reason the interviews gave the clients a chance to voice considerations and stances that were not brought up in the sessions. The clients did not depend on their interviewer for a good therapy as they did on their therapists and that accentuates this difference. Though, of course, there were topical overlaps between interviews and sessions, their contents were surprisingly different. The interviews gave the clients an extra chance to reflect on their everyday lives, their problems, and their sessions but in a different way and with somebody else. Besides obvious overlaps, all these differences meant that different things were said in the two fora. Certain things stated blankly in the interviews were not said and, to my best judgment, would and could normally not have been said directly to our faces in sessions. As therapists, we would not have asked them in sessions because we would have found no proper occasion and would not have believed there was time for it. After all, session time is limited, and there is not time for much else than what is seen as immediately relevant in a concentrated work on their troubles. The clients would not have told us either because they would have found no proper occasion or not found it relevant for our work on their troubles.

3.4. Studying the Everyday Lives of Persons Attending Therapy

Which relations are there between the materials from the sessions and those from the interviews? Of course, we go into many events from their everyday lives in the sessions. Unless new angles on these events turn up, they are not elaborated in the interviews because what was said about them in the sessions is a self-evident background for the conversation between the clients and the interviewer. In this respect, the interviews supplement information from the sessions. Yet, some experiences and events are told only in the interviews because we do not go into them in the sessions and/or because they do not want to mention them there. So, some things from the sessions are not covered in the interviews and vice versa. There are also clear – and intended – overlaps, but even then precisely the same is rarely said in the interviews. In addition to the different meaning, place, and coparticipants in the interviews, the interviews take place later so that the clients may draw on the sessions as a prior resource for understanding and talking about these things again and include whatever relevant events or ideas may have occurred in the meantime. Across the interviews there are ups and downs and other changes just as there are across sessions, and a session figures more in what they tell the interviewer if the interview takes place shortly after the session.

Because the two sets of materials do not cover the same topics and overlaps hold interesting differences in points of view, they must be analyzed in combination. Still, because of the differences between them, I shall indicate whether particular materials stem from interviews or sessions. In analyzing the two sources of materials, I bear in mind that personal experiences are situated and relational, and that the clients express their experiences from two contexts: sessions and interviews at home. I have no direct materials from the other places in which they live their lives. This gives my study of their complex social practice a particular focus. Aside from the two special contexts of sessions and interviews, I get to know most about their everyday lives in the context of their family since I study family therapies. I come to know less about their lives in other places, such as at work and in school, even about their problems and states of mind in other places. Moreover, what I come to know about their lives in other contexts is as seen from the perspective of their family life and their therapy, and this affects what they tell about these other parts. Conversely, I do not get to know much about their family life or their therapy as seen from the perspective of their lives in school, at work, and so forth. The study shows how fruitful it might be to conduct projects with an even broader scope. In the last case in the study, I added interviews with the schoolteachers of a referred child. It is easy to imagine how such studies can be extended to other parties as has been done in other later studies inspired by it (Højholt 2001).

Two further limitations follow from my design: First, I can only follow closely the lives of those members who attend sessions and who are, therefore, illuminated in sessions and in the next round of interviews. When a family member drops out of focus in the therapy for a time, he or she falls into the background of my study. Second, the focus of therapy on problems affects what I get to know about. In the interviews the clients also find it most relevant to tell us about those aspects of their everyday lives. I come to know about other aspects of their everyday lives as they are linked to their problems. As a study of everyday life, this is limited and skewed. The professional practice in which the study is anchored leaves its marks on what is highlighted and what tends to fall into the background.

Exploratory studies are used to develop new understandings of their subject matter. This study is no exception. It enabled me to note aspects of the materials I had previously paid no attention to or understood differently. The meaning and relevance of my materials changed and grew, and in some respects it became obvious where I now wish they had been elaborated. Especially in an exploratory study, some interview questions proved to be more fruitful than others. The responses to some questions surprised me; they made me expand the interview guide and later revise my frame of analysis. I shall point out some of those surprises and expansions in presenting my analyses. As our experiences with these interviews grew, we increasingly emphasized topics about states of affairs and events in the clients' everyday lives outside sessions. We were struck by how much uncovered terrain we entered, and that made us increase the decentering of our study of therapeutic practice. This change drew our attention away from looking too much at the sessions. Nonetheless, the study is still perceived from the point of view of research and professional practice. It originated from the position and stance of researchers and practitioners with their usual emphasis: sessions, having problems, treatment, change, and so forth. But the study went beyond a more restrictive framing, reaching further into other places and perspectives. This led to new insights and concepts.

Though I analyze materials about the course of therapy for a particular family, it is not an ordinary case analysis of therapy. Research materials are always used selectively and in this case I have other objectives and issues in mind. I do not highlight all that would have been included in an ordinary case analysis of therapy. Rather, I selected and organized the materials to show particular things about the practice of therapy that are normally conceptually and technically overlooked. Thus, I do not focus on the processes and workings of sessions and therapists as such, even though I planned chapters on this as seen from my theoretical point of view. I chose to omit them as the book grew and my primary interests went in other directions.

My findings are about clients as subjects. The interviews highlight how clients are the main agents of their changes and what aspects of their therapy they choose or do not choose to put to use. But interviews can only capture what participants are able to articulate stimulated by the questions we pose. Confusion and obscurity are seen in their statements, which are highly interesting. During the course of their therapy, the interviews reflected changes in clarity, confusion, understandings, and evaluations of their lives and the role their therapy played in it. Because we posed the same questions in repeated interviews, we could register when a particular clarity or confusion over an issue arose. In this way, we approached processes of change in personal perspectives, understandings, and evaluations, together with possible links between these changes and the ongoing sessions and events in their everyday lives. Of course, we could not be sure that the clients in their everyday lives did precisely what they told us in the interviews. But they reported what they did, and other family members overheard these reports and responded to them or gave us their reports too. Children are not as good at articulating issues of therapeutic changes as adults, and we certainly got more out of interviews with older children than younger ones. But what they could say was often supplemented by their parents, and at times that triggered further statements from the children.

Because the interviews were less frequent than the sessions and covered a broader range of topics, they tended to cover topics in less specific terms. Sessions were often superior in their wealth of details. I had to combine interview statements with session materials to follow up on interview questions.

3.5. The Chosen Case and Its Therapy

I chose the first case in the project for analysis in this book. It was the longest, starting in April one year and ending in October next year, that is, lasting one and a half years interrupted by two summer breaks of two and three months' duration, respectively. There were twenty-six sessions (including the intake session), which is rare because of the work pressures in this field. But in spite of its complications, it is a very ordinary case. The problems are very ordinary, and so is the treatment. The family lives a very ordinary life in close accordance with ruling ideologies of the family. Its members are ordinary people, small folks in the greater dramas of social practice in Denmark. But all this has great advantages for my study because I want to throw new light on common issues and phenomena of family life, individual lives, family therapy, and social practice. My purpose is not to demonstrate an extraordinary therapeutic accomplishment or to describe a clinical case with unusual features. Of the cases in my study this case also contains the richest materials and the most interesting interviews. Still, compared to much clinical casework, they live a very withdrawn family life. They are tied down to a very isolated family life and keep on being so to an unusual extent. They hesitate to seize new opportunities to move beyond their isolated family life, even when opportunities are worked out in their therapy. The parents deal with their work in quite instrumental ways, and the mother's employment is reduced for health reasons. Education does not seem so important for the two children either, and none of them have many close friends and leisure time activities outside home.

The younger daughter Angie is the cause for the referral of the family to the unit. At that time she is twelve years old and attends sixth grade in public school. Her older sister Donna is just fifteen years old then and attends ninth grade in the same public school. When the treatment finishes, she has recently finished tenth grade in public school and entered vocational school. The mother Mary is thirty-six years old at the time of referral. For many years she had an evening job in the service sector but had to give it up two years ago because of back troubles. Now she has a half-time employment assisting in a nearby public agency. The father Paul is of the same age and a full-time skilled laborer in a large state service agency. He often has to work overtime because he is a member of an important unit in the agency and state policies at the time did not allow hiring more personnel. They live in an apartment complex in Copenhagen. Each daughter has a small room; the living room doubles as the parents' bedroom. The family owns a small summer cottage and a car, and their financial situation is very tight.

At the time of referral Angie has complained for some time that visual symptoms suddenly make it impossible for her to read. An optometrist refers her for examination at the eye-division of the hospital where the outpatient unit of child psychiatry is located. Having hospitalized her for some days and finding nothing wrong with her eyes, they refer her to the outpatient unit of child psychiatry. We call the whole family, and in the intake session they tell us that Angie's visual disturbances are often accompanied by headaches. In addition, they tell us about anxiety symptoms that greatly restrict her life and say that she gets very aggressive over trifles.

Of the twenty-six sessions, eight are conducted with the whole family; four with Angie and my cotherapist, the chief-psychologist of the unit Ingrid; six with Paul, Mary, and both therapists; four with Donna and Ole; two with both parents and Angie; and two with both parents and Donna. Thus, Angie and Donna participate in fourteen sessions; Paul and Mary in eighteen. Two school consultations take place with both therapists, Paul, Mary, Angie and two of her teachers three months apart after session 12 and 18, but they are not recorded.

Eleven interviews are conducted in this case over a span of twenty months. The final interview takes place six months after the last series of sessions but only two months after a pending session with Paul and Mary. The therapy has faded since before the summer, and the interviewer's employment runs out shortly after. There are three interviews with the whole family, three with Paul and Mary, three with Angie and two with Donna. Thus Paul, Mary and Angie participate in six interviews each and Donna in five. (See Table 3.1.)

The interviews take place after sessions 2, 5, 10, 18, 24, and 26. They are spread in six clusters in order to cover everybody who participated in separate sessions in each round. The intervals between the interviews reflect the fact that they are conducted after the clients have agreed to participate in the study. Additionally, practical constraints and the mix of joint and divided sessions that

Table 3.1. *The course of sessions and interviews in the three periods of treatment in the case*

	Angie	Donna	Mary	Paul	Ingrid	Lisbeth	Ole
First Period							
Session 1	+		+	+	+		+
Session 2	+	+	+	+	+		+
Interview 1	+	+	+	+		+	
Session 3	+				+		
Session 4	+				+		
Session 5	+	+	+	+	+		+
Interview 2	+	+	+	+		+	
Session 6			+	+	+		+
Session 7	+				+		
Session 8			+	+	+		+
Session 9	+				+		
Session 10			+	+	+		+
Interview 3			+	+		+	
Interview 4	+					+	
Session 11	+	+	+	+	+		+
Session 12	+		+	+	+		+
Second Period							
Session 13	+	+	+	+	+		+
Session 14		+					+
Session 15		+	+	+	+		+
Session 16		+					+
Session 17	+		+	+	+		+
Session 18		+					+
Interview 5	+					+	
Interview 6		+				+	
Interview 7			+	+		+	
Session 19		+					+
Session 20			+	+	+		+
Session 21		+	+	+	+		+
Third Period							
Session 22	+		+	+	+		+
Session 23	+	+	+	+	+		+
Session 24			+	+	+		+
Interview 8	+	+	+	+		+	
Session 25	+	+	+	+	+		+
Session 26			+	+	+		+
Interview 9	+					+	
Interview 10		+				+	
Interview 11			+	+		+	

make the number of sessions each participates in vary in relation to the total number of sessions since the previous interview were a guiding factor. The ratio of interview participation to session participation is approximately 1:3 for everybody.

I shall give a brief summary of the treatment of the case sticking to the contents of sessions, as in an ordinary case summary. My purpose is to give readers an overview and some information so that it becomes easier to understand my analyses in later chapters. I divide the therapy into three periods. The first period comprises the first twelve sessions and lasts seven months, including a two month summer break. Here Angie's anxiety symptoms are in focus in a mixture of joint family sessions and individual sessions between her and my cotherapist Ingrid. We work with enabling her to address the risks of anxiety attacks in new ways and to find ways to re-open activities and friendships outside the home. We also work with the impacts of her anxiety symptoms on their family life at home. Furthermore, we work with her intense pestering of her parents and with her tendencies to get cross at the others over trifles. Finally, some of these issues make us work with the parents' practice of upbringing and with their changing understandings of their own situations and of the relationship between them. The second period lasts four months, from October to January and comprises sessions 13 to 21. While Angie's changes had come under way in the first period, problems surrounding Donna suddenly surface. It turns out that she had been in individual therapy for half a year two years ago because of problems emerging from being bullied in school for years. Her relations with friends are still very fragile, and this has led to serious problems in relation to her parents, which she now wants resolved. While working intensely on this, we see Angie a couple of times to follow up on how she is doing and work on issues between the parents related to all these troubles. The third period lasts for seven months, interrupted by a three-month summer break, and comprises sessions 22–26. In this period, we seek to stabilize changes especially in relation to Angie, but even more we address issues concerning the parents' reactions to setbacks and instability in the ongoing changes and to the changing perspectives on their future lives as a family wherein the daughters are beginning to leave and the parents remain as a couple.

The period of therapy is, of course, only part of the unfolding lives of this family and its members. Like a short story, it picks up at a particular point in time and ceases open-endedly at another point in time while their lives continue without therapy. Let me add that if this case had not been selected for the project, the unit might have stopped its treatment a little earlier. And let me finally say that the case was not conducted according to any particular, well-known tradition of therapy. But since the conduct of therapy is not the topic of my book, I shall not take that up systematically.

4   Clients' Ordinary Lives Plus Sessions

The practice of therapy complements other arrangements people use to get through the day and as parts of their life trajectories (Foucault 1997; Hook 2003; Strauss and Corbin 1988). Attending therapy means entering its structural arrangement which has been infused with the ordinary understanding of therapy that emerged from practicing in it so completely that it is taken for granted and its impacts ignored. Like many other social practices, therapy is carried out in one place with a particular set of participants, even though it primarily deals with issues from other times and places. Its tasks originate elsewhere, and its effects are to make a difference elsewhere. It is arranged as a sequence of secluded sessions that are to allow particular experiences and activities. This then ought to be the most suitable arrangement for promoting its purpose across contexts. When clients begin therapy, they get involved in this arrangement which frames their experiences and participation in sessions. They enter an extra, personally unknown practice with personally unknown experts and for a period of time add participation in it to their ordinary lives. I shall begin my analysis of the practice of therapy from the clients' perspective in the same way. Drawing on materials from the early parts of therapy and following up with later events I shall look at how their participation in sessions begins to unfold and how they begin to link it with their ordinary lives.

4.1. Getting Outside Help

The family's path into this therapy was presented in chapter 3. They were referred to it and did not seek it out. In interview 1, Mary says, "We had talked about it earlier because she suffers a lot from claustrophobia. So we had talked about that we should contact a psychologist to have something done about it."

To get this kind of help clients go to a place other than where they live their ordinary lives. In terms of their ordinary social practice, it is outside help. When therapists, in rarer instances, come to clients' homes, it is also in specially arranged situations set off from their ongoing everyday activities. This arrangement turns sessions into a special context with particular separations and links to other parts of clients' everyday lives. It also creates intervals between the sessions. If something important happens in these intervals, the clients must decide whether they want to bring it up in sessions and how they want to do so. Likewise, if something important happens in a session, the clients must keep at it during the intervals. The arrangement calls for client activity to link what happens in sessions and in the other contexts of their everyday lives.

In the interviews, we ask what the sociospatial arrangement of sessions and intervals in relation to their ordinary lives means to the clients. They note that they talk better with people they see frequently. The quality of their contact is then better and more easily maintained. In interview 2, Paul points out that it is annoying to have to interrupt the talk when a session is running out and "one has gotten well into something." They then wish they could have continued and that the interval until the next session is short, but it doesn't matter much if they didn't get well into something. They repeatedly point out that so many other things happen in their everyday lives that session topics and issues easily get out of focus, are not attended to, or are even forgotten after some time so that they "come close to relapsing into our old habits," as Mary puts it in interview 8. It can be difficult or seem impossible to continue on their own after sessions. In effect, intervals may interrupt their concentrated work with each other on the issues they deal with in sessions.

Two further aspects of the meaning of attending therapy stand out when we stop looking at therapy by itself and see it as a particular part of clients' everyday social practice. First, seeking outside help generally presupposes that you cannot manage your current problems on your own in the contexts of your everyday life. Why else would you be in need of therapy? Asked what they hoped to get out of attending therapy, Mary states this plainly in interview 1: "I hope to get the help I can't give Angie myself." Second, the people outside who provide help are "strangers" (Reimers and Treacher 1995, 120; Dreier 2000). The interviewer, Lisbeth, asks them, "How it is to talk with strangers" about this kind of problem. In interview 2, they respond. Mary: "But it would be difficult also if they were no strangers." Paul: "But I think, you know, like Ole and Ingrid, I don't take any notice of them." Mary: "No." Paul: "I don't consider them strangers." Mary: "No, they are very . . ." Paul: "I think they slide in very easily." Mary: "The problem, like yesterday, is difficult, you know. It is very difficult to explain how it occurs." In interview 3, they both say that the talks are cozy, they laugh together, but they do not get a clearer picture of the therapists as persons. Paul: "They are still strangers to me, but nice to talk to." The whole arrangement rests on a strange intimacy with intimate strangers. This concept of strangers has several dimensions that the clients do not distinguish clearly between, but from their statements we can discern the following.

Strangers are people whom you "take notice of." You do not behave in the same way in front of strangers, or interact and talk with them in the same way. You must also explain things differently to strangers than to people you know well. But these strangers are a special kind of strangers who "slide in very well" so that you "don't take any notice of them," and yet "they are still strangers." After all, clients tell therapists about their personal lives, but therapists rarely tell them about their own lives. This creates an asymmetry of knowing about each other that prevails throughout therapy and that turns therapists into strangers with an intimate access to and knowledge about clients' lives. In interview 11 after their therapy ended, Lisbeth asks them: "Do you have any idea whether Ole and Ingrid have a definite point of view about what your troubles are related to?" Mary: "Yes, I have. I am absolutely certain." Lisbeth: "Do you also have any idea about what point of view it is?" Mary: "No." Lisbeth: "You haven't? Why are you then so certain that they have one?" Mary: "I can sort of feel it. Because, I almost said we laugh at the same things, but, you know, we have talked so much with each other that I feel they know us completely."

By being strangers, therapists, at least in the beginning, do not yet know clients' problems and lives, and clients do not yet feel they know what kind of persons their therapists are. The therapists and clients have not yet established a relationship with each other. Paul states in interview 1: "We also have to size each other up a little." The therapists also need some time to come to know them and some opportunity to "put themselves into our situation" in order to "understand us," he adds in interview 2. Therapists can only accomplish this if clients report about their current everyday problems and allow them access to the concrete ways in which those problems for which they were referred to or sought therapy appear. Clients must more or less willingly put themselves at their therapists' disposal and allow them some time to come to know them so that the therapists may find out what can be done. In interview 1, Mary says: "I got the understanding that one was to talk so much about that morning to find out what goes on between us and things like that."

There are also advantages to therapists being and continuing to be strangers. Strangers may more easily introduce other perspectives on the clients' problems than the clients themselves and the people they know already have thought of. Strangers are more likely to introduce "new perspectives." What is more, as we have already reported, Mary mentioned, it would be difficult if therapists "were no strangers." Strangers are not directly involved in clients' everyday lives in between and afterward. On the one hand, clients then need not follow their advice but may do otherwise or nothing without telling their therapists about it and without their therapists finding out about it. This gives clients quite a leeway in whether and how to use therapy in their everyday lives. On the other hand, clients are not stuck with their therapists afterward as with people with whom they share regular contacts, personal bonds, and relations of dependency. This allows clients in sessions to feel freer to open up and experiment with ideas and perspectives. The same commitment and personal bonds are not at stake for them as there would be if the therapists were somebody with whom they were to live closely afterward. Even though they are willing to tell therapists things they would not tell, say, friends, it is easier to keep therapists in the dark about some things because they remain outsiders. All the same, therapists may have various indirect relations to their everyday lives through institutions such as schools and social agencies.

Strangers are not necessarily already allies of one person rather than others or against others, though clients may fear this especially in institutional or other third-party referrals. So even though clients may be deeply divided, they mostly join cautiously in relating to their therapists hoping that the therapists are much more neutral than friends or other people they know. These strangers have their practice of therapy, but much less other parts of their lives, at stake with their clients. Not to know where these strangers stand, means to be interested in finding out. It also means to anticipate that they might come to stand for this or that, which may certainly have the one or the other set of consequences for me and us. This provokes cautious attention and the need to "size each other up a little," as Paul said. It may also provoke a kind of jealousy as McLeod (1990) shows in a case where a couple beginning joint counseling watch their counselor with a jealousy he compares to school children depending on their teacher understanding them and taking an interest in them.

To sum up, relationships between therapists and clients gain special qualities that differ from, say, their talks at home and when confiding in close friends. It makes us ask in which particular ways these qualities in the relationship between clients and therapists in sessions allow clients to take care of themselves and each other as compared to, combined with, or besides the other ways in which they take care of themselves and each other in other relationships in other contexts.

4.2. Having Problems

At the beginning of therapy, the family presents Angie's problems as visual disturbances often accompanied by headaches. In addition, they mention anxiety symptoms: Angie is very afraid in the dark, has claustrophobic anxieties, and cannot be at home alone even during daytime. Finally, they say she gets very aggressive over trifles. Because of these troubles, she is isolated from children of her age. She cannot take a bus on her own. A parent has to bring her and fetch her if she is going someplace not nearby or after dark. She cannot even go down in front of the block after dark, or into the basement accompanied by a family member. She cannot take escalators and does not dare to use rest rooms in other places. She has great trouble going on excursions with her school class, among other things because she cannot sleep without lights on in the dormitory and fears to be bullied if other children know about her anxieties. Aside from going to school and to sports nearby once or twice a week in the afternoon, she stays at home most of the time. Especially her mother, who reduced the working hours of her part-time job due to back troubles, helps her out and stays at home with her. Mary denies that all this means sacrifices to her and says that she is glad to do it for Angie.

At the beginning of therapy, problems are typically perceived in a personalized manner as internal states and properties of a person, which cause that person to feel and behave in problematic ways (Holzkamp 1983, chapter 7). That is, they are seen to cause problems for her and for the others with whom she lives rather than to arise from and as a problematic part of their common practice. This understanding does not explain how these states and properties arose in the first place and how they may be modified and develop into other qualities in and through their ongoing practice. Personalization is an everyday mode of understanding that places problems within the skull of one person. Some psychological theories of personality have taken over this mode of understanding uncritically in their conception of personal properties and mental states (Holzkamp 1985). Nonetheless, problems and properties do have practical, social, and contextual grounds.

Somewhat hidden behind the clients' personalized accounts of Angie as having problems, they feel anxious and confused about her problems and compassion for the troubled person they care about. They also feel caught up in these problems because they must endure them and bear the burdens of repeated troubles and the ensuing constrictions on their lives. At times they feel a greater necessity or readiness to address them while at other times they pay less attention to them, do not consider them to be so serious, or avoid them. In fact, at the time of referral, this family said in interview 1 that they have problems, but "it's better now" and "not so much of a problem any more." They show a remarkable degree of satisfaction.

Confusion, ambivalence, and avoidance of the current problems shine through for instance in interview 2 when the referred patient Angie asks: "Mum, why do we really see a psychologist?" Mary: "They had to find out whether it was an eye disease or psychic." Angie: "Psychic what?" Mary tells the interviewer that Angie never understood. She talked to Angie about this lack of understanding a hundred times in addition to mentioning that the other family members might have something to do with it too and hence participate in the sessions. Mary: "We may create something in you which we shouldn't." Paul: "We end up seeing a psychologist afterwards." Mary: "I've always wanted that. That would be quite right. You should be able to afford it." Paul: "There bloody isn't time for that." Mary: "Nonsense." Paul adds in response to Donna: "Many people think it is terrible if you need outside help." At that time, they only mention their part in Angie's problems as an external cause creating a not well-known effect in her. They do not understand it themselves but fear that it may be the case, or that their therapists will insist that it is.

There is, in fact, an interpersonal dimension to personalization. Personalized properties are attributed to others, from a third-person perspective on that person (Holzkamp 1985). This reveals the divisive character of personalization, which places the responsibility for something that is the matter in somebody else and thus declares that something is the matter with somebody else. At least, a personalized description pins a person down and makes her behavior seem predictable. The targeted person may take over the attributed notion, but frequently does not and certainly does not do so completely and identically. Her personal reasons for getting into these problematic states and for developing these problematic properties, as well as for re-producing and changing them now, are glossed over or reinterpreted from a third-person perspective of other involved members. But these reasons still matter to her and affect her activities and points of view.

Paradoxically, personalized problems may seem desubjectified. Persons rarely address the problematic properties thus defined as their own problem from their first-person perspective and rarely pursue therapy as a part of overcoming a problem thus defined. In this family, the problems are considered to be Angie's and located in her, but Angie did not go to get therapy. She did not decide the referral for this therapy, nor does she see herself as having the problems that the others define – even though she may see herself as having problems for which she may use the same label. Indeed, although children in general are the referred subject of family therapy, they do not count as legal subjects in these decisions. The prevailing pattern in family therapy is that the referred patient does not consider herself the agent seeking therapy and more often than not has no clear reason why she should be – at least not for the officially stated reason. That is why Angie remains puzzled, or at best vague, about why she and her family are going through therapy. In interview 8, more than a year after the therapy began, Angie says: "Well, I am not so sure why I really had to see a psychologist. I have never understood why I had to.... I was just told that I was to begin to see a psychologist, but I didn't know why." What is more, when the therapy begins, the other family members do not see themselves as having problems for which they want therapy either. To them Angie has problems – they do not. As Paul puts it in interview 1, "I thought it would be the kind of talk the older one had," referring to Donna's earlier individual therapy. In interview 8, Mary says: "I didn't have so many ideas about it because at first I thought that only Angie and nobody else were to go there. But I was asked whether I was interested in taking part, and, of course, I said that we would help any time." Their primary reason for taking part in therapy is that they care about Angie's problems, are affected by them, and will "help any time." They do not see themselves as part of the problem, which they locate in Angie. Even more so, they do not see themselves as subjects of treatment though Paul fears the therapists may turn them into that. In fact, none of them see themselves as having the problems for which they are subjects of therapy as long as their personalized notion of the problems as an internal state in Angie prevails. In this sense, the clients' relation to their therapy is desubjectified (Dreier 1993a).

Personalization and desubjectification are linked because a personalized understanding of problems abstracts from the attributed person's abilities and reasons to take part in overcoming these problems as well as from others' part in creating, re-producing, and overcoming them. The person to whom the problems are attributed is seen as incapable of changing her problematic state of mind and behaviors. Due to desubjectification, no individual or joint subject is designated who is or could become able and willing to address and overcome the problems thus defined. Change seems to have to be introduced from the outside – in this case, help comes from those intimate strangers called therapists.

I must add a conceptual distinction: In the practice of therapy, therapists and clients mostly talk about clients as having problems. But in order to understand clients' troubles and the ways in which they relate to them, we must distinguish between problems and symptoms. Problems refer to a broader range of issues and include a greater variety of troubles than symptoms. "Always being cross," which is a major problem in this family, may hardly count as a symptom, but it could certainly be considered one of the family's major problems. Besides, symptoms are labeled and characterized from a professional point of view. They are mediated by experts and the state, which run treatment institutions where clients must be subsumed under recognized symptom categories in order to be entitled to a (particular) treatment. Symptoms are closely tied to historically developed regimens of accountability. But the practice of therapy has changed and encompasses more than the treatment of symptoms. This fact has created tensions and ambivalences in its definition and accountability. The category of symptom is rooted in the category of disease with its assumed signs (symptoms) and appearances (syndromes), specific diagnoses, and matching specific treatments (Jensen 1987). But the category of problem is not. We may consider symptoms to be a subclass of personalized problems: peculiar mental states and personal properties somebody else claims to be characteristic of that person. In spite of historical revisions and extensions of the list of approved diseases, far from all personalized problems may be labeled symptoms. Again "always being cross" is an example. Family therapy is a case in point that treatment practices have expanded to encompass a greater range of troubles than symptoms. The most widely used professional category is here problems. But the area still borrows the concepts of diagnosis and treatment – even of specific treatments for specific diagnoses – to account for its professional activities. All the same, professionals assess and treat many family problems that are not peculiar (personalized) characteristics of individual persons but, for instance, peculiar patterns of interaction, communication, or power.

The distinction between problems and symptoms has implications for the clients' relation to their troubles and therapy. The subjective experience and relation to various symptoms has common features. To detect these features, we must consider symptoms from a first-person perspective as opposed to the third-person perspective of expert diagnosis. When Angie refers to their occurrence in session 13 and says, "But I can't help it," she expresses a typical attitude. To the subject, symptoms appear suddenly. Signs of forewarning may be experienced, but that is not the case for Angie. Symptoms are also experienced as arising from within the subject and as processes over which she has little or no command. There seems to be no clear and coherent first-person agency behind them. Rather, there is a split between the experiencing subject and other internal states and forces. Besides, to the subject – and to others too – symptoms mostly appear incomprehensible. The members of this family did not believe that they understand what brought the symptoms about, what re-produces them, and what it takes to overcome them. They experience the symptoms as a fact they must reckon with and abide by. The symptoms just happen, and they see them as something the subject is not able to overcome.

Hence, they do not quite trust their experiences and practices in relation to symptoms but consider their experiences and practices insufficient or problematic. When they acted on a belief about a symptom in order to overcome it, the belief usually turns out to be problematic in that they are not able to overcome the symptom but instead re-produce, modify, or aggravate it. They are stuck with the symptom and may take its occurrence as a sign that something else is the matter – as in the professional concept of symptom. But they are not certain what this might be and what the symptom might be related to. Each person may have several, competing and contradicting hunches about it. In addition, they often disagree over how to understand the symptom and what it may be related to. Their notions and practices may be fragmented and contradictory. And if it was is not clear how the symptoms are linked to their social practice, how can they overcome them by changing their practice?

At the beginning of therapy, the troubles these clients expect their therapy to deal with are symptoms. Though they do not use this distinction to talk about their troubles, they list Angie's symptoms as the problems they feel disoriented about and unable to handle on their own; they also expect these problems to be treated by handing them to the experts. Of course, the family and its individual members have other problems, but they do not think they belong in therapy or that the problems should be mentioned or even suggested for treatment because they are of another kind and are to be dealt with by other means in other places. So, they select some problems for presentation and treatment and set aside others. The symptoms they present seem to be the most relevant troubles to present for therapy, but they need not be the most severe problems in their ordinary everyday lives. To them, there is an important difference between visual disturbances and anxiety, on the one hand, and, say, always being cross, on the other, which makes only the first but not the latter a reason to accept and begin therapy, no matter how much the latter troubles their everyday lives. We shall conclude that at the beginning these clients want their therapists to do something to make their symptoms go away. They believe that if these symptoms did not get in their way, they would be leading a good life. The symptoms disturb their lives. They are the sole cause of their troubles. Once this disturbance is removed, their good life will unfold again without hindrance. So, they do not want to change their lives; they simply want to have the symptoms lifted. Since they do not see the symptoms as arising from their practice, there is no need to change that practice. They are explicitly satisfied with their present life, appearing in the beginning therapy sessions and interviews as a smiling, happy family meeting their therapists to have some symptoms lifted – now with the second of two children referred for therapy.

4.3. Orientation toward Therapy

Where clients are referred to for help depends on institutional categories of problems and symptoms. Diverse problems are linked with diverse
kinds of help that can be obtained in different institutions that are delineated and divided according to the boundaries of disciplines and subdisci-
plines, which are presumed to have a distinct set of problems to treat and
tasks to perform. The major hospital where the unit of child psychiatry is
located is organized in that way. Its unit of outpatient child psychiatry is to
help with a particular kind of problems, and therapy is its standard means of
help. Nonetheless, the distinctions behind the institutional divisions are not
maintained in the practice of the hospital. Its divisions collaborate on an ad
hoc basis on so-called complex cases with complex problems. They are con-
sultants for each other, refer cases to each other and several divisions and institutions are often involved in treating the same set of problems. In the fields of
work dealt with in this book, (sub)disciplines are analytic distinctions between
various dimensions and levels of problems and symptoms, which cannot be
separated in the realities of clients' lives but are linked or even part of the same
complex, practical, everyday troubles. Clients' orientation toward their therapy is complicated when their troubles in their everyday lives are compounded
in constellations other than the analytic distinctions between them drawn by
institutions and experts. The therapy becomes even more complicated when
clients discover that their therapists, in conducting the treatment offered, also
cross these distinctions into other aspects of clients' everyday troubles.

This ambiguous institutional arrangement has consequences for prospec-
tive clients' attitudes toward therapy. Based on the institutional divisions,
clients go to get help for a particular kind of problem in a particular unit – in
this case, outpatient child psychiatry. They take a particular kind of problem
into therapy – not other problems, which they believe are not serious enough
for therapy or should be dealt with somewhere else or with something else
other than therapy. For this reason, we cannot expect clients to raise these
other problems in sessions. They do not see why they should. Yet, their therapists may consider some of these other problems relevant for the treatment
they conduct and address them in sessions. That may confuse clients. Thus,
Mary wonders why they need to talk about the fights between her daughters
in the morning since she sees no link between that and Angie's symptoms.

In fact, this challenges clients' attitudes toward what therapy is about and
their problems. The challenge may aggravate their confusion over what to
do about their problems, which help is needed to overcome them, and which
help different places and experts offer. The increased confusion may reduce
their influence on the content and course of their therapy further compared
to their therapists. It may push the clients into shopping for the advice of
different experts, or they may simply let the experts lead them from one place
to another and just follow suit as in this family's path into therapy. What is
more, symptoms are frequently obscure and abstract; hence, clients are not

sure about the nature of therapeutic expertise and what to expect from therapy and how it compares to other places they know or have heard about. The discourse of symptoms is an institutional one. Institutional experts define them, distribute them across divisions, and define and arrange what counts as adequate treatment. On the other hand, the challenges to the clients' prior orientations make them wonder exactly what their therapists think about their problems, that is, how their problems are seen from their therapists' perspective and stance. These challenges encourage the clients to wonder anew about their own notions about their problems and develop other notions.

As mentioned in section 4.2, Mary says in interview 8 that at first she had no clear idea what it would be like to attend therapy. She did not consider herself – or any other member of the family but Angie – to be part of the problem to be treated, but she was glad to help in the treatment of her daughter's problems. Paul adds: "In the beginning we each grappled more with the problems on our own, maybe also because it was something new." So, they have no clear common understanding of the problem and what can and should be done about it that might serve as a common ground for a joint orientation and stance toward their therapy – aside from having hopefully uninvolved, and in that sense neutral, expert strangers present new suggestions to them.

What does therapy then mean to them from their point of view? Asked in interview 1 whether they have any hopes about what the therapists can do for them, Mary answers: "Yes, certainly. Maybe not tell us, but maybe teach Angie that you can talk things over because it helps a lot to talk. You cannot always find a solution, but just talking about it." At the same time, Mary wonders: "One may think about how to help, how – for instance with Angie's claustrophobia – how on earth can one talk about things like that?" So, Mary, and the others too, have no clear idea about how the kind of help they are offered, namely "talk," and the kind of problems it is to help them resolve, namely Angie's symptoms, may be related. How does talking do away with visual disturbances and sudden attacks of anxiety? Paul ventures that the talking may be an initial phase that merely sets the stage for the real treatment: "They have to pin down the problems first, right. See what's really there, what's going to happen."

In the beginning, their therapy means that they have somebody to talk to about the problems that concern them. In interview 1, Mary calls this opportunity "wonderful" and "a privilege." They all say that, for various reasons, they cannot talk to anybody else about it. Friends may use it against them and tell it to others. Most friends do not want to hear about problems because their friends are "superficial." In this sense, therapy means they can go to a secluded place outside their ordinary practice and relations where they may talk with expert strangers about personal problems.

Indeed, throughout their over a year-long therapy, these clients state in interviews what they first said in interview 1, that they "have no idea" about what will come in the next sessions, but believe their therapists know, although they have no idea what that idea might be. Mary adds: "They are just nice to talk to. . . . Maybe I am pushing it a little away from me because I hope to get the

help I can't give Angie. So I wait and see what happens, then I take part myself."
Although they gradually begin to anticipate what they want future sessions to
be about and bring about, they continue to be reluctant to influence them
and act in anticipatory ways in them. These statements raise questions about
how clients understand therapy, therapeutic expertise, and their participation
in therapy.

4.4. What Can Therapists Do?

Though it has become more common to see a therapist and Donna
attended an individual therapy two years ago, the clients have no clear understanding of therapeutic expertise. Because sessions are secluded and participants hesitate to talk about their experiences in therapy, a public understanding
of therapy is difficult to cultivate. Many see therapy as somewhat mysterious.
The clients' uncertainty about their therapists' expertise stands in the way of
making demands on the therapists and making up their minds on where they
stand in relation to their therapy and therapists. Their use of sessions becomes
more uncertain and hesitant.

Their notions about their therapists' professional powers are charged by
their sense of what they believe they cannot do on their own and by the fact
that their therapists are strangers. In interview 3, Mary says: "I hope that the
therapists can tell the children what I cannot tell them myself, what they won't
listen to if I tell them." Her powerlessness in wanting to get "the help I can't
give Angie" is about being unable to trigger certain actions and changes in
the children, which the therapists can because they are strangers and not their
parents. This attitude comes across strongly in Mary's statements about the
family's prior contact with a therapist around Donna's earlier therapy: "There
it is again. It was a stranger who told them. The psychologist sort of turned
Donna's thoughts in the direction that the solution for her simply was to move
to another school. And then Donna told us that now she wanted to move to
another school. We had talked about that for years. But the psychologist could
turn it so that Donna said that now she had really had enough. And then Donna
found out it was simply the right thing, and then she felt annoyed she hadn't
agreed to it many years ago." So the therapists are perceived as being able to
do something that the clients cannot do themselves. That capacity is closely
linked to the fact that the therapists are strangers and that the clients will listen
more to them in particular significant ways. Consequently, the therapists can
gain such an impact on the clients' thoughts that they reconsider and change
their practice.

Yet, the clients do not quite understand how the therapists can do this, and
they wonder about the complexity of the therapists' competence and impact.
In interview 1, Mary says: "I don't really understand because it must be difficult
for them." Paul: "It must be difficult for them to put themselves in our situation
right here and now, right." Mary: "There must be a lot of things you must
know to find out what to do to be able to help. And find out which treatment

to give and how." As they see it, the therapists must be able to understand not only their symptoms but their situation to find out what might help. And they believe that must be difficult for strangers who do not know their situation and ordinarily do not take part in it.

During major periods of therapy, the clients' hopes that the therapists will change them primarily mean hoping the therapists will change other family members – but not themselves. Yet, since all members have this hope, there are hopes that everybody will be changed. Concerning themselves, on the other hand, the clients hope that the therapists can give them some advice about what to do. The difference between the two modes of change is one of being changed by others versus deciding yourself whether you want to go along with a proposed change.

In several respects the clients stress their status as subjects and their influence when they delimit and characterize what the therapists can do. Even though the clients believe the therapists can be quite influential, they also believe that if they disagree with their therapists, they can "correct their impressions," as Paul puts it in interview 3. Therapists, Mary adds, are "people with other points of view on things." Asked what they will do if they disagree with their therapists, they respond: "Then we just don't do what they think." There are several striking instances when they do not follow what their therapists believe, or hope, they will do. The clients also say that when their therapists are getting too deeply into what they prefer to deal with on their own at home, it is "not hard to stop them."

Still, there is widespread ambiguity and discord over the relative influence of therapists and clients on what takes place and on how they each matter for the ongoing changes. During this long therapy the clients are not able to resolve whether what the therapists can do is something they do to their clients or something the clients take part in bringing about so that the therapists' competence is to act in such a way that therapists as well as clients bring about the changes in a collaborative effort (Dreier 1993a). Mary often believes that therapists can make changes in others, and Paul often opts for the second notion. Thus, he says in interview 2: "I think we talked very well about how she could tackle it." He includes themselves in what triggered Angie to change. Everybody takes part in bringing changes about.

Much later in interview 8 Paul talks about what the therapists can and should do: "They are to help us to do it by our own means." By contrast, Mary says: "The only thing – I won't say I'm dissatisfied but I wish it were different – is that when we are there, it's on our premises. They don't say they think we need this and that. We decide what to talk about. I wish they'd say more directly, 'This is your problem.' . . . It took me a long time to find out it's really not the children – it's us. And I wish to have that thrown straight to my face, to be told that this is why. . . . I think they are competent to do so after all those talks. . . . You get some advice along the way. But I wish they'd tell me more directly, 'You do this and that wrong.' . . . It's not nice to be told, for example, that you do something wrong or said something wrong. . . . Today

I simply think we were too weak, too inconsistent, we simply didn't express our wishes toward the children because it was all about them." Paul: "Well, I don't agree fully with Mary that it's only our fault because there were problems with the children too. . . . We've been too weak too, but it's only because we wanted to do it as well as we could for the children. . . . On the other hand, it must be difficult for Ingrid and Ole to hand something out, telling us, 'Do this and that, try this.' I guess it varies from one family to another. . . . I guess it's smarter it comes as you go along when it becomes obvious that this is something to go into. . . . It's up to us to try to do things better. You know, they are not the ones to . . . They are to help us on our way, but from there to tell us, 'Do this' and look it up in a book saying it says so black on white. Maybe they can do that in exceptional cases, but mostly I believe one should do it the way we do." The argument between them continues. Mary modifies her stance to something we ought to do all along: "Or else, I've also thought that maybe they want it to sort of work. They make us feel as if we resolve it all without really thinking about that it's with their help. And maybe that makes you strong." Paul: "I'm more inclined to agree with you that it sort of has to come from ourselves. They just help us along." Mary: "I think we simply decide ourselves. And if something does not suit one of us, one just drops it, simply, right away. And there, maybe, one might take it up in an individual talk." Here we see uncertainty and discord among the clients over the professional powers. In some respects, they attributed greater powers to the therapists than the therapists have and the clients would accept if they were subjected to it. In fact, Mary vigorously disagrees with her therapists' interpretations and stances on several occasions.

When clients emphasize that therapists can do what they cannot do themselves and that all impacts stem from the therapists, they attribute all differences between what happens in sessions and in other contexts of their everyday lives to the presence in sessions of one extra person, the therapist (or, as here, two therapists). They reduce differences in their own ways of participating to mere reactions to what that person does, and all other differences are ignored. Mary says that impacts stem either from the therapists or from themselves – though the latter is a mere belief that the therapists instill in them. Impacts are not composed by the contributions of many parties but are divided so as to stem from one party. Yet, Mary's beliefs about the workings of therapists are precisely what she believes makes sessions different from how things are brought about in the context of their family at home. Here everybody has to play a part – and so they should. From Mary's point of view, their modes of participation in the two contexts differ. Indeed, through her particular participation in sessions, Mary appeals to a constellation of the therapists as expert-providers versus the clients as lay-consumers which she will not adhere to anyhow. She takes part in creating the way sessions work but attributes their success to the therapists.

Even in the final interview with Paul and Mary, half a year after their therapy ended, Mary says: "They sort of create the thought, the change in you. Or is it ourselves? No, I don't believe I had come to where I am today if I hadn't been there. Some very different lines of thought are opened up from the ones I believe – I believe we would still have been dawdling around here, like some old-fashioned housewife if I hadn't come there. I would still have been sitting here when it suited Angie, nursing her. . . . If I hadn't been there, I wouldn't have said that it's me too; I'm also a human being with a right to . . . So they don't directly tell you, 'what you do there, is simply awful; try this or that.'" Paul: "No, they wouldn't say." Mary: "But still they think about it." Mary considers it is probably too much to ask for an answer. Sometimes she even thinks that perhaps there are no solutions, and that very thought makes her feel powerless. Here the belief in the therapists' competence to know and to find an answer relates to her own sense of power or powerlessness. Persons who feel powerless to overcome their own troubles may hope that somebody else, here a therapist, is able to do it for them. The more they feel able to overcome their problems on their own accord, the more they may discard the notion that their therapists have a solution and can set it through for them. The ambivalence over whether the therapists create the effect or everybody participate in its creation is unevenly distributed among the members of this family. It is part of the power structure between them and of the clients' hoping that the experts know and can do what the clients cannot do themselves. It also reflects living under circumstances in which events are attributed to one party or to another – but not to everybody participating in joint action.

4.5. Participation in Sessions

The clients' initial confusion over the problems to be treated, the help they might get, and the nature of therapy leads to confusion over what they are to participate in, how they are to participate, and why they want to participate in one way rather than another. Their personal stances on participating in therapy are uncertain, and they have not adopted a common stance on participating in their shared therapy. Paul is of the opinion that they are to participate in such a way that their therapists can "pin down their problems" and then propose a treatment, and Mary hopes that their participation will lead family members to "learn to talk things over" though she is not certain this will resolve their problems and especially wonders how it can treat Angie's symptoms.

Let us rephrase Mary's puzzlement as follows. Which crucial links are there between the practice of talk between persons and Angie's symptoms seen as problematic internal states or properties, and how might these links bring about a cure of Angie's symptoms? This puzzlement over the links between their symptoms and the help they are offered leads to disorientation about how and why they are to participate in session talks. Mary especially considers it a general good to be able to talk about things, but she cannot relate it to the cure of symptoms in a way she and the others can understand. The disorientation gives their initial participation a quality of waiting and placing themselves at their therapists' disposal so that the therapists might come up with some advice or measure for treating Angie's symptoms. It also puts them one down compared to their therapists when it comes to exerting influence in sessions to get the treatment they believe they need and can use.

The confusion is also triggered by recognizing that the practice of their therapists, to talk with them, suggests that their therapists must consider talk to be the practice of cure or a means to get at the real cure. There is a further difference between them. Mary's notion of talk as a general good or treatment fits most closely with the assumptions about the talking cure among therapists and in the literature from the field.

When treatment is mediated through talk, whether and how the therapists seek to understand the clients and how the clients can make themselves understood becomes a major issue in clients' participation. This concerns both clients and therapists over long stretches of time in and between sessions. In interview 1, Mary states: "Because you don't know us, one has to, I won't say we wasted an hour or more on that morning." The clients' confusion over the problematic aspects of their everyday lives that are talked about in sessions makes it more difficult for them to make themselves understood. Seconded by Paul, Mary says in interview 3: "The worst thing is to explain what you mean. . . . We sometimes talk about that they judge us a little, or maybe rather misunderstand us. And maybe that is because we find it difficult to explain how it happens." Their worry may increase when their therapists introduced new and different angles on their problems. But their confusion may also make them more susceptible to new ideas and influences from their therapists, including ideas that might not be in their best interest.

In sessions the clients shift between placing themselves at their therapists' disposal to enable the therapists to come up with some advice and taking part themselves in finding a solution and bringing about the treatment. These shifts between different stances of participation in sessions persist throughout the therapy.

In interview 1, Mary compares the present therapy to Donna's prior individual therapy. They were not informed during Donna's therapy while "here we are making corrections as we go along. We take part in creating a solution here and now, right. . . . Because you [the psychologists, OD] are used to see things in a different way than we are. . . . In Donna's therapy I'd say I felt a bit . . . I don't think we were sufficiently part of what went on. . . . It is a bit difficult because you don't follow the development. You are sort of not a part in it yourself. You sort of have to adjust to be different because the child suddenly changes." Taking part as a family is a venue to get influence on family affairs – and on each others' lives as members of that family and as somebody you care for and may be in conflict with over the issues being treated. They would be unhappy to give this up and want it strengthened in the pursuit of influence on their own affairs.

The clients' shifts between considering therapy to be a matter of receiving advice from experts or something you take part in bringing about as you go along are fed by the ways in which they seek to utilize their therapists as a means to influence the power relations in their family. When persons feel stuck in their problems and relatively powerless in relation to other family members, they may want the therapists to put forward some authoritative advice about how the family or, more precisely, other family members, should behave and be willing to change. Relatively powerless family members may opt for an authoritative expert power as a means to change other members and, thereby, the family as a whole and their own situation in it. They may play out one source of power against another in order to get the impact they want. Having power and wanting to participate in creating a change may go hand in hand just as lacking power and wanting authoritative expert advice and intervention pair up.

That was a major issue in this case. Thus, Mary participates in sessions in such a way that the therapy may become a means for the other family members to learn to talk things over, which is her preferred way of dealing with things. In this respect she definitely perceives their therapy to be in her interest and to play a role in pursuing her power. But in so doing she concentrates on changes in the others first, and her stakes in the therapy primarily depend on the willingness of the others to change. When they do not agree on the direction and range of changes she wants, Mary hopes they will change their minds as the therapy proceeds. On this background, she acquiesces in sessions to the therapists' competence and to Paul's changing willingness to address further changes, spurring the process along with subtle suggestions. But as the therapy progresses, Mary increasingly wants to change vital parts of her life and needs especially for Paul to go along with these changes. In interview 8, with Mary and Paul about one year into therapy, Lisbeth asks whether they considered individual sessions for themselves too. Mary: "No, because Paul wouldn't, and I would very much like to. I think it's very exciting and they've been a big help. But, again, if they don't tell me, 'We think that would be a big help', it doesn't happen. Again that's something we decide ourselves." Asked for her opinion of whether they needed individual talks, Mary answers: "I think we needed it. Maybe not so much now because things developed very positively." Lisbeth asks Paul for his opinion: "I don't think I needed to talk to them alone." Asked whether she suggested it in sessions, Mary responds: "No, because I only thought about it after our latest talk. . . . I've thought about it quite a lot because I've begun to have to think a lot about my own life."

The stances family members adopt on who is to participate in sessions, why that combination of family members is to take part, and how this is to be decided change during their therapy. Their reasons for a particular con-stellation of participants are linked with which problems (seen as individual symptoms or interpersonal troubles) are to be treated in these sessions. Think of Mary's statement in interview 1 about Donna's earlier individual therapy – that it feels strange to witness major changes in a family member you care for, but not to know why and to be put out of influence on it.

In contrast to Mary, in the beginning Angie wants individual sessions for herself or sessions only with Mary. Rounding off session 2 and arriving at an appointment for the next session, Ole asks Angie whom she thinks should take part. Angie responds that it is to be only she and Mary. Ole prompts her: "What about Paul?" Angie insists on only Mary and herself: "Mary understands me better, for instance, my problems with darkness." Paul accepts her stance, but Ole pushes for reasons why only particular members are to be present, and it is decided to continue a mix of individual sessions with Angie and family sessions with everybody. Later in session 11 while negotiating future sessions after a joint meeting with some of Angie's teachers at her school, Ingrid asks Angie which appointment should be made for the next session. Angie starts out: "I don't know." Paul intervenes: "You can't keep on saying you don't know." Angie: "But it's difficult." Asked whether Donna should participate, Angie prefers her not to be there: "I don't think she's got anything to do with it. She doesn't say anything anyhow." Angie now argues, hesitantly but persistently, about who is to participate and why. Her reasons are explicitly related to the treatment of her symptoms, and to whether members contribute to resolving them in the sessions.

At the beginning of therapy, Angie is eager for individual sessions with Ingrid. But she soon loses interest in such sessions. Therapists easily interpret such changes as an indication of bad work (but the range of changes for Angie and her family speak against this). It may conjure up professional insecurity overshadowing another important reason why clients' interests in sessions may shift. After four individual sessions with Ingrid, Angie wants a joint session with her parents. She had been preoccupied by wanting a therapist to herself and be the unquestioned center of attention, which was difficult for her when the others were present. Now she wants sessions with her parents to deal with issues calling for joint consideration and negotiation. "It is very good we all talk together," she says in session 7 and flatly turns down Ingrid's proposal for another individual session: "It doesn't matter. I don't care." Angie wants to negotiate her needs, for which her parents' acceptance and support are crucial, in sessions with her parents and the therapists present as a means of gaining influence on her parents.

Four months later when individual sessions with Donna and sessions with Mary, Paul, and Donna about issues surrounding Donna have started, Angie says in interview 5 that she thinks it is strange that "now they talk with Donna." But she has no idea what the therapists were to talk with her about, except "if I had some problems." Lisbeth: "Yes, what would you then talk about?" Angie: "I don't know. I have no problems now." In interview 8 six months later, Angie says she has not been to sessions much but has not given it much thought. She is only curious to hear "what they are saying about me." Asked to look back and compare, Angie says there was a time when it seemed strange to her that only Donna, Mary, and Paul participated, since originally talks were arranged because of her problems: "I only thought it was about me, but apparently it was also about Donna, a lot about Donna, in fact." Paul: "It was about all of us, wasn't it?" Mary says that Angie never understood though she tried to explain it to her, and Angie confirms. Lisbeth: "Does it make you cross sometimes?" Angie: "Yes, sometimes." Asked whether she considered talking to them during the same period as Donna, Angie says: "But I don't bother to.... It's boring.... If they only talk about Donna, I don't bother to be there." The meaning of participation in sessions has changed for Angie from wanting to have the therapists to herself and being the center of things, which the others should stay clear of, to not bothering to take part any more. She is not sorry about it "because I think they've helped me a lot." In her last individual interview 9, half a year after the therapy ended, Angie admits to still not understanding why Donna got involved, but also to thinking "who cares then." These statements from across the therapy show that clients' reasons for participating in it and their stances toward it change. Other courses of changing reasons and stances about participating in their shared therapy are seen in the other three clients.

4.6. Diverse Perspectives, Modes of Participation, and Stakes in Sessions

In the remaining sections of this chapter, I shall highlight differences between the clients concerning their shared therapy. First, I shall look at differences between them in sessions. It is already obvious that the family members participated differently in their joint sessions and that their joint therapy has different meanings to them. The following chapters will show that, although members' perspectives and participation in sessions change during their therapy, they remain different from each other. Such differences speak against interpreting family therapy as having only one definite meaning and effect. They speak for recognizing the importance of diversity in the creation of meaning and in the dynamics and effects of therapy. In fact, these differences create a changing constellation and dynamics of participation in the sessions. They also challenge each member's understanding and participation in changing their problems and are important sources of personal learning from each other (Dreier 2003).

Differences between members' experiences and participation might be interpreted as expressions of different stable personality properties. Because each individual's experiences and participation change on the way, these changes must reflect characteristic individual patterns of change. But there is an interpersonal dimension to the formation of personal meaning and participation, and relations between persons are situated in their participation in local contexts and are part of their trajectories of participation across contexts. So, differences between them in sessions arise from their relations with each other in sessions and other contexts. They spring from these persons' positioned trajectories in relation to others in their complex social practice, including the interpersonal dimensions of participating in a joint therapy. Individual family members' different perspectives and participation in sessions, as well as what is at stake for them in these sessions, are mediated by events and concerns in their diverse everyday lives in other contexts.

But these mediations do not stamp out the situated character of experience, participation, and concerns. They are still a person's experiences, participation, and concerns in a particular context and situation that differ from her experiences, participation and concerns in other contexts. Thus, Paul and Mary do not take part and experience themselves as father, mother, and spouse in the same way in sessions as they do at home. In sessions, their experiences and participation are linked to being in a therapy that is a particular part of their lives and to their coparticipants in sessions – the therapists whom they only encounter here and the other family members with whom they share their family life at home plus these other experiences in sessions. What they "take notice of" in sessions, as Mary puts it, rests on their linking events and relations in sessions to experiences and concerns from home and other parts of their lives into a complex set of personal reasons to experience and participate in a particular way in sessions. Indeed, they have other situated reasons for participating other ways, in other places.

That Paul's and Mary's experiences and participation as father, mother, and spouse differ between sessions and home shows that the concept of position is insufficient to analyze their practice. While their positions as father, mother, and spouse matter to them across different contexts, they matter differently and make them participate differently. A position does not make a person act in the same way in different contexts. The concept of position must be linked to the concept of location to situate a person's experiences, reasons, and participation in her trajectory in a structure of social practice. Then we may ask in which particular ways a person's positions as, say, parent, spouse, and client are played out in different contexts. Positions matter and are realized in situated ways, and persons have different stakes in them in different contexts. Their realizations do not vary arbitrarily as discursive theorizing would have us believe by playing down the significance of our situatedness in structures of social practice (Harper 1996; Harré and Gillett 1997; Potter and Wetherell 1992).

4.7. Diverse Re-Interpretations of Sessions Elsewhere

In this section, I still look at differences between participants' experiences and ways of dealing with their therapy but now outside sessions showing that clients also re-interpret sessions differently elsewhere between and after sessions. Besides contributing to my general argument that persons deal with aspects from other contexts as part of the way in which they participate in any context, this section points out that we misinterpret sessions if we merely take them for what happened in their time slot and place. The meaning of a session's events and experiences is not a fixed product, which persons then merely carry around with them and apply accordingly. On the contrary, if session events and experiences are not discarded and forgotten, their meaning continues to change. And the ways in which their meanings are changed are part of persons' concerns with ongoing events and opportunities in their lives later in other places. So, sessions gain a different meaning across times and places, between and after sessions than they had when the clients took part in them and the therapists were present. If therapists do not realize that clients continue to re-interpret sessions in various ways and, thus, change the meaning these sessions have for them in their everyday lives, therapists may easily believe that the meaning they witnessed is the one that lives on afterward when they are no longer there to discover the ongoing changes in clients' interpretations.

These phenomena are overlooked or downplayed in research and conceptions about therapy because access to materials about clients' practice outside as well as inside sessions is a precondition for discovering, or at least documenting, that clients continue to re-interpret sessions and attribute other meanings to them afterward in other places. Yet, there is every reason to believe that continued processing and interpretation is a widespread and significant feature of the workings of sessions. We should, indeed, hope so; sessions continue to live on and are not just left behind because they are re-interpreted and put to other uses. It indicates that the clients consider aspects of the sessions worth pursuing further in their everyday lives.

Just as the meaning of a text emerges from the interaction between the text and an interpreter in a specific context and does not adhere to the text as its property (Alcoff 1996, 58), the meaning of the session talk emerges from different participants' interaction with it in different contexts; consequently, it does not adhere to the talk itself. Thus, clients interact with their sessions in other ways in other contexts and come to see the meaning of their sessions differently. One reason is that there are other constellations of participants in other contexts; for instance, the authoritative voice of their therapist is not there. The clients occupy other positions, or their positions matter to them in other ways in other contexts, and that makes them interpret the meaning of session talk differently. They also have other concerns in other contexts so that session talk may gain other meanings to them.

Obviously clients re-interpret pieces of advice from their therapists. They may even re-interpret other session events and therapist statements as if they were pieces of advice. In session 1, we talk at length about the recurring morning quarrels between the daughters. The therapists' intention is to get a more concrete understanding of how problems play out and the role each family member takes in them. Ingrid asks the daughters what they think about a solution Mary proposed, and they both say it is a good idea. Mary is surprised because she had mentioned it earlier at home and they ignored it. In the following interview, it becomes clear that at home Mary re-interpreted this sequence from the session. She now attributes her proposal to Ingrid – as Ingrid's advice on how to solve that problematic situation. But our intention in the session was just to get a better understanding of typical problem situations at home; we had no idea that we had put forward a piece of advice. Interpreting and using our explorations as a piece of advice from her expert allies in a context where we do not take part lends authoritative power to Mary's pursuit at home of a proposal her daughters were unwilling to listen to when she suggested it.

At the same time, by seeing it as the therapists' advice, Mary may attribute the responsibility to the therapists if an attempt should fail.

Clients also re-interpret expert statements and stances to use in struggles with others elsewhere and later. Drastic and far-reaching changes in their experiences and participation may come about by relating to session events elsewhere and later. In session 5, the therapists call into question that Mary and Paul take responsibility for Angie by doing things for her. Angie then merely learns to bring things about by making others do them for her and is free to criticize them for the results afterward if they fail to guess her wishes to her satisfaction. This displacement of responsibility from Angie to Mary and Paul often leads to disagreements between the parents over how to be coresponsible with Angie for her wishes. Interview 2, which takes place shortly after, shows that in the meantime Mary and Paul have re-interpreted what the session was about so that they now learned something important. They had paid too much attention to the children when they were cross. They had not cut them off and made demands on them, but now that must change. Paul: "Instead of showing consideration for them, one should perhaps show more consideration for oneself because we have never done that. We have always shown too much consideration for the children. So now it is perhaps time to show consideration for ourselves." Compared to the way things were in the session, the parents have reversed that the children were demanding on them and are now making demands on the children instead. This change in stance is quite a contrast, especially compared to Mary's earlier very considerate mode of care, and we therapists were taken aback by the authoritarian and retaliating turn they had made of our work with them. In the new polarized constellation between them, everybody is increasingly blaming somebody else – or at least the parents are blaming the children, and the children are blaming the parents. As is typical of family therapy, the parents are the first to grasp this and use it for their purposes, while the children gradually follow along, among other things provoked by the parents' new reaction. But first the children also have "to learn something new." In fact, the polarization changes the situation into one in which they all have a similar notion of a major problem and come to agree on a common label for it – though they locate the problem differently: in the other party of the newly formed polarity. They come to see "being cross" as their major problem. In the interview, Lisbeth asks them in turn: "Looking back at that session, what was the most important thing that happened?" Angie says she does not know and wants Lisbeth to ask one of the others first. Donna ventures: "I know. It was about being cross. . . . We were tired of our mum and dad being cross, especially dad." Mary: "It is not fun to be accused of something one isn't." Mary complains that they cannot talk calmly with their children without their getting cross or accusing their parents of being cross. "As soon as you say a word that doesn't suit them, then we are cross." Donna: "What else should one call it?" Mary: "But that's because you won't discuss. . . . Like dad says, you want us to sit around with a broad smile and be happy no matter what you do and offer us. You don't like it when we make demands on you at all.

If it doesn't just suit you, then we are cross." Donna: "Sometimes one can also make you shout, you know. You always say we should sit quietly and discuss." Mary: "Well, I don't tell you, 'You are so cross.' But you turn everything around no matter what one says, 'Oh, you are so cross.'" Donna: "You are damned cross!" Mary: "But I'm never cross!" Donna: "Yes, you are!" Mary: "No, I'm not!" Donna: "Yes, you are!" Behind the parents' drastic change of mind lies their discovery that they have let themselves be divided by their troubles with the children and that this has damaged their relationship and their practice of upbringing. So they extract a topic from a session talk, work it over in their everyday practice, and put it to quite contrary uses. The heated exchange in the interview also changes Donna's stance on being cross. In response to the same interview question about the significance of the session, Donna says: "I think I've learned not to say mum is cross." Evidently she did not learn that during the session, but came to realize it in dealing with the session afterward. Angie rounds off the heated discussion in the interview saying that she did not get anything out of the session. "I think we should talk about it again so that we could get more out of it."

However, to re-interpret sessions is only one way of using them in other contexts. In fact, if we only emphasize the re-interpretation of sessions, we construe a one-sided understanding of the links between sessions and other contexts and of the complex ways in which persons configure their everyday activities. We only look at how the clients deal with sessions in these other contexts and forget that they are concerned with much else than sessions. In other contexts, sessions are not the center of concern but rather a limited part of the experiences used in particular everyday situations. The opportunities and issues of their everyday contexts primarily configure which session events and experiences the clients reinterpret and use. So we should not overlook the particular local practices the clients are involved in and how re-interpretations of sessions are a part in the way they configure their participation in them. In the preceding instances, the re-interpretations at home were not simply trail-offs from the sessions or, as Bergin and Garfield call it, ways to "absorb, utilize, and follow through on the facilitative efforts of the therapist" (1994, 826). On the contrary, they were occasioned and motivated by events, social relations, and concerns at home, which gave these re-interpretations a particular role and meaning.

4.8. Struggles over Sessions and Their Uses

Some differences between clients coexist quite unproblematically, while other differences contradict each other because their experiences, participation, and concerns are in conflict. Indeed, they may be in conflict over their therapy, and sessions may become an instrument in these conflicts. Many readers may consider a conflicting way of experiencing and dealing with therapy an extreme and unfortunate way to participate in sessions and to use them, but the significance and frequency of such conflicts may be widely underestimated.

Conflicts over sessions may be played out in particular ways already in sessions. An instance occurs in session 13, half a year into therapy, when conflicts between Donna and her parents come to the fore. The family had just agreed that they have improved the ways in which they deal with Angie's symptoms. Ingrid then asks: "Are there other things we should take up?" At first Angie and Paul agree there is not. Paul then adds surly: "That's just wonderful." Ingrid asks him whether he is ironic. He responds that he needs a special style to survive at home. Angie: "Yes, you are special." Mary explains that a couple of days ago Paul "almost flipped totally out over those two." Donna: "We talk about Angie over here." Angie insists that they do; then she adds: "You can tell them if you want." Donna: "No, I don't bother to. But there was a lot I could say." Paul: "Good lord, I'd better go outside." Ingrid: "Is there anything you'd like to say to the others?" Donna: "Especially him over there. There are lots of things I think are wrong." Paul: "The two of us don't have the same point of view on various things, that's right." Mary: "But certainly one needn't have that." Following an exchange about that there still are problems at home Donna says she would not mind talking about it here while Paul wavers: "Donna and I don't agree very well, I can tell you that. That one then sees everything I do as wrong isn't everything there is to it. She probably thinks I am totally crazy." Paul suggests that one of the therapists take a session with Donna, and Mary protests "because Donna sees it in one way, I see it in another way and you in a third way. Donna shouldn't just (talk to the therapists, OD) without you. Donna is always very negative, always. And she is very dominating, and she believes she can do everything." Paul: "If she says something, then she is right, I can tell you. And then I stop talking because once in a while I flip out because then I've had enough, and then maybe I shout. But that's a natural reaction because one cannot discuss with Donna." Mary: "The two of you cannot discuss." . . . Donna: "Do you know what makes it so hard, dad? It's because we aren't fond of each other. I don't feel you are my father." Mary: "You won't." Donna: "But I don't feel you could never come over and give me a hug." Paul: "But remember then that during the last three to four years you've lived only for your friends and nobody else. And if one talked to you, one got a cross reaction. And then maybe I say, 'then it doesn't matter, then you can go on living your own life.'" Shortly after Donna says she wants to have these things talked over and agrees to see Ole for a couple of individual sessions. Paul tells about things Donna does wrong and spells out his distrust in her, sided by Mary, while both Donna and Paul, sided by Mary, tell the other that he or she is hopeless and how hurt and let down they feel. Angie says that the therapy was to be for her, and she does not want to take part in sessions with that kind of discussion between the others. "They should have their own psychologist, then." After talking with the therapists about that for a while, Angie says that she does not mind if Donna talks with Ole. Looking at Donna, Paul says: "I bet you have a totally wrong impression of me."

Here the clients not only have their usual conflicts with each other. They are also in conflict over the sessions: Is there to be a sequence of sessions about the problems concerning Donna? If so, who is to take part in them and what should they deal with? Besides, they are in conflict over the therapy: How are these problems to be understood, who is to blame for them, and who and what should change? Furthermore, they are in conflict over their therapists: How do they understand these issues? How can I win them for my side of the story and be sure they do not believe my opponent, blame me and side with him or her instead? These conflicts in sessions are not the same conflicts they have at home, which are played out in quite other ways and, during the period of therapy, include their sessions and therapists differently. They are particular conflicts in sessions. But the reasons for these particular conflicts in sessions do not just stem from their sessions. They emerge, first of all, from their conflicts at home and the way in which they hope, or fear, that the therapy may come to matter for these conflicts at home. The reasons for their particular conflicts in sessions are mediated through their conflicts at home. That is why they are particularly concerned in sessions about which understanding of their troubles the therapists may get and even fight over that understanding, trying to insist on their side of the story, reminding the therapists that it is important, and fearing that the therapists may fall for their opponent's story if they do not get a chance to tell their own.

These conflicts between Donna, Mary, and Paul continue for some time. Here I shall follow them a little longer to throw more light on conflicts about their sessions and their therapists. After a session between Ole and Donna, we all meet again in session 15. In that session, Paul is very much on guard over what Donna says and might want – and so is Mary. They both fire back at Donna and, thereby, take part in re-producing a gap between them that cannot be overcome in that way. Instead, they say that they are deeply disappointed in her because she created serious trouble for all of them a couple of years ago. Donna admits this and says that it is now in the past and that she has changed, but they insist that it continues and, in Mary's words, "She has done everything to ruin our trust." What happened was that during a period when the parents went to their summer cottage on weekends while it was literally impossible to get Donna to come along, Donna had a group of friends in their flat. Many things were damaged or destroyed, and complaints from neighbors ended in an official warning from the city authority overseeing the apartment block that they would be evicted from the flat if it happened once more. Donna wants them to give her another chance to prove that now she can handle what she could not then, but they insist that they do not believe her and trust her. After about half an hour, Donna leaves the session, hurt by how disappointed and bitter her parents still are and shocked by how much her mother feels that way too. The session continues without her. At the end Paul says: "That was just bad luck. I was the one to be shot at, not her. She had set the stage for us to talk about me. But, you know, I don't feel I'm that much to blame." Mary jumps in complaining that "It always ends with both saying that now they leave."

Conflicts in sessions about the sessions, the therapy, and the therapists may arise spontaneously as a session proceeds. But they are often anticipated and prepared by (some) clients. Paul believes that too. "She had set the stage for us to talk about me." Clients conduct these conflicts in sessions in ways they hope will make their conflictual maneuvers less obvious to the therapists and the opponent clients present. If they did not, other participants might discover and reveal their intents and counter or block them. Their therapists might do so too and come to side less with them and more with others. We may call this kind of behavior scheming, though it need not always be clearly premeditated, and a participant may even do it without paying much attention to it or being aware of it – in the course of pursuing his or her concerns and stances as he or she sees them. For instance, in the individual sessions with Ole, Donna says that she wants his support to resolve the conflicts with her parents and make them take her seriously as "a big girl. . . . It's hard to be alone against them. It helps just to know there is one to support me." She also wants Ole to tell her parents "to watch what they say because it will hit me hard, . . . and I believe they think more about it when you tell them." Yet, she never says directly in any session what she reveals in the next interview that her goal is to have her therapist make her parents allow her to stay at home alone during weekends. "That I get permission to be at home alone. That they allow me to show them that they can believe in me. . . . I believe Ole could make them allow me to, at least once. Then if that weekend went well, maybe they'd allow me another." Lisbeth: "How do you think he could make them allow you?" Donna: "By telling them he thinks they should give me another chance." By not telling me directly what she is trying to make me do for her, she does not run as big a risk that I might not do it, or that I might do something else instead of what she hopes.

There are other instances when some of the clients report particular episodes (or versions thereof), which they believe to be incriminating to their opponents. They may do so while the opponents are present or when they are separated in individual sessions or couple sessions. For instance, Donna uses individual sessions to reveal secrets about Paul that she believes will make the therapists side with her and do something about him. Likewise, Mary attempts to turn sessions into a means to promote her goal of more talk between family members and an understanding in line with her beliefs. These attempts to pursue conflicting interests and stances turn into fights between them when they are countered by other family members who defend their own interests and stances or maintain and strengthen their hegemony. That happened in all these instances. It shows a crucial condition for this kind of scheming to succeed, namely that the others do not discover the scheming or that it is disguised as not being a scheme but a move out of common concern resting on common grounds – which those advocating them may (in part) themselves believe. Such scheming belongs to a life in contexts and relations ridden by conflicts, which make any plain articulation of these intentions risky.

Conflicts over their sessions, therapy, and therapists also take place outside sessions. We saw that in the interview where the family fought over what they learned from the previous session, which demands should be made on whom, and what being cross meant. The clients also turn the meaning of sessions and of particular therapist statements and stances or presumed interpretations of clients' problems into objects of struggles at home and in other places. In the previous section, we also saw that such incidents may be widespread.

The instances in this section show that conflicts not only impede change but also trigger changes by lending dynamics to their dealings with the issues of the therapy (Dreier 1993b). Conflicts are the cause of therapy, such as launching sessions with Donna. Beyond that, conflicts throw light on their problems, and both therapists and clients learn new things about clients' lives and troubles because of these conflicts. Furthermore, conflicts give the clients reasons to want changes. The conflicts between them and for each of them are also inextricably connected with their being linked with each other in a joint family life. Indeed, that gives particular meaning and dynamics to their conflicts. For instance, they all share the common concern to participate in this therapy in order to help Angie and to improve their family life with the understanding that they will have expert strangers intervene between them and that these strangers will be given access to problematic aspects of their everyday lives, experiences, and concerns. But that common concern is surrounded by a set of diverse and conflicting individual concerns and stances of accomplishing what I cannot at home: teaching the others to talk, getting even with my father, and so forth. And it is not possible for an individual member, the family as a whole, or the therapists to separate the common concerns and stances from the diverse and conflicting ones. Still, they may and do disagree over these different and conflicting concerns and stances. When they establish how and why they want to participate in their therapy, they must hence balance off these various concerns and stances.

5   Therapy in Clients' Social Practice across Places

In the first two sections of this chapter, I go into the meaning of participating in sessions for clients on the basis of their participation in other contexts. In the last three sections I turn to how clients may link their participation and experiences in sessions into their social practice across places. The structural arrangement of sessions makes it necessary to understand how clients may accomplish this linking across places before going into the course of therapy-related changes in the next chapters. The fact that clients' participation and experiences in sessions and other places differ adds to its importance.

5.1. Diverse Modes of Participation in Diverse Contexts

As argued in chapter 1, research on therapy generally assumes that clients act in identical ways inside and outside sessions. That understanding is crucial to the prevailing idea about how sessions and clients' everyday lives are linked, how insights gained in sessions matter, and how therapy works. It also plays a key role in therapists' ideas about how a "good client" should behave. A good client hides nothing from her therapist and can be trusted to act in identical ways inside and outside sessions. In doing so, she allows her therapist comprehensive access and penetrating insight into her life from within sessions so that the therapist may reach a good understanding of his client on the basis of information obtained here. Therapists may, thus, assume to know from within sessions what their clients do outside sessions. Conceptions of therapy and evaluations of its effects and change processes assume that clients' practice and problems are identical across contexts or even surface in their purest and deepest form in the practice and interpretation of sessions. All this is part of more widely held assumptions that persons are insightful, rational, and skilled actors if and only if they transfer what they learned in places of expertise to act accordingly elsewhere (Lave 1988). These assumptions make the topic of this section controversial. Still, I want to push the argument further rather than to characterize clients negatively when they do not live up to these ideas and their behaviors are labeled "non-compliant." I contend that persons, here clients attending therapy, normally act in different ways in different contexts and for good reasons. This claim was partly documented in the last sections of chapter 4. I shall now show that clients participate in a particular way in sessions compared to in other contexts and that such differences are significant for understanding how therapy works. If this is so, we must understand how therapy works on a broader basis than sessions.

In our interviews we asked the clients whether it is different to take part in sessions compared to the interviews at home. If they answered affirmatively (which they did), they were asked what they considered to be the main differences. Their responses to these questions went as follows.

The clients all repeatedly emphasize that in sessions they "listen" in quite different ways and so they do not just to their therapists. What strikes them most is that they listen to each other in different ways in sessions than, say, at home. From early on in therapy, this difference makes sessions stand out as special and significant to them. In interview 2, even the rather inarticulate Angie claims that the others listen more to her and not just because she says more. Mary responds: "Angie listens more when Ingrid and Ole are there." Angie retorts: "You also listen more when they are there than when . . . " Paul interrupts: "We have always listened to you, but . . . " Angie: "No, because you keep interrupting me, right." Evidently, if talk – which is the dominant practice in sessions – is to lead anywhere, people must listen to what each other say. Thus, at home Angie keeps bringing up a particular topic and wanting to talk about it to put pressure on her parents to make her wish come true. In sessions, as Angie sees it, her parents at least listen to her talking about it, which they do not at home. Mary responds: "Well, it's also because you can sometimes talk about it at least ten times an hour so we may have seemed a bit as if we don't listen." In response to the interviewer Mary admits: "Honestly, it is very tiring to listen to." Talk leading nowhere wears out your readiness to listen and continue talking.

The next difference the clients emphasize is that because they listen to each other in quite different ways, talks with each other and their therapists in sessions become very different from talks at home. Early in their therapy, they notice this as a difference in how other family members take part. To listen is what others hopefully do when I say something in a conversation. To notice changes in listening, then, is to notice changes in others and not in how they themselves talk. Shortly after in the same interview Lisbeth asks Mary why she thinks Angie listens more. Mary responds: "Because she takes it all calmly when they are there. If they weren't there, then we would . . . she may turn somewhat . . . " Paul: "Then she turns peeved." Asked the same question, Angie first says she does not know why they listen more and then restates that they interrupt her less. Mary says that Angie behaves differently when the therapists are there. "We haven't explained anything else to Angie that day {in the session, OD] than we usually do." Paul: "Angie listens more to our points of view when somebody else is hearing it than if we explained it like we have always done; then she does not listen." In other words, they do not think Angie listens when they explain things on their own, but she does when the therapists are there. Paul: "Here it's as if maybe she considers it a little, all of it." So, they may even talk about the same topics in both places but in very different ways, and talks in sessions may lead to points they might never reach at home.

I shall now point out other differences between talk in sessions and at home which the clients mention during their therapy.

In interview 2, Donna says she got the impression that the therapists hope she might come up with suggestions about their problems but, "Sometimes there are things I don't say because it wouldn't suit one of them too well. . . . I also have to watch out when Ole and Ingrid are there. I don't know them that well. After all, they are still strangers to me a bit, you know. . . . You sort of have to formulate your ideas a little before you express them." By contrast, when the therapists are not there, "then I tell it point-blank." Paul and Angie recognize that they consider things more before saying them. Donna continues: "I believe we never talked so nicely to our mum and dad as when Ole and Ingrid are there." Mary takes up on that: "That's one of the major problems. One can't sit down and talk quietly with you. You don't lose your temper, get mad and crazy and what else you usually do when we are to talk about something." Donna: "No, you can't allow yourself that when they are there." So the clients watch more how they behave and what they say in sessions. The question remains whether they always succeed in participating more deliberately and watchfully or get caught, saying all the same what they had planned not to say in response to what other family members and the therapists say during a session. Thus, Donna's troubles were taken up in their therapy because she happened to say more in a session than she had in mind to do. Be that as it may, in sessions when "strangers are there," clients consider more how they articulate something, they treat each other more nicely when talking to each other, and talks are not so easily interrupted by conflicts and quarrels. All this makes it possible to pursue quite different concerns and problems by means of talk in sessions as compared to talk at home. Let me illuminate this further.

In the individual interview 6 with Donna after some sessions between her and Ole about halfway through therapy, Lisbeth refers to the interest of our study in changes in their everyday lives and in the part sessions may play in bringing them about when so much else happens in their lives. Donna responds: "Well, it's something quite different when you just live an ordinary life and don't go to sessions. You become quite different, I think." Lisbeth: "In the sessions?" Donna: "Yes, because when somebody else is sitting there, you can't just yell and shout." Lisbeth: "Is it mostly you who behaves differently, or do you also think the others do?" Donna: "I think everybody become different. . . . My dad also gets quite funny. Suddenly he becomes understanding, and he may agree to everything. It is even different when he returns home." Here Donna includes herself – not just other members of the family – among the persons who act differently in sessions, pointing to the feature of her behavior at home which the others complain most about: she "just yells and shouts."

Because of this difference between her participation at home and in sessions the other family members may get a quite different impression of Donna as a person in the two places, and a quite different understanding of the problems she is involved in and their meaning to her. For instance, Donna then cannot simply be the kind of person who always "yells and shouts" whenever problems occur and who is unwilling and unable to take part in dealing with problems in other ways. Likewise, while talking in interview 3 about some sessions for the couple since the previous interview, Mary says that she thinks the couple talks "have been better than I expected" because "Paul talks a lot more and is much more open when we are there alone. I also think we get around things in a better way when we are there alone, and new angles on things stand out." Reflecting on the same issue in session 24 with the couple more than a year into therapy, Paul and Mary concur that for a long time Paul said the most in sessions so that session talks often centered on him without it being because he was more wrong. Paul responds: "You know, what I said over here, I might not have said at home." Sessions make him stand out as quite a different person, and many of his points of view and concerns become much clearer to other family members.

Much to our surprise, in interview 1 the family says that two years ago, when Donna attended individual therapy for half a year, they barely talked about her therapy at home. Mary: "We didn't hear much about it because Donna didn't talk much about it.. I didn't think I should make her say a lot about it if she didn't want to talk about it." This contrast between concerted problem talk in sessions and no problem talk at home might be more pronounced because Donna attended an individual therapy. Nonetheless, the family states in interviews throughout their therapy that they barely talk about their therapy at home, not even about sessions in which they all took part. For instance, Donna says in interview 6 about halfway through therapy that they still barely talk about her sessions with Ole. She decided to change in some respects, but did not tell them so nor why she did it. She does not even notice whether they react to her changed behaviors. On second thought, though, "I don't know, maybe my dad does a little. I also think he is pleased about it." Donna thinks he understands why she changes. But they do not talk about it at home so the others may not realize it or may come to a different understanding of it than Donna intends and believes. It continues to be the case during their therapy and as far beyond as the interviews go that the whole family rarely gathers at home to talk – especially not at length and about problems. Lisbeth asks Donna in interview 6 whether she talks about problems at home, and Donna responds that she does a little and is able to do so with Mary but not with Paul because she and Paul are both stubborn. Angie also talks a little with Mary, and so does Paul. Mary is the only person involved in all these dialogues at home.

Why is this contrast so strong? It is primarily because they are not able to resolve problems by talking about them at home. In session 4, Mary characterizes the talks that occur between them at home: "I wouldn't even call it discussion. It's more like quibbling. You can't talk." At various times they report in sessions how attempts to talk about problematic topics at home soon lead to raised voices and yelling and shouting in which case at least Angie retreats to her room and stays behind her door. Doors are slammed, accusations fill the air, Donna and Angie often slap each other; so does Paul occasionally. Far from leading to resolutions these attempted talks are explosive, lead to various open conflicts and new problems in which they then get stuck. As long as this is so, there is no good reason to try this way again.

There is a further important reason why concerted problem talk at home is rare. In session 24 with the couple more than a year into therapy, we talk about their current notion of differences and similarities between sessions and their practice at home. Paul points out: "Sitting over here talking about it, it's more concentrated. At home when we talk about it, things happen in between, and you really don't get it back in focus again." Ingrid: "It's easier to evade." Paul: "It's also difficult to talk with everybody, that is, with the children, at once because they have a lot of things going and we are rarely all gathered like when we are eating. We almost never are any more. So we have no time when we can say, 'Now we are going to talk'. It's incredibly rare." In other words, even if they got the idea to transfer the practice of concentrated talk to their everyday lives, it would be difficult. There would be many obstacles that have to do with the complexities of their ordinary practices at home and elsewhere. It is not easy to organize a regular practice of gathering at home for concerted talks about problematic issues. But the sociopractical arrangement of sessions creates a secluded place and time for this. The therapists take the main responsibility for making it happen in sessions, and the clients want them to though not unconditionally. Whose responsibility it is, whether the others accept this distribution of responsibility, and the burdens of carrying it make practices in sessions and at home different. In the same session Mary says: "It's so wonderful to come here. He's never said so much in his entire life as when we were here." She adds another major difference between sessions and their practice at home. At home, "it's me who has to get the conversation going." That is a heavy burden to her and this difference between sessions and their talks at home remains important to Mary, even at this late stage in their therapy. Sessions are "so wonderful" to her because she does not have to carry things ahead alone.

In summing up, the following features of the clients' participation in sessions stand out as being especially important: the others listen more; they do not interrupt and yell and shout at each other; they consider things before saying them; they gain other impressions of each other and of their troubles; they come to talk more with each other, which is wonderful; they gain other experiences from concerted problem talk; and it is not the responsibility of an individual member to make such talks happen. None of these features of session talk are universal features of human conversation irrespective of time, place, arrangement, and purpose. On the contrary, these features stand out for the clients because they differ from how things go in their lives in other places, and the clients see these differences as useful for their pursuit of concerns via sessions. Sessions, home, school, work, and whatever else these clients participate in are particular contexts in which they take part in particular ways. Their participation in any of them is grounded in their selective linking of a set of present concerns to concerns from other times and places. Thus, participation in sessions is "wonderful" to Mary because of the way it differs from how they do things at home, and this wonderful difference makes her participate in a particular way in sessions where she holds back in order to let that difference unfold. The fact that activities and experiences in sessions are mediated in a cross-contextual way is in line with the purpose of sessions to be helpful primarily for clients' lives outside sessions.

5.2. Particular Features of Sessions Work in Conflictual Practices

Indeed, according to the clients, sessions work because of important differences between practices in sessions and in their other contexts. First of all, the clients emphasize that they get a chance to talk with each other in sessions. Halfway through therapy Mary says in interview 7: "The important thing has been that we get to talk with each other. . . . Now when both we and the girls go there and we don't talk much about this with the girls, they get a chance to talk about it, and we talk about it over there. I think that changes quite a lot. Especially the children think more about what they do and what they say, and when they react strongly, they stop sooner because they have begun to think about what they do and why they do it. And again that makes it nicer to be here. You still can't sit down to talk a problem over, and they also get very aggressive, but it stops very soon, and it is not as often as it used to be." The chance for a concentrated talk with each other in sessions about significant and problematic issues stands out as being important because it is not given or successfully realized in their conflictual practice at home. Given that background, talk in sessions allows them to come to a different understanding of each other's points of view, and that urges them to consider more what they do and how this is linked to what others do and to their points of view. They more clearly understand each other's points of view as grounded in their interactions with each other and in their respective parts in their everyday practice at home and elsewhere.

In sessions, the chance to talk with each other in a concentrated way and the therapists' presence as a particular kind of stranger with other perspectives and stances have a combined enabling effect that Mary points to: "The important thing has been that we get to talk with each other. It is as if one talks better when there is somebody else who can see it from a different angle than we can." They repeatedly point to the importance of having new angles introduced to their problems. Already in interview 2 Mary states: "I think things are turned over for us because it is other people who look at things differently. And they try to explain to Angie or Paul how one can do things differently to do it better. That's a good thing to get out of it." These new angles may turn their thoughts, that is, make them see things differently and get new ideas.

In interview 3, Angie expresses similar points of view about her individual sessions with Ingrid: "I like to sit and talk." She says it is different to talk with Ingrid compared to other adults. The talks are more about her, Ingrid listens more to what Angie says, and Angie gets something else out of what Ingrid says. Session talks focus more on the clients. When Angie says that the therapists "listen more to what I say," it also concerns the focus of their conversation and the direction of the therapists' attention and involvement. The conversation is concentrated more on talking about what concerns the clients, about what they do and say, their points of view and mental states, what is difficult for them, and so forth. That is unusual in their ordinary lives and makes sessions stand out as a peculiar experience and a privilege.

In all these respects, there is an intersubjective dimension to their experiences of participating in sessions. To be an immediate witness to the perspectives and reactions, troubles and hopes of the others bear important personal meaning to everyone present. They also hear what the others say about my problems, how they are affected by them, what they feel about them, and they witness their concern for resolving them. In addition, they care to learn about the others' perspectives and concerns – including their perspectives and concerns about me – because their relations with each other are embedded in a history of family bonds and a joint family life that affects each member's well-being and possibilities. This is the basic reciprocity of intersubjective relationships (Holzkamp 1983, 325–332). Listening to each other is imbued with recognizing each other as persons in general and as these particular persons with these particular points of view, concerns, and mental states and with this particular history of a joint family life. Because they do not talk well with each other at home about their current problems, it is a special feature of sessions that they get to talk about things and hear things they would normally not come to know about and get each others' perspectives on.

But because of the close bonds with each other, session talks can also be very hard on them. Their own problems involve other people close to them, and that may make it harder to confront these problems. In a retrospective study of user perspectives on family therapy, a client put it like this: "It made her aware of the effect of the problems on the family" (Reimers and Treacher 1995, 124). As mentioned in section 4.8, Donna only finds out how disappointed and bitter her parents are when they have a joint session about their mutual problems, and this really shocks her. Sessions then confront Donna in a direct and concentrated way with what these problems mean to the other family members whom she cares about and how they feel about Donna's part in them. Besides, what they say in sessions is not just said behind closed doors at home. It is said in the therapists' presence. That makes a difference because it matters how their therapists see them. In the next individual session, Donna tells Ole that she felt ashamed in relation to her therapists. That her parents tell these intimate strangers adds to what hurt her in the session. In fact, it makes a difference to everyone what other family members choose to say in sessions because it reveals what they hold to be particularly significant, serious, and problematic. What is said in sessions, hence, carries a particular impact and meaning for them.

The personal meaning of the intersubjective dimension of participating in sessions includes whether they think they get to play their due part in the talk. Thus, in interview 2, Angie says that she is dissatisfied with the decision at the end of a session about who is to take part in the following sessions: "I think that I, you know, it was I who was to see a psychologist." She wants to be the center of attention but finds it difficult to sustain that position during sessions. In the following interview, Donna adds: "Angie gets a little cross if I start talking. She is the center, you know." Mary counters by insisting on the advantage that Donna hears what goes on and what, among others, Angie has to say, that is, on the personal significance of the intersubjective dimension and on the intersubjective significance of Donna's potential contribution to improve things for everybody and Angie in particular.

In interview 2, Paul states: "We dug quite well into all that about being cross." Digging into things, in particular into their problems, is another important feature in the clients' experience of participating in sessions that is related to the intersubjective nature of its proceedings and to the therapists' introduction of new angles. By digging into things, new aspects of their life and new links between its aspects are realized so that new understandings emerge. But digging into things also entails that the course of session talks is unpredictable to individual family members, and that they get caught in unexpected turns of events, reactions, and dilemmas during the talk. In fact, if they could control the course of a session fully in advance and as it goes on, they would lose the new, unknown angles it brings forth. In the final interview with Paul and Mary, they state in general terms about participating in sessions that they both "got very engaged while sitting there." Mary: "One quickly gets into something different from what one had in mind. And then one just talks."

The clients see digging into things as an important aspect of what therapists can do, and the ensuing unpredictability of sessions has consequences for their modes of participation. Thus, they appreciate a session because they dig well into something, and they must allow their therapists opportunities to dig into things, for instance, by reporting and talking about particular situations. At the same time, they must watch out not to be enrolled by the therapists into revealing things they do not want them to dig into. While the digging brings about a different understanding of each other and oneself, it matters which understanding this is. The new angles should be ones the clients recognize as relevant, as a step toward a better understanding of their problems and as an opening of possibilities to resolve them. Besides, the digging must be done in such a way that the clients take part in addressing and dealing with these problems. A talk between them in sessions about problems at home can then run differently, with other ways of listening and reacting to each other, of involving oneself in others' concerns and points of view, and of joining and opposing each other. This creates experiences of other qualities and possibilities to their relationships and of being linked and joined in new and re-established ways.

The content and direction of the digging is often a matter of negotiation and conflict between them. The therapists' digging may be related to discords between the clients about which points of view should be presented, considered, and emphasized, or even about which topics from their lives in other places the therapists should help them with. In interview 3, Paul and Mary agree that the topics of the previous sessions were relevant and that they did not miss anything relevant, but Paul thinks the therapists sometimes dug too much into their spouse relationship. Mary started talking about it in a session, and then the therapists dug into it, but Paul did not want to deal with that topic. He got caught in it and was faced with deciding to go along with it or trying to stop it. He went for the latter alternative and found that it was no problem to decline talking about it. This shows that the therapists may take a topic over by digging into it and that when the clients disagree among themselves about whether a topic should be pursued, sessions may more easily proceed the way the therapists want. On the other hand, disagreements often spur the sessions and the digging on as the troubles between Donna, Paul, and Mary show. Here conflicts between them are played out in particular ways in sessions by using session talk as a means to affect their relationships and practice. While they all hope that session talks can resolve their problems at home, they opt for opposite resolutions so that participation in sessions turns into a struggle over what to dig into and which ends to pursue. In fact, the issues therapy is meant to deal with are basically conflictual, so the clients must turn their sessions into a particular part in their conflicts in order that the therapy may come to work. On this background, the clients have different experiences of the meaning and of the way their joint sessions work. These experiences become controversial too. And because sessions work by means of talk, session talk becomes a matter of conflict, of gaining and maintaining power, of insisting on talking about a particular matter or wanting to avoid it, and so forth.

Clearly sessions are particular argumentative contexts. Clients do not simply repeat the same arguments and stances in sessions as, say, at home. They unfold in a different context, with added strange participants, in a different constellation of arguments, counterarguments, and stances, with new ones added and discovered as they proceed. Even when the same things get said as at home, they do not have the same meaning. As Mary puts it in interview 2: "I only think it is because they are there [i.e., the therapists in sessions, OD] because that day we didn't explain anything else to Angie than what we've normally explained to her." While the contents of what they say may be essentially the same, it is articulated, adopted in response to others, insisted on, and becomes meaningful to them in contextually different ways. Indeed, in sessions they all pay attention to the special ways in which they articulate their stances compared to the ways they use at home because that tells them whether they may now be ready to reconsider their stances and embark on changes. Thus, Donna notices that her dad becomes quite strange and understanding in sessions.

Looking back at the features of sessions that clients find significant, there is an often overlooked and striking communality. The features that stand out and make a difference to them tend to be precisely those they cannot realize elsewhere on their own. They point to complementary features of sessions in relation to the features of the other contexts they take part in, namely what lies outside their combined objective possibilities and subjective abilities to do elsewhere. We misinterpret the features the clients see as those that make sessions work if we take them to be universal properties of human conversation and understanding, a particular set of techniques conducted in sessions, or the like, which clients then transfer and apply in identical fashion elsewhere and later. Rather, it takes a comparison between the clients' practice in other contexts and in sessions to define what makes a session work well. Contrary to the prevailing assumption in the research literature, a particular set of properties of sessions as such does not make the sessions work. It is the way the sessions are different from what clients can do in other contexts. What makes a good, significant session depends on what may make a relevant difference in relation to their circumstances and practices in other places.

Rather than universal properties of human communication and reflexivity (Bennett 2005), the properties of session talk reflect the structural arrangement of therapeutic practice. Sessions offer a secluded place for concerted problem talk from which emerges a particular form of session practice that may lead to perspectives and understandings that cannot be had elsewhere. Nonetheless, the working of therapy does not just rely on what goes on in sessions. Sessions are primarily to make a difference in clients' lives elsewhere and later and work by being linked with their everyday practices. What is more, it is left to the clients to include perspectives and understandings of their secluded sessions into their other practices. The fact that sessions are secluded and different from those other practices complicates this inclusion.

5.3. Ways to Include Sessions at Home

My analysis has now reached a point where I may begin to look closely at what it involves for clients to include experiences and understandings from sessions into their lives in other contexts. So far I have argued that it involves including session experiences and understandings into practices that are different from session practices. I have also argued that the inclusion does not proceed as a universal human process but in ways affected by the therapeutic arrangement of concerted problem talk with intimate strangers in a secluded context. Though sessions are not external to clients' ongoing everyday lives, they are a special, secluded part in a temporarily changed composition of their trajectories of participation. However, even though a proper study of therapeutic practice must focus on how clients link experiences and modes of participation across places, this has not been studied systematically. My project cannot compensate fully for this disregard or cover the range of everyday practices needed to comprehend the social practice of therapy. Many blind spots remain, and many issues must be illuminated further. All the same, my study launches an analytic transition toward a new, still incomplete, framework of understanding.

Three further assumptions frame my analysis. First, for therapy to work, session experiences and understandings must fit into the different scopes of clients' other contexts, and clients must have developed personal abilities to realize them. This constitutes the usability of session practices (Dreier 1998a). Second, therapy never works alone – although it is mostly studied as an isolated factor. It always works by becoming a part of something else, that is, in combination with other circumstances, events, activities and experiences. Therapy works by being combined with, or merged with, other influences in clients' lives. This makes it harder to describe and evaluate its particular impact. It calls for differentiated knowledge about how therapeutic and other influences hang together in clients' lives, that is, a more comprehensive conception. Third, only some of the pertinent experiences and understandings from sessions are used elsewhere and later. Uses are partial and selective, just as all personal attention and activity are (see chapter 2).

These complexities are reflected in therapists' uncertainties about how their practice works across places and in clients' statements about it. In fact, based on the clients' statements about it, I initially did not think they quite grasped how their therapy works across places. But gradually it became clear to me that this was partly because my understanding of their statements was affected by the prevailing framework of therapy and that I had to look anew at the materials. It also became clear to me that the clients too are affected by the prevailing framework, which makes it difficult for them to articulate experiences not fitting into it. After all, they are clients in a form of practice where that form of thinking reigns, and they have taken part in other social practices of institutionalized expertise with similar structural arrangements. I had to look in detail at what they said to appreciate their experiences and understandings as personal responses to taking part in a social practice with such a structural arrangement. That gradually enabled me to build a different analytic framework about their experiences of including sessions into their everyday lives in other places. So, I shall stick closely to the terminology the clients used in talking about it.

I start with the clients' vagueness and uncertainty about it. At the beginning of therapy in interview 2, they are asked whether anything changed at home. Angie responds: "I think nothing changed." Mary says that the mornings changed because they got new advice about them in a session, but Donna rejoins: "I think it came by itself." Mary: "I don't think so. I think it still, eh, it can also be unconsciously, but still it sits, it does something." Aside from their uncertainty and disagreement over whether anything changed at all, they are not certain how to identify whether a change was linked with the sessions or not, and they disagree about it. Surely, there may be different reasons for a particular change. There may, in fact, be several reasons for it. It is a complicated question to answer.

In the individual interview 5 with Angie halfway through therapy, Lisbeth asks: "What else happened in the period since our latest interview?" Angie: "Well, now I'm getting a horse. . . . And I got a job. . . . And then nothing else happened." Lisbeth: "That these things happen, does that have anything to do with the talks?" Angie: "Yes, I think so." She tells about Paul's role in helping her find a job as an outcome of the talks, but she cannot express in concrete terms the role of the talks: "I believe they have also been a part in helping it along." Lisbeth refers to the fact that Angie talked the job arrangement over with the owner of the plant, which was quite different from her earlier hesitation to take initiatives and talk to strangers. Angie: "I guess I have become more confident about asking. I'm not so nervous any more." Asked about a possible link to the sessions, Angie responds: "I guess it's because I've talked about it." Again Angie is uncertain and vague about the role of the talks, and she sees the talks as "a part in helping it along." There are other causes and reasons than those stemming from the talks. In fact, the causes and reasons from the talks become part of a configuration of causes and reasons outside sessions, such as Paul finding her a job and Angie taking part in making the job arrangement by acting in new ways in that unknown context. I shall discuss their vagueness further by adding other aspects of the complexities of including session experiences elsewhere and of understanding this process.

At home mostly several things go on at the same time. This is a major contrast to the practice of sessions where we focus on one, or a few, issues at a time and bracket everything else. Experiences are hence processed and pursued in quite different ways in these places. At home there are generally several, quite diverse options for what to do and engage in, and it is not possible to set aside and ignore all but one. Other options and concurrent activities compete for the clients' attention and engagement or even conflict. Their various concerns then overlap and may interfere with each other, and they must balance off, combine, or create a sequential order that takes their diverse activities, concerns, and obligations into consideration. In all this, they must find ways to link a session experience with their other concerns and situate it in the activities of a particular time. In so doing, it gains a particular meaning for them in that situation. Its place and meaning in relation to other aspects of contexts, thus, vary, and so do the clients' reasons to act on it in different ways suited to different situations.

This makes it impossible to hold on to a notion of session experiences as isolated pieces of knowledge applied in the same manner in essentially identical situations elsewhere – as in the prevailing framework about the application of expert knowledge in everyday practice (Lave 1988). On the contrary, they are included in varying ways by being linked with varying other features in different situations in clients' ongoing practice across diverse contexts. If we compare a suggestion or an idea as it was experienced in the session with its situated inclusion at home, it does not emerge as a replica; rather it is somehow transformed (Bohart and Tallman 1999, xv and 19). This is already true in a very plain sense that is, nonetheless, overlooked in the literature. Whereas sessions mostly work by means of talk, it mostly takes other means than talk to bring about the desired changes at home. And when talk plays a part in bringing them about at home, it is a different kind of talk than the concerted problem talk in sessions. We do not see a direct transfer of problem talk or a direct application of its insights and proposals. They are transformed into other kinds of activities that call for other abilities and modes of participation. The insights and proposals of session talk are reconsidered and worked over many times afterward on different occasions. To identify session insights and proposals with what occurred while the session lasted is too simple and narrow. It underestimates the significance of the continued work afterward and of the affairs outside sessions in interplay with which they actually may come to work.

Much to our surprise, the clients repeatedly state that they do not talk about sessions at home, as they did not talk about Donna's earlier therapy. It takes something else to bring about the desired changes, and, as we have seen, they have reasons not to talk at length about their problems with each other at home. First, there are no mediating expert strangers present. Second, they do not listen to each other; instead they interrupt each other so that the talk does not succeed but explodes in open conflicts. Third, there is no time slot set aside for such talk. Fourth, too many things go on at the same time, overlap, and interfere. Fifth, they are seldom all gathered at home. And sixth, they talk at length in sessions also because their therapists do not know them and are not present to witness what goes on between them at home. This calls for a more elaborate talk, which may then make clear to the clients things they had not realized before. But at home they often do not have to say so much because they know each other well and are familiar with each others' ways of doing and negotiating things. A quite different shared background exists between family members. Their intimate knowledge is not the same as the strange intimacy evolving in sessions. Indeed, the word for the special quality of their intimacy at home is familiarity. In this familiarity, much is taken for granted, and other things are said. The intimacy at home has qualities stemming from a history of close bonds between them. It is deeper and contains qualities they normally do not express or undertake in sessions. In other words, though much session talk deals with their life at home and sessions matter to them (among other things) for that reason, other things matter to them at home. Life at home is filled with other concerns, first of all with reproducing (or complaining over the disturbance of) the qualities of familiar intimacy amidst all the things that need to be done and all the problems that exist and occur at home. It would seem like a nightmare of family life if they turned it into a practice of concerted problem talk. Instead, they need to find other ways to address and work on their problems at home. In order to do so, they must work over their session experiences to find ways to make them a part of this other intimate practice at home with its less segregated and more turbulent ways of dealing with troubles and confusions. In fact, they cannot rely on the fact that they will all keep acting and responding as they did in sessions. Even if one person does, others might not. Thus, while Paul, according to Donna, acted in a funny and understanding way in sessions, it only lasted a while afterward. At home family members must acknowledge one or some members' attempts to use session experiences to change their ordinary practice, or they must accomplish it against passive or active resistance from other members.

When Mary says in session 24 that it is "so wonderful" to come to sessions because Paul has "never said so much in his entire life as when we were here," Ingrid responds: "But sometimes you can take that into your everyday life." Mary: "Well." Ingrid: "Like when you said you talked during the weekend." Mary: "I'd say we are more affected when we've been here. You sort of think it over more afterwards." Mary does not buy Ingrid's idea that she can simply transfer the practice of these wonderful sessions to her everyday life. Instead, she points to another way in which she includes session experiences, namely to "think it over more afterwards." This other way is not a direct transfer, but a more complex and contextual, occasioned and continued reconsideration of issues, which I shall now look into more closely.

In order to use sessions at home, the aspects of sessions they want to use must be on their mind for some time as a recurrent preoccupation. In interview 2, when they expressed uncertainty about whether and how the sessions had worked, Mary continues: "As late as last night you [directed at Paul, OD] used it. . . . You said to Angie, 'why are you like that?' There you already used what we have been talking about. . . . She remained seated and talked on. . . . Angie and dad both had it on their minds. I do believe that you give more thought to what you might say or do." Angie concurs, and Lisbeth asks what they have on their minds. Mary: "The things that were suggested you might do, isn't it." Paul: "You think things over once more before saying what you want to say. Like yesterday, it actually also did go better. Maybe that's what it takes." Angie confirms that she too turns things in her mind before saying something. They claim that nothing else changed. They started to think things over more, each on their own, all noticing that the others do the same, and nothing else changed. Instead of talking about it as in sessions, they each think about it on their own. And these thoughts make them react differently in particular situations. In this instance, it makes Paul ask for Angie's reasons for behaving in a way he finds problematic and does not quite understand. Because of the way they talk with each other and their therapists in sessions, they have come to hear about and understand reasons other than what they had previously known or assumed for other members' actions and to gain a different interest in each others' reasons for doing what they normally do and may want changed. Now that feature of session talk makes Paul ask for Angie's reasons in order to reach a better understanding of why she might become willing to change her mode of action. Here sessions do not re-emerge as a ready-made answer, but in the reasons for asking questions in order to make change possible between them at home. These questions concern how the interplay between individual members' reasons in particular situations re-produces particular constellations of participation between them which reproduce their problems or, if changed, may lead to their resolution and the realization of blocked goals.

However, I must make some important distinctions concerning what being on one's mind and thinking more about it refers to in linking sessions and life at home. First, something from a session may stay on one's mind for some time. That happened when Donna got home after leaving the shocking session with her parents. She set aside all other concerns and spent the rest of the night preoccupied by it. She even stayed home from school the following day because she was still very affected by it. But many other things go on in their lives so their attention is gradually diverted or interrupted. So, they can normally only remain preoccupied by the same issue for a limited time. Here we see a second way of being on one's mind: They can come back to it again. Their pursuit of it is then not continuous but intermittent (Crossley 1996, 95). Earlier, Ingrid called it a recurrent preoccupation, and that is precisely what it is. A third kind of thinking more about it consists in following up on session experiences and working on them in order to take the experience somewhere other than where it was when the session ended. The clients need to clarify certain things for themselves about the experiences, find out more about what they mean to the clients, determine whether and how they want to use the experiences, and adopt a particular stance on what they want to do with the experiences.

A fourth way in which thinking more about it may be related to the clients' practice at home is, strictly speaking, not to have it in mind but to have it come to mind. Obviously, this occurs later outside sessions. The clients' reasons to include session experiences and proposals then stem from their life in another place than sessions. The nature of the other practice, its scopes and limitations, problems and concerns, events and occasions determine the particular relevance of including session experiences. Just as their lives outside sessions determine which aspects of sessions stand out as being significant, the contexts and scopes, concerns and problems, situations and occasions of their lives outside sessions determine that a particular feature of sessions may be included and put to a particular use. The use of sessions is occasioned by ongoing events and situations in other places. A large part of the use of sessions consists in how they are invoked on the spot when possibilities and troubles arise or are anticipated. It comes to a client's mind in the midst of things. In interview 7, Lisbeth asks: "Do you sometimes go on thinking [after sessions, OD]? Do you get some ideas yourself sometimes?" Mary: "I don't know whether you can call it ideas, but I believe at least I think more over things when something's up, whether, or I may think, 'why did you say that?' ... Just like with my wishes and needs. Sometimes I'm just about to say like I used to, right, that of course, I'll do it or stay home, or what else I might have done. And there I've started, 'hey, if you don't want to, don't do it.' And then I say what I mean." Here the coming to mind and reconsidering is occasioned. The client does not set aside a time slot to realize it, but somehow she manages to do it while things are going on. She corrects and changes her participation in the midst of things as she goes along. I mentioned another instance of this earlier when Paul was in the midst of something and suddenly said to Angie: "Why are you like that?"

This mode of thinking more about things is not so much thinking in order to anticipate and plan things. It has to do with many things not being predictable, but also with waiting for things to occur, rather than bringing them about, and then using the opportunity to react on them in a particular way. Furthermore, it has to do with finding the right occasion to do something about it. Certainly nobody wants raising issues and addressing problems to get too much in the way of other things that they need or want to do or that must take place in their family life at home. They need to find the best time to raise them so that they do not disturb other necessary and desirable things too much. Sometimes it is a bad idea to do something about a trouble precisely when it occurs, as Mary reasoned at the beginning of therapy. She had to wait for things to calm down before she could find an occasion to raise an issue. A joint life riveted by disrupting troubles and tumultuous conflicts may even interrupt and get in the way of addressing and working on troubles. Clients then need to find ways to get back to them and pick them up again. All members learn their lessons about when and how what sort of trouble may be taken up and with whom. Indeed, getting beyond a disrupted family life into an interweaving of activities and concerns is what "makes it much nicer to be here," as Mary puts it, and thinking about things is seen as a main reason for this change. Asked about changes at home in interview 8 more than a year into therapy, Mary responds: "Everybody thinks things over much more. They are much more considerate." Paul: "Yes, we do not grumble so much at each other any more." Thinking things over involves taking each other more into consideration. Finally, things happening elsewhere and later may make an experience they did not pay much attention to in a session stand out as important.

To think more over things stands out as an important change for all of them throughout the one and a half year they attended therapy. It seems as ubiquitous in the clients' experiences of how they use their therapy as notions about transfer and application of session insights and results are to therapists. But, in contrast to these therapist notions, it involves the clients making up their minds about session experiences and proposals, and clarifying and adopting their own stance in relation to them. It involves re-situating issues in new contexts and situations and reconsidering how participants may agree to approach them in new ways. For these and other reasons, the clients continue to be preoccupied by these issues and, thereby, think them over.

5.4. Pursuing Concerns and Gathering Stances across Times and Places

The previous sections made it clear that if we only consider clients' inclusion of session experiences into their everyday lives, we comprehend the workings of sessions in clients' ongoing social practice in a too simple and professional-centered way. Instead, I draw on the concepts introduced in section 2.3 about persons pursuing concerns and stances across contexts in their trajectories of participation in structures of social practice. For a period of time, the session becomes one of the clients' contexts, and they must find ways to pursue some of their concerns into and out of it as a part of their pursuit of concerns across varying sets of contexts. The concept of pursuit denotes a complex, often cross-contextual and intermittent engagement with particular concerns that may reach across long periods of time and a complex set of occasions and contexts. There is a direction to pursuits, but it may not be well-defined and may be changed on the way. It involves a move toward more of particular situations and experiences and getting closer to particular states of affairs, or, if negatively defined, toward less of particular situations and experiences and further away from particular states of affairs. The concept of pursuit has the advantage over the concept of goal in that the latter implies a degree of definition ahead of time that does not always fit with how activities and engagements proceed. We have already seen some features of the clients' pursuits of concerns and stances across contexts, and we shall elaborate it as we use these concepts to analyze client changes in the next chapters. Thus, we have seen clients pursue concerns in their present context in such a way that the concerns are mediated by the links with other contexts where they take part and pursue them at other times. We have also seen that, in their pursuit of concerns in the present context, the clients re-interpret and transform features from their pursuit in other contexts and, more or less deliberately, pursue them in a way here that will allow them to pursue them further elsewhere and later. Furthermore, the clients' pursuits of concerns into, by means of, and beyond a particular context such as the session depend on what it is arranged for, as well as on their position, scope of possibilities, and coparticipants in it. They may then preferably or exclusively pursue some concerns into and through sessions but not in other contexts. Such contrasts in the arrangement of social practice make their pursuit of concerns across contexts partly discontinuous and divided.

When a troubled family begins therapy, members tend only to a limited degree to pursue across times and places those concerns that are closely involved in the problems for which they seek therapy. Rather, their ongoing practice is repeatedly interrupted or disturbed by recurring or new problems. When problems keep piling up on them, they may never catch their breath and jump from one safe spot to another in a continued struggle to thwart off the worst. It may seem too much most of the time, and when it is not, they may use the opportunity to take time out. They may also feel confused over what to do about the recurring problems and over why their attempts to deal with them do not succeed or are countered by others. In such a situation and state of mind, it may be difficult to identify possibilities for overcoming their problems. They may be of two minds about their problems and what should be done about them – according to the Danish saying they may even be of seven minds about it. When it is difficult to find ways to pursue problem-related concerns across times and places, family members may avoid them, neglect to pursue them, and just follow suit with their changing circumstances. That restricts and fragments their problem-related practice, and it becomes a difficult first step to make up their minds about how to start pursuing their concerns about their problems in a way that hangs together across times and places. The concept to follow suit denotes that, rather than pursuing concerns, persons are just following along with things as they happen. It comes close to Garey's term "drift," which refers to persons letting external events and other persons determine changes in their ongoing life (1999: 189).

At the time of referral, the clients in this family mainly go along with suggestions from others about the problems to be dealt with in therapy. They find it very difficult to pursue their problem-related concerns in a concerted way across times and places. In interview 1, Mary says: "One ought to write it down when one goes to therapy and comes to think of something." But she soon forgets what she had thought of when the session starts. The difficulties of explaining so that their therapists understand, the confusion over the problems, and the need to think over many new angles and optional stances get in the way of her pursuit of problem-related concerns across places. A little later Mary writes a note to remember to talk about the things she wants, but the session quickly leads into so many other issues that she forgets. This shows difficulties of pursuing concerns into and through sessions. About sustaining their pursuit of concerns out of sessions afterward, Mary says about the designated patient: "I notice in Angie, I believe in the first days after [a session, OD] it is better." But after some time, session topics vanish in the background or are forgotten amidst the many occurrences of the day. Throughout their therapy, there are many similar statements and full agreement about this. In the final interview after their therapy ended, Paul says about going to sessions that they "showed up and thought things over shortly before and a lot afterwards." In other words, their pursuit of therapy-related concerns peaks around the time of their sessions. It is affected by the sequential ordering of sessions and intervals lingering on for some time afterwards and then gradually receding into the background. In interview 7, Paul says: "I also think Angie has become more independent during the time she has been going there, and it is as if there is more initiative in her. She takes initiatives on her own she wouldn't have taken before." Mary: "She often takes initiatives when we have just been there. It's as if it pushes her, like last time we were there. She did something she would never have done and when she returned home she told us very proudly."

As long as they are confused and in doubt about what may be done about their problems, it is difficult to unfold sustained problem-related pursuits. Clients are often shaken by their troubles so that they find it difficult to gather where they stand in relation to them. They need to make up their minds about what matters to them about these troubles and what they want done about them. In other words, they must find out where they stand in relation to their problems in order to become able to unfold sustained pursuits of problem-related concerns. By adopting stances on their problems and the direction in which they want to pursue them, they may commit themselves to what they want and do not want to do about them and link their pursuits across contexts. These problem-related stances hang together with other personal stances about their practice across contexts. So, a client's pursuit of problem-related concerns is mediated by her stances, which she may change or hold on to for a shorter or longer time and over a narrower or broader range of situations and contexts.

Like all persons, clients do not pursue their concerns and stances isolated from others, but jointly, allied with some, and in opposition to others. For instance, Angie only wants to talk about her problems in sessions, not at home, hoping that session talks with the therapists may make her parents agree to things at home. Returning from an individual session, she tells her parents that they are to talk about a particular thing in the next joint session, but she will not tell them now at home. Mary, on the other hand, wants the others to learn to talk in sessions so that it may become possible for her to talk things over with them at home. Donna wants sessions with her parents so that the therapists can make her parents agree to treat her differently at home. In these instances, they pursue concerns and stances that are their own against others. An instance of an alliance is Paul coming to want joint sessions with Mary so that the therapists may get their side of the story about the troubles with the children. Like many alliances, it does not rest on entirely identical concerns and stances. Mary goes along hoping that it may also get Paul started on talking about their spouse relationship. So, many personal concerns and stances presuppose particular other concerns and stances in their coparticipants. They are adopted and pursued in particular, shifting constellations of participants. Besides, concerns and stances of different contents imply different options for pursuing them in relation to particular contexts and coparticipants. We have seen that contrary concerns and stances must often be pursued indirectly, as more or less hidden agendas, while common concerns and stances can be pursued more openly since they can be combined with those of others. Thus, the clients' pursuits of family-related concerns and stances are linked so that they afford or prevent each others' pursuits, and many family-related concerns and stances must be pursued jointly because they are about what they share or want to share with each other.

Addressing confused concerns and elusive stances plays an important part in dealing with client troubles in therapy sessions. In session 8, Ole asks whether the focus on Paul in working with the problems around Angie in the two latest sessions makes Paul think that the therapists are correcting him. Paul responds that he may feel uncertain about "whether I am all wrong, whether I am no good at bringing her up or anything. I must admit I have thought a great deal about that. And, I don't know, I think I have my way of doing it." Paul is more certain about his concern for Angie than about which stance to adopt in bringing her up. He characterizes his changing stance retrospectively: "I have been too vague sometimes. I've always preferred no quarrels.... It is very likely I haven't made myself clear, or my stances." When his stance is not clear to others, they may interpret his actions as being led by other reasons and interpret his concerns accordingly. In fact, his uncertainty about his stance and about how to articulate and pursue it in relation to the others appears to them as an uncertainty about his concern. Angie and Donna often take Paul's reactions to mean that he does not care about them and recognize them as the persons they see themselves to be but ridicules and restricts them (which he also does at times) even when he is trying to support a change in their situation and practice.

During the period of their therapy, confusion persists in some respects, and some concerns and stances are only pursued for a short while and then dropped or changed. However, the clients increasingly pursue problem-related concerns and stances across wider ranges of times and places. Some of these concerns and stances do not involve their therapy in any significant way. But it is precisely because they come to pursue concerns and stances across the context of their sessions and other contexts of their lives that their therapy comes to work. It would not work, if they did not. They must bring its impacts about by involving it in their pursuit of concerns and stances. By doing so, links between sessions and their lives in other places emerge and change. To coordinate their pursuit of concerns and stances in sessions and by means of them, the parents adopt a common stance of interrupting and ignoring the children when the children pester them, yell and shout, and so forth. What that means and what they then do is taken up in sessions as well as at home. It is not something they simply decide to do. They must explore and reconsider what it involves and how to do it, and in so doing they modify and change their stance further. They are changing their minds and watching how they do it, and they draw on their therapists' help in clarifying and reconsidering it. Though key impulses for their new stances may come from sessions, they must find out what to do about them by pursuing them for quite a long time and in different contexts. In session 16, Donna says about a change of stance in her participation across contexts: "I've got to speak my mind more, say what I think. It's a difficulty I have from my old school. I don't just get rid of that. It will probably take many years." She was severely bullied in her former school and had to change school.

Being preoccupied by these stances is a vehicle for pursuing and developing them across times and places. The clients stress that they get a lot out of doing so. Their growing concern to develop their stances is also seen in their asking for their therapists' help to sustain and elaborate them when they cannot make it. These pursuits across longer stretches of time and a wider range of places imply that particular concerns and stances are on their mind or pop up easily and repeatedly as something they are committed to pursue and reconsider. They also need to find ways to keep at these pursuits when they are about to vanish in the background among all the other things that go on and concern them, and they need to find ways to get back to them later in the same and other places. In addition, they need to find ways to counter relapses into old stances and more confused modes of living or into just following suit. Furthermore, they need to attend to their reasons for changing their new stances and the ways in which they pursue them. Finally, when they pursue a stance across diverse contexts, such as in sessions, at home, at work, in school and in other activities outside home, they cannot pursue it in the same way. Thus, it does not take the same for Paul at home, at work, and at meetings in Angie's school to pursue his new stance of being more consistent. It does involve working on changing his usual modes of participation in these different contexts and finding out how he makes it clear to himself and others in different contexts where he stands and how he may influence what goes on in them. But even what it takes and means to be consistent is not altogether the same in different contexts with different coparticipants. Stances are participatory and involve how a person relates, balances off, opposes, and combines his concerns and stances with those of different coparticipants, even others who are not present. The meaning for Paul of being consistent and which particular mode of participation it refers to varies across contexts with different stakes and possibilities for pursuing it. He may compare how he does it in different places as part of thinking about it and finding out how to do it in these places, but it would not be right for him to turn it into the very same pursuit. After all, in different places, his commitment to specific others, specific relationships and activities, arrangements and practices are at stake for him and different contexts hold different standards for appropriate participation (Taylor 1995a). So, it takes partly different abilities to pursue the same stance in different contexts, and he must practice how to do it in different places. To adopt a stance introduces some similar features in his participation and abilities across contexts and transforms other features, but it does not lead to an identical mode of participation.

5.5. Experience, Reflection, and Talk across Contexts

As clients pursue concerns and stances across contexts, they gain other experiences, notice other things, have other thoughts and reflections about them, and talk differently about them with different others.

In sessions, the clients gain special experiences that are affected by the arrangement of secluded sessions with intimate strangers. But the clients' experiences are not just related to the immediacy of the present context. What stands out in their experiences here is affected by contrasts and links with their experiences in other places in their trajectories of participation. Since their embodied practice takes place in different contexts with different social and personal relationships, their immediate experiences in these places differ and are mediated differently. Thus, they notice other things about the phenomena and events of sessions when they are at home and in the interviews as yet another arrangement to reconsider prior experiences from elsewhere in particular ways. Having other experiences then challenges and enriches their experiences, and they may relate their diverse experiences from diverse times and places, configure them locally, and generalize them by linking multiple experiences.

This conception of experience contrasts with the prevailing notion of experience as grounded in the local immediacy of a situation. As Calhoun reminds us,

> Appeals to experience easily slide into appeals to a kind of phenomenological immediacy that has been popular in counter-rationalist arguments from the earliest Romantics. . . . It is at the heart of the "metaphysics of presence" that

Derrida (1982) criticizes in many versions, and which he sees as an almost trans-historical intellectual problem dating from Socrates. . . . Heidegger's discourse is dominated by an entire metaphorics of proximity, of simple and immediate presence, a metaphorics associating the proximity of Being with the values of neighborhood, shelter, house, service, guard, voice, and listening. (1995, 182)

In this vein, the received view of therapy considers sessions a privileged place to gain deep personal experiences. But clients gain various experiences from different situated perspectives on different occasions in different contexts. Attending sessions merely means that the clients are going to another place that is not part of their ordinary practice and that affords other experiences so that they notice other things. What clients notice and observe in sessions is but a particular part of their complex reconsiderations. Indeed, what they notice and ignore varies across contexts because of differences between these practices and their participation and concerns in them. What they can observe immediately also varies from one place to another along with what they must include in a mediated way from other times and places. In their trajectories of participation across different contexts clients may then re-cognize phenomena and events by emphasizing other aspects of meaning, other links between phenomena and events, and other possibilities.

Persons can only capture with their senses what lies within immediate reach, and that varies across places. A person's experiences are also selective, and what he notices or ignores depends on the purposes of the context he is in and his concerns in relation to it. Besides, he combines perception and thinking in his observations (Holzkamp 1983, chapter 7) so that his knowledge affects what he notices and considers in a situation and his attunement for acting in it. Thinking includes in particular those aspects of social practice that are not immediately observable reaching into other times and places and linking personal experiences across times and places. But a person's thinking is not all-comprehensive, and it is affected by where it is carried out. It is located and spurred by its links with his ongoing perceptions and actions in a local context. On his position in the present context, the analytic aims and the significance of his thoughts depend on what other participants do and think. It depends on the analytic aims participants set themselves in this context and on the way they distribute and coordinate them. Participants' thinking is not merely individual or distributed. It is linked, negotiated, coordinated, and disputed. And because persons participate on different positions in a context and in other contexts, they bring different thoughts to bear on the issues of their shared context, thus, spurring an exchange of thoughts between them. In short, persons configure and pursue their thoughts across contexts and negotiate, coordinate, and dispute them intersubjectively in their positioned participation in the ongoing practice in a context. What is more, personal thoughts articulate personal experiences, understandings, and stances by drawing on existing social and cultural forms of thinking (Holzkamp 1983, chapter 7) as resources. These forms of thinking offer pre-understandings of aspects and links that persons have not yet been directly engaged in and made up their minds on. Persons may take over such pre-understandings, make them part of their personal knowledge or maintain personal reservations toward them. Finally, since personal knowledge is partial, persons relate to much social practice by imagining what it might be.

The received view on therapy also stresses that sessions offer clients an opportunity to reflect on their lives. The session is often held to be a privileged place to unfold a general human capacity for reflection (Rennie 1990; 1994a; 1994b). But clients' reflections in sessions are a matter of being in a particular practice where they notice other things, which they relate back to their life in other places so that these practices may be seen in a different perspective and reconsidered. Clients also reflect in diverse ways in different contexts. It is misleading to consider these processes as the mere execution of a general ability for reflection (Dreier 1999b). Personal reflections amount to re-collections, to gathering oneself anew at different times on different locations. They reassure me of the situations, concerns, and stances of my trajectory of participation so as not to get lost in my complex social practice and remind me what matters most to me. Persons cannot complete their reflections once and for all or confine them to a particular place. Because of the heterogeneous, linked, and changing qualities of personal social practice, persons reflect in different times and places triggered by the complexities and variations of their social practice. Their reflections are intimately and variously related to directing their trajectory of participation in structures of social practice. In the course of their trajectory across contexts they re-flect, that is, re-consider and re-configure their concerns and participations. They also re-flect and re-configure their participation and concerns in relation to those of others in hitherto un-re-cognized ways. In so doing, phenomena and events are re-cognized on the basis of changing premises foregrounding other aspects of their meaning, other links and possibilities.

Though the seclusion of sessions may make us believe so, reflection is not a matter of creating distance from the world or secluding oneself outside social practice lifting one's reflections off the ground of practice onto higher levels. Holzkamp's (1983, chapter 6) notion that gnostic distance enables knowledge is indebted to this metaphor of distance. But when a person reflects in one place on her practice in other places, she is not simply at a distance. She is in a particular place that allows her to notice particular other things that she may relate back to her practice in other places so that these practices may be seen in a different perspective and re-considered. Being at a distance from a place is being somewhere else, not outside everything in a privileged nowhere of pure thought. Such a notion blinds us to the social qualities of knowledge and its part in social practice. In my framework, the diversity of situated practices and perspectives replaces distance as the key condition of possibility for reflection. Relations between diverse practices allow reflection to unfold on a horizontal axis. Reflection need not be seen as lifting oneself off the ground of practice onto a higher level. Second-order processes are not a fixed level in a stable hierarchy, but a complex and shifting constellation of contrasting and comparing, which may lead to generalizations based on perspectives from local participations. This conception takes reflection back into personal trajectories of participation in social practice where it consists in seeing things from the perspectives of different locations and positions, be it my own perspectives in other contexts or others' perspectives in our common or other contexts. Having different experiences challenges and enriches reflection. Multiple, linked participations and concerns call on persons to address these links, and that involves a complex probing of realities and self-understandings. Social practices are rich and many-sided. To come to understand this calls for a many-sided personal practice and reflection. This multiplicity in diverse contexts allows persons to reflect on their commonalties and contrasts, and these reflections enable broader and richer understandings of the complex relations in social practice and in our personal social practice. On various occasions, we are urged to observe, think things over, and try things out from the perspectives of our local participation in different contexts.

Being a full participant in one community of practice easily blinds a person to aspects of it. Core blindness (Lave and Wenger 1991) arises when participants take particular key premises and functionalities of a social practice for granted and no longer see them. Participants may also overgeneralize premises of this practice and understand other practices with these, poorly fitting premises so that they are blinded to core features of other practices. While they are fully taking part in one context, they easily forget what is involved in taking part in other kinds of contexts. The phenomenon of core blindness shows that it is important for our understandings that we take part in several, diverse contexts and that comparison across them promotes our understanding. We may break with core blindness by participating in other practices and contrasting and comparing our experiences from them. The cross-contextual diversity of personal practice allows persons a leeway of reflection and change in relation to their core blindness. Indeed, there may be several, distinct, and interrelated core blindnesses in the social practice of a person and a society. This differs from Bourdieu's overarching culturalist notion of habitus (e.g., Bourdieu and Wacquant 1992).

Similar points can be made about the practice of talk. Talk is provoked by something else in the social practice of which it is a part (Hanks 1996). It is not a purpose in itself, but it has purposes and functions in relation to other aspects of ongoing everyday practices. When the clients talk at home about the issues dealt with in sessions, they talk about what they have later thought about them, now have doubts about, worry about, and are engaged in, and they talk about upcoming events they hope or fear will turn out in particular ways. But this kind of talk is done more in passing and does not presuppose that they all gather and set off a time slot to talk particular things over. The parents talk things over a little with each other at home. In line with the significance Mary attributes to learning to talk things over, she says in interview 3: "And then I think we [that is, she and Paul, OD] have started to talk more about it after we started sessions than we ever did. I'll say that is very positive." When Donna and Angie talk with each other, it is another kind of talk pursuing other concerns and topics: girlfriends, boyfriends, jobs, places to go, and so forth. The few occasions when the family does talk things over are dialogues between a parent and a child.

For this family, talking with each other carries other functions than when they all think things over on their own. In session 8, Mary appreciates the fact that because they now talk more about things, she comes to see her own behavior in a new light and does not have to bear the uncertainty of closed discussions. Talk highlights the interpersonal dimensions of their lives and problems. It allows them to develop their notions about their relations with each other, about the problems and possibilities in these relations, and about how to bring particular qualities and links about among them. This is a vital part in changing their notions about psychological phenomena from mentalist state and trait notions to relational, practical, and contextual notions about reasons for feeling, thinking, and doing what they do, including for the existing problems. Their thoughts about this become broader. Yet, talk also highlights differences and conflicts between them, and this may make it hard to talk and easier to avoid talking. Besides, talk may serve the function of anticipating and coordinating what to do, also when they disagree or expect problems to turn up. In interview 3, Mary says: "We started to talk things over in advance so that one of us does not say one thing, the other something else. We have had a bad habit of reacting to the children without agreeing or talking it over." Again this is most pronounced between the parents.

Nonetheless, the talking they begin at home during the period of therapy is not the kind of talking things over that Mary wishes they would all do and that comes closer to the concerted problem talk in sessions. In the final interview, half a year after their therapy ended, she declares: "The others did not learn to talk." In fact, the others do not want to talk about problems with each other. They talk about their problems with other people – friends, relatives, therapists – rather than with members of their family. It is more difficult to talk about their problems with each other precisely because of their interdependencies, personal bonds, and involvements. Even the not very talkative Angie talks with girlfriends about problems with their mothers. Friendships are a different kind of relationship with other practices of talk.

Reflection and talk create interplay between intrapersonal and interpersonal dialogue. As Calhoun argues, because we "engage ourselves through interior dialogue, we are better placed to come to understandings of others and to bridge significant differences than if we were only monological speakers of self-sameness" (1995, 50). Dialogues between people and with ourselves spur each other on but may also be related in problematic ways (Leudar and Thomas 2000). Both work by contrasting and comparing transposed perspectives, though this is often not recognized about internal dialogues.

6   Changes in Clients' Practice across Places

In this chapter I characterize the main features of the changes in the clients' practice during the period of therapy. On this background, I shall focus on changes in relation to their problems in the next chapter.

Therapy is meant to promote changes that the clients bring about by linking aspects of their practices in different contexts. In comprehending client changes, we must, hence, capture the varying coincidences and links between sessions, life in the family, and other places in the clients' ongoing social practice. But the main parties in the practice of therapy spontaneously understand these complex, cross-contextual change processes from different locations in social practice and consider the role of circumstances and events in what from there appears as other places. Clients spontaneously view the changes from the location of their family and consider circumstances and events in other places, such as sessions, as playing a part in enabling and inhibiting changes here (Dreier 1991). Therapists (and researchers) view the changes from their location in sessions and must try to understand how what goes on here interacts with what goes on in other places where they are not present to observe and affect the changes. Besides, many circumstances and events are not mentioned in sessions because sessions cannot cover everything, therapists select some topics for examination, and clients do not mention what they consider irrelevant for curing their symptoms or do not want included in their therapy.

6.1. Understanding Change

Change may consist in more or less long-term alterations of social conditions that affect persons on a wider or narrower range of locations. Such external changes have a determining impact on the scopes of possibilities for these persons. These changes happen to them, and they are subjected to them in varying degrees and ways. Still, if we want to study persons in social practice and not merely social conditions, we must add that persons may react in varying ways to such changing circumstances and, thus, modify the impact of these changes on their lives. Persons may also have varying sorts and degrees of influence on their circumstances. They may even take part in changing their circumstances. From the point of view of persons in social practice, we must make a basic distinction between being determined by circumstances and determining your circumstances, that is, between being objectively determined and subjective determination (Holzkamp 1977). These two kinds of forces always interact, and their relative strengths vary. Indeed, how and to what degree persons may increase their determination or whether their prior determination is threatened and restricted are important features of personal and social change.

Of course, persons may just go along with their changing circumstances and adapt to the changed situation without paying much attention to their mode of participation and understanding. They may do so without changing them deliberately, by continuing to function as they did or by making small alterations they barely notice. But persons may also change their abilities and understanding so that they become able to address other aspects of the existing scope of possibilities or address the same aspects in other ways. As mentioned in chapter 2, there are three basic classes of personal change. First, persons may become able to participate in a different way in an otherwise unchanged situation. Second, persons may change their abilities and understanding to keep up with a changing situation and utilize its changing scope of possibilities. Third, persons may change their abilities and understanding to bring about a change in their situation and its scope. In all three classes of personal change, persons modify their abilities and understandings, and they must pursue and accomplish this in various ways and more or less deliberately. Still, even if persons pursue a particular change deliberately, there is no guarantee that it comes about. It may turn into a different change from the one they had in mind or even a contrary one that they would prefer to be without. Besides on their own pursuit this depends on their changing situation and on what their coparticipants do.

I must now add the concept of learning. My framework is in accordance with Lave's conception of learning as changing participation in a changing social practice (e.g., Lave 1988; 1993; 1996; unpublished manuscript; Lave and Wenger 1991). More specifically, I stress that learning refers to those aspects of changes in which persons modify their abilities and understandings for participation in social practice (Dreier 1999a; 1999c; 2001; 2003; Holzkamp 1983; 1993). Those processes of change and learning that enable persons to increase their determination in a changing situation and to counter threatening decreases of determination are called development (Holzkamp 1983). Hence, not all change and learning implies development.

The distinctions introduced in chapter 5 are also part of my analysis of change and learning. Thus, most personal change and learning come about through pursuits across places. In this chapter, I shall address the clients' pursuits of changes during the period of therapy stressing how their changing abilities and understandings (i.e., learning) increases or decreases their determination in a changing social practice.

My analysis of this case provoked two further distinctions in relation to change. First, people's situations as well as their modes of participation and understanding may vary, strictly speaking, without changing. Their situation just fluctuates between being in one way on one occasion or for one period of time and in other ways on other occasions or for other periods. Their modes of participation and understanding also fluctuate periodically or as they move from one situation into another. I call this variation rather than change. This distinction is in line with my argument that a person's pursuit of concerns and stances across contexts calls for varying modes of participation and foci of awareness. Later we will encounter a special type of variation, which I call a shift, where we see pronounced periodic alterations in a person's modes of participation and understanding. In fact, variations and shifts may occur without any changes occurring. Social conditions and events may vary and shift, and personal variations and shifts are afforded by alternative possibilities in a situation and by moving into other situations and contexts. It follows that the range of variations and shifts in a person's practice may increase with an increasing scope of possibilities and decrease with restrictions in their scopes. But variations and shifts also occur alongside ongoing changes. The co-occurrence of variation and change makes it difficult to discern whether things just vary and shift or which changes really take place, all the more so since some variations may lead to a change in a not always obvious way. In addition, a changed practice still incorporates variations and shifts in situations as well as in participants' modes of participation and understanding. In fact, changes bring about other variations in persons' ongoing practice.

This conception of change recognizes that a person's world does not stand still except when she changes it. Her situation also varies, shifts, and changes when she does not change her participation and understanding. In fact, a person may prefer just to vary and shift rather than to change. This may seem just as efficient in dealing with existing problems especially when her scopes of possibilities are wide.

The preceding distinctions point to important issues for the analysis of personal change: How are we to comprehend the relations between a varying, shifting, and changing world and the personal pursuit of change? What is the meaning of personal change in a world that keeps changing and varying? How do persons find out that they accomplished a change when the social practice they take part in keeps varying and changing? Do other qualities develop in the relations between situational changes and personal changes as a consequence of a person's pursuit of change? That is, in which respects do the relations between a person and her world change when she pursues changes? For our purposes it is also important to ask what increased stability to a person's life and modes of participation and understanding means, as opposed to a high degree of messiness, confusion, and chaos? After all, stability cannot be the opposite of change. In a varying and changing social practice, it must involve personal variation, shifts, and change in a more stable and less chaotic way.

6.2. Changing from Different Angles

Three issues dominate the relation to changes concerning Angie in the first seven months of therapy including a long summer break.

First, activities with friends outside the family matter most to Angie's state of mind. In session 2, she tells Mary: "You say I'm cross in the morning. There may be a reason for it. If I've been on bad terms with somebody or if I didn't have anybody to be with, which I almost never have, then I may get irritated when I am bored." Angie's isolation and dissatisfaction with her contacts with friends affect her state of mind at home in the morning and when she returns from school to boredom in the afternoon. Her symptoms play a part in holding her back in this unsatisfactory and isolated situation.

This restriction is also conditioned by the second issue. Angie has no clear notion of being able to influence her relations with friends so that she may sustain and develop them into what she wants. She sees herself as a minor figure who is easily dropped, and this happened several times in the social relations between the children she knows without her really understanding why. So she just follows suit, waits, and complains or hopes for better times. Other people make her day a good or miserable one. It does not seem to be much of her making how her days turn out. Things change for her without her believing that she can do much about it.

Third, Mary and Paul encounter Angie's state of mind at home. They have no direct – and only limited indirect – experiences with the concrete significance to Angie of her activities in other places and with Angie's lack of influence on them. Given this background, Mary and Paul feel uncertain about what is wrong and why, and they disagree over the troubles they encounter and what can and should be done about them. These disagreements divide the parents and make them less able to help Angie. The constellation of this division between them is seen in an exchange in session 1 about who takes care of Angie's breakfast. In spite of being met by strong bursts of irritation from Angie in the morning if the toast Mary makes is not as Angie wants, Mary says: "But we take care that Paul doesn't make breakfast. He is not so good at it. That's why the mother does it all." Angie: "And you understand it much better." Mary insists on being the key figure in the care of her children, disqualifies Paul's ways of doing it, and feels burdened by the responsibilities she then carries alone. These disagreements hinder the parents from joining each other in supporting Angie. Paul wants to put pressure on Angie to make her do things, while Mary insists that Angie learns nothing under pressure, especially due to her anxieties. In this constellation, Angie's part in what they are trying to do with her and for her does not become clear. She may even avoid doing anything and feeling coresponsible for bringing about what she wants and, instead, lean on her parents to get it. They have no clear, common understanding of how to pursue such things jointly. So, attempts easily disrupt and fail.

As we see, the troubles that matter most to Angie are not located at home, but in other places such as in school and in the places where she might be with friends. They are outside the parents' immediate horizon and reach, and this complicates the parents' understanding of them and what they can do about them. When Angie starts individual sessions, Ingrid urges her to begin doing things herself and suggests that Angie tries taking the bus alone to and from individual sessions. In session 7, Angie finally says: "Yes, I think I dare to try it." And she did one day when Mary could not accompany her. But she does nothing else about the things that bother her because she is waiting for her parents to fulfill her one big wish: to get a horse. She is also quite disengaged in how she is doing in school. What concerns her most is that she spends her afternoons without friends at home reading. Yet, she is resigned to things as they are "because I am used to it being like that." That Ingrid prompts Angie to give it a try is an influence from outside her family. Still, she only makes concerted attempts to become able to move around on her own when she can link them to the pursuit of relations with friends and the loved activity of riding with friends. In session 8, Paul says: "She found a girlfriend in the countryside who has a horse. And they are taking a train from here to X-town where they change to another bus. And she simply does that." Mary: "In connection with these farms, she does things which she would normally never dare to do or imagine." To have a chance to do things with friends sets Angie off into new terrain. Her primary reasons for change lie outside her family and outside her sessions. If these other possibilities had not turned up so that Angie can link her new attempts to move around on her own to them, she would probably have discontinued her attempts again as she did with regard to so many other things. Variations and changes in her possibilities in other places primarily drive her attempts to change. What occupies her is the new activity of riding with her girlfriend in the countryside; taking the more than one and a half hour long trip to the farm is just a means of getting there. Attending therapy may trigger her to try it, but the occasion to pursue it and the drive to continue stem from elsewhere. These other activities turn, say, taking a bus alone, into a subjectively important possibility for Angie. They make her really notice possibilities and find out what it takes to do things she did not dare to do before. When these activities are not available, she does not really notice possibilities and find out what it takes to do things. In other words, when she just follows suit, she may change somewhat and learn something, but not so much. Most change and learning must be pursued.

In spite of Angie's increasing pursuit and accomplishment of changes, she takes surprisingly little notice of changes and hardly talks about them. In session 9, Ingrid asks her: "How do you think it's been lately?" Angie: "It's gone quite well." Ingrid: "Has anything changed?" Angie: "I don't know. I haven't noticed." Ingrid: "Do you, now that we talk about it?" Angie: "I don't think so." And in interview 4, shortly after Lisbeth asks her: "Has anything become different?" Angie: "No, I don't think so." But when Ingrid and Lisbeth prompt her further, it turns out that Angie has begun a number of new activities, has a job, new friends, and started riding a horse, which is what she wants most of all. In particular, she does not notice changes at home. Though she says that "we are not so cross any more," she does not believe that she changed at home, nor can she see any changes in her parents. It is not on her mind, and she does not pursue it. Her wish for a change in her situation is "to get my own horse. It's something different from riding somebody else's." In fact, she says that she has no other difficulties now besides getting a horse, and she has taken a job in order to get one. In saying so, she discounts her anxieties, visual symptoms, and so forth as "difficulties." Nonetheless, she would "like to talk about my claustrophobia and whether one can talk it away. Because when one is on a school trip, one can't be with the others when they do things at night." Again, troubles and activities in places outside home primarily matter for Angie's wishes to change and make her start pursuing changes and learning. Likewise, she begins to use the restrooms in school, while earlier she did not dare to and was at the breaking point when she returned home.

Angie pursues these changes over a period of time. Thus, she finds a place to ride a horse close to home so that not only does she have time to ride on weekends but she also pays half the costs with money she earns from her new job of distributing newspapers once a week. In session 13, Paul says: "I think it's better now with Angie. She does not pester us as much any more. Of course, it's also because of these various changes. Now she also has two girlfriends from her class. She's almost not at home now, or at least much less." Mary: "She's at home during weekends with her older sister." Paul: "With her alone." Last weekend she was in town at a party and slept with a girlfriend, not minding that no lights were on. Angie says she started to turn out the lights in her room when she goes to sleep "to get used to it." So, her activities outside home are expanding and changing rapidly, and she pursues the changes and learning it takes to be able to participate in them, even if it takes practicing at home and being at home alone without her parents. It is on her mind to do these things, and she combines her various pursuits of them across diverse contexts. But Angie is quite inarticulate about it which makes it difficult to capture her changes in interviews. She is also better able to articulate factual changes than changes in her state of mind and abilities. Thus, when Angie returns from school, she is often irritable. Ingrid asks her if she remembers how she reacts when her mother then asks her something, and Angie says no. Ingrid: "But when you answer her in that way, how are you then feeling?" Angie: "I don't know. I don't notice."

At home, Mary and Paul face Angie's symptoms and the troubles she causes them. In contrast to Angie, their reasons to change are primarily located at home. This is where they begin to pursue changes. Their pursuit of changes at home runs parallel to Angie's pursuit of changes in other places. There is a different composition and trajectory to their pursuits of changes. The three of them do not always clearly understand and link their parallel attempts though new understandings and links do develop between their attempts.

There is a second difference between Angie and her parents. While Angie pursues changes linked with her activities and relations with friends, at first Mary and Paul pursue changes linked with – their disagreements over – how best to help Angie. Their changes are mainly part of their practice of care for somebody else. A major change in the parents' practice of upbringing is a turn in their understanding of the link between making demands on Angie and supporting her. At the beginning, Paul sees making demands as the way to cause changes in Angie, while Mary sees it as working against Angie's change and as contrary to caring for her. But they change their understandings and practice and come to adopt a different stance, which evolves via a complicated set of changes throughout the period of therapy. These changes preoccupy the parents for long stretches of time. They must think about them, keep coming back to them, and stop themselves from relapsing into the old understandings and practices, which they want to discontinue. The therapists also keep coming back to these issues in sessions during the rest of their therapy and keep "digging into" them. At home Paul and Mary talk a bit about these disagreements to help each other and to forestall acting against each other. Their disagreements concern what they see as an enabling way of bringing Angie up. In the course of reconsidering this, they search for other ways to pursue it and to collaborate with each other about it that are better suited to their changing understandings of their part in her development. But for long stretches of time they both feel torn between different understandings and practices of upbringing. While they try out other ways and reconsider their old ways of doing it, they are in two minds, uncertain, and confused about it. Mary primarily feels torn over what it means to take care of Angie in a loving way, and Paul is primarily torn over how to become more consistent in his practice of upbringing. Only little by little do they make up their minds on a different practice with a new, clarified personal stance and collaboration between them. The first move in changing their practice of upbringing is to stop Angie when she pesters them or gets cross, and this reduces her pestering. In interview 3, they say they have both "started to be more consistent." In session 11, shortly after Ingrid asks them about Angie's pestering, Mary responds with a laugh: "I don't think I've heard it any time the whole week." Paul: "It's simply fantastic. . . . After we talked about running a different line, it simply just turned almost perfect." Mary: "And then she was lucky to get a horse to tend." Paul "Which is almost her own." Mary: "She was allowed to tend the wife's horse in another farm she visits now." Paul: "We can afford to let her go up there to ride it." Paul: "But it is also related to that I've started to say more." Asked by the therapists, Angie responds that she did not notice that her parents changed, but she confirms that the three of them quarrel less. However, she thinks that is because she has a horse to ride. In other words, Angie only notices the changes she pursues, while Paul and Mary believe that their and Angie's pursuits of change interact, or that their own part is most important. Still, stopping Angie, which is essentially what Paul and Mary now do, would not have worked as it did if Angie had not at the same time been engaged in pursuing the other changes.

There is a third dimension to the changes in Paul's and Mary's reactions. They begin to stress a polarity between themselves as parents and their children instead of their old division between Mary, Angie, and Donna versus Paul. This creates new disagreements and conflicts, as we saw in sections 4.7 and 4.8. But even though their earlier disagreements tended to get in the way of pursuing changes, the new division between them transforms the dynamics of their conflicts in ways that drive them toward further changes. Some conflicts stand in the way of changes, while others fuel them.

The parents are very impressed by the changes Angie pursues in other places, and it changes their understanding of her potentialities for development. They begin to recognize that Angie's changing activities lead to a changing state of mind and affect her anxieties and whether she gets cross. This recognition is also fostered by their therapists' "digging into" their practice of upbringing and raising questions about the impacts of their reactions on Angie and the relations between them. In interview 3, Mary says that "it has become better because she is more relaxed, and I think that's important. But again I suppose it has to do with that she started managing things herself and things like that. This gives some self-confidence, right, and this then makes her change." Now, according to Mary, Angie changes neither because they show consideration for her symptoms nor because of external pressure but because she is given a scope and opportunities to change her abilities, which increases her self-confidence. Their concerns for Angie are changing in the direction of how to support her pursuit of such changes and directed more beyond the family into Angie's life in other places. Again these changes are linked to session talks where we explore possible links between Angie being cross when returning from school and how she is doing in school. In interview 3 Paul says: "We really don't know. Sometimes she is very sad when returning home. And she is not really close to her schoolmates in any ways. So we would like to hear how she feels she is doing and so that Ole and Ingrid also know how it is." Here Paul shows greater interest in Angie's perspective and recognizes that he knows too little about it. This lack of knowledge is partly due to Angie not being very talkative but also typical of parents' knowledge about their children's lives in school compared to, say, in kindergarten. Yet, it is striking in a family where both children had to change school because they were bullied. Now we arrange a consultation with the parents, Angie, and her main teachers in order to be informed and follow up on the parent's suggestions for support in school. Shortly after, the parents take a stand for Angie in relation to troubles in her class. This is new and calls on Paul and Mary to develop their abilities. It takes abilities other than those practiced at home or in sessions to pursue their stance of saying what they stand for and acting consistently in negotiations with the teachers and other parents at school meetings about the problems in the class in such a way that they take good care of Angie's situation in the class.

The parents' personal changes are linked to their relation to Angie's changes. Thus, earlier Mary insisted on being the key person to define and carry the care for her family including the burdens this creates for her. In session 8, she begins changing her mind because, as Ole puts it, when this responsibility stays with her, it binds her around the children and the home. Mary: "That's how it is, yes. But then I've started, like tonight and tomorrow night, I am going out. And I've told Angie. And I haven't asked her where she wants to be." This issue of being tied down if she does not state her needs and pursue them grows out of Mary's changing stance in relation to the care of her children and turns into a major preoccupation for her throughout therapy. In session 12, Mary says: "It's something you must overcome. Something that is very difficult to learn. I've never said a word at a parent–teacher meeting. But I can't bear that any longer. Now I'm over that. You better believe I say what's on my mind." It also involves a changed understanding of what might be in Angie's best interest. Mary hopes that Angie will not spend twenty years overcoming her reticence as she did. Mary recognizes that her understanding of Angie changed, and she now believes that she and Paul must try to give Angie more self-confidence. They have done so for some time, and it works well. Earlier she considered Angie to be very sensitive. "But maybe I've shown her too much consideration so that I've made her weak." She realizes that this may not be the way to strengthen her because now Angie does things on her own. Ingrid asks if this means Angie does not need to be taken so much care of any more, and Mary responds: "Right, or maybe I've begun not to speculate so much about it." Ole continues: "When your relation to Angie changes, it changes your everyday situation at home." Mary: "Yes, but I don't feel sorry about that. Like with Donna, right, one gets used to their growing up. I think it's wonderful for Angie, even if I don't see her for a whole week." Ingrid: "What do you then do? Do you have more time for each other?" Paul: "Yes, we have. Now we've just been in the countryside a whole weekend alone." Ingrid: "It's also a new period for the two of you." Paul: "Yes, that's difficult to get used to, no doubt about that, suddenly to be able to allow yourself to do something without asking the children and bringing them along. It's just as difficult as all the rest." Ole: "You have to start to think about this now." Paul: "Yes, that's precisely it." Mary: "Much more time for yourself." Ingrid: "Do you take that up together, or does each of you pursue your own interests?" Mary: "I don't attend anything at all. Paul has his own." Mary says there is not enough money for the others when Paul has his sports activities, and she does not quite know what she prefers to do. Angie steps in as Mary's spokesperson suggesting things that Mary told Angie she would like to do. Mary responds that the money has not been there for her or the children, but she will take this up later because she does want to do something: "It's not fair." Asked by Ole, "Do you think you are the last in the line?" She agrees. Paul's control over most of their money is illuminated, and he says that something drastic would have to happen if more money was to be wrenched out of their budget, like selling the car or the summer cottage. Mary says that is what makes her refrain from stating her needs. It would put her in a moral dilemma and make her feel guilty. But, she adds bitterly, Paul does not have to ask for money for his sports activities while she has to ask for money to pursue her interests.

Looking back at their lives during the first period of therapy, their pursuit of changes already led to a changed situation. It may not have changed as they intended, and they did not share the same intentions, nor were they completely clear and consistent about what they intended. In fact, they changed their intentions on the way. Still, their situation now holds new possibilities and difficulties, and their awareness and use of these possibilities changed along with their changing understanding of their difficulties. New concerns and stances, agreements and disagreements, problems and conflicts exist for them and between them. Changes involving conflicts often do not overcome all conflicts, but transform them so that some are dissolved while others arise, change, or gain a different significance. Their relations with each other also changed. New links and ties between them have become possible and new understandings, stances, and conflicts between them are brought to the fore. This involves new understandings of what each person experiences, needs, wants, and does so that their understanding of the relation between their own and others' concerns changes. They have become able to oppose and combine their own and others' concerns in new ways. And they have reconsidered and changed their understanding of their own part in these relations. This involves changing one's understanding of what is at stake for oneself and of how to pursue one's concerns and stances together with the others and on one's own. In these respects, they have learned, that is, changed their understandings and abilities for participating in changing relations with each other in a changing practice at home and in other places. As a result, they are able to link their modes of participation, understandings, and concerns in new ways. Their conflicts and disagreements do not disrupt and hold their pursuit of concerns and changes back as much as they did earlier. They are better able to continue pursuing their concerns and changes in spite of disagreements and conflicts. Their pursuit of concerns and changes now reaches across longer stretches of times and places and is increasingly directed toward and involves further changes, learning, and development. Furthermore, they re-appreciate their present situation and concerns in new perspectives when they come to see it as a part of a new understanding of their past and possible futures.

In the last session episode discussed previously, a child actively supports her mother's concerns and changes. Angie mentions things Mary told her, suggests things to Mary, and insists that she has grown older and would now like to and is able to do this and that so that Mary may gain new possibilities. Aside from what Angie overhears in sessions, she must have thought about it and talked with Mary about it at home to be informed and motivated to pursue it in the session, perhaps hoping for something similar to what she pursued for herself earlier, namely that the therapists may set things right for Mary – with a little help from Angie. A child here tries to play a part in the development of a parent and not just the other way around, and this concern for her mother is part of Angie's changes. In the next session, Donna gives further evidence of the increasing reach of Angie's changes saying that the two of them now talk a lot with each other because Angie has grown so that new links between them have become possible. Yet, in the same session we are reminded that however widespread Angie's changes may be, they are not simply general and permanent. It is now mid November in the dark season in Denmark, and

Angie is afraid when she distributes newspapers in the dark late afternoons in an inhospitable industrial area. As conditions change, prior personal changes may not be sustainable, or further personal change may become necessary.

6.3. Continuing Pursuits and Other Conflicts

Now I turn to the changes in the next four months when sessions focused on problems surrounding Donna. Of course, changes occurred for Angie, Paul, and Mary too in this period, and I shall mention them first since I just dealt with them. It will be brief because the new focus in sessions leaves less material about them and because their changes are a continuation of what began earlier.

Two months later Angie takes part in session 18 because she complained to her parents over not being involved and because we want to follow up on how she is doing. She says it goes quite well. Her parents agree and add that she is more irritable, but they can now all laugh about it, and the parents do not mind it so much when it happens. It passes sooner, and she thinks it over when they ask her why she gets cross. The understanding between them has improved. It is easier to say things to each other; they understand better what each other means and know better where each other stand. In relation to friends Angie says, "It doesn't go well." She lost the girlfriend from her class whom she was riding with in the summer and who often withdrew from other relations. Once more Angie's increased irritability coincides with increased isolation from friends. But Angie now sees that she may do something to repair and sustain such relations. She has taken the initiative to talk about the making and breaking of cliques with her girlfriend and a boy from her class who has known this girl for a long time. In addition, Angie gave up her job of distributing newspapers now that it is dark in late afternoons. Paul then found new jobs for Angie and Donna in the same workplace, and this created a new kind of link between the sisters. Angie still sleeps with no lights on at home and goes out with friends and rides at night. So, in this period, she still pursues her concerns for changes though the triggering function of sessions decreases as time passes between them. Of course, Angie still runs into events beyond her control, but she now looks for ways to influence them and is able to gather others' support. Her abilities and understanding for taking part in relationships are changing. This enables new qualities in her relationships with new things to talk about and new understandings of each other, as her parents and sister report.

Interview 7 indicates continuity in Paul and Mary's pursuits of changes. Paul says that he changed from giving in easily to being more consistent and that he shows more clearly what he stands for. He changed in the same direction at work too because in general he thinks things over more. Mary says that she states her mind more, sticks more to what she wants and feels, and goes out on her own in the afternoons and evenings. Both say that in a way they have been too good to their children never showing them that they have wishes and needs too. Therefore, they forgot them. Paul says that Mary always stood more by what she said and that the children pestered him in particular because they could bend him more easily. The children knew he and Mary differed in raising them, but now they talk about it. He adds: "Already that we can start to do things on our own without telling the children that now we do this and that; it's something completely new to us." Mary says they are going to live a different life now. They spend more time alone since the children are off doing things, and Mary is still left behind frequently, which she thinks more about now since she began to pay more attention to her own needs and wishes. While the parents' pursuits of change initially focused on their care for Angie, it gradually turned toward changing their own stances and ways of life. They search for possibilities to expand their situation. It has become more important to pursue their personal concerns and to expand their personal scopes of possibilities and, thus, to live more freely and improve their well-being. They increasingly recognize the importance of this for the others too. So, the personal dimensions of change are closely linked to interpersonal dimensions. Thus, Paul describes his change as one from being a quite peripheral participant in family life to becoming a fuller participant where he is more concerned with his part in the lives of other family members and their part in his. He sees himself more as a participant now. Their relationships have gained new meaning and qualities. Their understanding of where and how they may join and disagree with each other has changed. In other words, their understanding of which relationships are possible between them has changed including the possible qualities of their future relationships. Their understanding and participation in family relationships now reach more into areas of their own and other members' lives beyond their family.

When this therapy begins, Donna considers it to be for Angie, but her parents put her under pressure to take part to help Angie, though Angie does not want her to. In interview 2, she says: "I'm just sitting here, listening to you, right. And maybe I say yes or no once in a while. . . . I might as well be with my friends instead of sitting here for two hours." Sometimes she speaks out very openly in sessions and draws attention to major aspects of their problems: "I just happened to say too much because it came over me." But she feels that she should not speak because Angie resents it. Seven months later, Donna takes the initiative for sessions about problems with her parents. In contrast to Angie, Donna deliberately pursues this therapy in the hope that it may be a better means to accomplish particular changes that she cannot bring about at home with her parents. Life with friends matters most to Donna as it does to Angie, but Donna's problematic relations with friends have burst into their family home, created serious trouble between Donna and her parents, and jeopardized their tenancy. Donna's life in the family and her relations with friends are not as separate as they are for Angie. So, Donna wants to straighten a situation with her parents, and she wants them to recognize that she has changed into a different, more grown-up person. The explosive conflict in session 13 (see section 4.8) makes her shocked over her parents' bitterness and deep distrust.

In session 16, she says: "I couldn't stand listening to it. . . . Because I know with myself that it has mostly been my fault. And then to have that thrown at me." Donna then decides to become "nicer." In interview 7, she says that after sessions with Ole it has become clearer what is difficult for her and that she "must learn to be a little nicer, listen a little more to what they say. I haven't been too good at that. But that's because I've been allowed to take care of myself. This room has actually been my small apartment." Now she agrees to more at home. Yet, for the time being, she is almost never home, and she does not notice changes in the other three. Lots of other things happen and occupy her mind. She got a new job, earns a lot of money, buys herself new clothes, is buying herself a moped, has come to know new people, found a boyfriend at work, and so forth. So, even though she is shocked over her parents' points of view about her and tries to change her participation at home, life in other places occupies her most.

That Donna does not pursue changes at home in a concentrated way is also grounded in her idea about what it takes to change. It is something you just make up your mind to do, and then you do it – it's as simple as that. If she does not succeed, it is because the others were not receptive to it or because she failed. Personal change merely consists in making up your mind. When she has made up her mind "to become a different person," she is a different person and no longer the person she once was. Personal change is like a switch. Because changes actually are more complicated than that, she switches back and forth several times when she has had enough of being one way rather than another. Thus, she sees herself as switching between what she calls being "a bitch" and being "nice" to other people. She uses these same terms about her relation to her friends and her parents, although what it means and what it takes to be nice or a bitch at home with her parents and elsewhere with her friends clearly differs. From her point of view, there are also marked distinctions between then and now, wrong and right. Now she looks at herself then from a distance because today she is different and can and will do things differently. Having to learn to do things differently vanishes behind sudden decisions to switch and is covered by the feelings of insufficiency, which occupy her when she cannot make her decisions come true. Still, she is working on being nice not just when she is with friends and might decide to go along with being treated badly for fear of losing them. And she breaks with most of the friends she feels let down by in connection with what happened in their apartment. She kept only a few after giving them a sound scolding. At home, Donna says in session 17, it goes quite well now because "we pull ourselves together more. We go a little more along with what they say. Maybe not so much Angie, but I do at least." She does so "because I want my mum and dad to get happy." She does things they tell her, like doing the dishes, and does not say, "I don't want to." When she pleases them, she feels better too, and when they all feel better, the problems recede into the background, and they start leading a different life. Donna wants to put the problems behind her and wants the others to do the same so that there will be room for a fresh start now that she has grown up.

However, the strong contrasts between Donna's and her parents' points of view on what goes on at home did not vanish. In sessions, they give their therapists very different impressions of what goes on at home. The parents emphasize Donna's "dependence on her friends." According to Mary, Donna hangs around at home waiting for her friends to visit, and if they do, Donna is unable to do anything other than let them in or leave with them. So, the rest of the family cannot make any plans to do or talk about things with Donna. The parents also still fear that the gang may turn up again in their flat. They say Donna is still very irritable, although now they have nice times with her and Donna is willing to do things with them there was no chance she would do earlier. By contrast, Donna says in session 19 that now Angie quarrels with Paul, while Donna does not. She does not know what changed it to become "quite good" between the three of them. At least she did not change her ways much. Paul is nicer; he bothers to talk and have fun. He changed, and Donna believes he did because one day she told him she wants to leave home to live in a boarding house for young people. Donna also feels better after she made new friends who are not linked to the gang, and she visits these friends on weekends. This makes her behave differently at home, which affects Paul and Mary too. The bitterness between them diminished. Again the parents' reports are different. Donna was infuriated when she told them that she wants to leave home. The parents took it as a threat because they did not instantly agree to Donna's plan to stay alone in their flat with a new girlfriend during all of Easter Holidays. On the contrary, they insisted to be informed before Donna made such arrangements. Talking about this in the session makes it clear to the parents that the key issue for them is that they feel powerless and let down, and that they regard Donna with distrust because she does not live up to the conditions and demands they set for her. Following a suggestion by Paul, we schedule a session with Donna and her parents about negotiating Easter Holidays. The parents neither want to give up going to their summer cottage nor let Donna do whatever she wants at home. Yet, they realize that there is no way around talking about it and somehow letting her try again to be at home alone on weekends.

Mary begins the scheduled session 21 saying that they talked with Donna about Easter Holidays: "It came all naturally one day while we were eating. We agreed very much on it." Donna will stay in their flat with a girlfriend for all five days. Paul says it "probably couldn't be any other way" and accepts it. They have set up conditions for doing it, which Donna believes she can live up to and finds good. They all consider the agreement a compromise and appreciate that they were able to talk it over quietly. Asked why they were suddenly able to talk about it in this way, Donna says she brought it up when she found out that she and her girlfriend could not be in the girlfriend's home, which is being reconstructed. She thinks they have become better at it "because we pull ourselves together. We must be able to talk about it now and not get mad at each other." She and Paul have become better at this, Donna adds. Paul does not think he has. He thinks that Donna found out recently when she was in hospital that she missed them and was willing to not be so quick-tempered. It was unnecessary for Paul to control his temper because Donna did not lose hers, and he always lost his as a reaction to her. Donna concedes that she changed the most and agrees with Paul that she thought many things over in the hospital. She is relieved that they were able to reach an agreement and to hear their appreciation of her. Paul and Mary say it is "incredible" and "wonderful" that they could agree on an arrangement. They have not told her so before, though, but she felt it. Donna talks in the past tense about herself, about having had a bad time in school and having brought a bad and irritable mood home with her. Paul adds that lately he has begun to see Donna as more grown-up than he did before so that he needs not tell her to watch out since she really knows. She is almost eighteen, and she has been much more relaxed and talkative lately, which both parents take as a sign of improvement and growth. Paul and Donna even gave each other a hug this morning for the first time in years. Paul voices his feelings and appreciation of Donna quite clearly – also that his fears are not all gone. Paul and Mary say they believe most of all that she can manage, and they are more concerned with their hopes than their fears. Last Saturday, Mary says, they only thought of getting into the countryside on their own leaving both girls behind, and that felt "wonderful." Donna gets her moped before Easter Holidays, and they agreed that she will drive up to visit them one of the days. So everything around Donna has loosened up, but last night Angie was cross because she was not coming to the session.

In view of the deadlock over Donna being alone on weekends and what is at stake for them if something goes wrong again, it is surprising that they did not wait to talk this over until the scheduled session. This shows a growing reliance in their abilities to resolve problems on their own. If we compare previous failed attempts with this successful one, three changes stand out. First, now all three approach the problem with a more converging focus and common goal, while earlier they were preoccupied with distrust and with insisting on being recognized as a different person. Their stakes in the situation then were more focused on getting what they wanted from their opponents and preventing what they feared from them. Differences and conflicts between them now coexist with the common goal of reaching an arrangement that allows them to move beyond the deadlock. To pursue a common goal, then, does not mean that diverse stakes and concerns have disappeared, but that they manage to keep the common goal in the center while they negotiate the arrangement. This change between then and now is linked to a second change. They have changed their understanding of themselves and of their participation in relation to the others. They have pursued changes that encompass – or are directed at – how they may all become able to make and sustain joint arrangements of their life at home. They all pursue personal changes aimed at enabling them to participate in other ways in this joint life. They pursue changes in relation to or with each other rather than in disregard of or (just) in opposition to each other. They all see themselves more explicitly as participants in bringing about a family life of a certain quality. The stronger linking of their own participation, understanding, and change to those of others and to their joint life does not preclude differences and conflicts between them. But they accept that (some of) these differences and conflicts coexist with joining around common goals and vice versa. Such differences then become legitimate and recognized (Fraser 1997). A third change between then and now is evident. Their concerns for themselves and each other are directed more at supporting personal changes and common arrangements that enable desirable futures for the whole family and each of its members at home and in other places.

6.4. When Have We Had Enough?

I have now come to the changes during the last seven months of therapy, interrupted by a long summer break. In this period we considered closing the case several times. Instead, we followed up on some problems. Intervals between sessions are longer than before because the clients need sessions less and because we want to see what happens when attending sessions recedes into the background. Therefore, I cannot follow their lives as closely in my materials.

At the end of session 21, when the problem with Donna is settled, Paul says, "There is still something with Angie." Mary: "She isn't easy to make out." She gets cross easily. They would like a bit more session talk with her. In the scheduled session 22, Angie says she is "fine." Paul adds that "she has taken a turn too in some way, maybe because she has suddenly grown older. I don't know. But all the pestering is completely gone. Now it's about girls and boys she knows. It's as if everything is completely turned around in her head. All the things about horses and all that, we hear nothing about it any more." Angie still has a horse to ride, though, and wants to stay home on weekends rather than to go with Paul and Mary to the countryside "because we have such fun." In many respects, then, Angie's situation and concerns are changing rapidly. Yet, Paul continues: "The only thing is that she is still pretty bad-tempered towards us, and then you can't talk with her." He fears that "precisely the same as with Donna starts now with Angie," referring to the trouble around Donna three years ago. Mary interposes that there were no problems with Angie or Donna in the past two weekends. Nevertheless, Mary is agitated over an incident when she prepared Angie's breakfast and put cheese on her bread, but Angie did not want cheese on it, which almost made Angie throw her glass to the floor. In contrast to earlier, all three argue about how each saw the situation and want it to pass. Then Mary says: "I bloody don't want them to get cross when I'm trying to make them happy." Again in contrast to earlier, she continues: "So I quit [preparing breakfast, OD]!" This is the core of Mary's problems with love and care in conflicts with her children. Ole points out that although Angie does not care whether she gets cross at her parents, the parents do care. Mary rejoins that she told Angie this morning that it matters to her, and then Angie fetched Mary's coffee, which she would normally not dream of doing. Mary continues: "You think you do everything so well, and what do you get for it? Nothing! Not that you must get something in return for everything, but, you know." Ingrid: "It's not being appreciated." Mary: "I think it is, but you never see it. So I guess I'm getting so old that I think they can stuff it 'cause nobody does anything for me, damn it; none of them. I guess that's what I am realizing." Notice that what pushes Mary to change her stance about caring for her children and paying more attention to what she needs and wants herself is not that Angie might as well prepare her own breakfast, but that Angie is preoccupied by other things and gets irritated over the help from Mary. For Mary it is a matter of a changed understanding of care with increased insistence on its reciprocity. She is not willing to continue caring for her daughter if Angie responds by getting cross. Mary's new stance of considering and pursuing her "needs and wishes" has made her reconsider how this can be combined with taking care of each other and balanced off with taking care of others. It has made Mary redefine her notion of love and care for the others so that it is no longer "no problem" for her to stay home with a grumpy Angie just because Mary loves her. These conflicts between them are other ones than before, and Mary's rising dissatisfaction with her position in the family and her pursuit of changing it are prominent in the remaining period of therapy.

In the following session, Paul is very upset over a disruptive incidence with Angie on the way to the session. It has discouraged him, and he wants to give up. This creates a situation where some are ready to continue pursuing change while others are not; consequently, they may need to individualize their efforts anew. Remarkably, Donna encourages Paul to continue and advises him about handling such situations with Angie based on Donna's retrospective views on the troubles around herself a couple of years back. Donna feels freer to draw such parallels because she looks at herself then as a different person. The main issue in the session becomes how Mary may help Paul get over such reactions. Another session is scheduled to talk more about this, and between these sessions Mary and Paul talk about how to react on Angie. In the scheduled session, Mary says that it is "awful" that Paul reacts by getting sad. It makes her "sad because he says nothing for a whole month, shuts completely off." Paul says he set himself the task to mind less, but it is difficult, and in their talk at home he asked Mary not to take so much notice of his moodiness. Mary responds that she can leave him alone and has done so for twenty years, but it is not easy, and she fears it will take longer if they do not talk about it. Paul concurs and adds that he is not depressed, but brooding, speculating over things and feeling inadequate, and then it is difficult to get out of it again. Asked how he does get out of it, he answers: "Usually by talking about it." Mary complains that she can leave him alone for some time, but then she has had it. She cannot stand that the other three cannot talk about problems and accept that there are problems. They must learn to talk about them, but she does not know how they may succeed. She tried by being a good example, but it has not worked.

In this period, the discord between the parents and the daughters about the importance of their joint family life is prominent, and primarily the parents address and pursue it. They are very concerned about what happens in their joint family life, while their daughters are preoccupied by the new exciting things going on in their lives in other places and do not pay much attention to their behavior and their parents' situation at home. This is obvious in the last joint interview during the therapy which took place just before the long summer break (interview 8). Lisbeth asks how their everyday lives are going, and Donna responds: "Well. I'm almost never home. I'm with my friends at the other end of the block." She finished tenth grade in school "super" and starts basic vocational courses to become a nursing aide. Donna stresses that it will not be like public school since they are treated as grown-ups. She has a cleaning job on Wednesday and Friday after five P.M. so that she can attend courses and still earn some money. The friends she spends all her time with are new ones. They hang around, talk, play ball, and go to the beach. She came to know them through Angie. They see them together, also during weekends. Angie says that her days go like Donna's, and that she starts eighth grade after the summer vacation. Lisbeth asks about the horse. Angie: "Don't laugh." Paul: "I don't; I smile." Lisbeth: "Have you dropped it too?" Angie: "Yes." Asked why she thinks less of horses, Angie says: "I don't know. Now I think more of being with my friends." She does not have her job any more. It was too boring. Donna and Angie both spent all the money they earned and find things at home "fine." One thing changed, though. Mary thought it unfair that they did not help out, made a list of household chores, and left it for them to divide and organize these chores between them, which they did well. Angie and Donna both think this is fine. Mary's part time job is now on all workdays, and Paul and Mary have taken a cleaning job "to earn a little extra; the children are never home anyway." Paul and Mary are alone at night and during weekends in the countryside, and Mary feels it is "quite lovely." "Thanks," Angie and Donna interpose. Parents as well as children find it wonderful to be on their own in separate places during weekends. Paul says that, with the exception of some extra evening turns at work, his situation is unchanged. Like Mary he enjoys being alone, and he and Mary look more ahead. He thinks that the girls have grown and become more reasonable, and he is excited to see how Donna will do in vocational school. Both parents are proud that Donna got a place in this vocational school and believe she will do well. Lisbeth asks about changes at home, and Mary starts out: "Everybody think things over much more. They are much more considerate." Paul: "Yes, we do not grumble so much at each other any more." Mary: "Yesterday we talked a little. We are going to the summer cottage on our own for three weeks, and Paul thought that was too long for Angie to be at home. . . . She is off for a week on an excursion with her school class, and then we asked them if they would like to visit us. We would very much like them to come for a weekend, and they said yes, for the time being at least. . . . Even so, I want to go on vacation for three weeks and not worry about it. We drop by home once a week, but besides that I don't want to worry about it." Paul: "We have a phone in our summer cottage, so they can call us if something's up." Paul voices clumsily and at first reproachfully that he will feel they are inconsiderate and be sad if they do not turn up. Mary states: "Quite deliberately I didn't tell them how to do things 'cause that's what we've done too much. One must learn to think for oneself, and then they ought to learn to talk about it." Paul: "We've learned to talk some more and not to give in even though the other looks cross. We've kept on talking about the problems anyhow until we reached a solution. We don't take it so hard any more, you know. We've got to get through, and then we must do it." He sees not taking it so hard and going on anyhow as one of his major changes. Angie noticed that her parents do not take things so hard any more when they get cross, and both girls say, "I believe we've changed a little." But neither Paul nor Mary believe that Angie thinks about these things. Donna says she found out that "I can't be without my mum and dad" when she was in hospital. Lisbeth asks her how she changed, and Donna responds: "I didn't reflect much on what I did. I just changed. I became nicer." Angie says she responds to Donna's change by being nice to her too, but she admits that "I can't understand how we can be together for so long now." Donna seconds her. Next Thursday all four are going to Tivoli. Paul and Mary asked the girls so that they may get a chance to be with them. Mary: "This is a really different situation. Well, I think it's wonderful and I'm not sorry about it at all. It's very, very different. You are going to spend your time in a quite different way."

We see that Angie's and Donna's situations and concerns are still changing rapidly. All four are concerned about pursuing the changes they are involved in and searching for and bringing about possibilities to do so. They are all committed to increase their personal determination in different ways. Mary and Paul are more engaged in changing their understanding and stances about their relation with their children than the other way around. The parents are also more engaged in changing the relation between their own future lives and their relation with the children. But all four are more concerned with granting each other scopes for development and supporting it. The conflicts and disagreements between them about all this are other ones than before.

Asked how they are doing, Paul responds in the final joint session after the summer vacation: "Well, when they are at home, it goes very well. There are no big problems, I think. I can only speak for myself.... Donna began vocational school and is going at it full speed and devotes herself to it heart and soul." Donna: "And I work." Mary talks about how proud she is over what Donna is doing in vocational school. Then she adds that Donna has an allergy that makes her fall asleep in school. She has been home ill for a week now, and they are seeing a physician from the worker's protection bureau because the school denies that there is a problem. Angie is in school most of the day and in youth school afterwards. She is doing OK in school but lost her friends who found somebody else while Angie was in the countryside.

In the final session with Paul and Mary, they say that things are about the same for Donna and Angie. They did not really manage to redistribute the chores at home. It hinges on the fact that nobody but Mary is planning their shopping, which is necessary because of their financial situation. Mary still carries the responsibility for and control over what needs to be done and is waiting for them to do it. That they do not do it, she takes as lack of interest. Mary takes notes about what needs to be bought and brought, but shows them to nobody and complains that they never got the idea of making their own list. Paul concedes but says that he does not want Mary to control what he is doing and missing. Mary: "That's all right if you make no mistakes." They gradually agree that Mary reduced her control over what they do, and Paul admits that it is OK that Mary checks up on them, but it makes him feel insufficient; therefore, he wants to avoid the chores. Mary keeps coming back to saying, "It's all no use. I've tried for so many years." She admits that here and now Paul says he is willing to make changes but adds: "Yes, he says so now, but he should also be able to tell me at home, right. We should be able to find out at home." Ingrid and Ole point out that Paul feels insufficient as a reaction to some of the things Mary does, and Mary feels let down as a reaction to when Paul does not help with the chores. The lack of belief in change hurts the one who is criticized, just as it did Donna, and they do not reach an agreement about how change is possible. Mary agrees and adds: "That's a general problem. Everything vanishes into uncertainty." Ole: "And that makes you bitterer, you feel more let down, and next time you talk about it, you say things like you do now." Mary: "Yes, you are quite right." Ole: "Yes, but that doesn't improve it." Mary: "No." Ole: "And no solution is found." We talk about making demands on each other and about ways of reacting to each other's mistakes. Toward the end of the session Paul says: "Some of our internal problems and the things with the children are gone so we don't need to take your time with this. We must grow up so much that we can talk on our own, and keep growing."

In this final session it turned out that they had not continued to change their participation in their joint family life sufficiently as their conditions changed over the summer. Mary got a heavier workload, Angie and Donna started school again, and Donna's allergies exhausted her. They are still variously committed to continue the ongoing changes, though. But they now stress that they should be able to accomplish such changes on their own without further help from their therapists. Mary has doubts about this, but these doubts only matter to her because she now thinks they should be able to do it, and at the end Paul reaffirms the same commitment. So, when their therapy ends their commitments to changes still differ, and there are still conflicts and disagreements between them over these changes.

6.5. Changing Understandings of Change

Some further considerations about the study of changes are in order. Because my materials are based on sessions and interviews, they mainly consist of the clients' reports and conversations about their changing practice and mental states in other times and places from where I have no direct observations. In my analysis, I extract and link instances of changing practices with each other and with other information about their ongoing practice. The procedure contains a risk of overhomogenizing their changes. If I confound the extracted instances with a new, general practice, I construct an oversimplified and abstract understanding of their changing practice. The occurrence of certain incidents of change is no guarantee of a general or permanent change. It just shows that a potentiality was created and that the clients may use it but that they might not use it in similar instances. It does not determine their future participation and understanding, but it creates new personal possibilities that the clients must seize elsewhere and later if these potentialities are to spread and continue to change. The use of prior abilities and understandings calls for the client to bring about similar events and opportunities elsewhere and later as well as to address these situations by means of those prior abilities and understandings. In a changing situated social practice doing likewise is a possibility that persons must re-collect and fit into their particular present situation – and even so they may end up doing otherwise. Uses elsewhere and later also depend on what their varying and changing coparticipants are willing to do. Besides, later changes in the clients' circumstances change their possibilities, call for other abilities and understandings, create other problems, or provoke what they see as relapses. Situations, abilities, and understandings change in complex ways and not in a cumulative and permanent manner. To re-collect and re-produce prior changes is an accomplishment involving various efforts and much work.

The many-faceted processes involved in personal changes in a changing social practice caution against an oversimplified understanding of the bringing about of changes. Many things need doing and re-considering across times and places to accomplish what afterward may seem to be simple, step-by-step accumulated changes. The clients certainly did not tell us all about it, nor were we sufficiently aware of all of it to ask them. Indeed, in response to our interview questions about what took place since the latest interview, the clients re-count something that already happened, and in sessions we often talk about things that took place. But when they re-count changes that already occurred, they consider them backward from the accomplished results. They re-construct the path that led there, that is, they mention what was involved in bringing about the given accomplishment, not all the other things that they considered and explored but that, as they now see it, turned out not to lead to this accomplishment. They will not tell us about all the failed attempts on the way to finding out how to succeed, nor will they tell us about all the different considerations and ways of going about it and bringing it up with various others that it may have taken on different occasions to come to do it and understand it as they now do. Meanwhile some earlier ways of doing and understanding it turned into their present modes and are forgotten as earlier variants. So the clients' re-counts of accomplishments appear more uniform than the paths they took to get there.

Still, in sessions and interviews, the clients not only tell us about instances that did occur, but they also tell us how they pursue, come back to, and anticipate ongoing changes for which there is no guarantee so far that they will accomplish. They want to tell us how they link ongoing changes across times and places, and they want their therapists to understand that they are having difficulties or are able to accomplish certain things in their ongoing efforts. By telling about it, they want family members and therapists to recognize their difficulties and accomplishments, and they hope to get some help in their pursuits. What is more, they must regularly pursue changes. Not that they must or should permanently pursue changes, but they cannot cease changing their participation and understandings because the social practices they are part of do not cease changing, and it then takes other abilities and understandings to participate in them. So, they must notice changing demands, possibilities, occasions, and reasons for change. They must be able to keep at, come back to, and pick up long-term changes anew. Thus, this family ran into new problems because they did not continue changing their personal social practice and interpersonal relationships sufficiently over the summer at the end of their therapy. This turned into a problematic neglect and looming failure.

Sameness and Difference, Routines and Variations in Changes

In psychology, change is mainly researched in the following way: While a particular behavior pattern, state of mind, or whatever characterized a person at time A, a different behavior pattern, state of mind, or whatever characterizes this person at a later time B – for instance, at the beginning of a therapy compared to at its end. At any given point in time, a person's behavior, state of mind, or whatever is thus assumed to be uniform and general so that change really means to replace one uniformity with another. In contrast to mere fluctuation, change is assumed to be stable, and stability is assumed to be brought about by establishing a different uniformity, for instance, by establishing new routines.

However, even routines are not entirely uniform and do not always represent repetitive behavior. They are affected by changes in a person's situation and concerns (Lave 1988, 189) and are re-produced in often not quite the same circumstances with changing resources and coparticipants. In this family, to change everyday routines is first of all a matter of changing their distribution and coordination among its members. It involves changing the place of these routines in individual members' courses of activity, the coordination between members' courses of activity, and their (dis)agreements about what counts as acceptable standards for their accomplishments. Routines are not merely part of individual courses of activity but of distributed and coordinated modes of participation in shared contexts with established and changing time structures of joint and separate activities. Even when not executed jointly, routines are subsidiary parts of complex social practices spanning diverse contexts and distributed across participants. So, routines must change as subsidiary parts of changing (personal) social practices, and we cannot understand individual activities and joint family life as made up of a set of routines. This claim runs counter to a widespread view of everyday life at home as quite repetitive (Lave unpublished manuscript). But whereas, say, in workplaces it may be important that participants (jointly and separately) re-produce the same outcomes over and over – though this is not all that matters about work achievements in all work practices – family life is primarily concerned with things other than re-producing the same outcome. For example, the mastery of a professional cook may be seen in being able to re-produce the same sauce over and over, that is, of intentionally producing sameness, and reaching the same result may vary with the quality of available produce and facilities; however, accomplishments in family life are normally not defined and pursued so strictly. A counterexample might be Angie's standard of acceptable morning toast. But even in such untypical instances, Angie's strict standard of outcome has a certain range. In contrast to work settings, a strictly defined sameness rarely matters to family members. At least they rarely agree on it and adhere closely to it. Contrary to widespread beliefs that family life is very routine, variation matters a lot to family members. They get bored if their family activities and experiences do not vary. They appreciate and treasure variation and, therefore, also change their routines (periodically), as when Angie became tired of having cheese on her toast. In many ways, family members dislike when members stick closely to doing the same and always want to have things the same way. They want varied meals, would dislike having to eat the same thing over and over, and do not want to have their meals strictly regulated and distributed. On the whole, they dislike having their family life too regulated and repetitive. When it is, conflicts erupt between them. Some members then feel that others are over-regulating how things are to be done and imposing it on them, as when Mary and Paul fight over the standards of household chores. It would be too rigid and violate their appreciation of room for variation in their everyday family life. To members, a good family life must hold variations, and so it takes varied activities to re-produce it. In fact, in my materials, members of this family only focus on sameness when it is a problem to them and they want it changed.

There are other reasons why family practice must vary. In other institutional practices, such as schools and workplaces, key activities are often arranged so that participants are to concentrate on doing one thing at a time while other activities and concerns are ignored and excluded. This gives rise to particular regulated ways of conducting key activities. But in most family activities and in many leisure activities outside home, many things go on at the same time. It is not possible to isolate one activity and address it in such a concentrated way, and participants often do not want to because they are concerned about and have obligations in relation to several concurrent activities. Instead, they prefer to pursue multiple trails of action concurrently (as in some work practices, Abbott 2001, 255; Engeström, Engeström, and Vähäahu 1999, 345). This affects how particular activities are performed in the family. They are also often performed with a varying constellation of participants and concerns. Hence, it is neither easy nor feasible to conduct an activity in strictly the same way. What we categorize as the same activity must be addressed and conducted in varying ways fitting with its particular place and weight in relation to a varying set of other activities, concerns, and participants. While tasks may be abstracted and activities distributed in a preregulated, fixed, and controlled way in work settings such as the one Hutchins studied (1993; 1995), at home and in leisure time activities the configuration of many tasks and the distribution of many activities among participants vary. The delineation of what to do and not to do, what to be concerned about and not to be concerned about, as well as the distribution of contributions among participants, must be accomplished in situ and may turn into a problem or a conflict. So, participants must find each other in varying ways of agreeing on how to delimit, arrange, and realize possibilities and obligations.

Finally, it takes different things to pursue changes in different contexts. After all, as persons move into other contexts, their possibilities vary, there are other standards for doing things and for what to take into consideration (Taylor 1995a), and other arrangements define other suitable modes of participation. At home other things matter, and things are to be done in other ways than at work or in school (Dreier 1979; 1980). In family life, members react against some forms of pressure and for some forms of leisure so that the timing and conduct of activities vary across contexts.

The prevalent emphasis on sameness in psychology and other disciplines is a result of the strong interest of science and professional expertise in establishing general taxonomies with a set of discrete categories of description, evaluation, diagnosis, intervention, and prediction. Science is seen as being aimed at identifying general phenomena and regularities; scientific findings must consist in such unchanging elements; and expert judgment must map concrete practice onto a list of discrete, general categories. All members of such a category are then claimed to be identical. But in concrete practice, particular instances of a category are not completely identical. They are similar. Unlike their representation as isolated entities in the realm of scientific abstractions, in concrete practice particular instances are varying parts of varying situations. Instead of operating with strict criteria of identity for all members of a category, we should look for "a complicated network of overlapping and criss-crossing similarities" and differences (Medina 2003; Wittgenstein 1953, section 6). Members of a category are similar in some respects and different in other respects. They display "family resemblances" (Toulmin 1996, 214; Wittgenstein 1953, section 67). When I point to the existence and significance of differences in this book, my intention is not to pit difference and variation against sameness but to insist that concrete instances are more or less similar.

Differences and variations are of little interest to mainstream research, which seeks what is general and stable. In their analysis of ongoing practices, they construe uniformity and repetitiveness. The experimental study of variables even considers variations as a disturbance to be ruled out as a symptom of the lack of control over the research situation where only the dependent variable may vary. Variation is thus highly restricted and controlled. But we must be careful not to lose sight of variations by subsuming them under empirical generalizations and the general, conceptual order of theories. Some researchers grant a limited role to variation. Thus, evolutionary theory since Darwin argues for the role of variation as affording selection in leading to the emergence of a new generality. Here variation plays a role in affording the bringing about of a new generality. Likewise, the developmental psychologist Valsiner (1984) distinguishes between the typological and variational episte-mological frameworks in psychology. In the latter, changeability leads to new generalities. But in these models, variations vanish in the new generality. In cognitive psychology and personality psychology, some researchers take the variety of situations into account by arguing for the development of an array of more specific generalities in individual functioning attuned to specific types of situations (Bandura 1999; Mischel and Shoda 1999; Wallin 2003). But this calls for the assumption of a mental switchboard that identifies types of situations and switches individual functioning accordingly. These models also confuse the flexibility of personal and social variability with a specificity of function-ing where uniformity reigns within each type of situation while difference reigns between them. My conception differs from these models in arguing that variability and changeability are features of ongoing practices and should be studied as such. I stress the personal concern for variation in ongoing prac-tices and for arrangements leaving room for varied modes of participation. I also emphasize that particular contextual scopes and arrangements hold par-ticular ranges of variability that change as these practices change. Likewise, I argue that the variability of personal functioning increases as personal abilities and understandings develop. The pursuit of changes requires variations too. Even re-producing a life that does not change much requires unending and diverse work.

Learning in a Changing Social Practice

As mentioned in section 6.1, personal change involves learning as changing abilities and understandings in a changing social practice. In everyday social practice, much learning is not conducted by isolating a learning activity and pursuing it separately from other activities and concerns. Rather, in much everyday, personal practice, learning occurs and is pursued as an intermittent or a concomitant part of activities that hold other concerns and purposes. It is an aspect of an ongoing, multifaceted social practice in the course of which persons also come to learn and sometimes pursue the learning of particular things. Holzkamp (1993) calls such incidental learning "concomitant learn-ing." Persons then learn in ways that are affected by being a varying part of varying, ongoing practices. When clients continue to learn about what they addressed in, say, sessions, the ways in which they then learn differ from their learning in sessions and continue to vary with the circumstances, concerns, and constellations of participation of their current situated practice. So, what the clients get out of attending sessions mainly consists in what they continue to learn in other ways in other places in between and afterward. "We got a lot out of that," as they say. To do so, involves changing the way they learn according to the current context, constellation of activities, participants, and concerns. They learn to utilize relevant contextual differences for their pursuit of learning, such as what they may best learn in sessions, at home, and in other places and how they may best distribute and combine a complex learning process across times and places. In fact, what is learned lives on because it is pursued and modified further while it may fade into the background and get lost when a person is no longer occupied by it.

Mainstream psychology, on the other hand, sees learning as the acquisition, transfer and application of knowledge (Lave 1996; unpublished manuscript). This point of view reflects the institutional epistemology of school learning (Dreier 1999a; 1999c), where learning is seen as being directed at a preexisting and predefined school knowledge and understood as the acquisition, transfer, and application of this knowledge. Strictly speaking, this presupposes that what is learned in the classroom remains unchanged when the learner enters other situations of use elsewhere and that it can be addressed in isolation from – and be unaffected by – other aspects of the situations of use. In my conception, the assumed identity between knowledge acquired and knowledge applied is replaced by a conception of varying and changing similarities and differences across times and places. Like the institutional epistemology in mainstream notions of therapy, the institutional epistemology in mainstream theories of learning reflects the positioned perspective of professional experts on the institutional arrangements of education. These arrangements affect the pursuit of learning related to therapy and education. Pursuits of learning in these practices are special and not manifestations of a general human learning process. The institutional arrangements incorporate arrangements of institutional learning trajectories in relation to which participants must pursue their personal learning trajectories. As a consequence, participants may learn particular things in particular ways in classrooms and sessions, and what they learn there matters because of particular significant and usable differences to what they learn in other places.

An important difference between learning in school and learning elsewhere is that school learning is supposed to have a well-defined endpoint in a fixed body of knowledge and that it can be determined when this point is reached and a learning assignment is finished. Much everyday learning has no well-defined endpoint. It is more open-ended and interminable. Though it may be interrupted, neglected, or given up, it is not entirely clear when and whether it is complete and finished. What a person believed to be an endpoint later often turns out just to be a point on the way. So it is difficult to make out whether he has learned it all or just some of it. Learning is incomplete, partial, and provisional. He can never entirely stop pursuing it. The open-ended nature of learning as changing abilities and understandings in personal social practice lies behind the clients' concerns about self-confidence.

Self-Confidence and Pulling Myself Together in Social Practice

In common usage, self-confidence reflects a person's appreciation of herself as being able to take part in particular situations and accomplish particular ends that are important to her and others. A person's self-confidence is believed to develop and vary accordingly. But there is more to an adequate concept of self-confidence. Because what it takes to participate and contribute significantly to an ongoing social practice is changing, a person's self-confidence also reflects her beliefs in whether she will be able to continue learning what it takes and possibly to improve. When a person's practice changes and her learning is open-ended, she cannot relate to her participation and learning merely as a matter of having reached a certain ability and understanding. Even more so, she must believe that she will be able to participate and learn what may be required and desirable in other, not yet well-known, future situations. The quality of this belief depends on her prior experiences of influencing and changing her situation, developing her understandings and abilities to do so, and seeing herself as a person learning and changing. A person's self-confidence increases when she makes it, especially in particularly difficult and important instances. It is shaken or turns into diffidence when what she had become self-confident in doing does not work after all or any more.

Personal change is not just a matter of acting and understanding differently. It involves developing her abilities and continuing to change them as her situation, concerns, and stances change. In doing so, her relation to her abilities, especially to her potentialities for changing and developing them, may change and gain the qualities of self-confidence. So a person's self-confidence is closely linked to her changing aspirations – in Mary's words, "needs and wishes" – about her participation in a changing social practice. Self-confidence is not a state. There is a more or less far-reaching and ambitious directing-herself-forward to it. Her aspirations are open-ended markers linking her self-confidence to change and learning. That is why Mary's self-confidence may be shaken by doubts as she raises her aspirations and her insistence on them.

In addition, there is an interpersonal dimension to self-confidence. It depends on others' recognition of a person's contributions to a joint practice and her development of understandings and participation in it, as we saw in the acute discord between Donna and her parents. Likewise, others' recognition may center on how a person is able to change in relation to unknown and changing situations, as we saw in Paul and Mary's changed recognition of Angie and of why self-confidence is important for her. The interpersonal dimension of self-confidence is also seen in how a person stands up for her perspectives and concerns in relation to others.

The notion of self-confidence is part of folk psychology and of the clients' self-understandings and pursuits of change. They stress the importance of self-confidence in understanding their own and each others' relations to change. However, they only begin to do so when their changes are already well on the way. Before that they use another notion that is also part of folk psychology, namely to "pull myself together" to "get going" and "make an effort." To pull myself together expresses a different relation to the pursuit of change where a person is less convinced about the qualities of the outcome of her pursuits and about being able to bring about an improved situation, participation, and state of mind. Rather, she is making herself begin to pursue change instead of just following suit. She is pushing and coercing herself, focusing on the moral dimension that she should do it even though or in spite of not being convinced that she will be able to bring about worthwhile improvements (Holzkamp 1983, 324; Osterkamp 1976, 115). It is a kind of self-coercive motivation sometimes confused with personal strength versus weakness (Bandura 1999; Dreier 1988b; Haisch and Haisch 1988). In contrast to these subjective qualities of getting started on unforeseeable changes, self-confidence reflects a pursuit of change accompanied by a belief in somehow being able to bring about improvements. During their therapy, the clients increasingly reflect on issues related to self-confidence. At the end, they raise the issue whether they now are confident in their abilities and readiness to continue changing and learning without further help from their therapists. Their reliance on their abilities and readiness to learn and their mutual recognition thereof are changing, and their doubts about it follow these changes.

In summing up, self-confidence does not merely mean that a person believes she is able to do certain things familiar to her. In fact, she feels self-confident in dealing with unfamiliar things, and not just increasingly confident in pursuing the more familiar things. The belief in being able to deal with unknown and risky situations is a stronger and more definite expression of self-confidence. Self-confidence does not presuppose the disappearance of uncertainty and unpredictability. It reflects a particular personal appreciation thereof and a particular personal regulation of one's relation to the open-ended nature of personal social practice and the non-pre-givenness of what things may turn into. It incorporates a measure of suspense about what may come. Nonetheless, feeling confident is different from feeling confused, that is, unable to find one's bearings and lay out a direction for one's pursuits, or feeling that one is in a mess, that is, unable to sort out many entangled things.

Stability and Hanging Togetherness in a Changing Practice

Stability in everyday lives and personal changes gains particular qualities and dynamics from the open-ended, varying, and changing nature of social practices and personal participation. Stability is not static and based on the regularity and repetition of the same activities. It must be changed and renewed, and in order to re-produce it, persons must continue to embrace changes and variations. Stability is open-ended toward possible futures. It may increase or decrease due to changes, and changes may occur in more or less stable ways. So stability and change are not each others' opposites. If persons live by this belief, sooner or later their lives will destabilize. If they do not continue to change and vary, the achieved stability disrupts and dissolves. But concrete changes are selective. They are particular changes of particular parts of persons' lives, while other parts are set aside for the moment. And because persons' lives are grounded in a complex of linked parts, the focus of their changes must shift if they are to be able to continue complex, long-term changes and sustain the ones they achieved. Having accomplished changes in other parts of their practice may open other possibilities for change in the part they changed earlier so that they may pick it up again. They must re-focus and re-locate their pursuits of change. Their pursuits of change must change.

In analyzing changes, I focus on the changing aspects of persons' lives and social practices, considering their emergence, transformation, and replacement. I also focus on the changing links between these aspects of persons' lives and social practices, that is, on the emergence, transformation, and disappearance of such links. In that way, I grasp the changing place of particular aspects and the changing strength and meaning of particular troubles, concerns, and pursuits. Consider, for instance, the emerging, and for a period of time prevalent, significance of being cross, which changes again and recedes into the background. Or the emergence and changing significance for Mary of attending to her needs and wishes, for Paul of being more consistent, and for Donna of being recognized. They are instances of response shifts where persons cease attending to certain aspects and emphasize other aspects instead or redefine the links between particular aspects and their meaning. Such changes in the strength and meaning of particular aspects and of what are important links between them are crucial to personal changes and to what therapy is meant to promote. The aspects and links of social practices and personal lives are not fixed. They are dynamic, and we learn about their dynamics by studying their re-production and change. Rather than seeking to gain knowledge about a change in isolated variables, events, and phenomena, I analyze changing links between events and phenomena and how they are re-produced, vary and change in changing *Zusammenhänge*. The sheer occurrence of an event or a phenomenon is not of primary importance, but its identification in *Zusammenhänge* and the dynamics of those *Zusammenhänge* are important. I seek to comprehend events and phenomena in *Zusammenhänge* rather than to document and predict the frequency and probability of their occurrence. In short, my aim is to characterize changing *Zusammenhänge* in social practices and personal lives.

Understanding Open-Ended Changes

Understanding open-ended changes in changing *Zusammenhänge* is complex. In sessions, we often work with different problem situations one at a time and explore a range of different, possible ways of proceeding in this situation and then in that situation. In each situation we deal with how the clients may oppose, balance off, configure, and combine a varying set of concerns and stances, possibilities and modes of participation. By doing so, the clients learn to distinguish between different situations or problems and to deal in similar ways with similar ones. They primarily learn to configure and combine a set of concerns and stances, possibilities and modes of participation in particular situations. They may gradually come to see and develop this as a situated approach to understanding and dealing with their lives and problems across contexts, as what Mammen (1983) calls a human "sense for concrete connections." This is why they are not necessarily at a disadvantage when facing dissimilar situations. Rather than taking their bearings from a repertoire of experiences from similar situations (Schön 1983), they compose their understanding and participation by linking multiple considerations of relevance in a particular situation.

As the clients' pursuit and understanding of changes evolve, they focus on other aspects of their present situation and on bringing about other links between it and imagined, possible, and desirable futures. These possible futures are understood as ones they may approach or hinder due to the ways in which they address their present situation. They come to consider their present situation more clearly as part of their own and each others' lives in other times and places and as reaching further into possible futures. The experienced horizon and reach of their current practice changes, and they re-appreciate their present situation accordingly. They change their engagement in possible futures and in bringing about other relations with each other, which may open these possible futures. They then approach their present relations in a new perspective reaching toward aspired futures.

To be able to expand their pursuits of change, participants must link their concerns to other participants' concerns and to everybody's stances on their joint life. After all, which changes are possible and meaningful to me depend on others, their changes, and their readiness for further changes. So, they must link their pursuits of change. This involves new ways of doing things, talking with each other, seeking each others' support, and negotiating differences in individual scopes, concerns, stances, and contributions. These changes in the interpersonal dimensions of their pursuits of change are brought about, among other things, through hearing what the others have to say in sessions. This brings about a clearer understanding of the others' concerns and stances, of how they want support and want to support others, and of which wishes for possible futures they share. It also brings about new understandings of the links between what they do, experience, and want, as well as new understandings and appreciations of their own and others' parts in their mutual relations and changes. They are then less dependent on orienting themselves only according to individual perspectives and concerns. Talk allows them to develop their understanding of how to bring about particular links and qualities between them. As the significance of talk for such purposes grows, they may begin to talk in order to anticipate and coordinate their pursuit of changes across times and places as Mary and Paul did. Furthermore, as changes unfold, they recognize each other's concerns to create possible futures and feel connected and supported in new ways in their pursuits of such changes, even though they recognize that they do not aspire to the same joint future family life. Their hopes and the realizability of desired futures are tied to the development of their relations, also when these hopes are not concerned with a joint life. Their feelings of hope and despair reflect the qualities of their relations and their trust in each others' readiness to join in pursuing change.

Obviously, the pursuit of changes presupposes an open-ended and changing understanding. But in a complex and changing social practice, changes have many causes and reasons, which makes them complicated to describe and understand. When asked in the interviews whether changes had occurred, the clients were often not certain how to answer. They even often held on to older understandings some time after changes of their practice had begun. After all, it is difficult to describe changes you are in the midst of. The impact of the changes may not yet seem clear, and they may turn out to be more or less passing or stable. It is difficult to describe possibilities you are still trying out so that you cannot yet tell how suitable they really are and whether they will bring about the stable changes you want. Besides, the clients do not stop changing when their therapy ends. Their changes are unending, and the end of their therapy is not the end of a story. What is more, the course of their changes may be full of twists and turns that re-open and complicate questions about how it hangs together. The life they lead may even change so much and so fast that they lose their grip on how it was earlier and seemingly forget it. Thus, in interview 9 after the therapy ended, Lisbeth asks Angie what happened in her life during the course of therapy. Angie cannot say much about it. Lisbeth then reminds Angie that she attended sixth grade when the therapy started and that she is now in eighth grade. Angie is highly surprised. It seems very far away to her. Yet, marking out this contrast enables her to come up with a number of significant changes in various areas of her life as seen from the perspective of her current situation. Finally, it is difficult to describe changes that also depend heavily on what others do, especially when their perspectives and reasons are not clear to you because they do not want to talk about it. The fact that changes also depend on others leads to questions for persons about the changes that occurred: What is my particular part in bringing about those changes? If I had done something else or nothing, what might then have happened? Would this change have occurred anyhow because the others would have done it for me, or would nothing or something else have happened?

Though personal understandings may become more comprehensive, they are always incomplete and partial. They are selective and have a particular, changing perspective, focus, and configuration. Being partial, personal understandings are easily challenged anew by what was not yet attended to and comprehended. Personal understandings are often searching, and persons need each other to resolve doubts and confusions about them. So personal understandings remain marked by varying degrees of uncertainty, of not knowing and understanding clearly, and of being confused over oneself, the others, and how and why things turn out as they do. Still, the clarity and certainty of the clients' understandings increase. We see that by comparing their statements in early sessions and interviews with later. At the beginning, they often respond to questions about their everyday events, needs, and feelings by saying, "I don't know" or "I am not sure." Later, they often present more elaborate considerations about why and how things occur and they feel as they do about them. Nonetheless, confusion persists and recurs about their everyday lives and changes. So do new and old disagreements about them. They still sometimes ignore each others' perspectives and concerns and feel ignored and not recognized as persons. But it happens less frequently and instead, they feel more closely connected with each other. As their concerns come to reach across larger spans of times and places, their practice of care for each other changes and unfolds new qualities. They become more concerned with issues about caring for each others' changing and developing lives.

7 Changing Problems across Places

7.1. Focus and Frame

In this chapter, I analyze client changes in relation to problems. It includes how clients' understandings and relations to their problems change and how changes in their problems are brought about.

First, I shall frame my analysis of changing problems in general terms. In section 4.3, I stressed the clients' tendency at first to view the troubles for which they seek therapy as peculiar mental states and properties in the referred patient Angie. They see these mental states and properties as external causes for the troubles they encounter in their ongoing social practice in the sense that these causes are seen as independent of their social practice and as intruding into it. To put it differently, it is incomprehensible to them how these mental states and properties are parts of their and Angie's ongoing social practice. I shall analyze these problems as dark sides of their social practice, that is, as obscure and troublesome parts of it, and point out how the clients gradually come to recognize their problems as they change their ways of dealing with them and understanding them. In my approach, problems are not given or resolved states; they are instead changing parts of their changing social practice with changing properties, meanings, and links in their ongoing practice. Therefore, chapter 6 frames my analysis of their problems. I focus on the clients' changing participation and understandings in relation to their changing problems, while keeping the broader structure of links in mind needed to comprehend problems as changing parts of a changing practice.

To claim that problems are changing parts of a changing social practice means that it takes a social practice to change them. This is their most obvious link to the ongoing social practice. Precisely this link challenges the clients' prior understanding of problems as abstract mental states and properties toward dealing with them and coming to understand them as aspects of social practice. Beyond that, I claim that problems *are* parts of social practice, that is, problems in, for, and due to social practice. This is their mode of existence. If they are a problem, how could they not be part of social practice? Whatever else we believe about problems, they are first of all parts of social practice – as, indeed, all mental states and personal properties are. And as parts of social practice, they disturb the realization of possibilities. They are linked to the realization of possibilities in disturbing ways. Problems exist when participants cannot overcome troubling situations and states of mind and cannot reach necessary and significant ends by bringing their abilities to bear on a situation or by developing their abilities and expanding their possibilities. Generally speaking, participants may overcome problems by joining other participants to expand relevant possibilities and develop relevant abilities. If problems, nonetheless, persist, the relevant abilities and/or possibilities cannot be brought about or participants' understandings of the problem and their relations with each other are problematic too. The existence of external constraints is no problem in itself. It only becomes a problem when these constraints are part of an ongoing practice in a way that disturbs the realization of possibilities. To designate something as a problem means to frame it in relation to possibilities and abilities in a social practice. It also means to frame it as something it should be possible to resolve (Lave 1988; Seidel 1976). Participants want it changed and believe it ought to be changeable, but they cannot quite see how. So, problems are involved in our pursuit of concerns in the scope of possibilities of our social practice, and as this scope changes, our problems change as internal contradictions to their realization. We address problems as part of our realization and expansion of possibilities.

When problems are part of social practice, they may have other meanings in other contexts with other scopes, concerns, and coparticipants and they may also be addressed in other ways in these other contexts. In this sense, the same problem varies across contexts, but there are also other problems in other contexts. When problems are parts of lives in a complex social practice, problems in other contexts may be unrelated or related and reach across contexts in complex ways. What turns into a problem may also differ from one context to another. So, when new problems turn up, they may have grown out of former problems, but this need not be the case. Problems may emerge for other, not closely related or unrelated reasons. They grow out of participants' practice, not necessarily out of other problems. Again we are reminded to understand problems first of all as parts of social practice, that is, through their links with other parts of social practice. This is also how we may understand the links between problems. In that sense, we must look beyond the problems in order to comprehend them. We must see them as problematic parts of something else.

7.2. The Course of Changing Problems

Relating to Angie's Symptoms and Problems

At the time of referral, this family says that they are quite satisfied with their lives and that Angie's symptoms are not much of a burden. Earlier troubles had disturbed them more. Her symptoms are not much of a problem because Angie is used to it being like this, and they see no possibilities for improving or overcoming them. This turns the meaning of her symptoms into a social fact in accordance with which they re-arrange and re-adapt their lives. At home, Angie's anxieties are no real problem for her primarily because the others take them into consideration and make arrangements for her.

Upon closer inspection, the clients have different points of view on the symptoms, even though they all present the same symptoms to their therapists, designate them by the same mental states, and illustrate them by the same events and behaviors. The differences concern their views on what reproduces the symptoms and what it takes to overcome them. Their preferred practices of preventing and handling them therefore differ. While the symptoms bother Angie most when she is in school, with friends, on a trip, and so forth, her parents do not know much about those aspects of her symptoms because they are not there, and Angie does not like to talk with them about it. Recognizing that the symptoms bother Angie most in other places, her parents are uncertain about what is the matter. Returning from school, Angie is often irritable and has headaches. Her parents do not quite know what this is about and have no other way to deal with this uncertainty than guessing. Because she often gets irritated over trifles, they guess it might not have anything to do with them. They would like to know what it is about, but because they do not know, what can they do other than to show consideration? This lies within their reach and powers.

They are all uncertain, confused, and worried about the symptoms in various ways. They do not believe they fully understand them and feel they somehow escape them. This belief makes them more ready to pick up what they believe the perspectives introduced by their expert strangers suggest. Mostly, though, it makes them do what they can to keep Angie's symptoms from recurring, especially because they do not know what to do to overcome them and fear that they may grow worse. Forestalling their recurrence involves avoiding particular situations, places, and events judged risky. It also involves not addressing particular topics and issues, not talking about them, and not participating in activities that might take them into such mine fields in the hope that it may encapsulate her symptoms so that they do not spread any further. Finding and agreeing on ways to prevent the symptoms from recurring turn into a problem of its own. The symptoms create other problems, and the other family members see no clear indication that they are involved in producing her symptoms, committed as they are to preventing them.

The family also addresses the symptoms in moral terms. Angie's anxieties are experienced and dealt with in terms of character. They pity Angie and believe her to be rather weak. They show her compassion and care, protect her and restrict her so that the symptoms will not recur. But they also blame her and hold her responsible for doing what she should and abstaining from what she should not. They help her, whether she wants it or not, and take over responsibility for her well-being in a more or less well-defined range of situations. They grant her conditional moral recognition. In addition, they believe they have a moral obligation to do all these things for her. This is why Mary insists that it is no problem to do these things, just as it is no problem to attend this therapy for Angie's sake.

The others have gradually found their ways to take care of Angie. First of all, they show consideration for her troubles. Mary is most engaged in doing so. As she puts it in interview 1: "We don't make a big problem out of it. It's more when we are not present, or I am not present." When Mary is there, she takes care that it does not become a problem. In the preceding session, Mary felt that the therapists turned it into a problem for her to watch over Angie and show her consideration, but she claims, "It's no problem. They made it sound as if I sacrifice myself, and I don't think so because it goes much smoother this way." Paul objects: "But I think you sacrifice yourself too much. I sometimes think you show too much consideration." This disagreement has made Mary take over most of it and keep Paul out for Angie's sake. In session 4, Mary adds that it is not too hard "when Angie is cross either. Of course, it's a relief when she isn't, but I don't think it's a burden." When Angie has her outbursts, "I don't get irritated; I get sad when I feel it's unfair, unjust."

Yet, showing consideration is a way of alleviating Angie's life with symptoms, not a way of overcoming them. Nor does it give them a deeper understanding of the reasons for her symptoms. In interview 1, Mary says, "I feel it's something I can't manage myself, in particular Angie's claustrophobia. I can help her by not forcing her to do things she is afraid of, but I can't get her out of it." Nor can she help Angie when Angie is in other places. For this, Mary needs the therapists from whom "I hope to get the help I can't give Angie." So, Mary wants the therapists to help Angie get out of her symptomatic states so that they will not bother her in other places.

When others take over for Angie at home, they bypass her agency and delegate to others what it takes to prevent her symptoms from recurring. They set and rearrange her scopes so that she does not learn to influence and expand them in relation to her symptoms. Instead, Angie wants her parents to do things for her and feels she "can't help it" when her symptoms occur. She does not trust her understandings and abilities in relation to her symptoms. Hence, she does not quite know what to tell us about them and often responds, "I don't know," when we talk with her about them. The responsibilities for taking care of Angie circulate between them in ways that often create disruptions and keep them from moving forward. In fact, they disagree over how to handle Angie's troubles and help her get over them. Mary and Paul disagree over whether showing consideration for her is the right way. So, even though they agree on labeling her symptoms, these symptoms are involved in conflicts between them. Still, as Mary sees it, disagreements between them are muffled: "Discord is their biggest enemy. They smooth out everything or stop discussions so that nobody gets cross. That is not allowed." All the same, they do get cross, which does not please Mary.

Being Cross at Home

In session 5, we point out that Angie also gets sullen when Mary shows consideration for her and takes care of things for her. Shortly after in interview

2, the heated exchange about being cross occurs (see section 4.8). Here they all agree that being cross is their major problem at home, and they all see the others as the ones who get cross. Indeed, they get cross at each other over the issue of who is cross. Mary adds: "We have to put up with whatever you say and do with a smile. We are not allowed to make any demands on you. If it doesn't suit you, then we are cross." The very person who out of consideration and care would do for her daughter what she feared her daughter might not like to do herself now marks out a polarity: "we" the parents against "you" the children. She has turned 180 degrees compared with her prior stance of being considerate. Paul picks up on it: "As soon as we say a word . . . " Mary interrupts: "Then they get cross. That's right. They both do." Mary now believes they have probably done what they believed the children wanted "because we mind them too much."

Notice that all family members still agree on a common problem – which is not the anxiety symptoms for which Angie was referred to therapy – namely, being cross as a pervasive burden on their family life. But they definitely disagree about their perspectives on this common problem. There is open conflict over it. Mary especially is changing her mind about showing consideration in relation to the issue of personal sacrifice. Aside from their continued agreement on a common problem, there is a further continuity in their understanding of their problems then and now. Being cross is seen as a mental state in particular persons. They still think about their problems and deal with them in a personalized manner. They still invert subjective states of mind into abstract determinants of personal behavior that intrude into and disturb their social practice. And they still think of personalized problems from a third-person perspective – as somebody else's problem, indeed, as somebody else being the problem. None of them describe themselves as being cross. All four point to somebody else, holding themselves victims of others and blaming those others for causing their problems. But they all locate the same problem differently so that everyone is blamed by somebody else for being cross. However, when they all hold somebody else responsible for their problems, they all wait for somebody else to do something about it. They all want change, but the change they all want is for somebody else to change. And while they are all waiting for others to change, none of them pursues changes. They all hold others responsible for the recurrence this troublesome situation and for overcoming it.

When they adopt contrary stances on the problem and want different things changed, the problem turns into a conflict or is grounded in an unacknowledged conflict. Like problems, conflicts rest on the need to change troubling situations and states of mind to reach necessary and desired ends by means of existing or developing possibilities and abilities. There are contradictions to the realization of such possibilities in problems and conflicts, but there are also contradictions between persons and for persons in conflicts. In short, in conflicts the concerns and stances of the involved parties are opposed so that when one party advances his concerns and stances, it will be at the cost of other parties' concerns and stances (Dreier 1993b; Osterkamp 1976). Persons are divided and struggling in conflicts; consequently, the concerns and stances of individual persons also become marked by contradictions. At first none of the clients wanted this therapy to resolve their own problems, but later they begin to be in conflict over it. Sessions now become a special part in unfolding their everyday conflicts, and session talks may assist in articulating muffled conflicts.

Compared to their initial presentation of symptoms as anxieties and visual disturbances, the clients have changed their points of view on which problems they have and how they matter. Nevertheless, a personalized understanding of the problems still ties them down, and their discords over them make them get in each others' way. The conflicting stances on their problems limit the possibilities of the family as a whole and of its members. They all face a particular, individual set of problems, and these diverse, not clearly linked problems with different individual priorities and stakes stand in the way of a concerted orientation and action. It makes them get stuck. Their understandings and stances on their problems are problematic in the sense that their acting on them will not lead to the resolution of their problems. It would rather re-produce them or make them worse.

Now they face the problems for which they initially sought therapy plus the other problems that turned up during the period of therapy. Lisbeth asks them in turn in interview 2: "Now some time has passed since you started therapy. If you were to say what your major problems are right now, what would you then say? If we start with you, Angie, what do you think is your major problem now?" Angie: "What do you mean – problem?" Lisbeth: "Well, what do you think is most difficult for you now, and what do you most need help for? What do you think something should be done about?" Angie: "My claustrophobia, I think. I don't think there is anything else." Turning to Paul, he at first says: "Well, I must still come back to what we discussed yesterday which I think is a big problem." He is referring to the session that focused on the divided responsibilities for Angie's difficulties and touched on Angie's being cross. Angie objects in the background, and he goes on: "And then it is, of course, also a problem that Angie has claustrophobia. That's what started it all. But perhaps one thing leads to another. Her claustrophobia is, of course, most important, that's for sure. It's a disease, her claustrophobia, it certainly is. It must be what matters most, what she hopefully gets rid of." Having just ventured that perhaps one problem leads to another, Lisbeth asks him: "Do you think it's sort of two problems?" Paul: "Yes, I guess it really is, yes." Lisbeth: "As you see them, are they linked?" Paul: "That's hard to say." Mary: "I don't think so." Paul: "I really don't think so either." Asked about what she sees as the major problem, Mary states: "It's to learn to talk with Angie. I'm quite certain that those episodes could be solved if Angie could talk with us about it. I think it would solve what they call being cross." So, Mary now stresses yet another problem as the major one. She sees being cross as a part of that other problem in that it could be solved if only they could solve the main problem, to learn to talk. Donna responds: "I don't really know. I'm almost never home. . . . It's probably being cross, but I think my mum and dad turn it into a bigger problem than it is." Paul: "Perhaps it's such a major problem for us." Mary: "We probably only realized yesterday that it's such a major problem for us." Paul: "You've never thought about how selfish you are. You don't think a damn about how we are."

What the clients see as their problem and what they think should be done about it, is part of their conflicts, and these conflicts over their problems add qualities and links to their problems and conflicts. This is indicated in their growing disagreement over what they see as their major problem. Now, not very long after their therapy began, they no longer present only Angie's symptoms to their therapists. They present several problems, which they do not see as being clearly linked but rather as unrelated, and individual members emphasize different ones. There is a new, strong trend to see being cross as the major problem in the sense that it occupies them most, and it would mean the biggest relief for them if it could be resolved. But they place it in different others and fight over how to interpret it and how big a problem it is. They also consider changes in opposite directions to be called for if it is to be overcome. They have reached no settled overall stance about their various troubles. Mostly they believe there are several distinct problems, but Mary's take on learning to talk is a candidate for an overarching problem in the sense that it might be what it takes to solve all the other problems. In interview 1, Mary said: "You can't always find a solution, but just talking about it" – that is, just coming to an understanding with yourself and others about how to live with it, would matter a lot. Now in interview 2 she links talking about things and being cross: "But that's because you won't discuss." In so doing, Mary takes their conflict to the level of talk, the main vehicle by which sessions are carried out. Donna responds sarcastically: "You say all problems can be solved because Ole and Ingrid are here." Mary interrupts: "All problems must be solved. No, they don't have to, but you can talk about them." Donna responds defensively: "Everything can't be sheer delight. . . . (–) You don't always bother to discuss it, do you?" Mary retaliates: "I realize that, but so do I." Donna: "Yes, you do, but I won't." "No," Mary responds in an unyielding tone of voice.

The clients must now find a way to share a therapy when they are in conflict over which problems should be brought up in sessions and what should be done about them. This conflict has also expanded their notions about what sort of problems their therapy might help them with. In the beginning, session talks were to treat Angie's symptoms, and they brought up certain topics and not others depending on whether they saw a link to these symptoms. Then they got involved in talking about other things without necessarily clearly agreeing on why they do so or why they should bring them up. And the therapists challenge their notions about their problems so that they come to wonder how their therapists see these problems. This leads them to re-consider their own understandings of their problems. Such re-considerations and disagreements continue throughout their therapy.

"Now I Must Pull Myself Together"

Parallel to and in interplay with these changes in their understanding and dealing with their problems, Angie begins to do something about the troubles her symptoms cause her. In interview 4, she says about her first attempt: "I took the bus now once alone when I went there [to the session, OD]." First she had to think about it after sessions, and then "I told myself, 'Now I must pull myself together. There really isn't anything to be nervous about,'" She is primarily motivated to pull herself together by resolving the problems her symptoms cause for her activities with friends in other places. But how do efforts to resolve her problems change her symptoms? Angie's inattention to her symptoms often struck us, and we sometimes wondered how serious they were. While they heavily constrict her life, she pays more attention to their consequences in the problems they provoke. These problems are more practicable to her. She can do something about them while her symptoms are quite incomprehensible and inaccessible. In fact, how can she change her symptoms when she experiences them as something happening to her beyond her doing? As a result, she cannot easily see herself as an agent in overcoming them. At best, she sees herself as an agent arranging for the symptoms to be encapsulated, avoided, and prevented hoping that they might "go away" if they do not appear. Thus, she brings a flashlight on a school excursion to prevent her symptoms from occurring. Does Angie, then, change her symptoms? For a long time she keeps saying that her symptoms do not change, even though many things in her life do change including the frequency of occurrence of her symptoms, their intensity and meaning for her. But she does not notice those changes much. Especially, she does not understand how those changes might be related to her agency, probably because symptoms appear as something outside the reach of her agency – as an "it" inside her that Freud fetishized into the Id. Instead, she notices that the symptoms may still occur, and if they do, they cannot be all gone.

In interview 4, Angie is asked what she would like to talk about in the coming sessions, and she responds: "I'd like to talk about my claustrophobia to see if one could talk it away. Because when one is on school colonies, one can't be with the others when they are doing things at night." The whole class knows about her anxieties, and they may tease her. Again she wants to talk about her symptoms because of problems they cause in other places. But she does not think we talk much about her symptoms in sessions and suspects it is "probably because I had something else on my mind." This is surprising in view of that in sessions we do talk about, for instance, what she might do to prevent her symptoms from recurring and how she might deal successfully with situations in which she fears they might occur. Thus, Ingrid talks in detail with Angie about how she might take a bus on her own to go to sessions, how she might overcome various threatening situations on the way, and so forth, and Angie pulls herself together to give it a try, succeeds, and uses it as a springboard to begin moving around much more freely and widely for things she cares about.

But in doing so, we too focus on the consequences of her symptoms in causing troubles and disrupting her activities and relations, and in so doing we pay less attention to the reasons for her symptoms. So Angie may think that she does not come to understand her symptoms any better because this would mean that she would have to understand the reasons why they occur. The family's personalized understanding of her symptoms also discards their reasons. In the sessions with Ingrid, Angie is quite inarticulate about the links between her symptoms, on the one hand, and her concerns and the circumstances, events, and coparticipants surrounding their occurrence, on the other hand. She is thus unable to clarify and concretize their reasons. Still, this does not prevent her from pulling herself together to change how those symptoms may get in her way when she has reasons to want them out of the way. In sessions, we go over her symptoms one by one in an attempt to clarify in which situations they occur, what she might do to prevent them, and what she might do about them if they occur, including changing how they play out. We make explicit what the symptoms have to do with the topics we go into and the appointments we make, such as talking to her school teachers to find out more about her visual symptoms and what might be done about them. In all this, we are also clarifying their possible reasons, so to say in a backward move, following the logic that when symptoms appear in this kind of situation in connection with those activities, there might be this kind of reasons for them. In this way, we launch the idea that symptoms have reasons, although these reasons now seem incomprehensible. When symptoms are understood as internal forces that cause troubles in their lives, these forces are perceived to be external to their ongoing practice while the understanding of reasons behind our questions in sessions assumes that reasons spring from their participation in social practice. Reasons emerge from the significance of their possibilities for pursuing their concerns in social practice (Holzkamp 1983; 1987; 1993). When this becomes complicated and problematic, their understanding of their reasons may become so too. It is then not only partial, as every other understanding is, but skewed, and they do not quite recognize how their reasons are embedded in their problematic participation in a problematic social practice (Osterkamp 1976). In sessions, we often prompt the clients for their reasons for doing so and so in this or that situation, and they hear reasons for occurrences in their lives they had not understood earlier – not the least from other family members. In talking about problem situations, we generally go into the links between the reasons and consequences of their actions in a situated way. After all, it is when the consequences of my actions contradict my reasons that they are problematic to me. When therapists challenge clients' understandings of their problems, it also makes the clients reconsider their reasons. So in various ways therapy sessions redirect clients' attention toward re-considering their reasons and the links between these reasons and the consequences. This is a key feature in the accomplishment of therapy. It challenges clients to ask themselves and each other which reasons they may have for these problematic states and behaviors. Still, despite turning Angie's attention toward the consequences and reasons for what she does and feels, she has not yet reached an articulate understanding of the reasons for those phenomena that seem most incomprehensible to her, namely her symptoms. The aura of not quite understanding them remains in spite of her increased command over symptom-related situations.

Angie seems not to attempt to overcome her symptoms directly because it is not clear to her how these symptoms are part of the social practice in which she would try it. But her statements about this are not clear. The most likely interpretation is that she merely attempts to gain such control over her symptoms that she can prevent their disturbing recurrence so that they may gradually recede into the background and, thus, hopefully "go away." For some time at least, gaining control over her symptoms seems not necessarily to imply changing her practice. Likewise, it is not clear whether Angie sees pulling herself together as a means to overcoming her symptoms or merely as a means to preventing them and getting them under control.

What, then, does it mean to "pull herself together"? It means ceasing to do nothing about it and just following suit. It also means not feeling certain that she will succeed and doing something in spite of it. And it means not really knowing how what she may accomplish will feel and whether it will be better for her, that is, doing something about it in spite of having no clear appreciation of the difference it will make. Besides, her problem situations hold difficulties, contradictions, and risks. So, she is motivated not simply by seeing possibilities for improvements in front of her (Osterkamp 1975; 1976) but by doing something in spite of having mixed feelings about it. It feels scary to do it, and she has other mixed feelings about it too. In pulling herself together, she relies only on her own force. That is, she tries to do something about it in spite of the lack of support from others in a situation marked by divisions and oppositions between them when it comes to doing something about it. Furthermore, pulling herself together reflects a situation in which she feels divided, torn, in seven minds about it and in which she is trying to make up her mind, that is, adopt a particular stance. It involves trying to resolve and combine various considerations and concerns. She may even try to lift herself out of such subjective complications by pulling herself together. Moreover, pulling herself together has the quality of not fully understanding the situation she is trying to command – that is, her concrete possibilities and whether she has the abilities it takes – but attempting to change it by relying on her own force instead. In short, it rests on an abstract and stripped down notion of individual agency. This is, indeed, what she may rely on as long as she is not more certain that she has understood the situation, has a more comprehensive command of it, and has relationships of other qualities to support her. Her understanding of the force in her that she relies on is like a personalized understanding of mental states and personal properties and of symptoms with the main exception that this force is at her command. These understandings also share a moralizing perspective and are rooted in the idea of character as morality plus inner strength. In that sense, pulling herself together appeals to the force of individual character when she cannot fully know what it takes and whether it will improve things. Attached to pulling herself together is a moral obligation to give it a try. Thus, Angie may feel that she should because she is attending therapy in order to get over her symptoms, because her therapists are in a situation to supervise what she does about it, and because she wants their recognition and support. Her parents also want her to "get going to make an effort herself," as Paul puts it. In fact, Angie takes care to tell her therapists and parents that she will now pull herself together. She wants us to recognize it and may feel under pressure to do it so as not to lose our recognition. Her earlier reason for just following suit, namely that, "I can't help it," has a similar dual root in morality and inner strength. Only here the moral obligation is on others because she lacks the strength to do it. But when others – and she too perhaps – begin to think that she might be able to do it, the morality turns around, and she begins to think that she should do something about it and that she is no longer entitled to expect others to take care of it for her. Actually Paul and Mary are gradually coming to believe that Angie may be able to do something about it. So, Angie is in a situation where she is both pulled – that is, motivated by the prospects of what she may become able to do – and pushed – that is, put under pressure to prove herself worthy of her parents' and therapists' recognition – to pull herself together and give it a try. In other words, when Angie pulls herself together, her situation has already changed in some ways. Her parents have begun to stop her pestering, that is, to prevent her from displacing responsibilities for achieving her wishes onto them. Mary has begun to reconsider showing consideration and taking over for Angie whenever something seems difficult for her. In fact, on the day when Angie took the bus alone for the first time, Mary was unable to accompany her for the first time. Or, to be more precise, her mother did not rearrange whatever else she had in mind to do in order to accompany Angie. So, the arrangements around Angie and her troubles are beginning to change. Raising and addressing the problem of Angie's dependence on her parents when she wants to go places is linked to changes in her scope of possibilities and in the contradictions for their realization.

Angie was very proud when she returned home after succeeding in pulling herself together. The usually not very talkative Angie told her parents about it in all detail. Still, going to this session alone is just an incident and not a guarantee that she will continue. The main reason why she does continue is that the incident coincides with the emergence of possibilities to ride with a girlfriend in the countryside more than one and a half hours away from home. In addition, there is no easy way back for Angie; she cannot stop doing these things and must pull herself together to do still other things. Her parents are taking it as an indication that she is or can become able to do things that were difficult for her. She is not as entitled to their doing it for her any more, and she might lose their recognition if she does not continue. Their belief in how best to take care of Angie is still easily shaken, but they are raising their expectations and demands at her.

So, Angie pulls herself together in part because her parents are beginning to change their practice of care and upbringing in relation to her. Some of these changes are abrupt, as in their changing reactions to her being cross, while others are complex, gradual, and nonlinear processes full of reconsiderations, doubts, and regrets on the way. Some of the parents' reasons for these changes are their changing understandings of Angie's problems and appreciations of her abilities. Already in interview 2 Mary and Paul emphasize appreciatively that Angie has started to make an effort of her own so that "There is more of a go in her." That Mary did not rearrange whatever she had in mind to do when Angie went to her session with Ingrid alone is a change. Earlier this would have been a mandatory part of Mary's consideration for Angie – especially when Angie is going to something as important as a therapy session to help her get over these difficulties. One reason for this change may be that Mary sees it as her support to the therapists' efforts to help her daughter. Another reason is her growing consideration of how important it is that Angie becomes able to do it or, perhaps, already is able to do it. A third reason is that Mary gradually pays more attention to her own situation. This opens a scope for Angie, puts pressure on her, and, thus, contributes to Angie's attempts to pull herself together. When Angie gives it a try, Mary is testing all this and feels confirmed that Angie can do more than Mary believed. Afterward, Mary says that she started to believe that she must show less consideration for Angie and think less of it now that Angie has begun to do more on her own. In beginning to do these things on her own, Angie actually needs a different practice of care and upbringing from her parents. She faces other problems, and this calls on Mary to reconsider Angie's symptoms and how Mary may react to her and support her.

It is worth noticing that because of Angie's changing practice and her parents' changing appreciation, certain situations cease to be a problem. It is not that these problems were overcome, but they, precisely, cease to be a problem for them when they change their understanding of what Angie is able to do. Certain things are then simply not a problem any more. Problems are raised and appraised in relation to the involved persons' possibilities and abilities, and they get past some of their problems because their possibilities and abilities change. Something else may then stand out as that which was the real problem all along, that is, they change their understanding of possibilities and contradictions and, hence, also of their problem. Perhaps other problems, which are not replacing the former problem or directly linked to it in any (significant) way, turn up or are raised instead. One such problem is the contradiction for the parents between drawing boundaries and making demands, on the one hand, and creating larger scopes of possibilities and granting more responsibility for their developing daughters, on the other hand. Though this problem does not directly replace their former problem, it takes its place as a key problem for them in their care for Angie and Donna and in their practice of upbringing. The parents now pay more attention to this problem and begin to raise and pursue it. They need to find a way in which making demands is not the same as narrowing scopes but instead allows for larger scopes and enables their realization. This entails new contradictions for the realization of possibilities, that is, new problems. It also calls on the parents to expand the horizon within which they orient their practice of upbringing and to pay more attention to ways in which they may pursue concerns of upbringing across times and places. Yet, this change in the parents' practice is complicated and must be pursued quite intensely over a long period of time. Thus, at this time – that is, in session 6 – Paul feels convinced that he has arrived at a new understanding, but he also has doubts about it. His feelings are a mixture of being self-assured and uncertain. He is torn between being convinced and wavering: "There is no doubt I try to be more consistent. That's maybe what one should have done from the beginning." There is no doubt about it, and then again, it is only something he should maybe have done.

Problems in Other Places

At first Angie addressed problems in other places, while her parents focused on problems in their family and only now begin to expand their pursuit of problems into other places. But in these other places their problems have other meanings and are understood in other ways because they take part in other relations with varying others and have other concerns and stakes. Indeed, they do not turn the same things into problems in different places, and if they do, these things do not mean the same, and they cannot do the same thing about them. Nor do their coparticipants in different places turn the same things into problems and understand them in the same way. Thus, Angie thinks about her symptoms in sessions but not much at home or in other places unless they threaten to turn up. When Lisbeth asks her to tell about her problems, Angie often does not mention her symptoms. And when Angie is with friends, the primary meaning of her symptoms is that they may get in the way of things she wants to take part in or of her possibilities to participate on equal terms. They are something to be ashamed of and must be hidden from the others so that she does not stand out as a peculiar person and is not ridiculed or excluded. At home, on the other hand, the primary meaning of her symptoms is that the others pity her, show consideration for her, do things for her, and arrange and constrict her scopes.

Are their problems in other places then simply other problems? Of course, Angie has other problems in other places. Among friends, she is most concerned with problems about her relationships. In school, she feels cornered by cliques in her class, is afraid to be bullied for not daring to use the restrooms, has math problems, and so forth. Even if anxieties play a role in these diverse problems, the meaning of these anxieties varies, as does the meaning of these problems and the possibilities of doing something about them. Yet, if the meaning of the problems and what it takes to do something about them differ, in what sense can it then be the same problem? To categorize diverse problems in the same, abstract symptom category of, say, anxiety may be partly misleading in understanding and dealing with them in concrete terms. Angie actually deals with her symptoms as parts of the various problems they provoke in different places. She notices them, needs to understand them, and wants to change them in those times and places. Problems have practical, social, and contextual grounds. So do symptoms, even when they seem incomprehensible.

So, a person comes across different problems as well as the same problem in different places. By the same problem, I mean instances of problems grounded in very similar possibilities, abilities, and contradictions to their realization. But regardless whether problems are the same or different, a person runs into them in her trajectory across places. They are first of all problems for her in her trajectory across places and she must address them in her life across places. This often involves including them in her pursuits across places. She must find out how to deal with her problems in different places and how to pursue their resolution across different places. In doing so, she must link her different experiences and pursuits of changes to her problems in diverse contexts (Dreier 2000, 248). The understanding of problems I argue for here does not abstract problems from their meaning, location, and relations in a person's ongoing practice in and across places. To insist that something is the same problem, though its meaning and what can and should be done about it differ, would be a strange way to understand a problem. It would turn the problem into a mere label. Even when the clients in this case use an abstract label such as claustrophobia for their problems, this label stands for different problems with different meanings for different family members in different contexts. In sessions, this label allows them to hand over responsibility to their strange experts for doing something about it, to feel relieved of the burden of being left to themselves with it, and, hence, to begin dealing with each other in other ways. But if they use the same label, say, among friends, it would not help in the same way. They would risk being stigmatized and excluded.

That persons pursue problems across places, affords displacement. Thus, displacement is involved when Angie is bad tempered at home. She is bothered by circumstances and events in other places, among friends and in school, but is unable to resolve what bothers her in these other places. She is also afraid to show her dissatisfaction openly in these places because it might be turned against her. Therefore, she does not do what is necessary to overcome those problems in these places. Instead, Angie takes her dissatisfaction out on her mother when she returns home. She reacts on her problems in various places by behaving problematically in other ways at home, using her mother and father as displaced targets of her dissatisfaction. Still, Angie changes her understanding of how she may deal with her problems in different ways in different places and pursue a resolution to some of them precisely by doing so. At first, she sees the meaning of sessions for dealing with her symptoms as talking her anxieties away, as if talking about them calms them down or exorcises them in some mysterious way. Gradually she comes to see sessions as a chance to talk about how she may handle her symptoms in other places. She may then begin to see how talking about symptoms in sessions can be used in considering how to get over some of her problems with friends. So, as seen from the locations of sessions and at home, Angie does most about her problems elsewhere. This creates particular difficulties of understanding and affecting her problems across places for her therapists in sessions and her parents at home. These adults' possibilities to understand and affect Angie's problems depend on whether she is ready to pursue her problems in and across those places or how she may become willing to do so. In interview 3, Paul says about Angie's life in school that "it's a problem to her now and a problem to us because we don't really think she functions well over there." While Paul's problem was not to know how she is doing in school, now it is how he may gain influence on it. There are two main avenues for this: (1) through Angie's pursuits across places and (2) by beginning himself to pursue these problems across places. To this end, meetings are arranged among the therapists, the family, and Angie's teachers at a time when other meetings take place between the parents of all children in Angie's class. In both fora, Angie's parents must find out how to gain influence on what goes on in school, and this raises challenges and problems for them. Mary states that she never before said a word at a parent-teacher meeting but "Now I'm over that; you'd better believe I say what's on my mind." This newly won self-assurance is not unlike Paul's because actually it is not easy. At this time, many parents are criticizing Angie's teachers in the larger meetings, while Mary and Paul are trying in the smaller meetings to build an alliance with these teachers to support Angie in school.

We see that they change the range of their pursuits of problems across contexts and the ways in which they pursue them. Their problems differ across contexts, but these differences are changing too and require that the family members change their pursuits across contexts. Divisions between contexts and parties must be overcome in order to enable pursuits of problems across contexts. But participants in different contexts may deal with overlapping problems concerning overlapping participants by placing these problems in a particular context, often not the one they are responsible for, so that persons representing the other context are held responsible for the problem and for doing something about it. Who is to be involved in doing something about it must then be negotiated and redefined. A problem may, thus, be displaced, or the participants from various contexts who are coresponsible for doing something about it may be linked in other ways so that participants may re-define their part of a joint responsibility. There may be struggles over this between participants representing different contexts and pursuing the stakes of one context over another. Thus, at first Angie's teachers claim that Angie is no problem to them, indicating that something should be done about it in the family, while Mary and Paul insist that there are also problems in school. Then the teachers argue for a division between school problems, such as Angie's math problems, and emotional problems, which should be dealt with by the family assisted by its therapists (Højholt 1993). This division reproduces an abstraction of Angie's anxieties from her life in school into mental states in Angie. Assisted by the therapists, a collaboration bridging the divisions between these contexts had to be established. As this collaboration unfolds, it changes the way

Angie's problems are dealt with in and across these contexts and parties. To be able to address such complex and varying problems, obviously, calls for other understandings and abilities, which Angie and her parents are challenged to develop.

Comparing family members' relations to problems at the start of therapy with their present relation to them, we see that while at first problems were mostly located inside somebody and imposing themselves on them, problems are now also increasingly something they raise and pursue. Such problems are not merely in their minds or their circumstances. They are in their practice, raised and addressed in practical terms by persons in their participation in and across places. Already the problem of being cross was raised because of changing possibilities and contradictions to their realization, and pursuing it changed their stances and modes of participation. Later, in session 12, Mary raises another wide-ranging problem of not wanting to be left behind but to do things outside home, though she does not know what, since she has been so out of it, it costs money, and Paul runs their economy. Linked to this problem, the couple raises a further wide-ranging problem of changing their joint life. Raising such problems implies changing their relation to their possibilities and abilities and their ways to pursue change.

Taking Care of Others and Your Own Life

Raising such problems is part of changing the ways in which they take care of their own and each others' lives. The changes in their ways of caring are related to changes in their agreements and conflicts with each other about their problems and how to pursue them. Their pursuits of problems change their relations with each other and with people in other contexts. Thus, their joint pursuits of problems into other contexts change the constellation and dynamics of conflicts between them in their family. While conflicts between them at home emerge from muffled and blurred problems, they are gradually polarized into new shapes of conflicts and eventually linked to perspectives of development beyond their present situation and to the mediation of their problems at home through their complex practice across contexts. Moreover, these problems and conflicts are seen more as shared problems and not merely as yours or mine. The division between Angie and her parents – implied in her parents' understanding of their relation to her problems as showing consideration and putting pressure on her – changes into a relation marked by negotiating, supporting, and distributing the pursuits between all three, with Angie playing an increasingly important part. The way they change problems is changing from relying only on individual efforts to relying on joint and distributed efforts. Of course, they are still anxious, worried, and confused over their problems and conflicts, but it is over other problems and conflicts. And they increasingly address and pursue their problems as problems in and for their participation in social practice, with each other as well as with others, at home as well as in other places.

7.3. Problems Subside, Vary, and Flare Up

In the second part of the therapy, Angie attends only two sessions and is interviewed a week after the latter. In session 13, a few weeks after her previous session, we work in detail with how she may handle her anxieties now that it gets dark before she can finish distributing newspapers. Angie is much more active and articulate in this talk, pursuing her concerns more vigorously by means of the session. This allows us to work differently with her. Everybody takes part in helping her, including Donna. Angie and Donna exchange experiences and possibilities for handling anxieties in the dark, such as what to do if they run into the disturbed, homeless people in the industrial area or around their block of whom one chased people with a knife and another is a flasher. Despite such disquieting circumstances and events, Angie's anxiety is less of a problem now that she does more herself. Mary still "shows special consideration for" Angie's symptoms, and it is no burden for her.

Two months later we learn in session 18 that Angie dropped the job of distributing newspapers. The problem grew harder in the dark season. But Angie still sleeps with no lights on and goes out with friends at night. Besides, distributing newspapers is not Angie's priority. It is a promise she made her parents to earn part of the costs for riding. Though Angie is just as isolated now, she gets cross less often, and it passes differently between them. Paul: "We've come so far that we don't mind so much any more." Mary: "It passes sooner. She has started to think more about it." It has turned into a less heavy problem, which does not need to be addressed in the same way. They can laugh about it because they reached a better understanding among themselves, which improved their basis for dealing with disruptions and problems. Rounding off this general evaluation of their present situation, Ingrid asks: "Does this mean that you really don't think there are any problems or difficulties left concerning Angie?" Paul: "I guess it's quite ordinary difficulties which one finds everywhere, at least.... The only thing left is the one we started with, her anxiety. She's still got it, for closed rooms, but maybe it goes away after some time." Mary: "And her visual symptoms." The symptoms do not bother them, but Angie did not notice that they changed. They all say that Angie occasionally works with her anxieties when there is something important she wants to do and that she has confidence in herself to take a further step so that she may gradually overcome them. A week later in her individual interview 5, Angie says it is strange that "now they talk with Donna." But she has no idea what we were to talk with her about because "I have no problems now." Lisbeth: "Then something must have happened because when we started, you had some problems." Angie: "Well, yes, I've only got my problems with darkness and things like that." Looking back at her problems, these were the major ones. Lisbeth: "What happened, what have you become better at doing?" Angie: "I don't know. What do you mean? ... Not very much happened." Asked what she expected to happen by going to sessions she answers: "If they could talk it away. Some say so." Lisbeth: "What else happened in the period?" Angie: "Well, now I'm getting a horse. And I got a job. And then nothing else happened." Lisbeth reminds Angie that she talked her job arrangement over with the owner of the plant which is different from her earlier unwillingness to take initiatives and talk to strangers. Angie: "I guess I've become stronger to ask. I'm not so nervous any more."

The parents say in interview 7 on the same day that they have less to do for Angie because she is more independent and there is more of a go in her. Mary now believes that when Angie is cross, it "also has to do with that she is bored. Then it hits down on us. She gets very uptight." They believe Angie is getting over this problem thanks to her increased independence and self-confidence. She has grown; they can talk more with her; she thinks things over a bit more. Lisbeth: "What do you believe Angie's problems are related to?" Paul: "I believe she has been very dependent, too weak. And by gaining more self-confidence these problems diminish somewhat." Mary: "She works with her difficulties on her own." Due to their changed understandings and stances, Paul and Mary know better how to get around an old problem if it turns up so that it does not become so serious that they get mired down in it. But family members' changing concerns and stances make other possibilities and abilities more important with other contradictions to their realization, that is, other problems. While some problems are waning, others recur, and new problems call for more attention and create more trouble.

"We Have to Find Each Other Again"

In the course of working on a case, therapists run into surprises. We are surprised to discover that while we focus on problems around Angie and her parents, very serious troubles go on elsewhere, and we may not come to know about them precisely because we are busy doing what we can to help with the problems for which the family was referred. In order to do so, we must be selective. We cannot go into everything, certainly not at the same time. But we happen to invite Donna to a session because, in her straightforward way, she is helpful and a good source for our understanding. This session is no exception. In it, Donna says in interview 6, "I happened to say a little too much since it should have been about Angie." Ole got interested and suggested talks with him. Had he not done so, she believes nothing would have come of it. We had been told that Donna attended individual therapy two years ago, but when we asked them what they needed therapy for and about their current situation they never mentioned problems for or around Donna. Now we realize that there were serious troubles concerning Donna all along but, despite the risks entailed, they were not brought into therapy. We had only heard Mary say in passing that she wished Donna's therapy had lasted longer, but it stopped because her therapist was fired when that division of the hospital was reduced in one of the Danish government's cuts of welfare services. We do not know whether the troubles between them are more intense for the time being, but

Donna spends much time at home now and then she thinks more about these troubles. So she might not have said that she wants sessions if she had not been invited at a time when she happens to be at home a great deal.

I can think of three main reasons why the family did not tell us about these troubles and propose sessions to deal with them. First, two years ago Donna was referred for individual therapy due to dramatic symptoms, but now she has no symptoms. As they see it, they simply do not get along, and it is less legitimate and more embarrassing to ask for therapy for this reason. So the nature of the problem may keep it out of therapy, although it is a very heavy burden on their lives. Second, the problems with Donna are more controversial. They are caught in open conflict over them. Paul is caught in the conflict of being Donna's main target and fearing that bringing these problems into therapy might be hazardous for him. To propose it, they must find out how to share a therapy over which and in which they will be in open conflict, but Paul and Donna are unable to negotiate this themselves. Third, Donna has doubts whether it will work and is in conflict over it. In her first session with Ole, she says that she and Paul do not get along. They are snarling at each other, she feels disgusted by him, and they are both stubborn. It would be difficult to start talking with each other again because they are not used to it. The confidentiality and intimacy between them is low. Nonetheless, Donna wants a new life for them, a fresh start to their relationship, although she is uncertain what this might be now that they are used to not being on good terms. They would "have to find each other again."

Donna's troubles lead to different problems at home, in school, and with friends in other places. But her problems in different places overlap in a way adding to her difficulties. Wherever she is, interferences between her participation in different places define her problems. In addition, these problems have different meanings for her various coparticipants in different places. They are in conflict over what the problem is and what should be done about it. How may participants, then, address such conflicting problems from their diverse locations and positions? I shall focus on changes in the conflicting problems for Donna and her parents in turn and then look into their resolution of these problems.

Donna insists that what happened belongs in the past because she is a different person now. She acted in one way then which was wrong, but now she acts in another way which is OK. In her first individual session she says: "When I was involved in it, I couldn't see that it was wrong. But now that I've gotten out of it, I can see that it was terribly wrong." Still, when her father mentions it now, she gets no bad conscience because she would not behave like this today. Paul's distrust and worry get between them. She changed by making up her mind to "become a different person" and feels let down by her parents' unwillingness to recognize this change. Deep distrust is a strong response to be subjected to. For Donna, it means they do not recognize her as the person she now is and what she now stands for. She feels erased as the person she takes herself to be. Mutual recognition of each other as different persons is constitutive of relationships. Donna insists that she be recognized as a person able to manage being alone at home on weekends with friends visiting.

But Paul is on guard in the first session between Donna and her parents about these troubles. He feels it is difficult suddenly to include Donna more again in their lives at home, while Donna feels it is hard to start over again because her parents are disappointed over her. Paul does not feel disappointed all the time, but Mary expresses strong condemnation: "She has done everything to ruin our trust." Paul picks this up, and both parents continue along this line. We ask whether they can still believe in Donna, and they say they do not know. Paul has "come so far out that I say to myself it doesn't make any difference any more because no matter what we say and do, it's lost on her because she does what she wants." Hearing how deeply disappointed her parents are, Donna flees the session feeling she has done something terribly wrong. Afterward, she takes their side against herself and feels she cannot make up for everything again. In session 16, she tells Ole that she feels she has let her parents down and let herself down as the person she wants to be. She feels small and stupid. We go into how this problem for Donna at home is tied to her problems with friends in other places. There she tries to be an accommodating "cheerful girl" who goes along with whatever comes up and attends to being on good terms with them, having fun, and not losing them. Occasionally, Donna feels she has put up with too much from her friends and gets mad at them, which surprises some and scares others. But mostly she does not state her mind much in relation to them. It is difficult for Donna to combine being on good terms with friends and having a say over things. She sees this difficulty as an outcome of being bullied in her former school until two years ago and believes it will take years to get over it so that she will dare to state her mind for fear of losing her friends. This conflict in relation to her friends makes it difficult to carry responsibilities toward her parents. She is caught in the problem of two intersecting conflicts of a similar kind in different places.

Donna shifts between being overwhelmed by the complexities of these problems, having them on her mind virtually all the time and pushing them aside to leave room for something else. She is preoccupied by them but cannot find a solution. So she must set them aside to get some relief, have some fun, look for a fresh start, and try to become a different person. But the problems then somehow return, and she must address them again. Returning from the first session with her parents, she stays home from school the next day brooding over her troubles in her room all day. "I'm thinking about it all the time, thinking very hard." But her preoccupation by these troubles varies periodically. In session 17, she says that she did not think much about them: "I've been so busy. I've been working and with my friends."

She tries to be really nice to get over the problems with her parents. In session 17, she tells Ole that things are going great at home because "I go more along with what they say . . . because it makes my mum and dad happy" and "then he [Paul, OD] listens more to what I say." She is proving to herself that she can do something to make them happy. As Donna sees it, this is linked to their problems in that when you do things that please each other, you all feel better, the problems move into the background, and you start to lead a different life. A measure of making up for what she has done and of showing regret without saying so directly may be involved, but Donna does not mention it. To her, being nice is a way to get around the problems. It is also a way of signaling to Paul and Mary that she wants improvements and is ready to take part in bringing them about without saying so directly and sitting down to talk about it; she will not do this, and they cannot. She hopes that when they are on better terms with each other, they will be better able to resolve their problems. It is harder to be nice to each other and listen to each other when you have been deeply divided by conflicts. Persons then do not feel very close and do not have much shared understanding to fall back on. Still, sometimes Donna does not quite know what she can do to make them believe in her again, and then she feels she may as well do whatever she feels like. It is no use anyhow. She then behaves accordingly. In other words, it gradually becomes too much to accommodate her parents and be nice to them all the time.

Parallel to these pursuits at home, Donna begins to state her mind more toward her friends. In session 17, she says that it is now going great with her friends too. She told them what she thought about their responsibilities for what happened in her home, kept only a few, and their relationship improved. Earlier she sometimes felt let down in her hopes for what might come of being nice to her friends because they, perhaps for that very reason, kept treating her badly instead of treating her better in return. Now she has set this straight and hopes to gain more respect from her friends. They know better what she stands for, and she will have more of a say on what they do together. Beginning to behave differently toward her friends is a necessary part in getting beyond the problem with her parents since these two problems are in conflict. When she was nice to her friends, it created problems at home, and if she wants to be nice to her parents, she must behave differently toward her friends. Though Donna uses the same polar terms in both respects, being nice and going against her friends and her parents do not mean the same and take the same to do. Being nice and a bitch are involved in participating in different activities in different places with different others, and changing her ways of being with them raises different problems for her. This complex of problems sometimes gets on her nerves: "Sometimes I feel it's damned irritating that I take things so hard. . . . Other people don't let that worry them, right."

The efforts to find each other again and get a fresh start seem to Donna to bear fruit. In session 19, she says: "My mom and dad and I are doing really well together for the time being." The relation with her dad "is very good. But I don't know what made it change. I haven't done anything for it or not thought about it. It just improved." Paul is nicer and more interested in talking with her. There was a turbulent episode, though, between all four of them, but Donna attributes it to trouble between Paul and Mary. Then there were some episodes between Paul, Mary, and Angie, but none with Donna, except "Once a couple of weeks ago we had a minor, not quarrel but discussion because I wanted to move out. After that it's as if he has become nicer, as if he does not want to lose me." Donna's statements draw heavily on her interpretation of others, which reflects the opacity of their relationships. She continues by saying that she did not change, but she has new friends and spends much time with them. This made her happier, and her parents too on her behalf. Ole asks if she believes their earlier problems are resolved now that they have been doing better for the last two weeks. Donna: "I don't think so, but I can't say because we didn't talk about it." Ole: "Can they be solved?" Donna: "I don't know. Right now I don't think we need to . . . It may turn up again later." In part, though with doubts, she hopes that problems may be overcome by letting them fade away and leaving room for something else. "Maybe we all think now we must be nice, now this must go well." At least, "When we have gotten into such a good cycle, I believe it will last a long time. I really think so. . . . It's crazy to bring it up now when we are doing so well. Then we should leave it alone or it will ruin everything." Judged by what usually happens when they talk about things, it might disturb rather than stabilize them. So it might be wiser to place your bets on pulling yourself together, continuing the good cycle, and hoping for the fresh start it may trigger. Besides, so much else is happening again in other areas of Donna's life, which she prefers attending to, and their quarrels are less embittered. "You know, we quarrel, and then we just forget it." Her view on their quarrels may be affected by trying to get them out of the way and being preoccupied by other things. But perhaps they do feel on better terms with each other and may find each other again without talking about it? At least, they feel closer and less divided though they do not know precisely where the others stand and what they want. In any case, coming to a different understanding between them is necessarily involved in overcoming conflicting problems.

"She Has Done Everything to Ruin Our Trust"

When the problems around Donna are introduced to us, Mary and Paul are full of distrust toward her. According to Mary, the problems do not belong in the past. It happened again very recently. Donna and/or her friends still steal and destroy their things when they are on their own in the flat, and Donna still tries to hide it and lies about it when Mary and Paul return. They hold Donna responsible, but believe she is too weak to handle her friends. So Mary and Paul see Donna's problems as cross-contextual, like Angie's. They face the challenge of understanding Donna's relationships in other places and finding a way to exert indirect influence through her. Even their home is disturbed when they are not there, and it takes a cross-contextual intervention to overcome it. Yet, it will not do to show consideration for Donna, stop her, go to school meetings, and so forth, as they did with Angie. If Mary and Paul are to accomplish anything, Donna has to change. But she will not listen to them, and they cannot talk with her about it. So they hope that she will listen to their therapists and that the therapists can make her change, though they fear the therapists listen to her instead. Besides, they have to change a problem with Donna in a place, their home, which in general is secondary to her. She is primarily concerned with things that go on, or she wishes would go on, elsewhere. While Angie pursued changes in other places that matter more to her, Mary and Paul must hope that Donna will pursue changes with them at home. Thus, that Donna decides to be nicer to them, agree to more, and listen more to them is significant. All the same, the parents feel deeply dependent on Donna's relations with her friends. In interview 9, Mary complains that Donna is too dependent on her friends and will not do anything that goes against her friends. It is all the more difficult for them to gain influence on these relations since they almost never see her friends, especially not after what happened in their home. Very few show up when the parents are home. The parents feel powerless because Donna will not listen to them, they cannot reach her friends, and they do not trust her readiness to change because they believe she only listens to her friends. These feelings of distrust and powerlessness are confirmed when Donna again arranges to have a friend stay with her in a weekend without talking to them about it first. They fear that they cannot depend on her when she ignores them and that she will ignore their concerns when the time comes. They are of two minds about how to understand that Donna has become nicer to them at home. On the one hand, they are not certain that she really changed. On the other hand, they recognize that she goes along with more, they spend nice times together at home, she goes on visits with them for the first time in years, and so forth. But if they do not readily agree with her on something, she may still cut them off and do what she wants. Donna still gets very aggressive over trifles, though they have nice times together in between, for instance recently during Christmas Holidays.

In interview 7, Lisbeth asks Mary and Paul which reasons they see for the problems around Donna. Having dealt with the problems around Angie, they now include their own participation in the problem, not just by taking the blame for their children's troubles but by including a contradiction in their own practice and a problem for themselves too. Mary: "I think we have taken ourselves too little into consideration, stated our minds and stood by our own stances too little, also in relation to the children because we have always gone by the children's needs and wishes, never by our own and we've begun to consider this much more." Paul: "We have probably, with too good intentions, been too permissive and, I won't say fussed too much over them, but we've always believed that we've done as well for them as at all possible. And this turns out to have been too much." They see Donna's problem as that "she is very quick-tempered," and they see their two daughters' problems as different and unrelated though they just pointed to a common reason in their own practice. Lisbeth comments that the therapy started with Angie, and then suddenly . . . " Paul: "It branches off." Lisbeth: "Is there any link, for instance, that you have changed your way of reacting to the children and then this turns up?" Paul: "No, it has nothing to do with that." They link Donna's changing state to having friends or being isolated and lonely. This is in line with their growing understanding of a reason for Angie's problems and with their view that Donna is very dependent on friends.

Making Joint Arrangements for Different Lives

In session 20 with Mary and Paul, they say that the quarrel where Donna threatened to move out arose when she told them she had arranged with a girlfriend to stay in their flat during Easter Holidays without asking them first. In doing so, Donna tries to avoid the trouble with them; nevertheless, she does things her way and on her own. Mary believes the quarrel arose because Paul stressed that he wanted no trouble and everything to be OK. He provoked Donna's reaction by "telling her it shouldn't be like before. And then I must admit it doesn't bother me much when she goes to her room. I take it ever more calmly because I'm convinced I'm right." Paul interposes that it does not affect him either. So they are not as easily off-tracked and have become more indifferent. They understand the problem differently, do not care in the same way, and do not let themselves be pulled down by it. Paul has become "more calloused," and Mary gets "less crushed." Mary found out that it's an empty threat when Donna says she is going to leave, and that "it's to make me stop talking about it or give in. . . . It also infuriates me because it solves nothing. We could sit down and talk things over instead." It gets in the way of her new stance of stating her mind and standing by it.

Nonetheless, the parents are afraid to let Donna live in a youth facility. They feel tempted by it sometimes but want to manage a few more years. When Donna breaks agreements, they feel powerless. Paul: "What the hell shall we do?" This is why he says "OK" when she tells them she wants to move out. What might make him agree to it is feeling unable to manage. "I don't think I can take it any more," he adds. But Paul and Mary do not agree where their limit lies. Then Paul says: "We've got to give her a couple of more chances, leave her alone some weekends. That's the only way if we don't want to stay home and give up our weekends." Again consideration for their own needs is an explicit part of relating to their children and of their stance on the problem. But when they make demands as part of an agreement, Donna does not comply, but she keeps it to herself and lies about it when they find out. It is difficult to make demands on her, which would grant her larger scopes and responsibilities if she followed through. The contradiction in this problem still brings forth changes in their practice of upbringing. As it is now, the parents still want Donna to ask permission for things, and Donna does not want to do so for several reasons: She may not get permission, and they may reproach her for this and that instead; she sees herself as a grown-up who is able and entitled to make her own arrangements; and her friends may look down on her for depending too much on her parents' permission.

On this background, we are surprised to learn in passing that Donna had been alone during a weekend a couple of weeks earlier – which, by the way, had gone alright. In session 19, Ole asks her: "Do you think there are any problems for the time being?" Donna: "No, not really. I've also been alone during a weekend." Her parents just said that they were going to the countryside and asked if she would like to have friends over, and she responded that she did not know. They did not talk much about it probably because they cannot and they believe everybody knows and appreciates what is at stake. Donna was surprised and wanted to prove that she can handle it, but she did not tell them. She did not dare ask any questions or offer much comment for fear that they might get into a quarrel and the whole thing would be called off. Donna believes she is also going to be alone during Easter Holidays, but her dad must think it over first. She thinks there is less bitterness between them now because they are better able to talk and help each other. "During the last two weeks" they have been on good terms with each other, and "then one doesn't think about it. Then everybody feel good, it's fun, and we laugh." In contrast to earlier, Donna says that "now I could" approach Paul. So when the problems become easier and other qualities and feelings emerge between them, it becomes possible to open up to each other and tell each other things they could or would not say or do earlier. However, they still avoid talking about the really difficult stuff. So the arrangement for Donna to be alone was made in a haphazard way because they were unable to talk about it. After the conflict over Easter Holidays, they did not talk about it either, but one day Donna hinted that she might stay with a girlfriend for a couple of days during the holidays. In doing so, she lets her parents know that she is trying to find a solution. We see that Donna is pursuing a solution along several lines, on several occasions, and in several places, some of which we do not know much about in sessions. She is also pursuing solutions which do not involve their flat.

Paul ends session 20 saying about Easter Holidays: "We've got to take it up again because we won't have it the way she wants." Despite the risks involved, there is no way around letting her try again or talking about it first. They must be able to talk, and we talk about how they might do it and how they might react while doing it. Paul and Mary also do not want to be unable to go to their summer cottage in the approaching summer season. It must be possible for them to leave for other places and experiences. Paul says Donna is more relaxed and talkative and takes it as a sign of improvement and growth. In other words, he responds to Donna being nicer and signaling readiness to change. But they are still anxious, hurt, and ambivalent concerning Donna. And they still feel compassion for her problems and avoid them for fear that they may be intractable and become worse. So they are all trying in various ways without talking much about it though Paul and Mary say that they gradually find it easier for everyone to stay calm when they touch troubled areas with Donna. All the same, both parents think they need a session with Donna to talk over an arrangement for Easter Holidays. Because of the risks which this conflict may entail, they all try to work things out on their own but still feel they need our help.

As mentioned in section 6.3, they start session 21 by saying that they already talked about Easter Holidays and reached a compromise that the parents accept and Donna believes she can live up to. They talked quietly about it but do not quite agree who changed to make it possible. They are all relieved, and Mary and Paul express their appreciation of Donna's part in it. The meaning of this conflicting problem has changed for them; they initially had feelings of lack of recognition, distrust, and dependence, but now they believe that there is no other way than to resolve it and that they must give it a try. It is probably also easier for Donna to be nice and agree to more when so many other things again happen for her in other places. This makes her more big-hearted, not as preoccupied by the problem, and more inclined to overlook some things that would have made her cross in the past. Donna says about the way they approached the talk at home: "We pull ourselves together. We must be able to talk about it and not get mad at each other." They set themselves up to reach an understanding. Their various prior indications of being more willing to consider each other and come to an understanding probably make it easier. It also makes it less scary to accept that they still disagree on some of the issues. They have a better platform for agreeing on this while disagreeing on other things, and they do not as easily let their negotiation drift into other areas of conflict so that they lose the chance of reaching an agreement. Still, they approach talking with each other about it with mixed feelings and an appeal to the inner strength of pulling themselves together as if their abilities were not linked to realizing possibilities in a situation with coparticipants.

Asked what else they need our help for, Paul responds: "One gets better at handling it, and then there is almost nothing more to talk about because then it gets solved by itself." He adds about Donna: "Had it only always been like this, then it would have been fantastic." Donna says she was not nervous before this session. Note that they did not reach the same new understanding and way of handling these problems, but they do not clash in the old way. They recognize differences and disagreements in a new way and are, thus, better able to make room for all family members. They focus more on themselves as participants with particular parts to attend to so that they may bring about a different joint arrangement. In relation to the complex problem around Donna, they first tried to solve it themselves, partly succeeded and then failed; then they asked for help from us, and finally succeeded on their own. The resolution of this problem opens new possibilities to raise and pursue other problems, such as how they can live a joint life, improve their relationships, reach agreements, and make arrangements that they also disagree on and have different concerns in relation to. Having made this arrangement, they now need to change other things. Thus, it does not come easy for Paul to say directly that he wishes Donna will visit them in their summer cottage on her new moped. He says so in a partly reproachful voice because he believes that she will not. Which changes are possible for each of them still depends on the others' changes and the changing differences between them.

7.4. One Problem after Another

We learn in session 22 that while Angie's pestering and anxieties have receded into the background, it still bothers her parents that she gets cross at home, though they all get over it sooner. Is this the same problem as earlier? There is some continuity, also in her parents' difficulties in responding to her, especially since they still cannot talk with her about it. But there are important changes too. Angie now gets cross for other reasons. The incidents boil down to Angie wanting to decide things herself without regard for what her parents might think. Mary adds: "She thinks many things are unpleasant. It almost doesn't matter what you say and do, you get the same reaction." While Mary believes they cannot behave to Angie's satisfaction, Angie wants to be entitled to be left alone and be preoccupied by other things. As she puts it: "Sometimes one doesn't feel like being happy." She gets cross over pressures from her parents to be in a particular mental state of presence and attention and not because of troubles with her friends with whom she is doing many exciting things. Rather, she wants her parents to leave her more alone and stay more out of the way of the other things, which she is engaged in independent of them in other places. As earlier, this leaves her parents with the difficulty of having to guess what may be bothering her and whether they have anything to do with it. It also leaves them with the burden of being subjected to her getting cross, her inattention, and her desire to have them leave her alone. What is more, it is no problem to Angie that she gets cross; it is only a problem to Mary and Paul. They disagree over whether it is a problem. That Angie does not mind is Mary's reason for saying, "So I quit!"

In sessions, they now often compare current incidents with similar problems and situations. Thus, Mary puts the current troubles with Angie in perspective by saying that it is ordinary behavior at puberty, which will pass in a couple of years as it did with Donna. In another incident Angie puts pressure on Paul for money, and he comments: "In a way we are back to the thing about the horse. You sort of just have to realize this first and then do it the same way around." Still, you cannot assume that similar situations simply are identical, and Paul and Mary disagree about it. To Mary, there is a difference because Paul sometimes does not want to give Angie money though she needs, say, to buy socks. Notice also that while earlier they often felt uncertain about their experiences of their problems, they have now developed broader understandings and stances on them. Moreover, working by way of comparisons between situations indicates that no single problem is so acute that it calls for all our time and attention in sessions. It indicates that the therapy may soon end. Their problems are less of a burden, less condensed, and more scattered. Session talks, hence, now pass through a wider terrain.

What may it then mean if something similar to what you believe you had overcome suddenly turns up again? Paul believed they were over the worst troubles with both daughters when Angie thoroughly disrupts their trip to the joint session 23. For Paul, this is too much to put up with: "What the hell can I do? I don't know. It gets me down as time goes, it does, very much so. And actually, up till now I think it went really well, until not long ago. I really think so." He realizes that relapses will occur but gets sad, withdrawn and broods over what to do. What affects him deeply is not just facing a similar problem once more. His reaction is provoked by the fact that things in general are going well and that they have done so much already. It is not acceptable to him any more to have to put up with this kind of trouble – especially when it cannot be resolved, and they must let Angie have her way if they are to make it to the session. The parents tell about another incident from the last couple of weeks when Angie became so furious that she ruined a weekend with them in the summer cottage. Angie felt cheated of things she now feels entitled to, and, in contrast to earlier, she argues her case vehemently. Again Paul's reaction was that he and Mary had a wonderful week and when they drove down to fetch Angie, it all fell apart. For Mary, when Paul says he has had it, it is as if she is getting another problem on top of the others and he is threatening to leave. She reacts much less to these troubles after she began going to sessions. It affects her more "when Paul says he's had it 'cause that's a strange solution and it's also 'cause none of them will talk about the problems." We ask what Mary can do to help Paul so that these troubles do not separate them and Mary is left to herself too. Paul believes these incidents are caused by his personal insufficiency. Mary jumps in: "You always say so. You always say it's only you. You say you are stupid, it's you." Paul: "Maybe it is." Ingrid: "Do you really believe this now that we talk about it?" Paul: "No, well."

Paul starts session 24 saying they have made progress over the last year. Last time he was somewhat despairing, but Angie has straightened up, it goes quite well, and they will not get much further. Mary, on the other hand, says that Paul has been the same since last session and this is "awful." He says nothing and wants her to mind him less. "But it is not easy to live with. It's very difficult, and it also depends on how long it lasts." She fears that Paul will dig himself down if they do not talk about it. Paul agrees and says: "I ponder over things, feel that perhaps I'm insufficient." Mary believes that a key reason for the problems has been that they did not state their minds toward the children, and, therefore, the two of them really are the problem. We see here that life in the family still holds different problems for the two parents and that their understandings of their troubles and of what should be done about them differ. To the daughters, Paul's reaction is an instance of being cross. Mary: "When he is like this, the children ask me, 'Why is dad cross today?'" She understands the problem in a broader perspective: "There must always be peace. That's what's wrong, simply. Everything must run smoothly. No problems. Don't talk about that. There aren't going to be any problems. We must always talk nicely and be nice to each other and all that. And that's not possible. I can't. The others can't either." Paul's reaction makes Mary insecure over whether she has done something wrong, and she gets angry when Paul says he has had it. It is not OK to give up just because a child flips out. "That's what I think is so awful because we really have no problems. It wasn't the children who should have gone to therapy. It should have been us because we've never understood to show the children what we mean and feel. That's really the problem in all of it. . . . That Donna saw a psychologist and now Angie, why do we take this so seriously? Because things don't just run smoothly. The child is impertinent. I thought there was something wrong with the child. There are no problems." Ingrid: "Now you are not as worried as you've been." Mary: "But I thought there was something wrong with the child." We point to the parallel difficulties for parents and children of stating their minds. Mary and Paul agree, and Paul adds: "Yes, it's not at all the same things today as when we started here. It has resolved a lot." At the end, we go into the fact that Mary still carries the responsibility for addressing issues and insisting that they talk about problems. Because it is a burden, she sometimes tries to see what happens if she does not do it. This difference between sessions and at home persists.

"We Don't Turn the Same Things into Problems"

While some problems are receding or overcome, they now raise other problems. Especially Mary raises and pursues several intersecting problems linked to her stance to "lead a different life," not accepting to be the last in line and left behind by the others. In order to become less tied down at home, she makes other demands on her children. She involves them in household chores in such a way that they must learn to take them over, and she tells Angie that she can stay home alone during weekends: "Once in a while I think of that Angie doesn't like sleeping alone, but then she must come along to the countryside." When Angie and Donna complain to their mother about each other, "I don't mind much because then they must learn to talk with each other about it." Paul: "Like Mary I think it is very nice to be alone [as a couple, OD]. We've come so far that we begin to be able to think a bit more ahead and see that it's really very nice to mind ourselves." Mary: "I can't get a bad conscience over it, at least." Paul says he learned not to give up even though someone gets cross and to continue until they reach a solution. "We must get through, and then we must do it." So, while Mary is concerned with the difficulties of raising and pursuing problems, Paul is more concerned with having become better at solving them. Angie still feels it is "strange" that the therapists talk so much with Donna because the therapy was supposed to be about her problems: "I only thought it was about me, but apparently it was also about Donna, a lot about Donna, really." Paul: "It was about all of us." Mary: "Yes, and you've never understood that." Angie: No, I haven't." Mary adds: "In my opinion, there hasn't been anything wrong with the girls, but with us. Today it's my understanding that we've simply been too weak. We haven't been consistent. We simply haven't expressed our wishes toward the children because it has only been about them. It took me a long time to find out it's really not the children – it's us." Paul: "I don't agree totally with Mary that it's only been our fault because there have also been problems with the children. . . . It's only because we've wanted to do it as well as we could for the children."

In session 25, this shift in their localization of problems persists. To Donna and Angie, things at home are fine, and their engagements in other places concern them most. In the session, Angie is much livelier than earlier, giggles and smiles, and follows the talk with greater presence and attention. Paul says about his recent reaction to the recurrence of problems: "I must say, I haven't speculated much about it." But Mary says: "I still think they've got a lot to learn. If you adjust yourself and keep your mouth shut, it goes quite well. None of them want to talk about anything, and I can't stand that forever. But I guess I almost have to because if I happen to say something and want to talk about something, they are no good and almost want to move out. It's still like that, precisely the same." For Mary, this is due to their unwillingness to talk about problems. Donna responds: "Well, then I'll have to learn to do it if I can." Paul says that sometimes when someone did not want to talk about a problem, they are able to return to it later; then he adds: "I'm not very good at discussing things. I never have been, and I never will be. Mary wants us to sit and talk about it for hours. I'm no good at that." Mary: "You can learn like we can." Paul: "I don't know. Now she's tried for twenty years and didn't succeed yet." We point out that only Mary raises problems, also joint ones. Paul rejoins that they are no problem to them. Ole adds that this is the biggest burden for Mary and that Mary's reaction is stronger because she is the only one to raise them. The discussion leads in the direction of sharing responsibilities and distributing chores for their joint family life. Mary doubts the others' abilities and readiness to change this and is hence unwilling to let go of part of her responsibility. Paul feels controlled and subjected to Mary's standards of how things should be done. He says they need not think about these things as long as Mary takes care of them. Then he offers to change their distribution of chores. Mary does not quite trust him and keeps heaping new issues on the table. A little later she says reproachfully: "This is one of the things I wanted to talk about, or to have talked about before, right. Because we are sitting here, you, we can suddenly try out a new solution. And that's what I've always wanted." Mary did not suggest rearranging these things after her workload outside home increased over the summer and declares: "It's no use." As the session comes to a close, the question of ending or continuing their therapy is raised. Donna, Angie, and Paul want to stop, and Mary says: "The family wants this to be the last talk." Paul responds: "Then I want, I would like to come here alone with Mary since evidently there are things we must talk about." This session also deals with Mary's dissatisfaction over Paul's degree of coresponsibility for family chores and his lesser inclination to talk things over with Mary. These issues are not overcome. Paul wants to end their therapy because those troubles are ordinary ones with which they should not take our time. Mary accepts it reluctantly, and Paul says they must "grow up" to become able to deal with these problems on their own. He ends the session telling Mary "Let's go home," in a voice suggesting willingness to continue on their own.

In Angie's final interview, three months after her last session, she responds to questions about how her life changed in the period of their therapy: "It's become better. I have more courage. I dare more to do things. . . . I have quite a lot of fun." The remaining difficulties about being afraid in the dark, and so forth, do not occupy her much. She has not thought about what she can do about them and does not mind much. In Donna's final interview, she says that in the period of their therapy she came to realize that she has "been very rude" to her parents. Now they are on good terms with each other, have nice times together, and do not quarrel all the time as they once did. Of course, they still quarrel. "It's not for real in a family. There must also be quarrels once in a while" or else "it becomes too sugary." About her friends she says: "All the friends I had were assholes, really, and they mean no more to me. Well, right at the beginning I was a little sad because I had no friends and stayed home for some time. Then, finally, I thought, they are just stupid. They are the ones there is something wrong with." About being able to break with them and build new relations she says: "I've become more confident in myself. Earlier people could knock me down by saying I was fat. Now nobody can get me down, not at the moment at least." Her former friends hurt her so much that she decided it was enough. Lisbeth asks if she could get down again. Donna says it depends on "what kind of period" she is in, "what terms I am on with myself." She adds that she showed her former friends she can strike back, which surprised them. Earlier she was so afraid to lose them that she would let them do anything, but now she does not care because they are not real friends. Lisbeth asks if she might come to care again, and Donna responds: "No, because in all the lives I've lived people always tried to get me down, ever since first grade, right. I was always bullied, and there isn't a thing that wasn't wrong. That simply grew inside me. I believe suddenly I thought 'Now, it's enough.' At that time I went along with everything. I didn't dare speak back." In the parents' final interview, two months after their last session, Mary and Paul express the same points of view about the changes in the period of therapy, although it does not mean the same to them. In Mary's words, "I take it much easier than I ever did. . . . It's as if you get a different way of thinking, you look at things in a different way, and you think things over before you do or say something. That's what we've gotten most out of." On her own behalf she adds: "I've also learned that I'm going to lead my own life. It isn't going to be on my costs like it's always been. It can't be the meaning of my life to sit here while Paul and the children go out. I simply won't put up with that any more. It's going to be me too, not just Paul and the children, because I won't sit here being dissatisfied and thinking that I'm missing something and not experiencing anything." Lisbeth: "Have you changed your view on the problems you started with?" Mary: "Yes, we look at them in a different way today." She refers to what she said about themselves being due to the problems adding: "What once was a problem is no longer a problem because you think differently and see differently." Paul:

"The problem is the same, but you handle it differently. You get around the problem in a different way, and you've learned to do something else and not to mind so much." Mary: "We don't turn the same things into problems."

7.5. Re-Considering Changing Problems

I shall now add some thoughts about changing problems. I analyzed problems as parts of the clients' changing social practice. We have seen that changing problems emerge from changes in their social practice so that some problems gain a different meaning or fade away, while others arise. Problem changes are brought about by the clients changing their social practice, participation, and understandings. We have also seen that the clients' problems covary with their circumstances as when Angie gains and loses friends and seasonal variations increase and decrease her fears of darkness. As with changes in social practice, much varied work is involved in re-collecting, re-producing, and changing their ways of dealing with problems. And as with changes, we must ask how the clients stabilize new ways of understanding and dealing with their problems. Moreover, since changes of social practice are open-ended, problems are open-ended too. The clients do not have either problems or no problems. They have changing problems. The open-ended nature of changing problems makes Paul feel he has had it when troubles recur. He cannot be certain that the outcome of his efforts will be that a problem vanishes completely, and while he exerts himself to solve a problem, other problems recur and emerge.

Numerous problems come and go, vary and change in the clients' changing everyday lives. Some problems are passing and specific while others are more long-term and comprehensive. They run into and raise different problems, which are different parts of their different participation in different contexts, and they understand and deal with these problems in different ways. In fact, most problems in the clients' everyday lives are not described in their therapy. While we help them with some problems, they encounter and deal with many other problems. They mention some of them in passing, but we do not go into them. Beyond what we know about their lives, there are even problems with important links to the ones we help them with. Thus, some problems in the spouse relationship are barely hinted at, and the haphazard way in which problems around Donna were included in the therapy warns against believing that we have more than a partial access to and understanding of the problems in their lives. As with changes, we must be careful not to overhomogenize and overgeneralize our analysis of problems. There is no guarantee that the problems we know of and as we come to understand them provide an adequate basis for understanding all their other problems and their lives as a whole. To claim so amounts to insisting that we have comprehended the essence of their lives from which "the rest" may be derived rather than that we have a partial understanding of something of which we do not know "the whole" and in which we, hence, cannot locate the parts we know precisely.

Since the clients' problems are changing parts of their changing lives, we can neither define nor treat them separately from their lives. Their problems cannot be separated in practice and subjected to controlled and well-defined interventions. They are not discrete entities that can be solved in themselves. They are messes (Reimers and Treacher 1995, 126; Schön 1983) with complex links to many concerns and to their participation with varying coparticipants in and across diverse contexts. Confronted with such problems, they are easily caught in dilemmas, and it gets complicated to make up their mind and adopt a stance on them. Nonetheless, there is more to everyday life than problems. Indeed, there had better be room for other things than problems. If there is not, it gets too much, as when Donna tries to put them behind her or Paul barely gets a grip on one problem before the next erupts. They need to find ways to keep their problems so much at bay that there is room for something else and more. After all, life is not first of all about dealing with problems. So they should not turn everything into a problem. Nor should raising and pursuing problems be all they do so that their life turns into one big problem. In addition, there are contextual differences concerning how much room problems may take up. At home, problems are not supposed to take up much room. There should, first of all, be room for enjoying each others' company and spending nice times together. Sessions, on the other hand, are a place to deal with (some) problems.

Subjective, and intersubjective, processes are involved in the constitution of a problem. "Something must first be transformed into a problem by the problem-solver" as Lave (1988, 59) puts it. Problems are not just aspects of external conditions but of an ongoing social practice, and participants must set particular aspects of their ongoing practice as a problem before it becomes a problem for them (Schön 1983; Seidel 1976). The clients call this to turn something into a problem, and having changing problems means to turn other things into problems. This aspect of personal agency is most obvious when persons raise problems, and it is more easily overlooked when something imposes itself on persons to become a problem. But for something to become a problem, it will always be linked to somebody's possibilities and abilities as contradictions to their realization. Participants may have different possibilities, abilities, and contradictions to their realization, that is, different problems. They then disagree about what should be turned into a problem and, if so, how, by whom, where, and when something should be done about it.

As the clients change their concerns and stances, other possibilities and abilities become more relevant with other contradictions to their realization, that is, other problems. Thus, in Paul and Mary's changing practice of upbringing and in Angie's changing reasons for getting cross, other possibilities and abilities become problematic. Likewise, at the time of referral they were satisfied with their lives because they had concerns and stances other than those they adopted later and they did not see possibilities to overcome what troubled them. But at the end of their therapy, they "cannot really understand how we could live like that," as Mary puts it. Now their concerns and stances have changed, and other possibilities and abilities matter more to them. They are now satisfied and dissatisfied with other aspects of their lives and turn other things into problems. Mary may express more dissatisfaction with their present life than she did then, though her situation has improved and she would not go back to the old situation because she now aspires to realize other possibilities. She may even express more distrust in the others than she did earlier. Distrust here means believing that there are some possibilities that she would like to realize but does not believe the others are willing to go along with. Mary now turns this contradiction into her problem while she and Paul disagree whether it is a problem for therapy. Such distrust in each others' abilities and willingness make them turn other things into problems, as we saw between Donna and her parents. As their situations, concerns, stances, aspirations, and demands at themselves and each other change, they turn other things into problems as shadow-sides of these changes.

Illness Problems in Everyday Life

Kleinman made a now classic distinction between disease and illness. Illness is

> the innately human experience of symptoms and suffering. Illness refers to how the sick person and the members of the family or wider social network perceive, live with, and respond to symptoms and disability. Illness is the lived experience of monitoring bodily processes such as respiratory wheezes, abdominal cramps, stuffed sinuses, or painful joints. Illness involves the appraisal of those processes as expectable, serious, or requiring treatment. The illness experience includes categorizing and explaining, in commonsense ways accessible to all lay persons in the social group, the forms of distress caused by those pathophysiological processes. And when we speak of illness, we must include the patient's judgments about how best to cope with the distress and with the practical problems in daily living it creates. Illness behavior consists in initiating treatment . . . and deciding when to seek care from professionals or alternative practitioners." (1988, 3–4)

In addition, "illness problems" are "the principal difficulties that symptoms and disability create in our lives" (4). I argued along similar lines that Angie and her family are more concerned with the problems her symptoms cause in various situations and contexts than with the symptoms as such. The meaning of Angie's symptoms is first of all their consequences in her and their everyday lives, that is, the contradictions they create for her and their realization of possibilities. Furthermore, Kleinman distinguishes between illness problems and illness complaints: "Illness complaints are what patients and their families bring to the practitioner" (5). The illness complaints in the family I analyzed come close to symptoms. Various other illness problems and life problems are filtered out and not presented as illness complaints, whereas some illness complaints are mainly addressed in sessions and much ignored in other places. These clients maintain a distinction between symptoms and illness complaints, on the one hand, and illness problems and other life problems, on the other hand. They do so although the distinction between disease and illness is less clear-cut and more difficult to maintain in psychosocial problems than in the chronic and somatic diseases that have Kleinman's primary attention. In contrast to some conceptions of medicine, no fixed baseline of an organism's normal functioning allows us to distinguish when people have psychosocial problems or not (Jensen 1987). Psychosocial problems are parts of people's varying, cultural-historical forms of life and understanding. They are delimited in practical terms for people's participation in an ongoing social practice.

It is also difficult to draw a line between illness problems and life problems, or, as Paul puts it, "ordinary difficulties." Kleinman's definitions focus on the illness assuming that people's attention remains focused on "it" and that their practice and experience are centered on and shaped by "it." He expands the significance of illness across people's everyday lives: "For in the context of chronic disorder, the illness becomes embodied in a particular life trajectory, environed in a concrete life world. Acting like a sponge, illness soaks up personal and social significance from the world of the sick person" (Kleinman 1988, 31). In his approach to life worlds and life trajectories, as in Strauss and Corbin's (1988) approach, the illness remains the center of attention and understanding. In contrast, I pointed out that the meaning of a symptom varies as it becomes a part of various situations and contexts in the clients' social practice and its meaning changes when what it is linked to in the clients' ongoing social practice changes. The meaning of an illness depends on its practical links and contextuality. This is so because "the life world" is not a homogenous environment but a complex ordering of diverse contexts, including the context of treatment, in and across which clients live their lives. The meaning of a symptom is also unclear, and there may be confusion over it when it is not clear what it is linked to. What is more, the meaning of a symptom is subsumed to other aspects of the clients' lives. It is not the center of experience. Only temporarily is the meaning of a person's life first of all the meaning of an illness. Even while attending therapy, in the intervals between sessions, the problems recede into the background. Kleinman's approach to illness in everyday lives is illness-centered, and this reflects a professional-centeredness (Dreier 1998a).

Angie experiences her symptoms as an "it" happening to her beyond her doing so that she does not easily notice changes in them as being linked to what she is doing nor see herself as an agent overcoming them. Instead she sees herself as somebody who must go up against her symptoms to (re-)gain control over them, encapsulate or avoid them, get around or compensate for them. The other family members also relate to her symptoms in a particular way. They feel insecure, show consideration for her, take over and arrange things for her to avoid her symptoms recurring. But they relate in other ways to problems that they see as aspects of their ongoing social practice. In practice, they have different concepts about symptoms and problems because they understand and deal with them in different ways. Their concepts of symptoms are also marked by their reactions to expert symptom labels. So they have different, coexisting understandings of their troubles. They adopt these understandings separately and alternately, or these understandings intersect, compete, and clash, and some troubles pass from one understanding to another. Their understanding of certain troubles thus passes from a symptom to a life problem when they come to understand how these troubles are particular aspects of their ongoing practice. For instance, their understanding of Angie's anxieties changes from a symptom to a life problem when they come to see her anxieties as dependent of her lack of self-confidence. No strict line can be drawn between those symptoms and other troubles. They take troubles to be symptoms as long as they cannot understand and address them as life problems.

Furthermore, they often do not share the same understanding of a symptom or other troubles. Though they may all be concerned about it, they disagree about how to understand it, what to do about it, who should do it, and why. Actually, such a disagreement and conflict often *is* their problem, that is, that which contradicts their realization of possibilities. The problem is then a different one for the different parties. Changing disagreements, conflicts, and joint understandings about their troubles are important dimensions of changing problems. There is a further difference. Symptoms and some problems are primarily seen as disrupting and as a burden to their ongoing practice. Other problems are primarily turned into problems because the clients aspire to changes that these problems contradict or in the course of which they must raise problems in order to succeed. Addressing problems is then part of realizing and expanding scopes of possibilities.

Seeing the life world as contextually differentiated explodes the understanding of illness as an "it," that is, as one and the same entity. Instead, problems are seen as complex with diverse meanings in diverse contexts, and these diverse meanings may intersect in various ways. Moreover, the varying meanings and ways of addressing them change as participants come to take part in these places in other ways, change their trajectories across them, or take part in other places. Problems arise and change depending on their modes of participation and coparticipants in different places. So, problems emerge from contradictions in the forms of participation in and across places. That is why it matters to find each other in new ways as coparticipants and come to agree or disagree on another understanding and way of dealing with these contradictions. Participants' ways of dealing with problems are mutually linked in and across places, and these links between them and across places change. For some participants, much of what is done about a problem may even be done elsewhere while they are not present, and they must find indirect ways to understand and affect it. In dealing with a problem, it is important where, when, and who is to be involved in which parts of it, and participants may displace their dealings with it to particular contexts.

In order to become able to understand and deal with her anxieties across places, Angie must come to see that their common qualities indicate her lack of command over her relevant circumstances (Osterkamp 1976). She must also realize that in her situated anxieties these common qualities are present in various ways with various links to various other aspects of her current location so that her situated anxieties mean different things to her and must be dealt with in different ways. In other words, situated anxieties hold varying configurations of similar and different aspects and links, and Angie must recognize her anxieties in situated ways as she moves across places. However, her experiences of her anxieties change in another way too, namely from being something scary to avoid as best she can to becoming indications that she needs to develop certain abilities and understandings. Indeed, the decline in her anxieties indicates that she developed her abilities and understandings so that she now has more command over her relevant circumstances and more confidence in being able to handle what may happen. In this sense, anxiety changes for Angie from being a symptom and an anxiety problem to being occasional emotional reactions to threatening losses of command over relevant circumstances to which she may react with new efforts at developing her abilities and understandings.

Changing Open-Ended Problems

When problems are open-ended parts of their changing social practice, the clients cannot simply stop attending to them as soon as they believe they have reached a solution, even though they want to make as much room as possible for other things. They must watch out that they do not recur. This involves attending to their ongoing practice and perhaps not quite trusting the others not to bring them about again. In this sense, these problems are still parts of their practice. In a more general sense, they must continue to consider their own and their coparticipants' situations and concerns so that there will not be good reasons for their problems to recur, and this calls for other ways of understanding and handling issues. The pursuit of changes to their problems involves much varied work, and they must keep these pursuits on their mind or find ways to come back to them even in order to keep resolved problems behind them. What is more, how much attention they pay to problems varies periodically. In some periods, the clients pay more attention to other things because they must or because they need some variation and fun and do not always want to feel burdened by problems. This reassures them of the qualities of their lives that they appreciate and why they want to overcome any problems standing in their way. In short, they want to make sure there will be room for other things than problems and for spending nice times together without attending to the problems. In part, they see this as a means to getting on better terms with each other so that they will be better able to reach an understanding about their problems, and in part they do not like to address problems, want a break from it, and have to pull themselves together to go on doing it.

Because they cannot and do not attend to their problems all the time, they may slip into ignoring them too much so that the problems easily recur and they may then see as a setback. This happened several times. One instance is the recurrence of the problem about the distribution of family responsibilities and chores over the summer at the end of their therapy. Perhaps set astray by the marked variations in their circumstances during the long summer vacation, they do not attend to picking up this problem and readjusting their arrangements after the summer when Mary's and her children's conditions change. Instead of pursuing a resolution further, they follow suit with their changing circumstances and arrangements at work, in school, and so forth, and those changes make them run into problems at home again. This problem recurs because they ignore problem-relevant changes in their situations. It reappears more suddenly because they ignore problem-related issues, and they are taken by surprise and getting backward into it when it is already a bit too late. As a part of raising it again, they remind themselves that they had ignored it. Hence, they are learning it the hard way, as we say about learning something we ignored until it imposes itself on us with the urgency of a neglected problem. They may, in fact, learn from this not just to follow suit, ignore and postpone issues. Still, they cannot pursue and anticipate problems all the time. The challenge is to find out which issues they need to pay attention to, and when they need to improve a problem compared to when they can let it pass and attend to other things because it will then cease to be a problem.

What do problems turn into in the clients' changing social practice? The prevalent notion of problem solving covers far from all problem changes. Closest to the notion of a solution come problems that are unraveled like a knot so that the clients may go on and get past them into other things. The threads that formed the knot, that is, the contradicting aspects of a situation, may still be there, but the contradictions between them are transformed so far that they do not stand in the way of realizing the involved possibilities. Other problems are, strictly speaking, not solved by participants. These problems cease to be a problem because participants' possibilities and abilities change. Participants then get over a problem because their possibilities, abilities, and contradictions to their realization change. Still other problems cease to be a problem because they change their concerns and stances so that other possibilities, abilities, and problems become relevant and call for more attention. Besides, while some problems are common problems for a set of participants, other problems are personal problems, but even these problems are not problems for an isolated individual. They are problems for individual participants and perhaps for their coparticipants. What happens to personal and common problems depends on the relations between participants in and across contexts. This is obvious in the significance of agreements or conflicts between participants for what may come of their problems. We saw that participants consider their dependence on each other for changing their problems when they feel let down by the others and distrustful toward them. They also try to develop confidentiality and intimacy; to signal willingness to go along with changes; to be nice to each other; to get on better terms with each other and come to an understanding with each other; to become big-hearted in relation to joint problems because other things matter more to them; to slip through minefields; to get over problems by not focusing on them; and to set problem changes through in a passing and haphazard way.

A further feature of problem changes has to do with the complexity of people's social practice and problems. Many problem changes are partial because problems are not isolated entities in relation to their ongoing practice and other problems. Participants may alternate between pursuing changes to several problems because they realize that partial changes in some problems open possibilities for changing other problems, and vice versa. They must then redirect their pursuits of problem changes, often with varying coparticipants and across varying places. They must also redefine their problems and their pursuit of changes on the way to prevent these pursuits from coming to a stop. And even though they pursue some problems, other problems may change or recur and call for a redirection of their pursuits. In a changing social practice, many open-ended problems may recur, although participants believe they had solved them and conduct their current practice so as to keep them from recurring. Because no absolute line can be drawn between ordinary difficulties and special problems demanding treatment, the same sort of problem may occur as an ordinary difficulty. Angie may still become afraid in the dark, get headaches, become cross, and so forth, even for a variety of other good reasons than before. No sharp line can be drawn between a "problem family" and a normal family either. Certainly, there is no line where families on one side of the divide have no problems, although it may seem to be the case for problem families who may even use this distinction to depreciate their problem-changing efforts. Finally, like other changes, problem changes are not permanent results that from then on remain the same. For this to be the case problems would have to be independent entities with separate and specific causes in a fixed practice. Yet, people sometimes evaluate the outcomes of their efforts at problem changes as if it were so. Thus, Paul devalues the changes they went through on this account. In fact, the idea of a relapse is based on an idea of problems as discrete entities with separate and specific causes. The occurrence of similar issues for other reasons in other situations does not deserve the term "relapse."

Changing Understandings of Problems

I end this chapter with some remarks about the clients' changing understandings of their problems. When they begin to see a range of options, their understanding of a problem changes. They can articulate it much better when they are already changing it or getting past it into a life with other issues. They then more clearly see this problem as but one way in which things can be and recognize it as belonging to a particular, problematic practice and understanding. It is easier to describe when they see that things can be otherwise. They are not as immersed and overwhelmed by it. Their understanding of a problem becomes more certain by virtue of seeing possibilities for dealing with it and seeing more clearly that it is grounded in their practice, has understandable reasons, and might be changed by changing their practice. They then develop clearer understandings of the reasons for their own problems and reactions to each others' problems. They also see more clearly how they may get around or past a problem. Their increased certainty is linked to a better understanding with each other about how they see the problem, what they want done and can do about it, and how they do not want to live with it. Even if they believe they cannot overcome it, they are more certain how it matters to them and what they may do in relation to it. Mary emphasizes talk as a means to reach a better understanding about problems between them. Still, the other three change their understandings and come to a better understanding with each other without talking so much about it.

The reduced confusion and increased certainty in understanding their problems change how they relate to problem situations. They do not mind troubles as much and are not as bothered and diverted by them. This is a crucial change in their everyday lives. When something turns up, they are more certain that they understand why and how they may deal with it. Their appreciation of their own, others', and their joint abilities for development changes. Their increased reliance on their abilities to realize possibilities, which they call self-confidence, changes their experience of the open-endedness and suspense of what things may turn into. The significance of self-confidence is apparent in that, at the beginning of therapy, they want help from their therapists for things they cannot accomplish on their own, while at the end they are concerned about continuing to make changes on their own, which calls for confidence in their own and each others' abilities. We also see the significance of self-confidence when Paul loses his. He tries to get over it by convincing himself that there is a way through and boosts his self-confidence by saying "we must go on."

Finally, their understanding of their problems changes as they come to see them as linked to certain aspects of their practice and to see particular links between their problems. Thus, their ways of dealing with the troubles of Angie's anxieties and being cross are put in a different perspective and change when they realize that they are grounded in her lack of self-confidence. Their more comprehensive and differentiated understandings link problems with other problems and with their complex social practice as aspects of personal and joint developments.

8 The Conduct of Everyday Life and the Life Trajectory

So far I have considered the social practice of therapy from the standpoint of clients living their lives across diverse places and participating with varying others in diverse practices. I stressed that for clients to begin therapy means that they are entering a structural arrangement in which they attend sessions at intervals with expert strangers in a way that sets off their participation in these sessions from their ordinary lives elsewhere. I focused on how therapy comes to work because clients somehow turn session phenomena into particular parts of their lives across places. And I decentered the understanding of therapy and the problems it is to treat by considering them as particular parts of the clients' ordinary lives. Now I take this decentering further by going into the conduct of everyday life and the life trajectory that all persons unfold regardless of whether they attend a therapy or not. This illuminates the workings of therapy as a part of the way the clients conduct their everyday lives and life trajectories. I already touched on phenomena belonging to their personal conduct of everyday life and life trajectory. But I did not analyze them as such. I shall now do so. It is easier to define this layer of analysis and link it to my framework after having dealt with therapy as a part of the clients' everyday lives and with their pursuit of changes and problems across contexts. In this chapter, I introduce the concepts about the conduct of everyday life and the life trajectory. I say only as much as necessary about them so that I may continue the case analysis in terms of a new, more comprehensive conceptual framing. In chapters 9–11, I use these concepts to ground and elaborate my framework and to reach a deeper and more comprehensive understanding of the case and the case analysis.

8.1. The Conduct of Everyday Life

The concept about the conduct of everyday life throws further light on personal trajectories of participation across contexts. It is inspired by a critique of the prevailing institutional epistemology in social theory, which stresses the role of institutional powers in the re-production of social life. This critique leads to a different interest in everyday life, which is no longer seen as "the rest" located outside the important institutions of work, politics, education, health care, and so forth, that is, primarily at home and in our leisure life (Lave unpublished manuscript; Smith 1987; 1990). Whatever counts as important for people is no longer seen as occurring within these institutions and merely being transported into the trivial "everyday" (Lave 1988). To this I add a critique of the conception of personhood that goes along with such a social theory. As I wrote in chapter 2, we need a conception of persons as living their lives in and across diverse contexts in a structure of social practice and not in a homogenous life world. We must understand social contexts not only as parts of structures of social practice but also as parts of the lives persons lead across them. We must comprehend the personal significance of what happens in a context within the complex everyday lives persons lead across diverse contexts with diverse possibilities, concerns, and coparticipants. Moreover, we must understand how persons live such complex lives by distributing and configuring their participation in the structure of social practice with its arrangements of possible paths to take in the pursuit of various concerns. Compared to earlier historical times, present social practices are less confined to particular places and regions. Places and practices are more densely linked, and people – not only just information – move more around in them and through them. In reference to Jurczyk and Rerrich (1993:26–27), Holzkamp (1995; 1996) argues that this complexity and diversity of social practice makes special demands on (1) the organization of time, (2) the organization of tasks, chores, and activities, and (3) the organization of social relationships. Such a complex social practice not only makes it necessary for persons to live up to multiple and diverse demands and expectations, as role theorists would have it. Managing such a complex life also calls for the special personal effort of conducting one's everyday life.

To get through the day and accomplish what needs to be done, persons must accommodate their activities to the sociomaterial, cultural arrangements of living in and across places where much of what they need and want can only be done and only makes sense in relation to various others in social contexts. Thus, in social practice, day and night are no mere physical properties but are built into social arrangements for doing things by participating with others in a coordinated way here and there and now and later. Persons must conduct their everyday lives in such a way that they can take part in these arrangements for doing things in relation to various others in the structure of social practice. In so doing, they bring about a personal ordering of their activities, relationships, concerns, and commitments that turns their everyday life into an ordinary life. They take part in and create ordinary sequences of activities, tasks, and relationships such as getting up in the morning at a particular time, washing, having breakfast, and leaving for work or school (Holzkamp 1995). They develop rounds and agendas of their ordinary everyday life and use schedules as an ordering device for participants coming together from different places in joint activities. So, persons cannot just burn their energies and fall asleep whenever they tire out. They must establish a personal conduct of everyday life with a regular ordering of certain personal activities in time and place and in relation to others attuned to the existing arrangements for doing things in the structure of social practice. The way a person conducts his everyday life does not merely express an aesthetic lifestyle. It is a personal effort that is necessary to get through the day and manage what he needs and wants done (Holzkamp 1995). Even continuing to live in the same way must be accomplished in practice through a personal conduct of everyday life.

The conduct of everyday life must also be composed. A person must select some possibilities, concerns, and commitments among her multiple options in relation to various places and coparticipants and compose them into a personal conduct of life. To compose them well is an accomplishment in which they may therefore also fail. Concerns and commitments linked to different places and relations may divert a person or pull her in opposite directions. She may feel torn over them or manage to compose them into a conduct of life in which she gathers herself around a set of activities and concerns that she can find a place for, link with each other, and focus on. The complexity and diversity of conducting her life may create personal and interpersonal dilemmas, conflicts, and crises. It is important to reach a personally suitable balance and centering, links and separations, variations and contrasts in the everyday life she conducts. Restricted scopes of possibilities may make this difficult. A person's degree of dependence and exclusion or participation in a joint command over her conditions and arrangements affect how she may conduct her life, including how she may go against such restrictions or along with them (Dreier 1999b; Holzkamp 1995; Osterkamp 2000). In other words, the phrase "to conduct one's life" does not refer to an autonomous, omnipotent superman whose life is fully under his control. It highlights the ways in which persons compose and unfold their everyday lives in complex structures of social practice with more or less restricted and expandable scopes for their pursuit of diverse concerns and commitments.

Each person must come to an understanding of her conduct of life. This understanding of the way I live my complex life in the structure of social practice frames my understanding of myself (Holzkamp 1993; 1996). It involves coming to an understanding of my reasons to conduct my life the way I do – or to change this. My self-understanding is grounded in my conduct of life and serves to orient and re-consider it. The concerns of my conduct of life fuel and configure my self-understanding. To reach a self-understanding, then, is no end in itself and serves no abstract need for contemplating the epistemological question of "Who am I?" Who I am is understood through my reasons to conduct my life the way I do in and across the contexts of my personal social practice. Though I may take a particular self-understanding for granted in my ongoing practice, I had to search and find it first. I come to a particular understanding of myself that may not always be equally clear, gathered, and well-balanced but marked by uncertainties, confusions, doubts, dilemmas, problems, and conflicts. What is more, in a changing social practice, my self-understanding is never altogether completed; consequently, I cannot take it for granted from now on and ponder no more about it. My self-understanding is both a partial and a particular one. It is both never concluded and always incomplete. Hence, it is always more or less unsettled and calls for further considerations. The functional grounding of a person's understanding of herself in her conduct of everyday life is missing in psychological theories of the self. Their characterizations of the self must therefore turn into a set of traitlike adjectives.

Since I conduct my life as a participant in social practice, my self-understanding is a social understanding. It deals with how I conduct my life as linked to and dependent on the conducts of life of my various coparticipants. Coming to a self-understanding hence involves coming to an understanding with my coparticipants about how we conduct our lives (partly) in relation with each other. In these relations with others, my self-understanding depends on others' understandings of themselves, on our understandings of us and the social practice we share, and on our recognition of each others' self-understandings. Our self-understandings are mutually linked, nonidentical parts of our social practice. In his work on identity and the self, Ricoeur (1992) makes a distinction between two meanings of identity. The first he calls sameness, in Latin *idem-identity*, and it indicates "permanence in time as opposed to that which is changing or variable" (2). Here the self or identity is characterized by an "unchanging core," as is often seen in psychology. The other sense of the term Ricoeur calls selfhood or ipseity, in Latin *ipse-identity*. It implies no unchanging core but is "used in the context of comparison; its contraries are 'other,' 'distinct,' 'diverse,' 'unequal,' 'inverse,'" and it "involves a dialectic of *self* and the *other than self*" with "otherness of a kind that can be constitutive of selfhood as such" (3). This second concept of selfhood is in line with the conception I present. However, Ricoeur's concept does not pay attention to the fact that intersubjectivities are part of social practices. The self-understanding I configure in relations with others is configured from my location and position in a particular context and as a part of my conduct of life across contexts with varying locations, positions, and coparticipants.

The concept of the personal conduct of everyday life is linked to other concepts in my framework such as the concept of situated personal experience. Since what matters to me in a context depends on the significance of this context with its relations and events in the life I conduct, my conduct of everyday life affects what I notice in particular situations and contexts. My situated experiences also serve my conduct of everyday life. I understand and appreciate my experiences as parts of the life I conduct and configure them so that they may orient my conduct of life from my locations in and across contexts. Furthermore, I gather experiences about how to conduct my everyday life. These experiences are personal in the sense that they become a part of my personal conduct of life.

Different participants may adopt diverse and conflicting stances on a situation and context because its status in their particular conduct of everyday life affects their state of mind and concerns in it. They may therefore also adopt different stances on which features and events it is relevant to consider in a situation, and which features in other places should be included in addressing and changing it. Arguments about justifying what it is contextually relevant and appropriate to consider and address may then emerge. Thus, the clients disagree about delimiting and linking aspects within and across contexts because the concerns they pursue in their present context are involved in the diverse conducts of everyday life across contexts and in changing these conducts.

As persons compare their participation, experiences, and understandings across diverse contexts, opportunities and challenges for learning arise. Much learning stretches across different contexts and draws on those differences as a resource for learning (Dreier 1999a; 1999c; 2001). For many issues and purposes of learning, persons unfold complex learning trajectories that may differ from and go beyond the institutional trajectories for learning arranged in particular institutions (Dreier 1999a; 1999c; 2001; Lave 1997). But persons must also find room, or rather rooms, for their pursuit of learning in their conduct of life in and across contexts (Holzkamp 1995). In addition, what they learn is affected by the status of the issue of learning they pursue in and for their conduct of everyday life. Indeed, establishing a conduct of life involves learning, and re-considering and changing it holds issues for further learning. Some learning is personal in the sense that it becomes a part of how persons conduct their lives. It grounds their stances on their conducts of life.

How the clients address problems and symptoms is affected by the meaning and status of these problems and symptoms in their conduct of everyday life. They must also find ways to pursue changes to their troubles in their conduct of everyday life in and across places. Because of the selective nature of personal attention and action, processes of change and learning turn into a mixture of intentional pursuits and unintentional involvement in events and arrangements that provoke change and learning. Existing social arrangements often challenge and necessitate learning even when participants did not intend to learn and were not pursuing learning about the issue in question. In this sense, social arrangements ensure some learning about common aspects of social practice of which participants were not aware. Many aspects of family life are learned this way. Educational curricula also affect participants' learning in unattended and backwards ways (Lave unpublished manuscript). Because we conduct our lives in arrangements that are parts of a social structure, a sociostructural impact on personal change and learning is provided for. Whether we recognize it or not, our change and learning is involved in aspects and issues of social structure through our participation in the structural arrangements of social practice.

Holzkamp (1995) emphasizes a duality in the conduct of everyday life between everyday routines and "the real life," that is, what really matters to us and arises from the ground laid by our routines. We must introduce routines into our everyday life, he claims, in order to get done what needs to be done. Routinization economizes our accomplishing the ordinary elements of our everyday life so that we have more time and attention to focus on what really matters to us. Routines are the little things in our lives that we normally take for granted and ignore but that, often to our surprise, turn out to hold important meaning. As in much social theory (e.g., Giddens 1991), Holzkamp sees routines as uniform elements. The claim that something becomes automated and taken for granted is combined with the claim that it thereby becomes uniform. Conversely, reflection is seen as breaking with uniformity. But there is a further claim involved that Holzkamp does not make explicit though he offers several examples of it: routines introduce trust and familiarity. In one example, a bunch of survivors, crawling out of the ruins after a bomb-raid, first try somehow to organize a cup of coffee so that they will be better able to face the terrible thing that happened and find a way to go on from there. In another example, a person returning from hospital treatment of a serious illness picks up (and perhaps adjusts) old routines at home for a (perhaps reduced) future conduct of life, experiencing these old routines as something that is deeply meaningful and as a reassurance that life will somehow go on. In these examples, the little things that are ordinarily experienced as quite trivial suddenly turn out to embody deep personal meaning; because they are deeply associated with the particular life we lived, they provide assurance as something around which we might conduct our lives.

Indeed, Holzkamp claims that the everydayness of everyday life is created by establishing everyday routines as a circle of activities every day, and this circularity makes everyday life different from the life course that has a direction. In contrast, I emphasize the existence of variations and the open-ended and changing nature of everyday life. Though regulated, our ordinary lives hold a measure of variation. Everyday life is too complex and changing for its conduct to be profoundly routinized. Indeed, routines are not identical, elementary building blocks of our lives that are re-produced in similar and not exactly the same ways of ordering things and getting them done. There are relatively important variations in the daily rounds of activities in the clients' ordinary lives. These variations are of a larger or smaller scale. Some are irregular while others have regular patterns. Thus, some variations depend on whether today is a weekday or in a weekend; others depend on which particular weekday it is. That is, some variations recur in a familiar daily, weekly, fortnightly, or monthly rhythm. Such rhythms combine regular orderings and variation into regular variations, just like the everyday conduct of life establishes an ordering of varying activities across the day. Variations of a larger scale, such as the coming and going of the seasons, lead to variations in the daily rounds of activities and everyday conduct of life. The clients in this case do some other things in the summer than they do in the winter. Their relationships outside and inside their family vary accordingly. Many institutional activities have seasonal rhythms. Attending therapy is a variation in the clients' ordinary lives for a period of time that is also involved in the seasonal variation of activities. However, while the conduct of life of this family varies with the seasons, the seasonal variations are parts of changing social and personal practices.

Our everyday lives also hold various shifts and transitory breaks or time-outs from their ordinariness. Alcohol and drugs may be used to create such variations and time-outs in activities, relationships, experiences, and pleasures (Valverde 2002). Holidays, vacations, travels, school excursions, illness, hospitalization, diversions, recreations, and distractions lift us out of the ordinariness of our everyday lives. But they can only do so incompletely and for a limited period of time before we reorganize a conduct of everyday life with the same or another daily round of activities. While in these time-out zones and upon returning to our ordinary lives, we may compare experiences from our associated conducts of life, and these comparisons may trigger changes and learning. Sometimes, and in some respects, these comparisons make us reaffirm our commitments to our ordinary lives, feeling that it is good to be back again and to get into our familiar places, relations, and modes of life. Special events, troubles, and problems may also pull us out of the ordinariness of our everyday lives by standing out as significant and different or provoking breaks in its ordinariness. They too may make us change or re-affirm our stances on the everyday life we conduct, re-configure what we attend to and pursue, re-compose the balance and links between its parts, or re-place parts of it.

Different cultures exist that specify the ways in which and to what degree our conduct of everyday life is to be routinized. Expressions that stress the link between arranging things in an ordered sequence and making them manageable reveal a particular culture for the conduct of everyday life. We see this in the German expression "*etwas auf die Reihe kriegen*" which Holzkamp uses, the English expression to "bring something in order" and the Danish to "*ordne noget*." But there are other cultures of the conduct of everyday life, and there are contextual and personal differences in its conduct. Some persons do not want to routinize so much. They prefer more room for variations and spontaneity, which, of course, takes a measure of routinizing to be possible. They do not feel at home in a tightly ordered everyday life. Persons have different preferences about how best to conduct their everyday lives, and such differences between them are the stuff of many everyday conflicts. Indeed, many everyday routines rest on preferences and are therefore sometimes changed.

Schatzki (2001; 2002) takes up the notion of order in social theory from the standpoint of a theory of social practice. He notes that in the positivist tradition, routines are seen as repetitions of the same and, thus, as a guarantee of order in the sense of regularity and predictability. This notion is indebted to considering particular entities as general causes in lawful events and predictions and believing that scientific cognition, or all human cognition, proceeds by grasping regularities. Regularity, prediction, and explanation are coupled in the positivist tradition. Only what is regular can then be explained and predicted. In a second conception of social order, indebted to functionalism, order is defined by its stability. Here the order of a complex whole allows some variation and changes in its minor parts. But the parts tend to be seen as continuations of the same, and there are problems of explaining the definition of the whole and its changes. In a third conception, social order is seen as an interdependence of the actions of individuals and groups that need not be reducible to regularity and stability. Schatzki argues for a fourth conception of social order as arrangement, that is, as "a hanging together of entities in which they relate, occupy positions, and enjoy meaning (and/or identity)" (2002, 20). This conception of order as arrangement may absorb the more restricted notions of order as regularity, stability, and interdependence, which then mark possible characteristics of arrangements. An arrangement can be regular or irregular, stable or unstable, asymmetrically dependent and interdependent in different regards and to different degrees. Let me add that arrangements order not only routine activities but what Holzkamp calls "the real life" as well. Arrangements allow us to coordinate and distribute our social relations, activities, and pursuit of concerns across places.

Schatzki focuses on order in social practice, but what about "personal order"? Theories of the person in psychology and beyond basically assume personality to be an integrated unity. Its structural order is seen as an internal regularity expressed in the consistency of individual behavior. Judged by its absence in the literature on personality, the structure of social practice is believed to be irrelevant for the structure of personality. When the social world is considered in theories of the person, theorists hold on to the assumption that human personality, identity, and the self basically are a matter of individual integration and consistency. Scholars, recognizing that persons take part in diverse situations, nonetheless consider the achievement of individual stability as regularity to be the "core problem for psychology" (Benson 2001). The preeminent function ascribed to our identity and self is the subjective construction of a meaningful individual coherence. Behringer (1998) even couches the conduct of everyday life as aimed at establishing an integrated individual identity. As Shoda and Leetiernan put it, "the core mission of personality psychology and our intuition compel us to seek an enduring set of characteristics that define the person across situations and across time" (2002, 241). A key assumption in the person–situation debate is that persons would behave consistently and uniformly if only their situations did not vary. Some, such as Bandura (1999, 188) and Mischel and Shoda (1999, 205–209), did introduce a notion of patterned stability triggered by situational variations. This includes the within-person variability characteristic of a particular person, that is, "patterns of variability that are stable and unique as individual behavioral signatures" (Shoda and Leetiernan 2002, 242). They do not discard variation but turn it into regular variations and thus subsume it to a notion of regularity and predictability. A statistical average can, of course, be calculated across these individual variations. But the question is: Which psychological and theoretical meaning should we ascribe to this average? Lamiell (2003) claims that the average expresses a particular individual preference of functioning, and Fleeson asserts (2004) that it is due to an underlying trait beneath a surface of momentary situational variations. A third possibility is that the kinds and degrees of consistency and stability in personal functioning are grounded in the kinds and degrees of stability in the personal conduct of everyday life across diverse contexts afforded by the arrangements of social practice. The kinds and degrees of personal consistency and stability then change along with changes in the conduct of everyday life and in those arrangements. In taking the arrangements into account, the personal conduct of life reaches a particular kind and degree of possible and preferred ordering to a person's life and functioning in structures of social practice. The personal functioning must be ordered so that it hangs together in and supports a person's conduct of everyday life in social practice.

As presented here, the conduct of everyday life is conceived of in primarily practical terms as a way of leading a life with different modes of participation across different contexts. A century ago the term "conduct of everyday life" was used, by Weber (1952) and others, to designate individual integration in relation to diverse demands by means of religious and moral values or by living in accordance with nature (Barlösius 1997). I hold that the impact of religious and moral values on the personal conduct of everyday life must be situated in the complex personal practice across places. Questions of values, life and death, and so forth present themselves in our everyday conduct of life in the structure of social practice. I also warn against oversimplifying what it takes in practical terms to accomplish complete individual integration given the complexities of a person's diverse participations across diverse contexts.

8.2. The Life Trajectory

Major causes and reasons for variations, shifts, changes, and developments in the conduct of everyday life stem from its involvement in the personal life trajectory that stretches across the individual life span. But theories about the life course, life history, and biography merely conceptualize the life trajectory as a process in time. This is a mistake because it reaches across times and places like the conduct of everyday life it is grounded in. Persons unfold their life trajectory as participants in several diverse contexts. In fact, some institutional arrangements for distributing and composing a conduct of everyday life across a particular set of contexts are arrangements for unfolding a life trajectory too. According to those arrangements, the set of contexts persons participate in regularly in the same period of their life and the personal significance of particular contexts are to change across the life span. They include arrangements for when and for how long in the course of a life trajectory persons are to participate in a particular kind of institutional context. They also hold regulations for the succession of contexts, that is, for what participants should have taken part in before and must or may take part in afterward. But while there are arrangements for life trajectories across the whole range of the life span, these regulations are not as tight for adults as for children and young people whose life trajectories are closely regulated and segregated by age-related entitlements and accomplishments. Furthermore, the practices of particular institutions are arranged so that participation in them is only a part in their members' life trajectory, often regulating which part, and sometimes which changing part, they should be. Institutional practices may also be arranged to affect a person's path through this institution, that is, how she may gradually change her participation in it and unfold her life trajectory by combining the way she takes part in it with a way of taking part in other contexts. In short, there is a directionality to many institutional arrangements that promote the unfolding of personal life trajectories and which participants must or may follow. Numerous institutional arrangements regulate and provide resources for composing and unfolding personal life trajectories.

The arrangements for activities and engagements in the conduct of everyday life and for participation and membership across the life trajectory are dimensions of social order. They must be included in Schatzki's definition of social order in a theory of social practice as "an arrangement of people in which they perform interlocking actions, are entangled in particular relations, and pursue specific identities" (1996, 15). The social arrangements for life trajectories and of specific institutional trajectories – educational trajectories, career trajectories, family trajectories, and so forth – exist prior to particular members' personal trajectories into and through them. So do particular cultural understandings of how to unfold a life trajectory in and through these arrangements. These social arrangements and cultural understandings affect how persons direct and prioritize their pursuit of concerns, compose their life trajectories, and develop personal understandings of it. In the course of their life trajectories, persons change the ways in which they compose, understand, and unfold their life trajectory in relation to the existing arrangements that afford more or less limited scopes for doing so. The arrangements furnish an institutional structuring and directing of people's life trajectories with many things left for participants to adopt stances on and accomplish. Since institutional arrangements, relatively speaking, hold more explicit and specific demands and regulations, it is left more to a person how to unfold "the rest" of her everyday life outside those arrangements, but she may accommodate the conduct of the rest of her life to those arrangements and, in so doing, adapt more or less closely to an institutional epistemology on her life. Still, the arrangements do not determine a person's life trajectory completely. As with the personal conduct of everyday life, there is a need for a particular personal accomplishment of composing, directing, and unfolding a life trajectory. Persons need to accomplish conducts of everyday life and life trajectory precisely because structural arrangements do not determine their activities completely. Which personal accomplishments are necessary depends on the structural arrangements, in particular the relation between their determination and scopes for action. This understanding of the relation between structure and agency differs from regarding structure as purely determining and constraining. If this were so, everything else that matters besides determinations and constraints must stem from something other than structure. Structure is then conceptualized as the opposite of agency and as devoid of agency. But we cannot understand structure as enacted, re-produced, and changed by agents if we see structure and agency as separate. We need to comprehend structure as incorporating, arranging, and affording agency so that we may comprehend that people are making history, but not "under self-selected circumstances" (Marx 1995, chapter 1). In relation to my topic, we must comprehend how structures may be so arranged that participants may become able to realize personal conducts of everyday life and life trajectories. This includes how structural arrangements afford participants' accomplishments of breaks, changes and developments in their trajectories.

Concrete personal life trajectories are, therefore, not identical with existing social and institutional arrangements for trajectories. After all, personal trajectories are accomplished in relation to more encompassing and general arrangements, and particular persons realize them in different, partial ways. These realizations are grounded in the concerns, understandings, and stances on the life trajectories that persons come to adopt and on their particular changes thereof along the way. Structural arrangements for life trajectories may, of course, also change in some respects like other aspects of the structure of social practice. Thus, personal educational trajectories change when they are realized in relation to new curricula, programs, institutional structures, and so forth. The personal impacts of such changes depend on their timing in relation to a person's life trajectory (Elder 1998). The same social event and change occurs at different points in different individual life trajectories and becomes different parts thereof. Individual biological changes are also folded into changing life trajectories in changing social practices. Finally, it is possible to break new personal paths in relation to preexisting institutional trajectories and thus contribute to changing the social and institutional arrangements for trajectories (Mørck 2006). In short, my general framework about life trajectories is suited to comprehend concrete life trajectories with varying and changing compositions, courses, dilemmas, and possibilities in a changing social practice with changing arrangements for life trajectories.

Persons must develop abilities to unfold their life trajectories. To unfold it freely, they must ensure, and if possible expand, their grip on it in a changing situation with changing scopes. This cannot be accomplished once and for all. Referring to the distinction between three kinds of learning in chapter 6, a person's conduct of his life trajectory may change and develop because (a) he aspires to become able to participate more fully in an existing social practice, (b) his social practice changes, or (c) he seeks to increase his participation in changing his situation. In other words, as his life situation changes, other abilities for unfolding his life trajectory are called for. He then needs to redefine his situation, that is, its changed possibilities for unfolding his life trajectory and which abilities it takes to realize them. Because relevant personal abilities can only be defined in relation to concrete scopes of possibilities, the fact that social practice changes implies that no fixed abilities or simple cumulative mode of developing them will do. In a changing social practice, we need a conception of personal development with other criteria for development. Critical psychology comprehends personal development as a change in the relative strength between (a) personal command over and (b) dependence in one's situation Holzkamp (1983), in other words, as a change in the relation between taking part in determining one's situation versus being determined by it (Holzkamp 1977). Personal development takes place when a person's participation in the command over his life situation increases and his dependence in it decreases. In a changing social practice, such developments are not completed once and for all and accumulated. They must be re-assessed and re-accomplished in a changing life situation. This conception of development stresses a general directedness in the pursuit of particular, concrete developments. Besides, personal developments often not only involve changes in one life context but also in the overall composition of a person's social practice, in the personal weight and meaning of various contexts, and in the links between them. Finally, personal life trajectories overlap and are linked with other personal trajectories (Elder 1998), and coparticipants have various understandings and ways of conducting their life trajectories.

As their life trajectories unfold, persons change their engagement in possible futures with other anticipated possibilities and relationships. Persons experience their future in a future perspective reaching toward a future horizon lying more or less far ahead. They deal with their futures as imagined future situations and life courses. These imaginations are concerned with the possibilities of future life situations. Holzkamp (1983, 340) calls this the personal life perspective, and it may represent varying degrees of realism, which matters for orienting the pursuit of possible futures. After all, even if their imaginations do not reflect it, their futures depend on the scopes of their evolving life situation and on the social arrangements for unfolding life trajectories. In addition, their relation to possible futures comprises their engagements and commitments in bringing about the lives they want to come true (Mattingly 1998; Taylor 1991). They care about their future lives and take care of themselves and others by doing so. What is more, the way they do so varies and changes across their life courses. Yet, there are limits to their future horizons and engagements. Their futures are not fully at their command but more or less unforeseeable depending on the degree of joint command over their social circumstances. Which consequences may they draw from realizing that they cannot rely fully on their anticipations? They may pay less attention to their possible future and pursue it less, which will reduce their influence on the direction their lives will take. Their future perspectives may also seem to be mere utopian dreams. The mixture of a realism that still matters, an uncertainty they are repeatedly reminded of, and a caring about their future lives anyhow implies a measure of suspense about how it will be (Mattingly 1998), that is, about its qualities and their likelihood. The suspense makes them develop various ways of conducting their life trajectory and dealing with its risks and unforeseen events (Sloan 1996). After all, they cannot not care about their future lives. Feelings of hope reflect their belief in and commitment to possible improvements of their current situation and to future lives with such improved qualities. Thus, feelings of hope reflect a personal belief in the realism of their anticipations, whereas feelings of despair, that is, of giving up hopes, reflect giving up realizing such commitments because they do not believe they can be realized. Still, feelings of despair also reflect that they cannot stop caring about their future lives. Why else feel in despair? Feelings of hope and despair are grounded in differences of the non-givenness of their future lives – just as experiences of self-confidence, or the lack of it, are grounded in addressing what they cannot take for granted.

Because it is not certain what the future may turn into, their anticipations are open-ended and incomplete. Without pre-given, precise endpoints to their trajectory, they cannot direct themselves toward fully specified goals and plan the courses of their lives as realizations of well-defined ends. Rather, they may adopt goals and plans in more general and vague terms defining appealing and attractive openings as well as directions for what more of and closer to what they want means in contrast to less of and further away from it. But goals and plans must be filled in, specified, and modified as persons move along. At times, persons may also be confused and uncertain about their direction and about how to realize it. In any case, they cannot successfully premeditate and intend their life trajectories as a whole. In subjective terms, their life perspectives are open-ended, not fully specified, and of a more limited reach than their life span. Its distant parts are vague and preliminary, perhaps also more indifferent to them. The futures they hope and fear are sketchy anticipations of future courses of life with associated conducts of life. They are projected from their present as a sketch of a future with a longer or shorter reach, and they may attempt to realize some of these projections as personal projects (Sloan 1996). In short, their future personal life trajectory has an emergent quality. Nonetheless, the way they pursue their future life and understand this pursuit matters for their self-understanding, even though it may lead to something other than what they now realize and much of what they now do is not intentionally directed at bringing it about. Think of the dual meaning of the term project. On the one hand, a project is something we throw out and may pursue. On the other hand, in a professional, educational, and managerial sense, a project is set up in order that we should complete it. But persons do not normally turn their whole lives into such a project, or series of projects, to be managed and completed; nevertheless, some professional interventions and institutional trajectories are based on this logic and seek to impress it on us.

To some extent institutional arrangements for life trajectories ensure that a personal life trajectory unfolds even when a person does not intend and pursue it much. Persons are often most concerned with their present situations and those links to their immediate past and future. As the social practice they participate in and/or their understanding of their life trajectory changes, they may change their direction, and some of these changes constitute breaks or turning points. However, due to their involvement in structural arrangements, they are making and realizing a personal life trajectory even though their concerns and understanding of it are of a limited reach, cursory, and unfold and change as they move along. But the nonidentity between personal trajectories, on the one hand, and structural and institutional arrangements for life trajectories, on the other hand, allows personal trajectories to change also when these structures remain stable – or personal trajectories not to change when pertinent structural features of social practice change. In using the term "life trajectory" we must, therefore, carefully identify whether we refer to structural and institutional arrangements or a subjectively pursued life course. The nonidentity between them affords various kinds of mismatch between being involved in structural arrangements and pursued life courses. As persons live their lives, they run into consequences of this mismatch between arrangements and their intentions, and this may make them revise their intentions or turn their lives in other directions.

Although persons comprehend their life trajectories incompletely, they do to some extent conduct it and develop an understanding of its conduct. Just as their self-understanding orients the way they conduct their everyday lives, it orients their engagement in their life trajectory. This raises some questions. When and how do persons realize in the first place that they are involved in a life trajectory and may pursue and conduct it in certain directions? How does this realization affect the ways in which they relate to their current possibilities, do things on a day-to-day basis, address and deal with problems, and so forth? How do they realize that they need to fill in or revise their understanding of their life trajectories with the various parts, links, foci and priorities? And how do they change their understandings of what it is important to pursue and what it takes to realize their life trajectories? They may tie themselves down if they do not revise their understandings of their life trajectories in accordance with their changing lives just like coparticipants may tie each other down if they do not recognize revised understandings of their life trajectories. Changing their understandings of their life trajectories is a necessary part of living in a changing social practice – all the more so since their self-understandings are partial, hold dilemmas, and need further clarifications. Still, changing their self-understanding may be a complex and prolonged process. At various points in their lives, persons realize and appreciate that they now see it in a different perspective, other things matter more to them, and so forth. They may then even find it hard to recollect and articulate their prior self-understandings and conducts of life. This is because their self-understandings are not superimposed upon one another as layers of bricks in building a house. New self-understandings arise by transforming older ones which then cease existing in their old guises and persist as transformed parts of the new one (Maiers 1996). It then takes special reconstructive techniques to recollect prior personal understandings.

Theorizing the life courses as being grounded in changing structural arrangements of social practice is an alternative to considering it in terms of a succession of general stages of individual development. In a theory of general stages, there is only one way: up the ladder of stages; and it is the same way for all of us. In relation to this one-way street of stages, no shifts in direction are possible, and no new pathways are discovered and won. The learning involved in personal development must be considered in fixed and cumulative terms as the means by which the stages are reached. Stage theories tend to study life courses and individual development in terms of abstract time categories of a number of years. Nonetheless, they implicitly rely on those sociocultural arrangements for trajectories in which boundaries and transitions are drawn according to age: transitions into kindergarten, into school and through its age-graded educational trajectories, out of school and into various career trajectories, retirement, and so forth. They often recognize that problems of personal development cluster in the transition periods of those sociocultural arrangements and, thus, implicitly acknowledge the sociocultural nature of personal development. But they draw no conceptual consequences from it. As persons begin to participate in new contexts with new demands and a new composition to their social practice, they become visible to new social agents and may not accomplish appropriate changes in their everyday conducts of life and life trajectories smoothly so that they may get stuck facing necessary changes (Højholt 1993; 1999; 2000). But stage theories see such practical, sociocultural transitions through the lens of their abstract categories. Thus, based on his general categories of play and learning, Leont'ev (1979) construes the transition into school as a shift in the leading activity in the development of the child. Functional categories – of play and learning – then define what to study in various stages of human development, and concrete personal life trajectories are subsumed under abstract functional units of analysis. That transitions in sociocultural arrangements for life trajectories concur with changes in stages of human development is taken as a mere coincidence, or the sociocultural arrangements of trajectories are re-construed as instantiations of a "normal biography" of natural human development. At the same time, the concurrent diversity to personal functioning, abilities, and their development is divided into successive stages.

A conception of personal life trajectories in a theory of social practice is positioned between abstract stage theories and social-constructionist theories. The latter assume that persons construe coherence into their life, thus turning their life into a constructed whole. They conceive the construction process as a purely subjective and intersubjective matter and accomplishment. Self-identity is seen as a person being constructed as and constructing herself as being the same. But these theories do not ground why persons should be preoccupied by and aspire for wholeness and coherence and accomplish it by constructing a narrative (Dreier 1999b; 2000). They claim that persons "tell" continuity and coherence into their lives. Life seems to be about the plotting and telling of a story rather than about the conduct and course of a life in structures of social practice. Bringing about a life trajectory is replaced by plotting and telling a story.

There are various versions of these theories. An example is the social theory of Giddens claiming that "Self-identity, as a coherent phenomenon, presumes a narrative" (1991, 76). He realizes that the life course contains passages but subsumes them to a coherent narrative.

> The life course is seen as a series of "passages". The individual is likely to, or has to go through them, but they are not institutionalized, or accompanied by formalized rites. . . . Negotiating a significant transition in life, leaving home, getting a new job, facing up to unemployment, forming a new relationship, moving between different areas or routines, confronting illness, beginning therapy – all mean running consciously entertained risks in order to grasp the new opportunities which personal crises open up to. (79)

In other words, Giddens plays down the significance of any real structure in personal social practice claiming that they are not institutionalized and that individuals turn them into matters of reflection. Based on these reflections, they are then turned into life plans. "Life-plans . . . are . . . an inevitable concomitant of post-traditional social forms. Life-plans are the substantial content of the reflexively organized trajectory of the self" (85). Although, in reference to Berger, he acknowledges the "pluralization of life-worlds," which have become "much more diverse and segmented," and that "individuals typically move between different milieus or locales in the course of their everyday lives" (83), the significance of this vanishes in his view on our construction of a self-identity and life trajectory. "The line of development of the self is *internally referential*: the only significant connecting thread is the life trajectory as such. Personal integrity, as the achievement of an authentic self, comes from integrating life experiences within the narrative of self-development" (80, emphasis in text). Surprisingly, a theorist of social practice claims that personal integrity and authenticity merely are a matter of integrating experiences within a narrative, and that the line of development of the self is purely internally referential, based only on reflections leading to life plans integrated into a narrative. In his narrative theory, as in similar theories, narrating has its own subjective logic from which narratives emerge; it does not allow the narrative to follow from the ways persons relate to their life trajectories in structures of social practice. The practice of narrating is then always essentially the same endeavor, which always leads to essentially the same accomplishment. In this way, Giddens plays down historical and structural variations in subject-world-relationships as well as the significance of discontinuities and diversities, breaks and contrasts, replacements of and changing links between contexts, relationships, activities, and concerns in our conduct of a complex life. He is bound to assume that a person always pursues and understands his life trajectory in basically the same way. The real complexities of conducting a life across times and places vanish behind his preoccupation with constructing coherent self-representations. Like stage theories, Giddens separates social structure from the person, creating a dualism between structures of social practice and the self as a narrative construct. In spite of Giddens's work on the duality of structure, he too believes that social structure must be determining and fixed in order to matter for personal life trajectories. When social structure calls for participant initiatives and accomplishments, choices and engagements, orientations and reorientations, and the moving into and out of particular parts of it, Giddens no longer considers this to be implied in a particular arrangement of structure. Instead, he believes that everything has turned into mere subjective constructions.

In other narrative theorizing, such as Polkinghorne (1988), stories are seen as unfolding. We are in the midst of our stories, not certain how they will end; hence, we constantly need to change and revise the plot. Yet, we are still preoccupied by the construction and plotting of coherent stories no matter which structure of social practice we take part in and how we direct our trajectories in relation to it. Other narrative theorists have replaced the idea about an overarching narrative with the notion of many small stories of varying scopes. But they maintain the same basic assumption about the need for subjective coherence as the driving force behind narratives. Postmodernist theorists too insist that coherence is the name of the game. They only add that it cannot be accomplished in a fragmented world (Dreier 1999b; Griffiths 1995), and so they are also blind to the significance of conducting one's life in a complex social practice with heterogeneous parts. Instead, they focus on recurring negotiations of different self-representations and self-presentations as discursive phenomena and interpretative outcomes. What remains is a sequence of fragmented selves/stories with fragmentary shifts between them. The significance of persisting and changing structural arrangements and links – even when persons are unaware of them – is lost behind an ongoing practice of interpretative construction. Because they negate these links, these theories end in a constricted intersubjectivist view of coconstruction. Still other social theorists are concerned with social changes that they claim increasingly lead to disruptions and discontinuities in life trajectories. Sennett claims that work trajectories are increasingly marked by disruptions and discontinuities. He fears that the tearing up of our career trajectories will make us tear up the rest of our lives too so that "People feel the lack of sustained human relations and durable purposes" and our characters corrode as a "personal consequence of work in the new capitalism" (1998, 98). But why should we tear up and replace all parts because one part is replaced or torn up? After all, different relations and parts of our lives have different durations. We might even hold on to other relations and parts of our lives in order to compensate for disruptions in our work life.

9 The Children's Changing Conducts of Everyday Life and Life Trajectories

In this and the next chapter, I go into the conduct of everyday life and life trajectory of each person in turn. The aim is to illuminate how their modes of participation and troubles are parts of their conduct of everyday life and life trajectory. My analysis elaborates their practical reasons for living as they do and for their current concerns. It shows how their individual subjectivities arise from their conduct of everyday life at the current points in their life trajectories. I go into those aspects of the conduct of everyday life and the life trajectory that appear in my materials, referring to what was described earlier and adding aspects not yet introduced. My analysis is limited because the focus of my materials is on the sessions and the clients' lives at home and on their lives in other places as seen from there.

9.1. Angie

Conducting a Life in Dependency

When my study begins, Angie is twelve years old. After school, she spends her afternoons at home alone with her mother, reading cartoons, doing home assignments, being bored, and becoming easily cross. Most children her age do things together in other places, and she would like to participate in this. But her anxieties hold her back at home, and a history of being bullied and a change of school to get over it less than two years ago have so far left her with no close bonds to other children in school. Still, her symptoms might not have become so disturbing and she might have gotten over them herself if she had not gotten into a conduct of everyday life tying her down at home. She does not understand why she gets cross so easily at home. It soon becomes clear that this tendency varies with her involvement in activities with children in other places, and that missing exciting activities in other places while being bored at home is an important reason. She spends most evenings at home too because of her anxieties in the dark. But being at home in the evenings is more in line with how she wants to spend her time because many children her age are also at home at that time of day so that she does not miss so much. Her everyday life leaves an impression of ordinariness with no real surprises. Even its major variation is regular activities. Twice a week a parent takes her to organized leisure activities, such as sports. The major contrast in her everyday life is being in the countryside with her parents in many weekends and during summer vacation. There she leads a different life.

In general, children's scopes for conducting their everyday life are quite tightly prearranged and regulated. The basic structure of Angie's everyday life is laid down by institutional regulations or arranged by the care of adults: her morning routines, school hours and time tables, when she is to come home, her meals, when she is going places, her household chores, her sleeping hours, and so forth. Children are, of course, afforded room to play, but in family life the separation of child play from the adult activities of jobs and housework fosters a view on child play as an endless activity that may always be interrupted by the call of more serious matters (Dreier 1980). The basic ordering by others of children's everyday life affects the development of child agency. Though children must follow these regulations, they do not have to realize their meaning nor attend much to organizing their everyday lives and commit themselves to the way it is organized. Taking care of organizing children's everyday lives is also crucial to what it means for adults to care for them, for instance, what Mary means by loving and caring for Angie. In general, adults do this in such ways that children gradually become able to take over conducting more of their everyday lives, that is, with an eye to children's development in their life trajectory. Because adults organize and regulate children's everyday life so much, adults' opinions about a child matter in a special way to the child. Thus, Angie wants to come along to school meetings and sessions to hear what the adults have to say about her, though she does not want to say anything. She wants to know how opinions flow and adults ally about caring for her across contexts. Listening to them may then, of course, make her re-consider how she is doing and perhaps do something about it.

All in all, children's everyday lives depend on adult arrangements and care for them, and children must conduct a life as dependent persons. How does Angie do this, and what does it take? At home she accomplishes many things through her parents, making them help her or take care of things for her. Having things done for her makes her dependence deeper. Yet, even though she wants her parents to take care of things for her, she does not want them to decide for her. She wants to have a say herself, but she still wants to rely on their competence to carry things out. She wants to be heard, but not to have to do things herself. They should do for her what she wants done. She is against Paul deciding too much for her: "He almost decides everything, I think; at least over me." In her opinion, she and Paul do not talk well with each other because he should manage things for her, not decide what should be done about them. So she sometimes talks with her mother first, and then they can make him do what she wants. Her parents should also take her places when she wants to attend leisure activities, is seeing a doctor or a therapist, and so forth. However, in addition to being dependent of her parents' help, Angie feels she can rely on them for help though she is often dissatisfied with the help she gets. She also feels she can rely on her parents to protect her against the unpleasantness of her symptoms and to compensate for her boredom in the afternoon. Angie understands and uses her symptoms, urging her parents to help her avoid them since she "cannot help it."

Children's attempts to make adults do things for them are in general grounded in discrepancies between the development of their wishes and their abilities and powers to carry them through. But Angie is not very concerned with developing her abilities and thus reducing Paul's deciding for her. Instead she pesters her parents to make them take care of much and fulfill her wishes for her. In doing so Angie replaces the need for her own efforts, and she does not consider whether her wishes are fair and realistic. Nonetheless, as a dependent person, Angie is quite powerless in relation to many decisions and quite peripheral in deciding the rhythms and foci of many activities at home. So she has to do something extra to attract her parents' attention and make them do things for her. She needs to watch for the right moment and find the right channels and ways of presenting things. Her lack of power, peripherality, and dependence easily turn her appeals and pressures into pestering, often for hours in a row. When her parents then try not to attend so much to her wishes or, out of consideration for her, just do things for her, they do not consider her much of an agent able to take care of herself. These reactions and the whole situation eat at Angie's confidence in her abilities and make it more acceptable for her to continue pestering them regardless what she wants.

Since Angie both relies on her parents and is dependent of them, she cannot be on bad terms with them for long. In session 2, she describes getting cross at Paul and having a row with him, but it does not last long because "I cannot keep on being cross. I cannot stand to go on being it." Instead she switches to other things and approaches others or him on other terms. The row then vanishes into the background and makes itself felt in her readiness to react with distrust when he says or does something. When she gets cross at her mother in the morning, she tries to make it up with her before leaving for school. Angie has learned a particular way to handle being cross and other troubles. She conducts her life in such a way across contexts that she has to get on good terms again before it feels alright to leave.

But the ordinariness already described does not resolve the complexities of Angie's everyday life. We should not lose sight of the variations and contrasts, tensions and ruptures, contradictions and symptoms in her ongoing life. First of all, Angie is caught in that the structure of her practice is distributed across places, while she is not very able to conduct her life across these places. Her symptoms hold her back, and she has no clear notion of having influence on the formation of friendships. Because she is unable to move around on her own, she is not very able to link her activities and relationships in different contexts into a conduct of everyday life. She can neither stay alone at home nor go out alone. In our forms of social practice, learning to move around on your own is a key feature in the developmental trajectory of children. In Denmark, children begin to accomplish this around the time of school entry. But Angie cannot conduct her life in accordance with the structure of social practice she takes part in. This discrepancy gets her into self-inflicted restrictions, exclusions, and troubles. Children unable to participate in the structurally arranged trajectory for child development run into problems, and become aware of them, if they do not develop appropriate abilities, seize opportunities, and move on. Another tension in Angie's everyday life is between being isolated from other children at home and watching friendships between other children unfold in school and at leisure activities and sometimes being pulled in as a replacement for someone for a time. This makes her realize and appreciate what she is missing and reminds her of her lack of influence on friendships.

In line with her self-understanding as someone who wants to decide for herself but cannot carry out her decisions, Angie easily gives up any attempt to realize her wishes herself, sees it as something her parents should fulfill for her and appeals to them to make it come true. Her main concern about her wishes is not whether and how it is possible to realize them but her impatience about their fulfillment. Thus, her parents cannot afford to buy her a horse, and it would take her a year to save money to buy one if she got a job. But Angie does not care about that, she simply wants it now. How to realize her wishes seems quite blurred to her, and her lack of belief in being able to make a difference makes much of her possible future vague. She is uncertain and easily confused when it comes to finding out and pursuing what she stands for and finding others in doing so. Because of this lack of clarity about where she stands, it may not even be clear to her that she uses her parents for comfort and compensation and as displaced targets of dissatisfaction, in line with the socioculturally widespread use of family life as a target of displacements and compensations. This makes it more acceptable for her to need comfort and compensation at home and still be dissatisfied and cross at the others.

While Angie is killing time, bored, hoping and waiting for something in a very ordinary everyday life, she does not clearly stand behind the life she lives. In fact, she does not really want the life she leads; instead, she wishes it would turn into something else. This makes her interested in interruptions and breaks, which then do not appear to her as interruptions and breaks in a settled ordinary everyday life but as attractions. Unlike Holzkamp's (1995) general assumption about the conduct of everyday life where routines constitute the basis for our engagement in the "real life," the routine regulations and arrangements of Angie's life do not have a so deep meaning to her. Though they are very familiar to her and structure her everyday life, she has not settled into them and does not stand behind them as really hers. Conflicts with the others at home around the routines of her everyday life frequently arise because she does not stand behind the life she lives. Besides, because she wants a different life but does not quite know what to do to get it, she hardly makes plans for what to do in case some opportunities suddenly turn up. It is important for her always to be open for opportunities. Indeed, she conducts her life in an open, hardly planned way and wants to preserve an open – in contrast to a settled and fixed – structure to her everyday life across times and places. She does not see the ordinariness of her everyday life as her own conduct of everyday life.

Moving Confidently around in Separate Worlds

The change in Angie's conduct of everyday life and life trajectory is triggered from places outside home. In sessions 2 and 3, she tells us that she prefers to be in the countryside where she may ride, has friends, and can pursue what interests her. She likes to ride because other people notice her and enjoy seeing her ride; children laugh and run after the horse, and their parents laugh too. In this other place, other activities and relationships are possible for her. Because of those opportunities, she makes an effort to become able to move around on her own. She may then elaborate her engagements in other contexts and link her concerns and relationships across places. This calls on her to become able to handle her anxieties, know her way around by various means of transport, and search for and sustain contacts and activities.

Besides other places than home, other people than her parents matter more for Angie's motives to do something about her troubles and symptoms. Thus, when she starts riding in the countryside on weekends with a girlfriend, she stops pestering her parents. Her parents believe that changes in their relationship with Angie at home are the reason for her changes, but for Angie the activities and relationships in other places count as a significant change. Angie's main concerns at the current point in her life trajectory are directed at being on her own with friends in other kinds of activities. These have not always been her main concerns, but their pursuit will probably strengthen them further. Still, these growing concerns do not replace all her other concerns, activities, and relationships. Her life in the family spans a longer duration and does not cease to matter to her, though its meaning for her is affected and may change or vary for a period of time. Precisely how, is too early to tell when these new activities begin. After all, the new activities are seasonal activities and a weekend variation in her everyday activities. For a while, she looks forward to those weekend activities during most of the week and considers what happens during the week dull and uninteresting. But while these activities still go on, Angie tries to change her everyday life in other respects too. These changes are an effort to establish a different composition in her everyday life, and they reach toward a future horizon. She sees these new activities and relationships as attractive and exciting – in contrast to being boring. She is getting into something new with a clear feeling of why but not yet of where it may lead her further along in her life trajectory. She has no clear idea of a definite direction and no definite trajectory in mind. Rather, as it evolves, she comes to realize and appreciate a new direction with its activities and relationships and get a clearer sense of what it means to be in it and stand behind it. This includes, among other things, coming to realize which qualities of activities and friendships she likes and prefers, which demands they make at her participation, and what she must attend to and be concerned about to sustain and unfold them further.

There is a further feature of the structure of Angie's social practice. Life at home, in school, and with friends in other places are to a large extent separate worlds for her, and she has come to want it this way. Parents know much less about their children's lives in school than in kindergarten. Their children tell them less about it and increasingly separate their lives in school and at home. Though Angie depends on her parents' support and spends so much time at home, she tells them little about her life in school. Children her age pressure each other to separate family and peer relationships and not to tell their parents so much about what happens in the world of peers and friends. In that way, it becomes more up to Angie to organize and conduct her relationships and activities across places. There are other differences in her concerns and ways to fulfill demands and take care of herself in her conduct of life across places and relationships. At home, others may fulfill Angie's wishes for her and take care of her, but in other places she must take care of herself in a different way. It's not that she cannot get any help from her friends, but they do not take care of her like her parents do. In fact, children of Angie's age ridicule each other if they need or want this kind of care from others. They tell her she is a small child wanting her mother to take care of her and that she should not conduct herself like this any more. Instead, she should change into managing more on her own. Outside home, Angie needs to change into doing things in a different way. In order to be able to unfold her life more freely in other places, Angie must diminish her dependence of her parents as well as her dependence on them.

About the United States, Bellah et al. state: "In a culture that empha-sizes the autonomy and self-reliance of the individual . . . , childhood is chiefly preparation for the all-important event of leaving home" (1996:56–57). Angie must, indeed, come to rely much more on herself. That is what she and her parents mean by her need to develop self-confidence. But, while Bellah et al. primarily locate this phenomenon around leaving home in "late adolescence," a similar demand at the personal mode of functioning and self-understanding arises much earlier due to the distribution and separation of parts of a child's life across separate contexts. What is more, it grows out of the fact that a person is not participating with the same other persons in different places. Angie must also come to rely on herself in other places because the persons she primarily relied on, her parents, are not present. Talking about autonomy, as Bellah et al. do, should not make us believe that Angie is alone in these other places. She is with other coparticipants. She is with others and at the same time "on her own" in relation to her prior primary reliance on others. In this sense, she must come to rely on herself. It includes that in school and with friends in other places she must take care of her affairs in a different way, and though she may get some help from her friends, she will be ridiculed if she still needs and wants a parental kind of care. Precisely in relation to those demands for self-reliance, Angie doubts whether she is able to gain influence on her participation with others. Though she may decide that she now wants to rely on herself, she might not be able to accomplish it. In other words, self-reliance is not a matter of autonomy of free choice. It is a matter of personal abilities and accomplishments in particular social relations in a particular structure of personal social practice. Because she has a history of being bullied, Angie doubts her abilities in such relations and places. But in a structure of social practice where persons participate with different others in different and sepa-rate contexts, self-reliance implies that persons must become able to conduct a life that pursues their concerns across varying and separate places, relations, and modes of participation. While Angie's participation in organized leisure activities allowed her to explore various activities, it did not contribute much to her development of abilities for organizing activities with others while taking care of her own concerns.

Which experiences and qualities of her participation in relationships indicate that Angie may have grounds for self-reliance? First of all, she has developed friendships with other qualities than her earlier peer relationships. Angie emphasizes experiences of friendships in which she and a girlfriend not only like to do the same kind of things together but confide in each other and ask each other for help in personal matters. In her final interview, she says about her relationship with a girlfriend: "You know, we can talk about our problems – if we have any. And often she has some because she has problems with her mother. And then she tells only me and nobody else." Angie takes it as a sign that this friendship will last and that she is becoming an important person for her girlfriend. So another kind of intimacy is developing in other places alongside the familiar intimacy with her parents. Such experiences work against Angie's doubts in herself as a person, that is, her lack of self-confidence, and against the marks of her history of being bullied. Angie's self-confidence is not strengthened by being an autonomous individual but by being able to take part in relations where others also seek her company, need her, and rely on her as a responsible and capable person. Having friends is beginning to matter in a different way due to the qualities of these friendships.

Two final remarks about the changing composition and qualities of Angie's personal social practice are in order. First, Angie also changes her conduct of her social practice because the demands on her and her concerns and self-understanding are changing. We see this in her changing relation to her symptoms. She re-frames her understanding and handling of her symptoms stressing other aspects of the troubles associated with them with a different meaning to her in other relationships in other places outside home. She is coming to a new understanding of her symptoms and associated problems as particular parts of her practice in various places. Second, because Angie is only about to enter a new personal social practice, she is far from having elaborated a comprehensive understanding of what it may lead to and mean to her, the qualities and troubles it may hold, the new demands it may make at her and how she may fulfill them, and the personal stances she will gather and adopt on it. She is still uncertain about where she stands in her new social practice and about how she may conduct her life in it. She has not yet found herself and others in the new structure of her personal social practice.

An Unstable, Varying, and Changing Conduct of Life and Self-Understanding

Are the emerging activities and relationships then changes or just variations in Angie's social practice? At the beginning, this is hard to say. After all, these activities and relationships are linked with marked seasonal variations in Angie's practice. In the summer, she does other things and is involved in other relationships in other places than in the winter when she is more at home and participates in organized leisure activities apart from other family members. In summertime, Angie can be out all evening because it does not get really dark, while she barely manages to distribute newspapers before dark in wintertime. Returning from the first summer vacation during their therapy, they tell us that when they moved to the countryside, they soon forgot all about their problems and therapy. They were leading a different life. Angie feels much better when she is in the countryside. She would, in fact, like to live there. In contrast to living in town, she almost never stays home in the countryside. Angie and her family are involved in a different structure of activities in which children are not as segregated from adults and the family is not as segregated from other fields of activity in time and place. Their family relations are hence different in the countryside. Still, these seasonal variations are not completely circular. They are parts of changing personal life trajectories. We see this in Angie's new way to build on and extend activities and relationships in the countryside beyond the summer season by continuing to go there on her own to ride with a friend.

Many of Angie's new activities and relationships shift and are replaced at short intervals. While the regular leisure activities Angie attends are arranged in seasons, she replaces one by another at even shorter intervals after having tried them for a while, exploring how she likes them and what they may bring. In doing so, she looks for whether an activity may lead to new friendships beyond its time and place and tries to create such openings. If she does not succeed, she drops the activity and shifts to another, perhaps because somebody suggested it to her and she took this as an indication that this person might become a friend. There are other reasons for the instability and shifts in Angie's activities and relationships. Organized leisure activities for children and young people are age segregated. Thus, the financially supported, publicly arranged youth facilities and activities seem very exciting to Angie, but she is too young to get access to them at the age of twelve. Next year she may, but will she then still have the same interest? Like most children and young people her age, Angie has not made long-term commitments yet. Her concerns, activities, and relationships shift after shorter periods of time. This is because it is important for Angie to try out new activities and relationships on her own. She is very eager to get into new things. But it is also because it is hard to sustain stable activities and relationships with young people her age since their activities and relationships are shifting too. Angie is involved in a group of people who, contrary to what Sennett (1998) claims to be characteristic of our time, find it exciting that many new things happen and that things may shift on a short notice. It goes with these shifting activities and relationships that friendships must change too or cease and be replaced by new friendships or the revival of old friendships that were inactive for some time. And since relationships with friends on her own matter most to Angie now and these friendships are quite unstable, from time to time she finds herself hanging around at home again after a friendship breaks up. She then gets cross more easily again though now it passes sooner. The instability of Angie's friendships is also grounded in the fact that she is in the process of developing her abilities to make herself heard and negotiate her part in a joint practice on her own. She is in the midst of learning how she may exert influence in other, linked practices.

Since the exciting new activities and relationships are just beginning to unfold and Angie gets new experiences and concerns and new perspectives on possible futures from participating in them in other places, it is still too complicated for her, and not so important yet, to settle on particular long-term future perspectives and concentrate on pursuing them deliberately. Her situation and focus of awareness shift and change frequently – and in different directions. It is even difficult for Angie to identify which changes will be sustained amidst all these shifts and changes and, hence, also difficult to discern stable personal accomplishments. How do self-made changes stand out amidst all this? And how does stability and change matter in lives subject to frequent, exciting variations and changes in contrast to lives marked by stable, long-lasting bonds? Angie is certainly glad to get out of a situation that appeared stable – staying at home alone with her mother every day, and so forth – and into one with frequent exciting changes. Besides, she still has a stable family situation to fall back on for a while if things go wrong for her on her own, and in this sense everything is not changing rapidly in her life. Finally, she has good reasons not to settle into a planned conduct of everyday life but to keep it open for shifting opportunities, for trying out various exciting options, relations, and directions, and for responding to the instabilities of her situation. In a personal social practice with frequent shifts and changes and with limited possibilities to anticipate them and have a grip on them, the intense learning involved for Angie cannot merely be deliberate pursuits of change and learning. Much learning must occur after the fact, triggered by things that were unforeseen or turned out otherwise than intended and by becoming concerned with other matters. Much open-ended learning must occur. Her learning will take many different directions and becomes more complicated to configure and direct.

These complications in Angie's ongoing life are reflected in her self-understanding. Most of the time much is going on in Angie's new activities and relationships though her unstable beginnings and recurring shifts provoke temporary relapses into her old conduct of life. But, when her therapists or interviewer ask her whether something happened since we last talked with her, to our surprise she says that she did not notice. In session 12, Ingrid asks her: "Has something happened since our latest talk, Angie?" Paul: "Don't look at me. Think for yourself." Trying in vain a couple of times to get an answer, Ingrid guesses that something must have happened and asks her: "When did it start?" Angie: "I can't remember when.... I've started to ride." My interpretation is that she does not answer in the first place because she is in the midst of all the new things happening and fully emerged in them. She does not quite know what to answer because particular events do not stand out as clearly when things are shifting fast. Getting into new exciting things is then what occupies her rather than a particular thing that happened and may be replaced by another later. And Angie's situation is changing into one in which many things happen. At this time she is fully preoccupied by riding and being on her own with friends in other places, and later in the fall by a week-long school excursion and by being alone at home on weekends with Donna. Perhaps Angie's answer is also to be understood on the background that she does not see the occurring events as consolidated and is not certain what matters most to her. At least, just as her activities, relationships, and concerns are shifting and not stabilized, her self-understanding about these matters seems unstable, vaguely configured, or hard to articulate. What is more, Angie's lack of attention to and articulation of particular events persists until the end of our study. In her final interview, Lisbeth asks her to consider what happened in other parts of her life than the sessions. Angie: "What do you mean by 'happened'?" Lisbeth lists areas of her life: her school, friends, leisure time, and home life but gets no response. She asks Angie what grade she attends now, and Angie says she is in eighth grade. Lisbeth then reminds her that this means she attended sixth grade when they started therapy. Angie is highly surprised at this; it feels like very far away to her. Helped by this contrast, she says that she is better now and dares more. She started youth school this fall, has new friends, visits a discotheque every Friday night, and comes to know a lot of people this way. "So I have quite a lot of fun." She picked the course she is taking in youth school because "it could be fun to try." Her new girlfriend is a revived acquaintance going five years back, but now they join in doing other things: playing handball, going to the discotheque, and taking trips to the nearest mall. When Lisbeth prompts her to think back into the time of seventh grade, Angie cannot remember anything that happened then. Lisbeth tries to be more concrete: "How did it come about that you started in youth school?" Angie answers in a matter of fact way: "I got a letter home with me to have my parents' permission, and then I registered." She does not have a job now, only her pocket money "which isn't too good." She put up a note for a job in the local supermarket, but she does not want to distribute newspapers and the job her dad got her and Donna is too boring, cold, and ruins her finger nails.

Being Away and at Home

Does Angie lose sight of her long-term relations in the family while all the exciting new things happen in other places and occupy her mind? It seems that, to a large extent, she does. She often does not notice changes at home, and if they involve her, she thinks it is because of things happening to her in other places, such as having a horse to ride. While earlier she was home every afternoon, later she just returns, throws her school bag down and leaves again. Is the significance of Angie's family relations then changing for her or just shifting for a period of time into a different personal configuration of participation across contexts? In considering this, we must remember that children need not commit themselves fully to the arrangements of their family life and may be inattentive to many family activities since family life is primarily arranged and ordered by their parents. Parents also tell their children which chores to manage and which arrangements to keep. Children may then not commit themselves much to these arrangements but consider them to be their parents' domain and responsibilities, which they delegate to their children and may withdraw again later. At present Angie does not attend much to "her" chores nor to the making and keeping of arrangements involving her. Rather, she conducts her life in a way that presumes she may drop her family obligations and commitments for a while when it suits her. It suits her that her conduct of everyday life thrives on embracing frequent changes, variations and shifts that make her withdraw temporarily from family life. Perhaps there is also a time lag at play in the way she relates to her family life in the sense that for some time she fears that her old relations may be re-installed if she does not stay clear of her family engagements. Be that as it may, the absentmindedness in Angie's relation to life at home is the reverse side of her preoccupation by activities and relationships in other places, and Angie clearly feels entitled to this reversion and absentmindedness. In fact, she gets cross over pressures from her parents for attention at home and for having to be present when exciting things in other places preoccupy her. Angie wants her parents to stay more out of her life, not to ask her how she has been doing when she returns from school eager to get out to her friends again, and so forth. She wants to be entitled to be left to herself with other things on her mind. "Sometimes one doesn't feel like being happy," is Angie's response to Mary's complaints in session 22. She reacts by getting cross over pressures for presence and for having to be in a particular mental state. Instead of wanting her family to compensate for her life in other places, she now wants them to stay out of the way of what matters more to her and what is hers in other places independent of them. For similar reasons, it is no problem to Angie that she gets cross at home; it matters only to Paul and Mary. As far as Angie is concerned, she thinks it is okay to leave her family life hanging for a while, even when it involves treating the others rudely in a way she would not dream of treating her friends in other places. In fact, she treats people in different relations and places differently. For instance, she loves to help an old farmer in the countryside, but she hates to help her parents at home. It is not just because the activities are different but also because helping others has a different meaning to her. "It is more fun to help other people." Nonetheless, she takes over new family chores to help her mother as Mary complains about increasing workloads, but it is no stable commitment for Angie, and it fades away again if her mother does not put pressures on her daughters from time to time. In summing up, we may say that as Angie's conduct of life and pursuit of a life trajectory across places change, the meaning of her relationships, concerns, and commitments in family life are changing too. Besides, there are deep contrasts between the meaning of activities and relationships while being away and activities and relationships while being at home.

Becoming Different and Changing Demands on Others' Recognition

An indication of Angie's changes toward the end of therapy is that she makes other demands of her parents. Most quarrels with her parents are now about her claims to be entitled to decide on her own and be recognized by her parents as a different person. At the beginning, she disliked when her parents, especially Paul, decided things for her but she wanted him to do those things for her anyhow, whereas now she insists more on deciding things on her own, wants them done her way not his, feels better able to and wants room to do them, and wants her parents to recognize those changes. This pursuit of a more self-determined conduct of life is marked by Angie's reaction against her parents' prior tight ordering in that she even emphasizes her right to decide by herself without much consideration for how her decisions affect other family members and what they think about them. Issues about this are what now most easily make Angie cross and which it is then difficult to talk with her about. Beyond such apparent similarities, we should not overlook that Angie sees herself as a different person now with other important activities and relationships, another main direction to her life trajectory and other main concerns and stances about a self-determined conduct of life. In fact, the recognition thereof by important others is a part of her realization – in both senses of the term – of this new self-understanding. For the same reason, Angie gets cross over feeling passed over as seen from the perspective of her present self-understanding and main concerns. She reacts strongly against what she sees as violations of her entitlement to a larger share of considerations, resources and part in joint family decisions and activities – when she is there and it is something she wants her fair share of. In reacting to these issues Angie finds new ways to pester her parents, and she is now able to continue her pestering argumentatively for longer stretches of time. She picks up what looks to her parents like an old reaction they hoped had been overcome. But Angie gets cross and pesters for other reasons and in new ways.

Reaching Toward What?

The fact that, in her final interview, Angie feels that her life when she started therapy is very far away and hard to recall indicates that many things have been on her mind since then and that she sees herself as a different person now. Angie's earlier concerns and self-understanding are hard to reach because they are different from her present concerns and self-understanding. They have been given up, transformed, reconfigured, or replaced, that is, her concerns and self-understanding have changed. We have less detailed information about them from the latter part of this therapy because Angie became a less central participant in what was originally "her" therapy and is moving into a whole culture of youth activities and relationships outside home. Despite being a less central figure in the last sessions and less concerned with family matters, when she does come along, she follows what is said with greater presence and attention and in a more lively and joyful state of mind. Her engagement in what goes on around her has expanded. When she does not understand something that is said, she often responds with a question, whereas earlier she would remain passive or, when asked, just say "I don't know." She wants to understand and relies more on being able to. Comparing her life in the countryside in the first and second summer we knew her, we see that while Angie's interest in riding increased again over the second summer, she now talks more about the qualities of her relationships with friends. She is realizing that creating good friendships calls for engagements in each other which make friends important to each other. As something new, she talks about living in the countryside as an adult, perhaps as a farmer tending animals, that is, about qualities of an adult life attractive to her. She has begun to imagine and consider possible future lives. The meaning of this seasonal variation in her life has thus changed from one year to the next as a part of her life trajectory. Still, in many respects, her future perspectives are far from specified and definite. In response to Lisbeth's questions about it, she merely says that she wishes to have a lot of money and that the other family members should be just the way they are. She is looking ahead, aspiring for a future, and primarily focusing on it being a life full of activities and friends she likes, thus reflecting her current preoccupation with trying new activities and friendships without attending to much else or seeing very far ahead. In spite of this vagueness and regardless of whether she realizes it or not, Angie is involved in social and institutional arrangements for life trajectories that will continue to affect her life trajectory and her concerns and pursuits.

Angie's self-understanding about how to conduct her everyday life and realize her life trajectory is not very articulate and will only become so as she gathers more experience in these accomplishments and becomes more certain about what she wants. In their final interview, her parents comment that she is not just dangling along any more. She has become more responsible and tries to get further ahead. Yet, they do not believe that Angie has developed sufficient abilities to conduct her life the way she wants it to be. They seem to believe that her ideas and engagements are ahead of her abilities in her present state of development. Actually, Angie may not yet have reached an appropriate balance and configuration in her distribution and pursuit of concerns and commitments across places in her current social practice. Perhaps she has moved, like a pendulum, from too much of one thing to too much of the opposite in an attempt to get beyond the problems of her former conduct of everyday life. This does, in some sense, make it easier to realize the peculiarities and limits of what she is getting into. That said, Angie still does not want to settle into a definite conduct of her life but to keep it open for exciting, unforeseen opportunities and future changes. There is a further duality worth noting in the way Angie now pursues her changing life trajectory. On the one hand, she lets go of some activities and concerns and projects a future life trajectory from her reappraisal of other aspects thereof. This leads her to emphasize self-determination, entitlements, recognition, activities in other places, and friendships – as a reaction against what seemed to her to be the problems in her former conduct of life and as her belief in what it takes to unfold a new and better conduct of life. In this sense, she projects her future life from her relation to her present life. On the other hand, her pursuit of a future life is directed toward something she does not know yet, but which she believes will be a better and richer life and which it is only possible to search and find by pursuing it and, thus, coming to realize its qualities (and problems). This presupposes an idea about development as the unfolding of a more encompassing and richer life. Indeed, there is a directionality of development in the ways in which Angie has come to relate to her problems and expects her parents to recognize these problems and support her in overcoming them. She increasingly addresses her problems as problems for her development and in her development. All in all, though, Angie has not yet gathered her perspectives in finding where she stands amidst her rapidly changing activities, relationships, and experiences. She has not quite come to an understanding with herself and the (changing) others in her life about what she stands for and about how to conduct her life and realize her life trajectory.

9.2. Donna

Being Away Most of the Time

When this family begins therapy, Donna is fourteen, that is, a few months older than Angie when the study finishes. Two and a half years earlier, a long history of being bullied in school led to Donna's hospitalization after which she attended individual outpatient therapy for half a year. As a result, she shifted to another public school. When the family therapy begins, Donna considers it to be for Angie and does not want to be part in it. She is busy living a life with friends outside the family but still has hang-ups with her family, especially Paul. Due to the focus of our study, we get to know little about her at the beginning of the therapy but get to know her better when she becomes a key figure in sessions about half way through. At that time, Donna believes the bullying she was subjected to still has an impact on her state of mind and self-understanding. In session 16, she says: "I've always felt bad about myself. Always. Ever since sixth grade because I was always bullied, and that has hurt me so much that I was hospitalized. . . . And then people think 'OK, she is easy.' They could always make me cry and thought that was fun. I was not strong, and I still am not. I am no strong person." Yet, she sees her change of school two years ago as an important break and turning point in her life trajectory. It made her get into a different conduct of life in which activities with friends are central. We do not know whether this break was more acute for Donna than for Angie. But we do know that it was due to a special institutional arrangement of her trajectory made by experts from several institutions. Be that as it may, in Donna's perspective it was a success.

In interview 1, she tells us: "And then at last I said that I would like to move to another school. And then it has just become super. I've been lucky. I got into a nice class, and we are on great terms with each other."

When we start working with the family, Donna is not much at home. What she notices about Angie in session 13 goes for herself too: "She's got something to do. . . . She is not so cross, happier." Activities with friends in other places are her main concern. As it was for Angie, these activities and relationships are exciting and fun, and Donna welcomes shifts as new opportunities in a shifting landscape of youth activities. Many exciting things occur in her life. In interview 8, she responds to Lisbeth's question about how her life is going: "Splendid, I'm almost never here" – that is, at home. And in interview 6, Lisbeth asks her: "If we set aside the talks for a while, did anything happen in your life in the last half year?" Donna: "Oh yes, lots of things happened, you better believe that. . . . I've got another job, right. And there I earn a lot of money, right. Then you can afford more, and buy new clothes, and now I am getting a moped. And then at work I've met some new people . . . and then I found myself a boyfriend out there, right. . . . It is funny to get to work one day, and then he's there and the others too, right, where I came to know them. Then I just wanted to go to work every day." She plunges fully into what goes on now. It occupies her mind so much that her earlier life fades away fast. The frequent changes in her activities and relationships make her change her conduct of life, configuration of concerns and self-understanding along the way. Just as it was for Angie, it is important for Donna to keep her conduct of life open to new opportunities.

Living in Separate Worlds

The different, recurrent places and relationships in Donna's current conduct of life are separate from each other. Donna takes care to keep family, school, and friends as separate worlds in her conduct of life. What is more, in the world of friends she is cheerful, while at home she is isolated and broody. According to her parents in session 15, Donna "is really well in school. . . . The teachers say so too. And she is very fond of going every day. The teachers also say there are no problems. Everybody loves her. There is nobody who doesn't like her. . . . Still, she sees nobody after school, only in school." Shortly after, in session 18, Paul and Mary are surprised by a note in Donna's grade-book saying that she is very quiet and withdrawn in class. Apparently, Donna's parents do not know her life well in this other place. In her next session, Donna tells Ole that she is cautious in school because she was bullied in her former school, whereas "As soon as I leave school, I am quite a different person." She is on good terms with everybody in her class and not afraid of being bullied again, though she never feels certain that she can trust them, is on guard about what she tells them, and is afraid that someone she is close to may suddenly turn against her. That is why she only saw a few outside school for shorter periods of time, but then it was no fun any more. The former bullying in school plays a part in making Donna separate her peer relations from school by getting involved with other groups of young people outside school. In fact, both Angie and Donna have their primary networks of friends outside school, and these relationships do not cut across school, other places, and their family. They keep their social relations in different places apart to be able to control unwanted links between them. While we have often seen that the members of this family establish and use links across contexts in the pursuit of their concerns, here we see the opposite: the deliberate pursuit of separations.

Eckert (1989) shows how young people in a U.S. high school, through their modes of participation in school, polarize into two contrary social groups and categories of identity: jocks and burnouts. Their participation in the social practice of school with its arranged educational trajectories thereby contributes to locate them in terms of social class and their life trajectory. While jocks organize their social relations and friendships around their participation in school, burnouts organize them apart from school and around other places and concerns than education. In this perspective, Donna establishes her position as a burnout by not building social relations around school but separate from it. The impacts of the former school bullying on Donna contribute to this. She lost a close girlfriend who now pursues an education-oriented trajectory in high school, and it is difficult for her to get new friends instead in school "because I have a bad reputation." Once a girlfriend in school accused her of stealing a purse, and this reputation still clings to her. Unlike Angie, Donna is entitled to get into the publicly arranged youth school facilities, but she no longer finds them exciting. She prefers hanging around with her group of friends in public places beyond pedagogical supervision. They want an exciting and fun youth world on their own apart from the worlds of children and adults. This world is made in particular places and relationships for a period of time in their life trajectories. In opposing school and family they re-appropriate such landscapes, and this then orients their trajectory (Eckert 1989). So Donna's group of friends only comes to her home when her parents are away. Referring to the troubles, which then occur at home, Ole asks Donna in session 16: "Perhaps a solution could be to meet in other places?" Donna: "But there are no other places we can be. Only my mum and dad have been so open to let us in. The other parents won't let us in, and that's why we hang out in the street, and that's just as bad. People also get crazy over that. Then we just hang around and feel bored. It's a wonderful world." Sometimes she attends youth school for a while but feels bored. Still, the acute troubles at home around her and her group of friends might not have arisen if other places had been available to them. Paul recognizes the unfairness of their having no places to go but does not want to carry the consequences as a private cost. Neither Donna and her friends nor their parents raise the political issues of urban planning, architectural design in public housing districts, and neglected municipal politics for young people that leave them with a few opportunities for paid participation in supervised, pedagogical arrangements.

Taking Care of Myself in My Room

Although Donna attempts to separate the worlds of school, friends, and family in her conduct of life, clashes arise between them anyhow. She has moved further into a world of activities with friends than Angie but participates in them in a problematic way in relation to her family home and relationships. Due to these clashes, Donna is less able than Angie to keep those worlds apart. Still, the conflict between those worlds is marked by their normal separation. From the location and perspective of Donna's parents, the conflict looks like this: "Donna is so far out, so preoccupied by all the other things that what goes on at home actually means nothing. It's only about her friends." And these friends are normally outside her parents' reach. Actually, this statement stems from session 15 where Donna wanted to revive their joint life at home, but her parents hesitated to join. Donna's parents recognize that she became much better and got some friends after changing school, but she is still far too dependent on them. From Donna's perspective, the conflict rests on overlaps between diverse, conflicting relations in her life across places. At first, she reacts to the escalation of the conflict by withdrawing into yet another world of her own: her room at home. In session 16, she says: "I sort of live in two worlds, right. Because when I'm in school and with my friends, I'm a happy and cheerful girl. As soon as I'm alone, right, my spirits go down. Then all the bad stuff surfaces, right. I can spend hours brooding in my room behind my door." In her room at home, Donna deals with the troubles with her friends from other places in other ways than when she is with her friends or her parents. Her way of dealing with these troubles in her room is grounded in that it affords opportunities to brood on her own at home withdrawn from direct confrontations. Still, her activity and state of mind while brooding in her room are concerned with relations across contexts. In her room, she works over her conduct of life across places and tries to take care of herself by imagining possible events and her moves and lines of argument in discussions. Persons may take advantage of and create such a room for brooding as an in-between place in the structure of their social practice, especially when something is up and in order to prepare, clarify, and gather themselves. Of course, it matters how realistic their imaginations and anticipations are because things may unfold and their coparticipants may react in other, unimagined, and unanticipated ways. Persons cannot control real events and real others like they control virtual events and virtual others by working them over in their imagination. At first, Donna's imaginations are quite unrealistic. But – in interplay with another special context for re-considerations: her sessions – the recurrent brooding gradually changes Donna's imaginations and anticipations. She comes to realize neglected aspects, concerns, and points of view and, thus, change and elaborate her anticipations reaching, and gradually gathering herself around, a more complex and realistic stance. On earlier occasions, Donna used a similar conduct of withdrawing to get over everyday troubles by staying in her room for the rest of the day. Then next day, "they are forgotten," she says in session 19. For a while, she even turns this withdrawal into an internal exile from her parents and most friends. In session 14, Donna says about Paul: "Maybe he likes me less and less.... But then I live in my own small world, right. And then I've got my friends when I return from school. And then I have my own small room, right. And they [i.e., her parents, OD] are just there." For some time she withdraws to the point of almost never being visible when her parents are home. "This room has actually been my small castle," she says in interview 6. Her plea to launch sessions to deal with the conflicts is an attempt to get out of this internal exile and, at the same time, an outcome of her brooding. Donna's isolation and the fact that she and her parents did not and could not talk with each other carries a special significance for them. Even though they all feel disappointed over each other, they also miss talking with each other and feel hurt because they cannot and do not. In fact, by not talking with each other, they cut each other off. On top of being isolated, Donna is then excluded and excludes herself. In the silence between them, she feels hurt by a wall of blame and by noticing that, all the same, the others are aware of the troubles she caused, that they pop up anyhow and that the others try to address them.

While Donna's relations with her parents are precarious, her friendships are thriving most of the time. In session 19, she says: "So much happens, and it runs around in my head. But I experience so much for the time being. I am with my friends in X-town and have such fun. Then I don't think so much about all the other things. Then there are lots of other things I am thinking of. Then there is school and home assignments and youth school." Nonetheless, in addition to the frequent shifts in youth activities and relationships, Donna's ambivalence toward unfolding friendships with trust and intimacy because she was bullied creates difficulties for her in expanding and maintaining a life with friends. But as long as her activities with friends are thriving, she does not think much about her life and troubles at home. So it is not accidental that her initiative to start sessions with her parents coincides with a period in which both sets of major social relations are not going well for her. She recently shifted back to being more at home because of a temporary break in her activities with friends. These shifts and breaks affect her state of mind and concerns and make her conduct her life in a shifting and unstable way. They also make it less important and harder for Donna to gather and sustain a sense of direction to her pursuits. Like Angie, Donna reacts to the shifts and instabilities by not planning much ahead in case opportunities turn up. It is important for her to find a way to resolve the troubles at home, which does not lead her into a very planned conduct of life because she wants, first of all, to be open for opportunities with friends. At first, this apparent contradiction between a resolution and her insistence on openness pushes her to be passive and makes her hang around in her room waiting for friends to call. After all, the changes Donna is beginning to pursue in her conduct of life and life trajectory involve complicated re-considerations about her relationships with others. In session 19, she says, retrospectively, that she came to realize that only a few of the gang were her friends: "They did not come to visit me. They came because the others were there, right." And in relation to her family Donna says in session 14: "It will be difficult to begin to talk with each other again after so long time.... We should stop snarling so much at each other. We irritate each other in some way, all the time. But I don't know why. It's just something between us. We are both irritating, right." Donna feels caught by her spontaneous emotional reactions to the others, especially to Paul, and this may be hard to change.

Struggling with the Way I Conduct Myself

Though Donna's parents reproach her for only being preoccupied by becoming able to get into new, exciting activities and relations with friends, like Angie is, this is not Donna's only concern. She is also concerned with not having been able to handle the troubles with her prior conduct of life. In fact, unlike Angie, she is calling herself to account in a deliberate attempt to re-consider and change her conduct of life and life trajectory. In so doing, she compares the current issues with her prior conduct of life in order to reach a different way to conduct herself in and across her troubled relations. She reacts to the shortcomings of her prior conduct of life based on the troubles it has led to wondering how she should change her former troublesome mix of separations, clashes, conflicts, withdrawals, and shifts. Since her troubles cut across relations and places, she cannot resolve them by re-emphasizing their separation. They must be addressed and resolved in complex, cross-contextual changes of her conduct of life, and she must change her understanding of herself as a person involved in complex relations across places. She gradually realizes she cannot avoid serious troubles in her relations across places because she cannot identify and hold on to stances that combine them in less troublesome ways. Her personal premises of participation had shifted beyond her control, and her pursuit of changes was marked by shifts and interruptions. But it is hard to pursue changes in a sustained way as long as her life is shifting, and in the periods when so much happens elsewhere, Donna is not keen to concentrate on changing at home and does not notice changes of the others either.

When Donna begins to consider changing, it is not clear to her in which direction she wants to change nor how she should do it. She considers and tries several directions and ways to change as possible future life trajectories. What is more, she is not certain in which respects she will be able to change. In session 16, she ruminates about changing her mode of participation with friends: "But I cannot stop being nice. I'm born like that, I am sure. I've always been like that, nice. I've always listened to people and given them good advice, and people could always come to me if they needed to cry or something.... It irritates me sometimes that I'm so nice because then they exploit me." On the one hand, she believes she cannot stop being nice, wants to be nice, and needs to be so in order not to lose her friends. On the other hand, her friends may exploit this, and it is hard to combine being nice with stating her mind more clearly in relation to them: "I don't think they listen to me if I say what I mean." Ole: "Why not?" Donna: "I usually don't say much about what I mean. Mostly I keep it to myself." This tension lies unresolved in her participation. Besides, it is sometimes difficult for her to make out whether she really changed or her situation just varied. In session 19, Ole asks her: "Have you changed too?" Donna: "I don't know. Well, I don't think I changed. But maybe I did. I don't know." Ole: "Is it that you don't think about it?" Donna: "No, it's because I haven't done anything to change myself at all." Ole: "Perhaps you feel different, or now that Paul reacts differently, you also begin to do things a little differently?" Donna: "It might also be because I've gotten new friends I visit every weekend in X-town, right. And then I feel better, right. Then my mum and dad get happy too because I am fine." Here for Donna to change means to do it deliberately – making up her mind to do it, and so forth – as she does when she decides to become nicer to her parents. If she does not do it deliberately, it is hard to make out whether she changed at all; perhaps her situation just varied, as it often does. In fact, sometimes she only realizes that she changed after she already did. Until then it is not quite clear to her. She realizes it in hindsight, and even then it may be difficult to make out. Her understanding of a change sometimes only becomes clear – or she only articulates and admits it – when she has gotten over the issue she wanted changed. In session 21, Donna says: "I don't think I've been on very good terms with myself and my friends and all." This is a big change in Donna's self-understanding, which occurs when she has gotten over something and into something else from where she is now looking back and realizing the difference. For such a change to become clear, Donna needs first to have reached a situation that is different in an important respect and thus holds a distinct point of comparison. But as long as she has not established a new situation, she still partly hangs on to her earlier understanding. Her new self-understanding also only stabilizes as her new situation becomes more stable. In her final interview, Donna says about her former friends: "Actually, all the friends I had were assholes, really. And they mean no more to me. They are the ones there is something wrong with." She continues about her present situation: "I've become more self-confident. Now nobody can get me down, not for the moment at least." If her situation varies, changes, or destabilizes again, she may get down again, but not for the same reasons and probably not in precisely the same way because her situation has changed, and she has changed her conduct of life and self-understanding. Meanwhile, she has learned that she needs to go up against attempts to get her down and concluded after years of being bullied, "Now, it's enough."

Switches as Changes?

The gradual and backward realization of changes contrasts with an immediate and deliberate relation to change when Donna switches to become nicer or pulls herself together. But it is not easy to make out whether a switch becomes a change in the sense that it leads her somewhere else and lasts. As deliberate attempts to change, switching and pulling herself together depend on the consequences of realizing these intentions. But intentions and outcomes may or may not fit with each other. They may turn out to contradict each other. The uncertainty of intentions depends on the degree of realism of a person's anticipations, including the situational possibilities and personal abilities to accomplish them. In addition, it is harder for Donna to make out whether she managed to realize an intention to change when her situation, concerns, and relations frequently shift and vary. It may not even matter so much to her. In fact, it can be hard to pursue a change in one's conduct of life in a sustained and concentrated manner, and Donna may prefer to vary and shift instead. As she puts it in session 19, "All the time to keep thinking 'Now it must go well' can suddenly become too much." While change can be difficult for Donna, for instance, when she pulls herself together, it can also have an easiness about it, for instance, when she just decides to become nicer or put something behind her. In session 19, when Ole says that change can be complicated, Donna responds, "It just goes really well." A few weeks earlier she wanted to leave home because things felt unbearable, but that is out of her mind now that things simply are different. Perhaps, then, Donna switches because she really cannot change but has to do something anyhow? That is, in a situation in which she is caught in a conflict and it is uncertain whether she will be able to realize her intention? To switch is to decide with a paradoxical easiness to make a break in relation to something hard and complicated. In this respect it differs from pulling herself together because this calls on her "to make an effort to make it work" as she puts it in session 19. Pulling herself together is associated with an effort and uncertainty about its success. Whereas putting problems behind her and having a fresh start are associated with believing that many new things happen and are easily attainable, appeals to her inner strength in pulling herself together are harder and may not succeed. What is more, if she fails, it proves she was too weak. It produces a personal failure (Dreier 1988b). Still, a person can always pull herself together and stop doing it later if it becomes too much of an effort. It need not imply a stable personal change, but it can be dropped again later. Furthermore, no matter how she changes her conduct of life and understands this change, it is not accomplished by an isolated individual with isolated intentions and efforts. Donna switches and pulls herself together in particular relations with particular others in particular places that make quite different demands on her and have different meanings. How easy or hard it is to change depends on the social practice in which it is to be accomplished. Different things are hard to accomplish in different practices with different relationships. Thus, issues and processes of change are put in different perspectives by the fact that some relationships may easily be dropped and replaced by others while she is committed to other relationships on a more long-term basis.

Donna's considerations about changing her conduct of life and life trajectory take a further direction too. She considers moving out from home. One set of reasons for this is that she is "very disappointed" in their family life, especially in her father, and fed up with it. Perhaps, she ventures, by moving out she may become able to return on better terms after some time? This may seem like an easy break in a complicated problem, and Donna hints at that it might be a too easy way out. In session 19, she says that things have gone really fast for her in the last couple of years, even more so because she was held back by her former problems and jumped ahead when they were resolved. It may, actually, "sometimes have gone a bit too fast." She recognizes this as a risk of taking it too lightly and adds: "I want to prove that I can take care of myself because I still don't think they really believe it." So, moving out is also related to affecting her parents' beliefs about her and her beliefs in herself. Furthermore, recognizing and considering the option of leaving home leads Donna to re-consider her relationship with her parents and stay anyhow with a changed perspective on her life at home. Realizing that there are alternatives often makes people re-appreciate their present situation. They then do not feel stuck with their present situation and may compare situations anew.

Resentment, Self-Confidence, Self-Respect, and Change

A key issue for Donna at the current point in her life trajectory is that her parents recognize her as more grown-up and as able and entitled to manage much more on her own. Her parents' recognition of what kind of a person she is matters very much to her. In her first individual session with Ole, Donna says she does not get a bad conscience when Paul talks about what she once did because she is a different person now and would not do so today. "I've tried to tell him that, right. But he doesn't believe it." Their lack of recognition that she has become a different person troubles Donna most. She sees the trouble from the standpoint of a person involved in a trajectory of development and needs her parents to recognize her change. She needs it for practical reasons – to gain room to do the things she wants to do in the way she wants to do them – and because it matters for her self-understanding, especially her self-confidence. But the troubles get between them and make her parents not recognize her as a different person and distrust her instead. According to Donna, the problem between them has even become worse in the last months "because my dad can't understand that I am growing up, and I answer him back." What is more, because Donna sees herself and her life as changing rapidly, she believes in getting over things and putting them behind her. When she first proposes joint sessions about their troubles in session 13, she says to Paul: "Last Friday you had to tell me all sorts of things which happened a long time ago. And in the other weekends where I've been alone after we got that letter, you did not say anything. Why on earth did you not do it the other times? One believes everything is fine and you are happy, and then suddenly all sorts of things are thrown at me." Donna believed they had put it behind them, and Paul's bringing it up again unpredictably hurts her and complicates dealing with the issue for her. In this session, both parents stress their strong distrust, even disbelief, that she changed and their serious doubts in whether she will be able to change. They hesitate to join sessions aimed at resolving the troubles between them. Paul says, "I just don't know if that will straighten out our relationship," while Donna's stronger hopes for changes make her say, "It's something that affects me really much. I would very much like to talk about this." She is more ready to believe that things may change, while her parents doubt it or feel all too certain that things will not change, anticipating futures on the basis of distrust and resentment rather than hope and openness. Donna registers this and says in session 14 about Paul: "He can't get over it." Earlier their lack of recognition and distrust made her shut herself off from them and try not to pay any attention to them and consider them. "They are just there," as she puts it. But it hurts her deeply anyhow because "they are so disappointed" that it is "hard to start over again," she says in session 15.

Especially for a person like Donna who is in the midst of many ongoing shifts and changes, self-confidence – in the sense of relying on her abilities and relationships – becomes an important means to regulate her practice. She stresses the significance of her growing self-confidence for her changes at this point in her life trajectory. It may be more difficult to find out about her self-confidence in a rapidly changing practice, but much of what Donna does is also directed at improving her self-confidence. In session 19, she says that she also tries to be nice to her parents in order to "prove to myself that I can do something for my mum and dad so that they become happy." Likewise, she wants "her own place to live" to "prove that I can take care of myself." Proving something to herself is linked with her own and others' recognition of her. But her parents' lack of recognition and strong distrust reflect a harshness of their family relationships that makes it hard for Donna to gain a stable self-confidence. On top of this, their depreciating reactions affect her self-respect (Mangini 2000). Mary and Paul accuse her of being irresponsible; they say they cannot trust her and that she lies when it suits her. All this plays into the history of Donna's problems with self-confidence and self-respect from being bullied in school. In session 16, she says about her reaction to hearing how disappointed her parents are that she feels she has done something terribly wrong and takes their side against herself. She will not be able to make everything all right again and has not only let down her parents but also the person she wants to be. She feels small and stupid, hurt and embarrassed, especially because her therapists were present during this exchange. She is strongly dependent on others' opinions of her. Self-respect comprises that others can rely on her, and that they recognize this. When she is confused about her self-understanding and uncertain about her self-respect, she needs somebody's reactions to what she is doing and thinking, and she may look for somebody relying on her and needing her. That Donna becomes better able to trust others goes hand in hand with the fact that she feels less vulnerable by finding out that they need her too and rely on her. This is also evident in Donna's changing relations with her friends.

Being Told, Deciding for Myself, or Being Heard

When her parents' lack of recognition and resentment make Donna shut herself off from them, it gives her special reasons to insist on deciding things for herself. This insistence interacts with the general arrangement of care between parents and children according to which parents take care of their children by arranging and, to a lesser degree, deciding things for them. Though parents reduce these regulations as their children develop, they do not completely give up this mode of care and responsibility, and parents may grant their children scopes to do things and withdraw them again as they find reasonable. Hence, children must ask permission to do things from their parents. Donna rebels against this regulation and insists on not having to ask permission to do and arrange things on her own because she believes she is not that much of a child any more and entitled to more self-determination. In session 14, she says about Paul: "He probably doesn't think that I'm old enough to decide for myself." Not letting her decide things on her own indicates to Donna that her parents do not recognize her as the person she now takes herself to be. In a mixture of shutting herself off as a reaction against her parents' distrust and of insisting more on deciding things for herself and opposing adult regulations more strongly as a grown-up child she says, "I simply don't listen to him," when Paul tries to interfere in her relations with friends. Besides, having to ask permission from her parents embarrasses her when she is around her friends. On the other hand, when she does not ask permission, her parents feel let down and think that she is beyond their reach. Donna does not even include her parents before making the risky arrangement for friends to stay in their flat.

To resolve this conflict, Donna must change from insisting on deciding for herself, that is, on total individual self-determination, to gaining an appropriate measure of influence on matters concerning others too, that is, to understanding herself as a participant in a shared life at home. Again the issue of personal change in Donna's conduct of life is closely linked to her relations with various others. These links imply that Donna must realize that she needs to state her mind more and commit herself to doing so. In sessions with Ole, they talk about how she may have more of a say and be taken more seriously and about how this as the common issue in relation to her friends and parents. Donna begins to pursue this but finds it hard to state her mind more since "It's also got to do with my old school. It's not so easy to get rid of. It will probably take many years." She is still quite tense when doing it. When she spoke out toward some of her friends, they got scared, but they also got closer to each other, and they respect her more now. Stating her mind is related to the dynamics of recognition, self-confidence, and self-respect. Doing it "made me feel better myself." It takes getting over some of her tension in doing it and feeling better about it to actually hold more on to her stances in relation to others. In other words, it takes more to hold on to a stance than just her decision to do so. Finding a personal stance and gathering herself around it is a complicated matter that involves re-considering and linking many concerns in new ways.

Stating her mind must also be accomplished in relation to the points of view of others and to how she may pursue her stances in interaction and perhaps conflict with them. In doing so, she and they must find themselves, each other, and "us" anew. Donna's reasons to state her mind more toward her friends are also marked by her revolt against the disrespect they showed her, among other things, in wrecking the family apartment and by her commitment to improve the relationship between them. She wants to be on better terms with some of them, and the difficulty for her consists in being able to combine being on good terms with friends and having a say over things.

The complex change in Donna's conduct of life involves changing from others telling her what to do and not being heard by them. This is a common issue across her relations with parents, with friends, and in school. It also matters in changing her understanding of her problems, which she comes to see as problems of having a say, of being heard and taken seriously. This changing understanding of her problems is a part of her changing life trajectory. At the end of tenth grade now, Donna tells us she has learned to fight back and feels stronger. But feeling stronger is related to more than fighting back successfully. It is related to that in school she is now considered a grown-up so that she feels she now wants her opinion to be heard and does not want to hold it back any longer. This change in others' recognition of her in school is related to her change of educational institution over the summer in leaving public school and pursuing an educational trajectory in vocational school. This is a major change for Donna. In interview 8 in the early fall, she says: "It's not like in public school. They regard us as grown-ups. In public school we are children, right. So that's very different." On top of getting new friends and a new job, she is proud of getting through the admissions process in the vocational school she wanted and has plans for further studies afterward. The current significance of these changes in Donna's life trajectory is evident in her final interview later in the fall when Lisbeth asks her to look back at changes in her life during the one and a half years of their family therapy. Donna: "Well, I've gotten new friends. . . . The biggest change was getting out of public school, really. At first I was a bit sad about it because I wouldn't see my old friends from my class any more. That was strange, but I got used to it now. And I very much like to be in vocational school because it's like we are all sort of grown-ups, and now I feel that my voice is to be heard, right. So we are not children to them, you know. And we are allowed to stay away if we feel like it. We decide when to be absent. And we must handle our things ourselves. And that's wonderful because then all of a sudden you really find out how much you can. . . . Well, I've got a job too, you know. Three times a week. I'm a check-out assistant. And I like that very much because you get a big responsibility because I'm handling all the money, right." What matters to Donna are new activities, new recognitions, new entitlements, and new responsibilities. Education, work, and friends take almost all her time. She is almost never home, not on the weekends either, and she feels that she is almost living her own life. This makes new demands on the way she conducts her life by coordinating activities and relations across times and places. She has to accomplish this more on her own than earlier when her parents took more care of her arrangements. She now expects them to let her accomplish it on her own and nonetheless understand well what is going on in her life. Her new emphasis and obligations in relation to education, work, and friends also lead to other demands on making and keeping appointments, responsibilities, and commitments at home.

Leaving School, Changing My Conduct of Life, and Future Perspectives

Evidently, Donna's future perspectives are changing. Leaving public school, entering vocational school, getting new friends and jobs, envisioning leaving home – all this opens a new future horizon and sense of direction to her life which makes her re-appreciate her present situation in light of it. The foci and places of her main concerns have changed, and family matters do not have high priority. This affects her pursuit of changes in her family relations. She is not so preoccupied by these changes as, say, when she was brooding over them in her room. She is also more inclined to let some of what hurt her fly and get past it into a fresh start. She becomes more big-hearted and finds it easier to agree to arrangements at home when so many important things happen to her elsewhere.

Donna re-appreciates her family relations in another sense too. While being in hospital for some days, she finds out that she cannot do without her family. The chance of experiencing her life from another angle in a different context makes her look back in re-appreciation of her family life with its long-term relations and commitments. She realizes that she needs her family; they also provide a haven in the background to return to for comfort and support in times of trouble. In the other circumstances of the hospital she misses the others for other reasons which she links to her life trajectory, and she remembers other aspects of their family relationships. Likewise, Donna re-appreciates her relationship with her mother because Mary likes to hear what happens now in Donna's life in other places, which pleases Donna. In general, Donna is attracted to moving away from home by an urge to get out. Moving out is directed at a future she envisions and would like. In session 19, she says that she considers moving out "because I would like to try to live on my own not too far from home so that I could come home every day and hear what's up." Considering moving also makes her redefine the relationship with her parents from a different perspective. "I want us always to stick together when I've left home. It isn't going to be like not seeing your mum and dad because you are on bad terms with each other. I won't have it like that." She deliberately wants to change as well as to maintain her family relationships.

Even though Donna begins pursuing her own life trajectory and not just throwing herself into various exciting activities and relationships, her conduct and pursuit of it are still marked by switches, discontinuities, and contradictions. She is in the process of coming to an understanding with herself about her conduct of life and life trajectory as something that can never be taken for granted but always has to be found and accomplished, and as something that is not always equally well gathered and clearly directed. In fact, she modifies and recomposes her conduct of life and life trajectory because new possibilities arise and because of dissatisfactions and troubles associated with her former conduct of life. In the course of a complicated process, Donna finds herself anew in a changing situation; she changes her self-understanding and stances on her conduct of life and life trajectory. She does not reach a complete self-understanding of her ongoing and changing life, though. Her understanding of herself in her life trajectory is partial, provisional, and changing. It is also personal in the sense that it is marked by the constellation of contexts she currently participates in and by her current concerns, stances, troubles, and so forth. Still, regardless of whether she realizes it or not, her imagined and pursued future life is caught in structural arrangements for life trajectories, and it changes as she moves along in those arrangements. Her change into vocational school illustrates this. The dynamics of Donna's troubles and conflicts, her understanding of them, and their resolution are part of her unfolding life trajectory and are tied to its changes. In fact, her unfolding life trajectory frames the emergence and meaning of her troubles and conflicts, and it gives direction to her changes of them.

A few concluding remarks on the children's conduct of everyday life and life trajectory are in order before going into the parents' different conduct of life and life trajectory in chapter 10.

Both children's situations and pursuits of a conduct of everyday life and life trajectory are marked by shifts, and they find it hard to gather themselves and their pursuit of a conduct of everyday life and life trajectory. It is crucial to them to reach out toward a different conduct of life and life trajectory though these are not well defined. When Lisbeth asks Angie, "Which goals do you have for your nearest future?" she responds, "What do you mean?"

In fact, both children want their conduct of everyday life and life trajectory to be provisional and not settled leaving much room for exploring and seizing new opportunities.

Accordingly, the dynamics of their changes are marked by a polarity between what is exciting as opposed to what is boring, and they go by what attracts them as exciting. By doing so, they are finding out what they prefer and developing their preferences.

They both struggle to change the balance and composition in the everyday life they conduct and in their life trajectory. This is accompanied by changes in their self-understandings.

They change their conduct of life because it is involved in their unfolding personal life trajectory which is involved in social and institutional arrangements for life trajectories. We see this in the significance of Donna's transition into vocational school; in the significance of which grade Angie attends in public school and of her access to youth school; and in the significance of issues about recognition, entitlement, and responsibilities. The links between social and institutional arrangements for life trajectories and the course of their personal life trajectories matter regardless of whether they realize this and develop a personal relation to it or not. But since they are not yet through their current transitions, it is not yet clear whether and in which sense these transitions will be turnings points for them, that is give their life trajectories a different overall direction (Abbott 2001, 249–250).

Their practice generally changes in a certain respect before they change their self-understanding in this respect so that changes in their self-understanding lag behind changes in their practice. But in some respects, changes in their self-understanding are ahead of changes in their practice. Their preoccupation by what they aspire to affects what person they take themselves to be so much that their self-understanding is ahead of their possibilities and abilities.

There is a difference between the current changes in the two daughters' conducts of everyday life and life trajectories. Angie is primarily involved in establishing and consolidating a conduct of life and life trajectory of her own, while Donna is calling her earlier conduct of life to account and changing it because she realized that her troubles are associated with it.

10   The Parents' Changing Conducts of Everyday Life and Life Trajectories

10.1. Mary

Being Strongly Committed to Leading an Ordinary Life

When we meet this family, Mary is strongly committed to the life she leads and pursues her stances on it emphatically. Compared to her daughters, she leads a much more settled life. It is also very ordinary. But, although it may seem very stable, it is really more ordinary than stable, for three reasons. First, Mary's outspoken stances and commitments leave an impression of stability though she has no firm grip on her life as the family problems indicate. The emphatic articulation of her stances may rather be a reaction against her lack of command over the troubles. Second, the ordinariness of her life is in part an outcome of Mary taking charge of compensating for the problems. Third, though Mary defends it so vigorously, it is not clear whether the life she leads is satisfying to her. All the same, it is very important for her to maintain a stable family life for all members of her family, and she accommodates her conduct of everyday life to serve this end, making it seem very ordinary, articulate, and stable.

Later Mary clearly is dissatisfied with the life she leads and wants it to change. This dissatisfaction arises from calling herself and the others to account on certain aspects of their lives, which gives her pursuit of change a particular dynamics and shape. It unfolds over a long period of time as recurrent re-considerations and confrontations with the life she and they have led. While Mary pursues changes by reacting to shortcomings, troubles, and dissatisfactions of their earlier and current conduct of everyday life, Angie's and in some respects Donna's pursuits of changes are primarily marked by reaching into and exploring possible futures. And while Mary's pursuits of changes are marked by searching for ways to get beyond the troubles and shortcomings of her current conduct of everyday life, her ideas about what she wants to get rid of are at first much clearer than her ideas about what she wants instead, that is, how she would rather want her future conduct of life to be.

Mary pursues many changes by adopting stances opposite to the ones she stood for earlier, thereby trying to counter the troubles and shortcomings bothering her. Yet, such counterreactions often do not transcend the issue in question. They are charged by reacting against something by holding on to the same basic definition of the problem and just adopting a contrary stance on it. Counterreactions are self-corrections within a given framing of the situation and/or just a more efficient way to combat one's opponents. They affirm and re-produce an existing conflict between parties rather than reach beyond it. But by adopting countering stances, everybody is put under pressure to attend more to the issue and address it. Others may react to this in countering ways too as when the members of this family turn being cross into a major problem between them and reshuffle their attributions of blame and what to do about it. In this way, counterreactions affect the dynamics of how the parties deal with the issue and may provoke changes. They may also make the parties find out more about the issue and become clearer about how they want to live instead.

The changes in Mary's conduct of everyday life and life trajectory are especially closely linked to and entangled with the changes of the other family members and the relationships between them. Indeed, in important respects, Mary just wants the other three to change and believes her life will change by virtue of their changes. She also changes to fit with her changing understanding of how best to help Angie. Only later does Mary begin to pursue changes grounded primarily in her wishes to lead a different life with a different future. Finally, the changes in Mary's conduct of life and life trajectory center on changes in their and her family life while Angie's and Donna's changes center on their activities with friends in other places. After this initial characterization I shall reconstruct the issues and changes in Mary's conduct of everyday life and life trajectory during our study.

"The Mother Takes Care of It All"

When our study begins, Mary takes care of most things at home. In session 1, we talk about the troubles between her daughters in the morning, and Mary says she takes care that everything runs well: "I've always had much time in the morning because I never worked in the daytime. I always worked at night. So it's never been a problem." Two years ago, she stopped working at night, though, because back troubles forced her into another line of work. Instead, she took an afternoon job twice a week that still allows her to take care of things at home. Taking care of things at home means doing the housework as well as taking care of her daughters. As working mothers often do (Garey 1999), she switched to her present, smaller part-time job when the problems with Donna peaked. Now she takes care of Angie in the afternoons, taking her places and often bringing her along to her workplace. Arranging things for her children is crucial to what Mary means by taking care of them. She insists always to be there for Angie and ready to talk to her. Being constantly accessible is very important to her (Garey 1999, 178).

When family matters are presented and interpreted to their therapists in sessions, Mary is the natural spokesperson for the family. She is in charge, concerned to get the right impression across and receive no unfair judgment, and she reacts strongly when she believes her therapists make a problem out of her care for the well-being of her family. For Mary, taking care of things at home means things should run well and "never [be] a problem." She sees the quality of their family life as mainly her responsibility and insists this is how it should be – in the future too. So she easily feels that she has not been there enough, has not done enough, and gets a bad conscience. On the other hand, she does not have much to do with her children's lives outside home. There is a gendered division of care between Mary and Paul, and Mary's part corresponds to her location, being tied down as she is much of the time at home. Given her location, what Mary can do when she feels uncertain and powerless in relation to Angie's life in other places is to concentrate on taking good care of her at home.

At home Mary also takes care of the troubles related to Angie's anxieties. She shows considerations for Angie and orders her life according to her. "But I suppose it is necessary, then it runs smoothly," Mary insists in session 1. In interview 1, she says about how much consideration she is ready to show Angie: "There's nothing we can't do because there's always an alternative option." Showing consideration, conducting her life according to her children, and making things run smoothly are also means for Mary to create a good atmosphere at home, and she sees this as primarily her responsibility. She insists that showing consideration for her children means that she does not mind Angie's insults when Angie gets cross at her because Mary knows that it has nothing to do with her but with Angie not feeling well. We may say that Mary does not mind out of consideration for Angie. Instead, Mary talks to Angie about it afterward. This way of handling Angie getting cross is a part of taking care that things run smoothly. Moreover, Mary takes care that things run smoothly and in ways she wants by acting as a go-between in conflicts between Paul and the children, for instance, by talking to them separately afterward.

Nonetheless, occasionally Mary criticizes the others, namely for doing too little and not being grateful for what she does for them. When Angie gets cross if the morning toast Mary makes does not suit her, Mary says: "I get sad if Angie reacts as she does if the toast is just a tiny dark. But I don't feel it's a burden because it's sort of a system we've found. I may get sad because she knows very well that I try to do the best I can. I get sad when I think it's unfair, unjust." Ingrid: "You might also get angry." Mary: "No, I don't. I'd rather sacrifice, or what shall I call it, I don't think it's a sacrifice that I make their breakfast." In interview 1, Mary comments that the therapists "were turning it into a problem, and I don't think it is." Still, she gets sad or hurt when the others treat her unfairly in return for what she does for them. The children claim she also gets cross, but Mary strongly repudiates it. So, besides taking responsibility for creating a good atmosphere at home, Mary wants it to "be nice to be there" for herself too since it is the most important place in her everyday life and she spends most of her time there. On the one hand, she carries the main responsibility for their well-being at home, and, on the other hand, they should treat her nicely in return for her efforts. This is no simple exchange relationship, though. For one thing, the others may not treat

Mary nicely for reasons that have nothing to do with their joint family life. For another thing, even if there are other reasons for not treating her nicely, Mary may still feel that it is indirectly her fault since it is her responsibility that everybody feels well at home. But, all in all, Mary insists that everybody should treat each other nicely at home; it is unfair if they do not.

"But I Think It's Unfair!"

Mary gradually changes her mind so that she believes there is no fair balance between the children's considerations for themselves and their parents, or between the parents' considerations for their children and themselves. She works over this complex problem for a long period of time saying in interview 7 about herself and Paul: "I believe we have considered ourselves too little, not said what's on our mind and stood by our opinion, 'I'd like that' or 'I don't want this.'" She comes to the understanding that she has not stood sufficiently by her "needs and wishes" and now gets cross and protests when she feels her needs and wishes are unfairly treated. In session 12, Ole asks her: "Do you think you are last in the line?" "Yes, but I think it's unfair!" Mary exclaims. It is not clear to what extent this is a counterreaction against what she now sees as a one-sidedness in a relationship where it is either them or her and she just wants to strike a better balance, or she aims for a new relationship with new common grounds. Be that as it may, Mary becomes deeply concerned to pursue her new stance of defending and taking care of her needs and wishes. From mainly being concerned about being there to take care of the others to insisting on her needs and wishes is quite a contrast, which means that she has come to center more on changing her own life. But this is, she says, a complicated change that cannot be separated from her concern for the others and her relationship with them. For a long period of time she is preoccupied by finding new ways to deal with these complexities and, thereby, change her life.

Despite Mary's new insistence on her needs and wishes, she holds on to the fact that the housework and care for the well-being of the others is primarily her responsibility. In addition, if the others do not do their fair part of the chores, it is ultimately up to Mary to take care of things anyhow. About caring for her children she now says: "But I've begun to do less of it, especially in relation to our older daughter. But from when I was a child I remember going to school without breakfast. Then I hung around with a rumbling stomach, and that's probably why [I continue to take care, OD]." Likewise, she says about Angie's bouts: "And the reason why I don't make so much of it is also that I know she has some problems." So, Mary's care for the others, especially for her children, holds back her pursuit of her needs and wishes and of what she sees as fairness. Ole points out that to carry the overall and ultimate responsibility for their family life is a burden that ties her down at home. Mary gradually lets go of some responsibilities but holds on to most of her overall responsibility and so has to deal with the agonies of the conflict between carrying the overall responsibility and being tied down in her conduct of life.

Mary stresses that she is changing to minding the troubles and her responsibilities for caring for the others less. But it is complicated because, although she adopts new countering stances, she will not let go of her concern for the opposite stances – for instance, she does not stop showing consideration for her children in order to pursue her needs and wishes. It is also complicated because, although Mary distinguishes more clearly between her various concerns and troubles, in practice they are mixed up in problematic ways and, hence, not easy to separate in her relationships, in their ongoing life, and in her conduct of everyday life. Often many things go on at the same time at home, and many concerns are involved in the same unfolding relationships. Mary even has special difficulties disentangling her concerns and troubles from all the other things as long as she holds the overall responsibility for their family life and ultimately makes the care for the various concerns and troubles her responsibility. This complicates developing a new relation to her concerns and troubles in practice. She is easily caught in regrets, second thoughts, and attempts to balance out opposed considerations, and she shifts between such opposite poles. On the one hand, Mary says in session 11 about her new reaction when Angie shouts at her: "I won't take that any more because then I get sad." On the other hand, Mary insists in session 12 always to be ready to talk to Angie and be there for her. But then it is difficult to mind Angie less. Likewise, although she and Paul try to mind Donna less, it is not easy because Donna and her friends cause troubles in their home, which Mary is responsible for. Mary and Paul also have a special personal relation to some things in their home which go far back into the history of their joint life and which they want to preserve, but Donna does not have the same relation to the things in their home and minds less if they are destroyed. This is one of the reasons why Mary and Paul have a grudge against Donna for a long time. So, while Mary in some respects certainly minds a lot because of her long-term commitments and ties to their family life, in other respects she gradually minds less. Thus, somewhat later she gives her children a list of household chores and tells them to take care of them because they do nothing and she has so much else to do which is "unfair." But she does not tell them how to organize and distribute the chores between them because "they must learn to administer it." Likewise, she minds less when she and Paul have been away on weekends and the daughters complain about each other afterward. In interview 8, she says: "I don't mind that much because then they must learn to talk with each other about it. . . . Now and then I come to think of that Angie does not like sleeping alone, but then she must come along to the countryside. I can't get a bad conscience over it at least." In sessions, we point to her overall responsibility for their family life as the crucial issue she needs to address and change to become able to unravel her various concerns and troubles and link them in new ways (Dreier 1980).

Mary's commitments to caring for and loving her daughters and husband span a joint family life of many years and are marked by the point she has reached in her life trajectory. This is seen in Mary's and Donna's reactions to each other when the troubles around Donna become acute. In session 15,

Donna says that the troubles she caused at home lie in the past now, and she wants to put them behind her for a fresh start. It is no big thing for Donna to try again and do something else instead. But her mother responds: "She's done everything to ruin our trust!" Mary's deep distrust makes her unwilling to give Donna a fresh start. It is not a believable and acceptable solution to her. Instead, Mary adds: "But I must continue to love them no matter what. She is my daughter." To Mary feelings of deep distrust and love do not exclude each other. The "no matter what" resonates with a history of hardships and disappointments and long-term commitments to loving and caring for them in which loving in spite of disappointments and sacrifices may be the ultimate proof of love. Her distrust is not merely a matter of being on guard for some time for fear that the old troubles may recur, or of not being certain that things really have changed and might not be taken back again by others. It is mixed with her continued love and care and gains particular qualities from this. On the one hand, people you love may hurt you in a special way, for instance, by not caring about what you hold dear, not considering you and not holding on to what you agreed on, as Mary thinks Donna does. The repeated violations hurt Mary in a way that creates her distrust precisely because Donna is a loved person and not a stranger. On the other hand, Mary's relation to Donna also contains other concerns, and she continues to love her for other reasons too. Thus, despite her deep distrust, Mary does not want Donna to move out because she is her daughter and "I can take a couple of more years." But the complexity to Mary's love for Donna makes her feelings shift so that her distrust sometimes surfaces more than her care and vice versa. It also means that Mary is deeply committed to loving Donna but not to changing her relation to her. She is unwilling to give her a fresh start, holding on to their old relationship – including her distrust. In fact, Donna and not Mary is the one to push for changes in their relationship. Because Mary is getting older, there may have been too many prior disappointments and failed attempts, and she may be losing her belief in such changes along with her nerve to pursue the changes she wants. In this sense, Mary may be disengaging to some degree and in some respects, even while she holds on to her love and care. There may also be minor changes in her stances on all this, or she may stand less behind their pursuit.

"I'm Going to Lead a Different Life"

Despite tendencies to hold on to her relationships and stances as they are, Mary increasingly considers herself from the point of view of her unfolding life trajectory. She also attends more to the others as involved in trajectories. This happens on the background of the prominence of issues of change in this period of their lives and of the close links between their trajectories. Thus, in spite of having insisted that the relationship with Donna is not changeable, a few months later they reach a resolution to the conflict with her, which is marked by considering Donna's life trajectory. Mary and Paul emphasize that

Donna is getting older and ground the resolution in their own future trajectories too. Here the conflict between Mary's needs and wishes and her desire to show consideration and take care of her children is present but changing. Likewise, when her children want her not to decide things for them but to do those things for them anyhow, Mary is still quite ready to see this as a discrepancy between their insistence on autonomous choices and development of abilities, which then makes her continue to show consideration and do things for them. But she changes her mind on making demands on them to seeing it as a way to promote their development of abilities and self-confidence. At the same time, it has become more difficult for Mary to care for her children's trajectories because she is located at home and takes care of them here while most of what they now pursue goes on in other places and they want those parts of their lives to themselves.

Mary's concern for her future trajectory increases on the background of having been held back by responsibilities of care at home, realizing that these engagements are becoming less significant for her children and herself and beginning to search for new activities and relationships outside home. She is beginning to change the composition of her conduct of everyday life and the relative significance of its parts. In a sense, Mary is forced into these changes by her children's ongoing trajectories (Garey 1999, 184) and the changing ways of dealing with and understanding their troubles. But even forced changes may lead to new understandings of what matters for her life and of the challenges, troubles, and possibilities she faces. In session 12, Mary talks about being at the beginning of a new period and having to learn to conduct her life in a different way. This is complicated because she does not know what to do and there is no money for new activities in their very tight, earmarked family budget. While "the children grow older and I get more time for myself," at first Mary does not know what to do about her changing situation. One side to this complex problem consists in changing the relation between the way she takes care of her children and her pursuit of her needs and wishes. In interview 7, Mary says: "Earlier when Angie went somewhere with me in the evening, I went home when Angie wanted. Now I tell her it will be when I want. You sort of start to think more about your own needs, and they accept it when you tell them. I've got a lot out of that." If she feels like going somewhere in the afternoon, she does so too.

A new problem for Mary emerges from this changing situation: "At the same time, one is going to lead a different life. Because the children, we haven't seen them since last Friday. Paul and the children have not been home, and one is sort of going to live a completely different life. I've been sitting here alone since last Friday, and nobody's been home." Mary sees the new situation as one in which she must find out how to lead a completely different life if she is not to be left behind. For a long period of time and in between many other things, Mary is preoccupied by re-considering what matters to her and imagining future lives she may lead and how they may fit with Paul's and her children's possible futures. This is aimed at clarifying what she stands for, gathering herself around it, and finding realistic ways to pursue it. She is dissatisfied with her current everyday life and searching for ways to accomplish a conduct of everyday life with a different composition that is part of a different understanding of her future life trajectory. She gradually changes her points of view and gathers herself around changed stances and future perspectives. She is changing her self-understanding as her orientation of her conduct of everyday life and life trajectory, and she must find this self-understanding by finding room for her life in her changing relationships and life trajectory. As Mary gradually identifies another future trajectory to pursue, she comes to appreciate being involved in it and looks back at her former life as something of the past. In interview 8, she says: "This is a really different situation. Well, I think it is wonderful, and I'm not sorry about it at all. It is very, very different. You are going to spend your time in a quite different way."

The urgency for Mary of changing her life trajectory is linked to her changing understanding of what is best for her children. Yet, her children do not agree on her new understanding, and she must hold on to it and find ways to pursue it in spite of these disagreements. Thus, when Angie gets cross at her now, Mary will not accept it any more and protests in various ways, among other things by not doing what she did earlier. And when, say, Donna and Paul feel hurt in family troubles, Mary says in session 20: "It's as if to make me . . . Well, either I should stop talking or just give in. Paul and Donna use this a lot. Then you should sort of smooth things out and not talk about this any more. So that's why I've begun to protest instead." Earlier Mary took it to be her responsibility to take care that things ran smoothly, but she now protests and complains that the others are not willing to accept the existence of problems. Mary's protests are a counterreaction against what the others do as well as an insistence on pursuing the changes that are important to her.

"We Created It Ourselves"

Mary's increasing focus on her and the others' life trajectories and her changing understandings thereof go hand in hand with changing her mind about the children's troubles and what led to their referral to family therapy. As she now understands it, it is in the children's interest too that she does not smooth things out and that she holds on to her needs while earlier she saw this as a conflict. In session 24, Mary says that she and Paul really are the problem and elaborates about the genesis of their problems: "There must always be peace, and that's what's wrong, simply. Everything must run smoothly. No problems, don't talk about that, there aren't going to be any problems, we must always talk nicely and be nice to each other, and all that. And that's not possible. . . . That's what I think is so awful because we really have no problems. It wasn't the children who should have gone to therapy. It should have been us because we've never understood to show the children what we mean and feel. That's really the problem in all of it. . . . No problems, no anger, no nothing. It's always been like that. We created it ourselves. And when the children grew up, they started to protest against it and don't do things the way we want." She and Paul then wake up too, and conflicts flare up. "That Donna saw a psychologist and now Angie has her anxiety – and I don't think I've got anything to do with that as such – and we complain because our child is a little impertinent. Why do we take that so seriously? That's because things don't just run smoothly." . . . Ingrid: "Now you are not as worried as you were." Mary: "But I thought there was something wrong with the child." In the final interview, she says that she takes it much easier with the children now than she ever did and that she learned that she is going to live a different life. "I've become much better at stating my mind, and I feel that at work too. I wasn't very good at that earlier. It's absolutely not the same. That suits me very well." She elaborates about her relation to Angie: "Well, during the time [we attended therapy, OD] Angie started doing many more things herself. She does not at all depend so much on me. And I've stopped fussing so much over her as I did, and that helps too. She makes up her mind about things. She really does, and she's become good at it. But again it is also because I, if you express yourself clearly, they are better able to make up their minds than if we arrange things for them and say and do everything for them, or for her."

Nonetheless, obstacles affect how Mary changes her conduct of everyday life and life trajectory. In session 22, she says: "But I've stopped doing it. I stop making her breakfast if she is dissatisfied again, simply. . . . I bloody won't have that they get cross when I'm standing there to please them. So I quit." She is "getting so old that they can stuff it because nobody does anything for me, none of them." Here, and in similar instances directed at Paul, Mary uses a further means in her struggles with the others about changes in their lives at home, namely stopping to do things. This reaction is grounded in her difficulties of disentangling conflicting activities and concerns in their family life. It is also grounded in her difficulties of affecting changes when the others continue to expect things to be done as before, do not attend to them and take over doing them. Still many things must be done one way or the other, and, if they are not, it is not tolerable for Mary. So she cannot hold on to not doing things if somebody else does not take over. Stopping is meant to provoke something to the attention of the others. As the preceding quote suggests, it may also be a counterreaction not directed beyond the current problem. Actually, it is not easy for Mary to get out of those problem situations at home. After all, it is her family life too, she is deeply affected by it, and she does not want to leave the family. But by stopping she questions that it is her ultimate responsibility to do those things. Thus, in session 24, Mary complains that she carries the responsibility and burden of addressing troubles and issues and of insisting that they talk about them. Because it is a burden, she sometimes tries to see what happens if she does not do it. Furthermore, because most changes Mary pursues depend on the others' readiness to go along with them and she does not quite trust their support, she may turn to stopping or other means of provoking them to move on. For the same reason, once initiated, it is difficult to stabilize changed arrangements. The others may gradually discontinue them, and from prior experiences Mary does not quite trust them not to. This is a further reason why it feels like a burden to accomplish those changes.

As long as Mary carries the overall responsibility for what is to be done at home, the structure of her activities will depend on the others because she is, literally speaking, waiting on them and this ties her down at home (Dreier 1979). But a new period is beginning, and she does not know what to do and must find out because she spent so much time at home for so long. Though Mary has led a life across the regular contexts of her family and work plus other regular and occasional contexts, her family is the center of her life and its complexities have created the complexities of her life. She has a very instrumental relation to her work paired with appreciating that it offers contacts with people other than family, but she does not want those contacts to stretch beyond the workplace. Yet, the significance of her family life is changing, and it is difficult for her to find significant activities in other places. She tries to go along to the sports activities Paul and some relatives practice, but her back troubles make her unable to participate fully. In line with her family-centered conduct of life, she tends to want activities with family members in other places, Paul being her preferred and most realistic option. The two of them gradually extend their joint activities somewhat – because she complains about it. They go places to do things and create contacts with others. Mary is not willing to work more than she does. She has her back troubles to consider, but she and Paul take a cleaning job together for a few hours two nights a week. They need extra money for Mary, the children are not home anyhow, and they like doing it together. Occasionally Mary also goes out on her own with friends.

All in all, Mary shifts the composition and balance of her activities somewhat away from being a mother and housewife, but the family remains the center of her activities. She holds on to caring for her family and to providing the glue holding it together, not believing the others will do so if she stops. When things go wrong for them and between them in their ongoing struggles for change, Mary is still the one to intervene as a go-between to keep them going and hold them together. There must still be room for continuing to take care of them in her changing conduct of life. But the changes in the life trajectories of the family members imply that Mary is faced with rising difficulties of maintaining their home as the center of her life and of caring for the others. She increasingly has to care for her children indirectly while acknowledging that they want those parts of their lives to themselves. This is in line with Angie's dual demands on her parents where she expects them to leave her alone yet continue to understand her well and care for her.

Changing Her Practice of Care

Mary is changing her practice of care. But while she emphasizes caring for her own needs, it is important for her to hold on to a sense of the others needing her, thus feeling that she matters to them. She tells us joyfully several times that Donna found out while in hospital that she cannot do without them. The care for each other also lies behind Mary and Paul's changing relationship, joint activities, and future perspectives. To Mary these changes make it "much nicer to be here." So, whatever changes in her practice of care for the others Mary wants, they must be appropriate for her as well as for their changing situations and trajectories. She must search for a way of caring they are ready to gather around at this juncture in their lives. Nonetheless, her changing practice of care for the others is more clearly than before seen from the perspective of her changing life trajectory and makes other demands on them. She demands of Angie to accept the new activities Mary engages in, including new activities for Mary and Paul alone even if Angie wants to join them. To Mary these activities are now legitimate parts of her pursuit of a changing relationship with Paul as a part of her future life trajectory. Likewise, Mary's new understanding of the importance of self-confidence changes how she cares for her children. She need not and should not do certain things because her children are to become self-confident about doing them without her with other people in other places.

Though Mary invests so much time, effort, and care in their family life, it is a secondary area for the others, and their engagements in it fluctuate with what goes on in other places. No matter how strong Mary's efforts at home are, they are easily overshadowed by other matters and may cease to work after some time. Mary then must renew her efforts, accommodate to other things not in her grip, and wait for the right opportunity. The secondary status of their family life for the others also places her at risk of being left behind. So she must strike a new balance between her engagements in different contexts and people that may be more satisfying to her in a future perspective too. Her priorities of time and obligations between contexts must change as well as her ways to organize and coordinate activities in and across contexts with different others. Thus, if she and Paul want a joint activity with their children, they must now ask them if they would like to do this or that and arrange it with them, which feels "very, very different" to Mary. On the other hand, parents and children enjoy doing more in separate places. To Mary it is "wonderful" to be less bound by a child-centered practice and enjoy other activities with Paul and others. She appreciates it as richness in her life like she appreciates what her children do on their own as leading to richer lives. This creates new qualities of mutual recognition between them and makes them leave room for these activities and join in creating possibilities for richer lives. But Mary is at a disadvantage in these respects because first she must find other activities and people in other places while the others are already involved, and Mary's back troubles prevent her from participating in the sports activities Paul and some of her relatives go to. She must search for other activities and relationships, and if she wants Paul to join her, she must persuade him.

In a study of changes in the life trajectories of working mothers, Garey (1999) highlights the formation of sequences in which a particular work and family pattern dominates. These sequences are "changing patterns over the life course" (165), which may be planned, situational, or involuntary (179). She argues that flexibility and variation over time is called for in the lives of working mothers because they cannot simply plan their lives successfully. In line with Duffy and Pupo, she points out that these women may drift, that is, "allow extraneous events and significant others to make major life decisions for them and not plan their lives" (Duffy and Pupo 1992, 136). Garey adds:

> The concept of a single trajectory, mapped out in advance and from which few deviations are made, is foreign to most of the women I interviewed. Nor does the 'career model', in which occupational status is central and all-consuming, resonate with most of them. The women I interviewed are weaving patterns in which employment and mothering are not two independent lines but are overlapping, interwoven, and entangled. (1999, 189)

The historical moment and geographical location of women's lives also affect their unfolding trajectories as does the "form of life" they are involved in, for example, as a "housewife" of a wage laborer (working part-time as Mary), a "backing wife" of a husband in a "career form of life," or a wife in an economically "independent form of life" (Christensen 1987). Health issues, as Mary's back troubles, have impacts too.

The impacts of the constraints and concerns of family life on Mary's changing life trajectory stand out in my materials because they stem from a family attending therapy. My analysis shows that she must weave together various changing family constraints and concerns and find ways to combine them with her engagements in other places. The sequential changes in Mary's life trajectory are not just provoked by reductions or increases in her work hours or by changes in the relation between her work and family life. They are provoked by differences between the conducts of everyday life and life trajectories of Mary, her children, and her husband. Paradoxically, Mary's need for flexibility and variation is provoked by being closely tied by complex family responsibilities. Mary's sequencing follows changes and troubles in her children's trajectories (Garey 1999). Her life trajectory is linked (Elder 1998) to those of others, even across generations (Moen and Erickson 1995). It is linked to other members of her family, first of all her children because children's trajectories are more tightly regulated so that Mary accommodates her trajectory to their changes. But at any given point in her life trajectory, Mary must consider many constraints and concerns so that some may overshadow others. Thus, she was at risk of being tied down because she did not sufficiently consider and pursue concerns about her life trajectory. She was holding those concerns back out of consideration for her troubled children and, therefore, finding out quite late that she needs to change her conduct of life and her relation to the lives of the others with greater emphasis on her needs and wishes and the others' recognition thereof. This is not unlike Donna's longing for her parents to recognize that she has reached another point in her trajectory. They both center on their changed self-understanding and their need for the others to recognize it.

Though Mary's life trajectory is less tightly regulated than her children's, necessities of changing it and her self-understanding arise due to existing social arrangements for life trajectories. Mary is faced with these necessities, and they turn into problems for her because she did not move on adequately in her trajectory, seize appropriate opportunities, and develop appropriate abilities. These necessities are not the impact of a biologically fixed life course but of a sociocultural arrangement for life trajectories, which includes biological dimensions. Taking care of the family, Mary is caught in such arrangements through the links between her trajectory and her children's trajectories. As the burdens and constrictions of her family life are lifting, Mary's scopes for unfolding her life trajectory expand, including her present and future relationship with Paul. The way she pursues her life trajectory changes in a further respect. She has some catching up to do while her prior experiences of only partly accomplished or failed attempts have made her lose some belief in the changes she wants. Urgency blends with disappointment, bitterness, and distrust. She is not as confident in being able to accomplish what she is striving for, and this minimizes her pursuits, at least periodically. Her pursuits of changes become marked by breaks, shifts, and new attempts. Where persons in other situations, for instance her daughters, may jump emphatically into pursuing uncertain changes, Mary sometimes stops waiting to be proven wrong in her expectations that the others are not ready to back her and come along, wavers and re-considers her possibilities. Nonetheless, she comes to a different understanding with herself about her conduct of life and the necessity of changing her life trajectory. And she increasingly understands it on the basis of her own changing situation, rather than what she considers best for her daughters. So her self-understanding reflects more clearly where she actually is standing and gradually gathers her around a changed configuration of concerns and stances. She increasingly sees her life trajectory as something that must be accomplished and recomposed with new parts and a new balance. Yet, if changes in her life trajectory are to be accomplished, they must be done in relation to those others whom her prior conduct of life revolved so much around taking care of, but who do not seem to Mary to be sufficiently willing to go along with the changes she wants. Hence, she must pursue her trajectory through pressures, struggles, and clashes with them.

Rising Aspirations, Dissatisfaction, and Disappointments

On this background, we can understand the paradox that although Mary is satisfied with her life when their therapy begins, when it ends she is both more dissatisfied and says her life has changed and improved a lot. Her aspirations have risen and made her dissatisfied with more. That is why her pressures on the others, especially Paul, increase toward the end of their therapy. It is grounded in her rising aspirations for the future of their relationship, in the existing asymmetry between them, and in his lack of support for her when it comes to changing their joint practice. In interview 7, Mary says she thinks more about this injustice now because she thinks more about her needs and wishes. "I express my dissatisfaction more towards Paul than I did because I think it's so unfair, really unjust. I fight more for it than I've ever done precisely because the children are growing." While earlier she held on to the overall responsibility for their family life in order to take care of all its members, she now holds on to much of the overall responsibility for other reasons, namely to insist on and push for the changes she finds important and does not believe the others will pursue if she does not hold the main responsibility for their joint family life. A mixture of doubting and insisting makes her push them. As she puts it in session 25: "I still think they've got a lot to learn. If you adjust yourself and keep your mouth shut, it goes quite well. None of them want to talk about anything, and I can't stand that forever. But I guess I almost have to because if I happen to say something and want to talk about something, then they are no good and almost want to move out. It's still like that, precisely the same." Mary sees herself as the only one to raise problems and pursue further changes, and this is a burden. At the same time, her tight control over things may keep the others from taking more responsibilities because sometimes Mary gets cross when things are not as she wants. This leads to complications and much reproach between them. So, Mary has new hopes for a different future, on the one hand, and feels let down by the others, on the other hand. This creates doubts for her, both in what is possible and in herself. After all, self-confidence also presupposes that others need you and recognize what you are doing. Since they do not, she must be on guard for some time, ready to re-introduce issues, before she may feel more certain. Her pursuit of changes becomes marked by shifts between insisting and pushing, on the one hand, and interruptions and giving up, on the other hand. In session 25, Paul offers to change their distribution of chores, but though Mary admits it would improve things, she keeps heaping new complaints and demands on the table because his offer does not reach far enough to her, and she states, "It's no use."

The life trajectories of Mary's teenage daughters are marked by rapidly changing and shifting personal practices where getting into new things matters most and seems the best way to move on. They are in the midst of many new beginnings and may try out one new thing after another without making long-term commitments. By contrast, Mary and Paul have to be prepared for their children's varying engagements and concerns in their family life, but the changes in their life trajectories are closely linked to their strong, long-term commitments and responsibilities. And even though stable relationships are hard to sustain in the shifting activities of their teenage daughters and certainly must change if they are to continue, the parents are not as ready for shifts and variations and hold more firmly and grumpily on to established relationships, which also contain disappointments. Certainly adults may, for other reasons, cultivate ways to conduct their everyday lives and unfold their life trajectories in which they value the unplanned and spontaneous, even shifts and breaks (Garey 1999, 181; Sloan 1996), but most adults, and definitely the parents in this family, settle into forms of life with a more long-term stability and ordinariness. On the background of a very settled and ordinary life, Mary then appreciates variations and time-outs as lifting her out of the ordinariness of her everyday rounds and obligations. Thus, she appreciates her wider scope for variations as she gets less tied down. There are also marked seasonal variations in her and Paul's conducts of everyday life. In the summer, they spend much more time together in their summer cottage, sometimes with their children, friends, or acquaintances, while in the winter they participate separately in organized leisure activities. Furthermore, Mary is pulled out of the ordinariness of her everyday life by extraordinary events and troubles. These disruptions are so powerful that Mary changes her stances on her life and pursues a different future trajectory. In the final interview, she says retrospectively that if it had not been for the troubles that occurred and the therapy sessions they took part in, "I would still have been loitering around here like some old-fashioned housewife." In the course of this, she re-configures what she attends to and re-composes her everyday life and the directions of her life trajectory. She changes some aspects of her relationships and parts of her everyday life and replaces others. But far from all parts are replaced or fully transformed. She deliberately holds on to some long-term relationships, commitments, and stances while changing their significance. Unlike what Sennett (1998) believes, the disruption of some activities and relationships is accompanied by holding on to other long-term relationships, concerns, and stances. Although Mary comes to adopt quite different stances and self-understandings, there is no deep discontinuity in her conduct of everyday life and life trajectory. Her everyday life is turned less upside down than her children's. She stresses that she must continue to love them no matter what and is not ready for a fresh start nor believes it to be a solution for her to leave them. Her life remains centered on qualities of a joint family life though she comes to appreciate other qualities. All this is related to the point she has reached in her life trajectory, to her position and commitments in the family and the conduct of everyday life across places she built around it. The crucial meaning in her life stems from her position in the family and is closely linked to being with and for them and sharing meaning with them. If this meaning crumbled, she might withdraw, leave, or file for a divorce. She gains self-confidence from the others needing her, appreciating and recognizing what she does, as well as from being responsible for and caring for them – though the meaning and implications of this for her change. In spite of these deep, long-term continuities, Mary does change her self-understanding and stances quite markedly and talks about living a completely different life. She re-produces a life of long-term commitments from the point of view of quite different stances and understandings of what matters about it and what it takes to accomplish it. She locates herself as being in the midst of a changed life trajectory with changed activities and relationships with others.

10.2. Paul

Changing from the Periphery

When we meet Paul, his position in the family is much more peripheral than Mary's. He is a full-time skilled worker in a public agency and proud of his work, though he is often tired when he returns home and sometimes has to work twelve hours a day in his special unit because the state cut funding for his agency. He talks with excitement and joy about his sports activities in the winter, which keep him away from home regularly some weekends and evenings; he spends his vacations with the family in their summer cottage or on trips getting into a different relation with them for some time. Paul does not take part in this therapy for his own sake but for Angie's and because he sees it as a family matter. Referring to his work pressures, he says in session 1 that "there must be time [to attend therapy, OD], I think. The family is to do this together. Then we must all take part."

We do not know all the history and personal reasons for his peripheral position in the family. But we know he was a more active parent earlier when he took care of the children alone in the afternoons and evenings while Mary was at work. The troubles with Donna a couple of years ago, disagreements with Mary about how to deal with those troubles, and Mary's job change around that time led him into his present, more peripheral position. Paul then also increased his sports activities. So he may have retreated as a reaction to the past troubles and disagreements and to become more disengaged from his family.

Besides being tired and withdrawn upon returning from work, his children say he is cross. His tone of voice toward them sometimes expresses resentment and having had enough. In interview 1, he says about the talk in session 1 about the troubles between the daughters in the morning: "Unfortunately, I'm not so much at home. So one might say I do not participate so much in the up-bringing, but I think I've found my way of doing it." In the morning, this means staying in bed out of the way of the ongoing troubles while Mary gets up to take care of them. While his daughters' conducts of everyday life overlap since they have to be in school at the same hour, he has to go to work later and takes advantage of the different rhythm to his everyday life. In the morning and upon returning in the evening, Paul conducts himself in a way that allows him not to be in charge and not to pay attention to the everyday chores of housework and child rearing but to leave it to Mary. He does take care of the family finances, repairs, and housing, and he helps his daughters with school assignments, finding jobs, and other extrafamilial activities.

My materials only throw light on parts of Paul's conduct of everyday life and life trajectory. He never wants this therapy for himself but is repeatedly, and often hesitatingly, pushed and pulled further into it as it unfolds. So he does not want to talk much with us or the interviewer about some of the personal matters of his life, and we have no data from his life at work and in his sports activities. Moreover, Paul's stances are quite vague and inarticulate, which makes it harder to come to know him. Nonetheless, as for Mary, Paul's changes during the period of therapy occur because he links his practice to that of other family members and changes his conduct because he wants to help somebody else and because of disagreements over family issues. His changes are primarily grounded in his relation to his family and centered on his family life. In this respect, they are like Mary's and unlike their daughters' changes. So, although his family position is peripheral, he is engaged in it. Besides, again like Mary and unlike their daughters, Paul's pursuits of change are directed at overcoming current troubles and less at bringing about possible futures, though this gradually comes to play a greater part for him too. Like Mary, his ideas about what he wants to get rid of are clearer than his ideas about what he wants instead. On the other hand, the dynamics of Paul's changes differ from Mary's in that he rarely pursues changes by adopting countering stances, but by becoming uncertain and needing time to reconsider his stances, thus, changing more slowly, with more confusion, doubts, and brooding.

Being Targeted in Disagreements over Changes

Angie's pestering and the conflicts with her and Donna are primarily directed at Paul. In this sense, he is not peripheral. His point of view on Angie in these situations comes across in a statement from session 8: "As soon as something doesn't work, Angie blocks. She gets cross." In response, he puts pressure on her, while Mary wants to show consideration for her. This disagreement between the parents on raising their children is widespread. Since they disagree, Mary remains passive and lets these conflicts between Paul and the children pass without supporting him. It then more easily becomes too difficult or too much for Paul, who is not very good at handling such troubles anyhow. Afterward, when things have calmed down a bit and the protagonists still cannot get over their unresolved conflict, Mary intervenes as a go-between. Besides, Paul is the one to take charge when troubles with the children peak. Perhaps he is more easily upset and less tolerant than Mary. At least, anticipating that he cannot handle it and will get no support lends his anger a special tone of impotence. He is easily overwhelmed, gives up whatever he intended, and sometimes declares he has had it and threatens to leave so that, again, Mary has to intervene as a go-between and glue to keep them together. Paul adds that it often worries him whether he and Mary agree on a certain thing in relation to Angie, and that this may make him refrain from doing anything and stating his mind, and Mary intersperses: "Also to have peace." Because this pattern has been repeated, they all recognize it. The children then do not take whatever he says and does in such situations so seriously because they expect he cannot carry his intentions into effect. Instead, they may place their bets on Mary's intervention afterward. This has promoted a pattern of exchanges between them in the shape of three against one. So while Paul is addressed in these troubles, he is also pushed into the periphery and excluded. His manners and tone of voice show that he does not feel the others take him seriously and recognize him, and this affects how he now and then insists on things.

So while Paul's position is peripheral, he is targeted as a key person in family conflicts. He has opinions about the troubles and what he would like changed, and he may try to set them through, but he is rebuffed. On the other hand, he also witnesses troubles he wants to help overcome and increasingly engages in doing so. The point is that for Paul there is no way around that helping the others entails being strongly criticized and that arguments from the others for changes in his conduct play a key role in the way the family deals with troubles. So while he wants to help others, others want him to change. In other words, in facing issues of change related to himself, Paul does not simply address them for his own sake but because the others want him to change, that is, for the sake of his children and wife, his relationships with them, and his family life. Mary does not join this therapy because she wants to change herself either, but because she wants the other three to change, so she is not met with similar wishes or demands from them. In short, throughout this therapy Paul is a central target of others' wishes and demands for change, and this affects his relation to changing and the dynamics of his changes.

On this background, Paul's interventions in relation to his children become marked by what he calls "inconsistency." Thus, he makes demands on Angie, which turn out to be too high, or at least too much for her, so that she "blocks." Though it irritates him, Paul then ends up doing for her anyhow what he had demanded that she should do and, thereby, gives up his demand. He takes over for his daughter out of care for her. From Angie's point of view, his taking over excludes her too much, she has too little of a say over what he does for her, and this makes her turn to Mary. This pattern of intervention from Paul does not help Angie develop abilities to accomplish things, and he believes that many of her wishes are unrealistic in the sense that her abilities are not developed sufficiently to accomplish them. Paul's "inconsistency" is then played out as switches between making demands resolutely, withdrawing, and being overbearing. Such switches in his stances are seen in many aspects of their family life. They are a result of Paul not having committed himself to clear stances and a consistent pursuit of them. Rather, his reasons shift in contradictory ways as the unresolved conflicts between them surface and wane beyond his control.

A division of responsibilities has grown between Mary and Paul's care for their children drawing on gendered social arrangements and making Paul focus on the children's activities and obligations in places outside home. This makes Paul's care for them more important as they grow older because more of their development is located outside home in relation to education, jobs, and participation in public life, while the same changes make it more difficult for Mary to care for their development. Still, though Paul is more familiar with those places than Mary, he too is faced with uncertainty about how Angie is doing in school and with friends, which she does not want to talk to them about. It may, hence, be difficult for him to find out how best to help her and resolve the inconsistency in his stances. He sometimes tries to support Angie's development in other places by arranging and organizing things for her and leaving it to her to fulfill his arrangements. In so doing, he switches from an active to a passive mode, waiting to see if she can make it and taking over at signs of problems. All in all, and more so than Mary, Paul uses planning, organizing, and arranging as ways to assist his daughters. But the daughters see that as his way of doing things which does not fit them, and this may make them fail so that he takes over again.

Being Pushed and Having Doubts about Changing

From being a peripheral figure, Paul turns into a key figure in sessions where they pursue changes to troubles in which he is targeted or has engaged. He feels supported by the therapeutic arrangement to take part in pursuing those changes. His therapists listen to him, and Mary and his children interrupt and exclude him less. Sessions, thus, constitute a different opportunity for him. Being in focus gives Paul more opportunities to profit from sessions, the others opportunities to experience him in a different light, and all of them opportunities to cooperate in new ways. All the same, this is hard work for Paul, and he sometimes feels burdened and guilt-riveted by it. He receives much blame and often blames himself. Occasionally, it is almost too much for him. This gives his change processes a laborious, toilsome character, which is also grounded in his need to gather a clearer sense of direction to his changes. On the way, he considers and tries changing in several directions.

Paul has doubts about changing because, in some respects, he is pushed into those changes and uncertain about their direction. Being criticized as the source of many problems, makes him doubt his abilities to change. In session 8, he says: "I've probably been too weak. Maybe I am not good enough to mark my stance towards her [i.e., Angie, OD]." In session 13, he responds to Donna's proposal for sessions to deal with the troubles around her: "I just don't know if that will straighten our relationship." But on this and other occasions, he lets himself be pushed into trying, thus, hesitatingly widening the scope of issues he and their therapy addresses. Like Mary, he does not put past troubles behind him as easily as Donna because of his doubts and resentments. He even sometimes intimates that the others should not push him too hard. Thus, when Donna says Paul does not show he loves her, he responds that he does not show it so much, not toward Mary either. "You cannot expect that of me. That's how I am. I just show it in another way, by coming home every day, by being home. Some don't bother to come home." Here he hints defensively at spending more time outside home or leaving home.

Trust and Clarification of Stances

Despite these doubts Paul gradually becomes a very engaged and articulate participant in sessions and in supporting his daughters. Though his daughters recognize his support, for some time they are not certain what he stands for (i.e., how to interpret his reactions). Thus, Paul grins in session 12 listening to Angie telling her therapists that she started riding in the countryside and what she did to bring it about. Angie, not being too sure of herself either, snaps back at him: "There's nothing to laugh about!" Paul responds that he is proud of what she did, and that, perhaps, he does not express himself clearly. Angie then tells us Paul helped her. While Paul is changing his relation to his daughters, helping them more and feeling proud of what they accomplish, he must expect expressions of distrust from them for some time alongside his pursuits of clarifying, articulating, and realizing what he stands for. The uncertainty is mutual, like the growing trust, and both have to be addressed and influenced in the relations between them. Until then, neither he nor they can feel certain that the changes they believe they accomplished may not be unstable or backtrack.

While in the process of changing and clarifying what he stands for, Paul's lingering uncertainties and doubts are often expressed in the past tense as a safer way of admitting to them. In interview 3, he says: "In several sessions we talked about that I'm not consistent enough, too reticent perhaps, [not] stating what's on my mind. I've changed this attitude somewhat. One simply has to manifest oneself more today, or else they'll run you around corners." Later, in interview 7, he tells us he pursues a similar change in other contexts, such as at work, indicating that his pursuits of change now reach across the contexts of his everyday life although at first they were family-centered: "I guess you think more about everything, really. I haven't shown my stances, which I really think I express more now, both at work and towards other people in general." As he articulates his stances more, it becomes easier for other people to understand what is on his mind and not be uncertain in relation to him or misunderstand him. Donna says in session 19: "He is often cross when he returns from work. If he told us what was the matter, we might leave him alone instead of everything coming down on us." Or as Paul puts it in interview 7: "I've always given in too much. [Now] it need not only be when I say 'no' but, you know, they know better where I stand and what I mean." This change in Paul's self-understanding and articulation is, in some respects, similar to Mary's change to "express my needs and wishes" more. The similarity gives rise to mutual support and goes hand in hand with a strengthening and development of their relationship as parents and spouses. But Paul is also aware of a difference between them that makes it harder for him to accomplish the changes he is pursuing. In interview 7, he says Mary always stood more by what she said, and that the children pestered him in particular because they could bend him more easily. He and Mary knew they differed in how to raise the children, but now they talk about it before introducing something new. So, although Paul is pushed and pulled into these changes, they lead to what he now sees as positive outcomes for him with a new understanding of which challenges he faces and of what matters most to him. Clarifying his stances is not simply a process of adopting them. He must compose them in relation to many concerns about their conflicts and to finding and understanding themselves and each other anew in their relationships. The stances rest on exchanges of points of view and on unfolding imaginations. As long as their relationships are marked by unresolved conflicts, his stances may fluctuate (e.g., between interfering in relation to his children and then regretting what he just did).

Even when Paul feels his situation has improved and his abilities to handle it developed, he is still marked by occasional doubts and uncertainties. But he emphasizes that he takes troubles much easier. Thus, in session 22, Paul says that when Angie gets cross, he puts it out of his mind sooner. Indeed, he sees not minding things so much as one of his major changes. Another, closely related, major change is not giving up as easily, but continuing to pursue an issue until he gets through. In interview 8, he says about himself (though he uses the plural form of "we"): "We've learned to talk a bit more with each other and not give up as easily even though someone looks cross. We have continued and accepted that there are problems. We've kept on talking about the problems anyhow until we reached a solution. We don't take it as hard any more, you know. We've got to get through, and then we must do it."

Being Good Enough?

Believing that his situation has improved and that both daughters changed, how will he react if – or rather when – similar troubles recur and they seem to be facing a relapse or setback? This happened when Angie created a major rouse on their way to session 23, and they had to let her have her way though they saw it as clearly unwarranted and unfair to Donna. For Paul, this is too much to put up with, and he says he has had it. How are we to understand his reaction? First, his rising hopes and aspirations make the recurrence of similar troubles more unbearable, that is, a heavier blow now that he has begun to believe they are finally over them. His reaction shows that, though it is true that he minds less, in other respects he minds more. This is similar to Mary's rising aspirations and dissatisfactions. They now both mind certain things more and for other reasons than before since their concerns and stances have changed. Second, Paul's reaction is grounded in the fact that he engaged in dealing with many troubles which were getting out of hand and worked hard to overcome them though much was directed at him. Third, his reaction is provoked by the fact that things are in general going well so he is not willing to put up with this kind of troubles any longer. It is not acceptable to him that they still occur, especially when he cannot resolve them and has to abide Angie. In his words: "What the hell can I do. I don't know. It gets me down as time passes, it does, very much so. And in fact, up until now I think it went really well, until not long ago. I really think so." It is a demoralizing setback to him. Fourth, this and a similar incidence happened just after he and Mary had a wonderful week in their summer cottage. All that fell apart, but he was not willing to let go of it. Fifth, without admitting it, Paul may have entertained the idea of finally getting rid of all problems, that is, of their complete resolution. Sixth, it gets Paul down that Angie shows similar problem behaviors. He focuses on the behavior she exposes him to, but her reasons for acting in a similar way are different. Now they are about Angie feeling unfairly treated and entitled to a greater share of family resources and about wanting to decide things on her own without much regard for her parents. It has become harder to act to Angie's satisfaction, no matter what her parents do and say. From Angie's perspective, these reactions are absolutely not the same. It is important that Paul understands that Angie gets cross for other reasons, although her similar behaviors affect him in similar ways and therefore are a burden to him. A consequence of Paul's reaction to this setback is that his commitment to pursue further changes diminishes for a period. That reduces his influence on the direction his and their lives will take and makes his hopes for his and their future lives appear more like unrealistic dreams.

Paul's changes are marked by dilemmas over whether his accomplishments are good enough. He doubts his abilities, and his criteria for what is good enough are uncertain, fluctuating, and problematic. Whether he is okay and right or wrong occupies him a lot; it seems to be a never fully settled issue that is difficult to ascertain. In retrospect, he often judges what he did and thought as wrong and insufficient, talking doubtfully and critically about himself in past tense. The consequences of his actions and stances often turn out other than intended so that he needs to correct himself and easily comes to consider himself problematic. When we meet him, his daughters and wife often find what he does and says problematic, and, having changed and elaborated his relationships with them, Mary criticizes him more again in her new pursuit of her needs and wishes. Paul is easily shaken and put off balance when the others do not find what he does and says acceptable and recognize him for it, and he may react by shutting himself off. Because he is often pushed into changing, he may believe the others are right in what they are pushing him to do, but he may also be divided between being convinced by them and having reservations about their demands and critiques. Then he does not stand fully behind his pursuits of change; he may feel that they are too demanding and that he cannot and will not accomplish these changes. The pushing and convincing facilitate as well as complicate finding and gathering himself around his stances.

According to Mary, Paul demands of himself to be perfect and, hence, feels he is not good enough: "You always say it's only you. You say you are stupid, it's you." Paul: "Maybe it is." Ingrid: "Do you really believe that now that we talk about it?" Paul: "No, well." Mary adds: "You must always be perfect, with no problems." Paul's reaction may also be facilitated by feeling he is on trial and not really recognized. At least he says in session 24: "I ponder over things, feel I may be insufficient." He also sometimes gets a bad conscience over being an insufficient provider not earning enough money for the family in a situation where the purchasing power of his salary is decreasing. The others increasingly express support and recognition of him while they continue criticizing him. Even Donna supports him in the recurring troubles with Angie, and Paul feels confirmed by it. Self-confidence presupposes that others need you, rely on you as a responsible person, and recognize that they do, and Paul's daughters and wife increasingly do so. The fact that he expresses his stances more offers them a clearer understanding of what they may rely on him for. Paul also searches for ways of participating in their family, which the others want and accept, and this contributes to new qualities in their mutual relationships. Nonetheless, as long as our study lasts, Paul is not fully gathered around his stances and settled in relation to them. They only become clearer to him as he realizes that he is able to hold on to them in his pursuits of changes. Like Donna, as long as his situation is not stable and he is not over his troubles, he cannot be certain that he accomplished the changes he pursues and stabilize a new self-understanding. And when it is not quite clear to him what he wants and how he may accomplish it, his pursuits of change remain somewhat shifting and discontinuous.

Becoming More Supportive Yet Remaining Less Central

All in all, though, Paul does change. In relation to his daughters, he engages much more in their development and supports their efforts much more. He makes demands on them accordingly and is proud of their accomplishments. It gradually changes his relationship with them and their recognition of him. As his understanding of their troubles changes, he recognizes that a key difficulty for them consists in influencing their circumstances, especially other people, in adequate ways. He focuses on how to support their doing so but it is difficult because their attempts mostly occur in other places where he is not present or are directed against him. Though he is ambivalent about risky changes, the resolution to the conflict about Donna being alone in their flat in weekends shows that he is able to hold on to his stance anyhow. This and many other instances strengthen Paul's sense that they still need him and he still matters for them – only now in other ways. The same holds for the changes in his relationship with Mary. His long-term commitments to his daughters, his wife, and their joint family life are strengthened. All this calls for his recurrent working over of old ways of doing things, including how he articulates his terms and wishes in relation to them. Thus, he has held his wishes back tongue in cheek in relation to Donna because he has been turned down so often. Talking about this in sessions, Donna says that she now feels his care and that he has to state it more clearly.

Paul comes to take a much more engaged and central part in their family life. Most of his changes are about participating in other ways in their family life and coming to understand himself and his participation therein differently. His position in the family changes; he takes care of himself, the others, and their family life in a different way; his feelings and stances and the way he expresses them change; and his relationships to the others expand. Mary and Paul find each other in new ways and increasingly do things together in other places too. They even take an extra job together. Nonetheless, Paul remains a less central figure at home than Mary, primarily because he has other obligations to meet than Mary. Working more than full-time, he is bound to make other priorities in order to accomplish his conduct of everyday life. He must order, prioritize, and coordinate his activities and obligations across the contexts of home and work in such a way that he gets done what he needs to do. He tries to accomplish this in a way that contains important qualities for him, joins him with important others, and is a life that he can stand for and that points toward possible futures. The moral issues involved are linked to his scopes for conducting his life and the manner in which he does so. When Mary increases her pressure on him to carry greater parts of the responsibilities for family chores, it coincides with a period in which his employer puts increasing pressure on him at work. The state agency he works in has put special pressures on Paul's work unit and reorganized its work schedules into shifts so that Paul must work extra hours in the evening every three or four weeks. This makes it more difficult to continue his pursuits of changes at home and seize opportunities for talking and doing things with his children and wife. His pursuits of family affairs become less intense and more discontinuous, and this may also have provoked Mary's new pressures on him. In session 25, he speaks about how things have been since he reacted to the relapse of problems: "I must say I haven't speculated so much about it." There may be several reasons for this: that he does not care so much about it, that he avoids it, or that he is preoccupied by other obligations. And it is not always easy for others – for instance, Mary – to distinguish. Clearly Paul believes he may reduce his responsibilities and commitments at home for a while because Mary is there to take over and be responsible in the end. So there are deep differences between Paul and Mary's conducts of everyday life and self-understandings. While their family life is the area of Paul's primary changes, it is not his primary area of responsibility as much as it is Mary's, and this makes the dynamics and processes of their pursuits of change differ. Paul insists less than Mary on combining taking care of himself in relation to things outside home and their family life at home. It seems all right to him sometimes to divide his engagements and not pay much attention to his family commitments.

Threatening to Leave and Recognizing Differences

In fact, on several occasions Paul threatens to leave home. How are we to understand this? First, it is related to his peripheral position in the family and the status of family life in his conduct of life with important engagements and commitments at work and in sports activities. Changing in relation to his family hence has a particular and limited significance for him, and he may feel it is not worth all the trouble it gets him into. But he actually engages more in their family life, also in taking care of their troubles. In so doing, he moves further into their family relations and attends more to their family life and why it matters to him. It thereby probably becomes more important for him. Threatening to leave may then express frustration of his new hopes. He has a history of little influence on his family relations, of Mary keeping a firm grip on them and of his daughters siding with her so that he may not believe he can bring about what he wants. As a reaction, he may return to a more peripheral engagement and position or say he is going to leave. By contrast, leaving is no solution to Mary, but Paul may threaten to leave because he actually can withdraw, leaving the care for their family to Mary, thus indicating that their family life is not his as unconditionally as it is Mary's who says she must continue to love them no matter what. Still, in view of the degree to which Paul engages in their family life, threatening to leave may not be a genuine move but a defensive reaction to troubles that are a heavy blow to him and against which he cannot find other means of asserting his influence. Leaving home might create troubles for Paul. He might find it very difficult to take – and perhaps regret it.

Personal differences between Paul and Mary persist though they both change and come to agree more on raising their children and other matters. It is important for both of them to reach joint stances on more aspects of their everyday lives, such as making demands on their children, minding less when troubles occur, insisting on room to pursue their own needs and wishes, and unfolding their spouse relationship. This changes the meaning of Paul's position in the family and of his relationship with Mary and his children, and it reduces his doubts in his abilities. It is also important for Paul to realize the similarity between his, Donna's, and Angie's difficulties of having a say and relying on themselves. This makes him address and pursue that difficulty differently, finding it more urgent to change and learn by comparing their difficulties. Furthermore, they all increasingly consider the personal differences between them and leave room for them in the way they deal with each other. Paul does so and feels the impacts of the others doing so in relation to him. They also live differently with their still unresolved conflicts. In all these respects, they change their conducts of everyday life to fit the new relationships and understandings between them.

Still, some differences in conducting their everyday lives and pursuing their life trajectories continue to create troubles because they cannot resolve them or because they will not recognize them and cannot find ways to live with them. Many of these troublesome differences involve Paul. One troublesome difference in relation to Mary is that Paul's pursuits of changes are less ambitious and far-reaching than hers. On several occasions, he sums up the changes they have made, indicating that they cannot and should not try to go any further. Thus, he starts session 24 saying that they have made progress over the last year and that the last time he was somewhat despairing, but now Angie has straightened up, they will not get much further, and it goes quite well. But to Mary, who wants them to change further, Paul's reaction is the same as giving in. She gets angry at him saying that it is not acceptable to give in just because a child flips out. The children are not the problem. The parents are the problem because they have never understood they need to show the children what they mean and feel, they left no room for problems and anger, and they have insisted that things should just run smoothly. In all this, she clearly considers Paul to be more of a problem than herself.

Needing Time to Ponder and Being Less Optimistic

Paul and Mary deal with troubles in different ways in their conducts of life, and that gives rise to troubles between them. Paul needs time to consider troubles, to ponder over them, even to brood on his own. Somewhat like Donna – though he does not have his own room and must hang around in the living room – he creates secluded spaces of time in which he imagines possible events and re-considers what he can do and should have done. In so doing, he includes the points of view of the others in an internal dialogue and may gradually change his mind. This is both a part of how Paul deals with doubt and insufficiency and of how he clarifies where he stands and gathers himself around it. But Paul is less optimistic than Donna about being able to change his conduct and may become downcast for some time while brooding over his troubles. Another reason why Paul needs time to brood is that, again like Donna, he is not good at stating his mind and asserting his influence directly. On the other hand, while he shuts himself off from the others brooding over troubles, he excludes himself from their help, and he may imagine things they might think and say about him, which makes it harder for him to get over it. In fact, shutting each other out like this gives rise to uncertainty for all of them. Mary says: "The children say to me, 'Why is dad cross today'" when he is pondering. After some time she too becomes uncertain that she might have done something wrong. Paul says he wants her to mind him less but concedes that he may dig himself down if they do not talk about it.

Paul believes that brooding makes him better able to deal with troubles and that he may then pick them up later. In many instances, he prefers this way to deal with troubles over confronting them directly when they are most acute. But to Mary it is difficult to live with, and she wants him and their daughters to "learn to talk" about troubles as they occur. Paul responds: "I'm not very good at discussing things, and I've never been, and I never will be. That Mary wants us to sit and talk about it for hours, I'm no good at that." Mary: "You can learn like we can." Paul: "I don't know. Now she's tried for twenty years and hasn't succeeded yet." So, while Paul is targeted and says much in sessions and talks more at home too, he is still less articulate than Mary, his stances are still more uncertain, and his position is still more peripheral. He does not necessarily want Mary to stop talking and pursuing particular issues. He just cannot do it that way. But while it is a pressure for Paul to continue, it is a pressure for Mary to stop, and she is not certain that she can rely on him to come back to it later.

Striking a New Balance and Beginning to Look Ahead

In interview 8 just after the therapy ended, Paul is again asked about changes in his life, and he says: "My everyday life is as it's always been, actually: getting up in the morning, going to work. No major changes there, but I've also noticed the changes Mary talked about. Then I've begun to work on evening shifts now and then." He has also begun to appreciate looking ahead at a different life for him and Mary. Notice that Paul points first to the significance of his work, which has not changed much and, hence, his everyday life is "as it's always been." Still, he agrees about the family-related changes Mary had just mentioned, such as that the children changed, they do not mind troubles as much any more, they place greater emphasis on their needs and wishes, and it is nicer to be home. In other words, the changes that occurred are not major ones in Paul's conduct of everyday life, but they hold other qualities for him, including the changed significance of his spouse relationship. This implies striking a new balance between his individually pursued activities outside home and joint activities with Mary plus occasional new joint activities with their children. Paul's understanding and appreciation of his relations with Mary, Donna, and Angie have changed. He feels more certain that he needs and cares for them and they for him. These changes are primarily family-related, and family life plays a different part in his conduct of everyday life than in Mary's. In response to Mary's complaints in session 25 over her burden of carrying the overall responsibility for their family life, Paul is willing to take more responsibility for family chores, but Mary's insistence on running things holds him back. He says that Mary sometimes gets cross because things are not as she wants them to be, that they need not think about things as long as she takes care, and that he does not like to be instructed and judged. Mary is probably right that Paul does not attend sufficiently to family chores. They do not matter as much to him as his work, his sports activities, and other aspects of family life. Though we do not know much about the significance of his activities and relations in other places, it must be substantial since he can threaten to leave home.

Nonetheless, Paul says in interview 8 that he is going to lead a different life now, referring to the changed significance of his family relations in his conduct of life. The meaning and priorities of his various activities and relations must be so much up for re-consideration and re-configuration that it feels like a different life. Their worst family troubles now being resolved, he says about the new perspectives: "But besides, like Mary, I think it's very nice to be alone. We've come so far that we begin to be able to think a bit more ahead and see that it's really very nice to mind ourselves." To be able to unfold these new perspectives, their children must accept them too, which they mostly do because it also grants them more room to pursue their perspectives and re-define their relation to their parents. But occasionally they do not, especially when they too would like to do what Paul and Mary did. For the most part, though, the parents and children both enjoy doing more on their own. But in the last session Paul says, "We are very much alone." He reduced his sports activities, and he and Mary have not (yet) found other group activities to attend jointly or separately, nor do they have any real close friends. Paul adds: "I have no parents, and Mary has a mother she can't really talk to."

All in all, Paul changes his conduct of everyday life and life trajectory but not as much as his daughters or his wife. He is not as engaged in changing either, saying on several occasions that he does not believe they will get much further and that it goes quite well and has become much nicer. His hopes and aspirations are not as strong as theirs, and he is more resigned about making them come true. Nonetheless, his hopes and aspirations have changed, insisting now on a different family life and on deserving something better after having put up with so much and realizing that he is in a situation where his needs and his relationship to Mary must be brought to the fore. Like Mary, he has many prior experiences of disappointments and failed attempts and less belief in and nerve to pursue further changes though they still matter to him. Unlike his daughters, he is not ready for a fresh start, so he holds on to many old beliefs, stances, and relationships. Still, he has not simply resigned. He pursues changes though less intensely and with interruptions and shifts. Indeed, one of his major changes is replacing a tendency to give in and not bother any more with keeping at it even though it is hard.

Paul's self-understanding changes too. First of all, he comes to see himself in new ways as, precisely, a participant in family life and in the lives of the others. His reasons to change his concerns and stances are triggered by issues in his relationships with them. In other words, these concerns and stances are intimately related to his relationships with others in which he grounds and adopts them. In that sense, they point toward the lives of Mary, Donna and Angie, and beyond the boundaries of their family into other areas of his and their lives. Indeed, Paul's self-understanding changes as his relationships change and his partners change their understanding and recognition of him. It changes as they find each other in new ways and reach new understandings with each other about each other and about their shared and separate lives. On this background, Paul addresses and pursues his life trajectory in new ways. His changes show how others and their relations to him are crucial in affording and preventing, grounding and accomplishing his life trajectory. The partiality of personal understandings, changes and learning are linked to others and supported or prevented by them. In his changing self-understanding, Paul is finding himself where he is standing in his current life situation with the way he currently conducts his everyday life and life trajectory.

Pursuing Continuity and Change

Paul articulates what happens in his life in terms of both continuity and change. His life is marked by more continuity and less change than his daughters. But, in one sense, this is a problematic way of looking at it. The life of his teenage daughters is shifting and changing fast. They are in the midst of many new beginnings where some activities and relationships replace others, and they have adopted less long-term commitments and responsibilities than their parents. These replacements of activities and relationships reduce the continuity in the daughters' lives so that continuity and change here are alternatives to each other. Either there is continuity or there is change. Nonetheless, not all parts of their lives are replaced. Some parts have a longer duration and are not torn up when other parts are replaced, though the replacements may affect them. This comparison with the daughters calls attention to differences in change processes and in the relations between continuity and change. Although change by replacement creates discontinuity, various transformations of existing parts combine continuity and change. Changes in sustained long-term relations are of this kind. Here continuity and change are not alternatives so that continuity would amount to no change. Indeed, there may be deep continuities and nonetheless marked changes. This is certainly the case when Mary says that she is now living a completely different life. Her practice and understanding of what it means to care for herself and the others has changed in the same way that she understands and pursues her life trajectory and contributes to their trajectories. In other words, we need to look more closely at the personal dimensions of continuities and changes, that is, at the personal modes of participation, understandings, concerns, stances, troubles, and the like. Evidently, this goes for Paul too, though he does not articulate these matters as clearly as Mary. On the one hand, he says his life has not changed much; on the other hand, he says he is leading a different life. There are many levels of being the same and transformed, and Paul is not clear on the depth of his continuities and changes. Furthermore, some stances – like stating his mind more clearly and being more consistent – may be continuous and, at the same time, have led to changes. It is complicated to articulate relations of continuity and change.

As the troubles with the children subside, Paul is relieved that he has more scope to unfold his life and think ahead. He then pursues changes of his conduct of everyday life and life trajectory differently, more deliberately – though still with interruptions – and in a more long-term perspective. Moreover, Paul comes to conduct his life in a way that both reacts to and corresponds with Mary's, Donna's, and Angie's. Though there is a tighter ordering of life trajectories for children and young people, social arrangements for life trajectories are not absent for adults. Regardless of whether Paul realizes it or not, his imaginations and pursuits of a future life are caught in social arrangements. The troubles he and his family have run into and become aware of arose because they conducted their lives and dealt with troubles in a way that did not fit the unfolding life trajectories of its members. In order to overcome these troubles, they had to change their conduct of life and self-understandings. This includes the fact that they all need to consider the unfolding life trajectories of the others too and to see themselves as participants in each others' unfolding life trajectories. Thus, Paul develops a new understanding of his life trajectory and the need to accomplish and change it. This new understanding is seen when he steps in to support his children's and Mary's trajectories, accepting their demands and critiques. When Mary is close to giving up in session 25, saying "It's no use," Paul insists that the two of them continue: "Then I want – I would like to come here alone with Mary since evidently there are things we must talk about." He has become more ready to consider and pursue his life trajectory and contribute to others. Paul changes by being criticized, by being pushed and pulled, and by wanting to help others even though he does so with hesitation, doubts, and uncertainty. These changes do lead to new issues and concerns, many of which are closely linked to the unfolding lives of his daughters and wife who, thus, contribute to changing his life trajectory.

11 The Changing Conduct of Everyday Family Life and Family Trajectory

In this chapter I shall go into family life by taking up the conduct of everyday family life and the family trajectory. Families are involved in different socio-cultural forms of life (Christensen 1987) with different conducts and understandings of family life. Other cases than the one I analyze would therefore show other links and patterns in the conduct of everyday family life and family trajectory. This family also withdrew into a particularly isolated family life and moves beyond it hesitatingly. The parent's relation to work is quite instrumental, and education is not so important for the daughters. This restricts what my materials cover.

In social theory, the family is seen as a social institution in a social structure. This institution predates and frames the formation of individual families and is pre-given in the material–practical sense of family homes as places arranged for family practices. A particular ordering is thus created as "an arrangement of people in which they perform interlocking actions, are entangled in particular relations, and pursue specific identities" (Schatzki 1996, 5). Besides, the institution of the family plays a particular role in individual life trajectories. It is a changing, long-term part of individual lives, and a break and replacement of family membership is built into the social arrangement for life trajectories in that children are born into a family of origin, which they leave when they grow up to create a new family at a later time.

In social theory, the institution of the family is also seen as fulfilling particular functions relative to other institutions and to society as a whole. But, rather than seeing the life of this family as a fulfillment of the social functions of the family and asking how its members accomplish the associated tasks, I focus on how it unfolds in a structure of social practice. In addition, I include its members' conducts of everyday life and life trajectories. This suggests considering how the family members conduct their everyday lives in and across their family, workplace, school, and other regular, occasional, and infrequent places in a structure of social practice. It also suggests considering the significance of the timing and spacing of activities in and across places in the structure of social practice, the means of transportation and communication between them, and the structure of family living spaces for the unfolding of family life and its links with and separations from other places. The relations between family members and the ways in which they take care of themselves and each other are then seen as aspects of their conducts of everyday life and

255

life trajectories. Differences between members' participation in family life can be seen as emerging from their personal conducts of everyday life across places and from the different points they are at in their life trajectories. The significance of life in the family differs between them and changes as a part of their changing conducts of everyday life and life trajectories.

Individual members' conducts of everyday life and life trajectories overlap in the family. In the scenes of everyday life, "except for 'isolated' episodes, several conducts of life always overlap or, to be more precise, an area of overlaps arises between more or less 'shared' conducts of life" (Holzkamp 1996, 43). We must bear this in mind in the analysis of family life. A family is neither a unit with the same significance for all members or a mere copresence of different individuals. Indeed, family members must somehow conduct an everyday family life and a family trajectory marked by overlaps as well as differences. This calls for mutual understandings of each other which recognize the different and changing meanings of family life for all members and which orient a conduct of family life that delineates, sustains, cultivates, and changes this area of overlaps.

Research on the family conceptually overlooks the conduct of an everyday family life and family trajectory. Moreover, in its conduct, the family is no autonomous entity. Family life is lived and understood in relation to its members' lives in different other places and as a part of their different individual life trajectories. The conduct of everyday family life and family trajectory rests on the family being a place and social arrangement for only partly shared everyday lives and life trajectories in sociostructurally arranged rhythms of activities and life courses. To create a well-functioning and rich family life, members must understand and conduct their participation in it accordingly. Their conduct of a joint everyday family life and family trajectory must leave room for the different and changing other parts in members' lives.

In the conduct of their everyday family life, members consider the significance and place of the family in structural arrangements, for instance, by changing their participation as they leave or return home (Dreier 1980). These changes are everyday shifts in their conducts of life grounded in that different places are arranged for different practices and afford different scopes so that different things matter to them. Persons come to realize and consider such differences as they grow up and are introduced to new social contexts in the institutional trajectory for children, and they must consider how to conduct their lives in and across those places (Højholt 1999; 2000; 2001). Sometimes persons hold on to the premises of one place after entering or returning to another, such as the premises of their workplace when returning home. This may go unnoticed, lead to displacements of concerns and to troubles. After all, other things matter in family life than, say, at work, things are to be done differently, and family standards allow other variations.

Individual members' understandings of their family life and their participation in it differ and are partial. They rarely share the same understanding of their family, each other's participation in it, and their relationships, troubles, and changes. Their understandings of each other's conducts of everyday life and life trajectory are also partial and different. Due to these different, partial understandings of their changing lives, their arrangement and conduct of family life can never be completely fixed. It is partly fixed and partly has to be found and changed, including changing the fixed parts. Members must delineate and distribute family activities and obligations based on their different understandings and modes of participation. This easily gives rise to conflicts about their participation and obligations and about the timing of joint and separate activities in establishing and sustaining suitable conjunctures in their activities as a family and as persons. These conflicts are about their participation in the conduct of their everyday family life.

Due to their changing individual conducts of everyday life and life trajectories, family members must change their shared family life in keeping with its changing significance in their life trajectories. This leads to new situations, meanings, and problems. To accomplish these changes well, members must recognize each others' concerns to change their family life and their current participation in it. They may then feel connected and supported in changing their family life and find each other anew in their changed conduct of family life.

11.1. The Changing Conduct of Everyday Family Life

In shaping, sustaining, and changing their conduct of everyday family life, this family must consider the given structural arrangements for family life. This includes the significance of the housing estate they live in with no nearby places for young people to meet, a dark basement, dark surroundings with a flasher and a hallucinating man for the anxious Angie, neighbors filing complaints against them, and no room in their flat for Paul and Mary to be on their own and Paul to brood. They must arrange their family life to fit these circumstances and the social rhythms of activity of their work, school, transportation, shopping, and so forth. Their conduct of everyday family life then organizes family time, tasks, chores and activities, and their social relations within and beyond it (Daly 1996; Holzkamp 1995; 1996). Thus, it organizes the necessary and appropriate time for activities, such as eating meals and needing the bathroom in the morning.

The conduct of everyday family life must fit their diverse individual conducts of everyday life. This involves issues of time planning, scheduling, and synchronizing family life in relation to other, separate parts of their individual lives. They must make and keep appointments with each other about family activities, tasks, and chores. But the parents complain that Donna should give family affairs a higher priority and not just drop them when friends call. In other words, when other opportunities emerge, family appointments may be broken, and in making and sustaining them they must consider their relations, appointments, and obligations to others in other places. They must also make arrangements regarding the presence, absence, and return of particular members. These include who should be present for particular activities, who should stay home with Angie, who should take her places, and what should be done when particular members are absent, such as what Donna should do when she is at home alone during weekends.

Making Open Family Arrangements

But their family arrangements can never be complete because many possibilities for their joint family life are not fully at their command. Unstable opportunities must be seized before disappearing again. They all have a keen eye for passing opportunities and are quite good at seizing them, except Angie at first. They must hence keep the conduct of their everyday family life open and flexible and be ready to readjust it so as to fit their individual conducts of everyday life and occasional possibilities: When do particular members go to work, school, sports? When might Donna or Angie want to leave to be with friends? When might they all meet at home and, for instance, have time to talk uninterruptedly? Contacts, care, and ties between them are enabled and sustained by conducting their everyday family life in an open and flexible manner.

Still, it is necessary to conduct their everyday family life in order to get done what they need and want done, and so as not to create problems, this conduct must consider the opportunities and concerns of all members. Every family develops regularities and routines as a way of getting some things done based on their experiences of how it is best to do them in their family. In this family, the morning routines of ordering who goes to the bathroom and so forth show how considerations for particular members and for troubles between them play a part in such arrangements. Regular patterns of some recurrent activities may thus exist for some time before being changed, replaced, or given up. They are patterns of sequential order in the conduct of everyday family life. Other regular activities such as shopping, paying bills, going to sports activities, to the youth club, and so forth must also find their place in the conduct of everyday family life. They are recurrent activities on particular days of the week or month or on a daily, weekly, fortnightly, monthly or seasonal basis. Going to therapy sessions must be arranged in their conduct of everyday family life for a period of time.

But doing things regularly has different meanings to individual participants. Some prefer tight regulations of certain activities or of their ordinary days while others are against it and prefer a more open ordering and want more room for variations. Members prefer to do things in different ways and have different preferences about how best to conduct their joint family life. On the whole, the members of this family do not seek to sustain a high degree of orderliness. They insist on variations and are against too strict regulations in their everyday family life. They appreciate that variations introduce other opportunities and especially resist strict regulations of family activities meant to express their care for each other (Dreier 1993b, chapter 2). They prefer varied evening pastimes, meals, and so forth. Some variations in their conduct of everyday family life recur at certain intervals so that certain activities show a regularity of weekdays or weekends or recur on a weekly, fortnightly, monthly, or seasonal basis. The family members do other things in the summer than in the fall, winter, and spring where they attend organized leisure time activities separately and go to school and work. In the summer, Angie can be out all evening and move around more freely because it does not get so dark, but she can barely distribute newspapers before it gets dark in the winter. In the summer, Donna goes to the beach instead of hanging out in front of the block with the gang. Their activities and social relations vary and shift with the seasons.

There are also shifts and breaks in the ordinary conduct of their everyday family life, such as travels, school excursions, and hospitalizations. They lift the whole family or some members out of the ordinariness of their everyday life for some time. Like variations, members may compare experiences gained during such breaks with the experiences of their ordinary lives and, on this background, be reminded of, reaffirm, or criticize and seek to change certain qualities of their ordinary conduct of family life. When Donna is hospitalized, she finds out how much she misses her parents, cares for them, and wants to maintain close contacts with them.

Their conduct of family life and family relations also differs between the contexts of their flat, which affords and delimits particular homely family relations and activities, and their summer cottage where they spend vacations and weekends. In the summer cottage, they can be together for longer stretches of time and participate in other activities and contacts. Joint family travels allow yet other conducts of family life. So their family relations are affected by being played out in different places. In the first summer we knew them, they stress that their family relations changed when they moved to their summer cottage on joint vacation. Paul says they got into a different way of life, and this affects the relations between all of them. Thus, they forget all about their therapy and problems, which only recur when they return to town. Angie feels much better in the countryside and would like to live there. She is in contact with other children and adults and does not hang around bored in their cottage. Activities and relations there are not as age-segregated. Like therapy sessions, doing things together or living together in other places shows them other aspects of their mutual relations and of each other. Indeed, they often remember their family life by variations or breaks from its ordinariness. At home, family activities and relations unfold in other ways and have a different feeling to them than in other places. There is a sense of familiarity, intimacy, and boredom about homely activities, whereas activities and relations – also family activities and relations – in other places are marked by another kind of openness to suggestions, by uncertainty, and by more excitement. Thus, Angie likes to help an old farmer in the countryside but does not like to help her parents at home. Sveen (2000) uses the sports metaphor of home field and away field to point to such differences in the unfolding and meaning of activities and relations. That said, the meaning of these variations changes as their life trajectories unfold and as changes lead to other variations. This goes for the variation between living at home and in the countryside too. Thus, soon Donna and Angie do not care to come along to the summer cottage any longer, and the meaning of being there changes for Paul and Mary into enjoying the tranquility and loosening constraints on them.

Arranging Family Life for Family Matters

As a social institution, the family is arranged for particular human concerns. Other things are important here than at work or in school while some things really do not belong in family life. Family life makes particular demands on its members' participation, commitments, and emotions (Bruner 1990, 133). Cultural understandings of family life serve as references for concrete families' conduct of their family life. The family home is a figured world with a culturally preshaped meaning (Holland et al. 1998). Leisure rather than pressure for efficiency should prevail with a greater range of acceptable performances. Taking care of each other is crucial to family life. As Mary insists, caring for each other should be reciprocal. They must like each other and show it, and when one member does something for another or for everybody, they should respond positively and not, for instance, get cross. Mutual sympathy is in demand (Dreier 1980). They should also attend to each other at home and be mentally present, not absentminded. These cultural pre-understandings and emotional commitments are not always on their minds, though. They may, in fact, be taken for granted and not attended to by some members for a while. Though they are obvious to everybody, they may not be apparent in the ordinariness of their everyday family life. Variations and troubles in their ordinary life, or opportunities for comparing it with experiences from participating in other places, may then remind members of these core qualities and make them re-appreciate them, that is, re-affirm or change them.

Though general cultural understandings and arrangements of family life substantially impact how this family is lived and understood, they have different meanings to individual members. Members' lives are affected differently by it since it is a different part of their individual conducts of everyday life. They occupy different positions in their family, and its shared arrangements have different implications for them. Family arrangements hold different responsibilities and burdens, considerations and support, recognition and exclusion, and relations of different qualities for them. Their commitments to it differ depending on whether it is their family of origin or the family they created for themselves. The parents relate to it with a feeling of having settled in it, which their children do not want. The parents are preoccupied by long-term commitments and responsibilities in relation to it, while their children are preoccupied by expanding their participation in other places. On the one hand, the parents do not think their children give sufficient priority to their shared family life; on the other hand, they enjoy watching their children getting into new things in the world outside and must be prepared for their children's shifting engagements and concerns in it. The children, on their part, do not feel responsible for conducting this family life. In a sense, they do not feel it is theirs' as much as their parents' who grant and withdraw permissions and chores to them. For the children, this family life is only the beginning of another as yet unknown life they will lead later apart from each other, probably in another family together with others. They expect to leave it some time, and at least Donna is looking forward to it. In some respects, members do not fully understand and recognize how other members relate to it. We see this in how they take care of family possessions where the meaning of past experiences and an emphasis on continuity play a greater part for the parents and make them distance themselves from Donna's and Angie's conducts. Another instance is the contrast between Donna's readiness for a fresh start and Paul and Mary's distrusts and doubts in whether changes and new arrangements can be accomplished. They find it hard to understand each others' different perspectives and are hurt by the lack of recognition of these differences. There are deep differences between the meaning of their shared family life for Mary and Paul too. While their shared family life is the center of Mary's everyday life and she is the key person in sustaining and conducting it, Paul is preoccupied by his job and sports activities, and, though his engagement in family life increases, he continues to believe he could reduce it if he so wished. For a long time, Paul has been a peripheral and targeted person in matters of raising their children while Mary took charge. In interview 7, Paul says: "Mary has always had very strong opinions. And that's why it's always been me who tried to bend a little because I've not stood so firmly. They've always been able to bend me. If they pestered me enough, I would give in." Their children have a keen eye for such differences between their parents and know how to take advantage of it.

Discords between them arise over the significance and boundaries of family life in relation to their lives in other places because it is a different part in their individual conducts of everyday life. Thus, for some time, Angie turns into a bored and irritable participant in family life who wants the others to show unreciprocated considerations for her because she is unable to conduct her life in the structure of activities across places that she wants. Donna's participation in family life is deeply affected by her conduct in other places, and she is unable to resolve the troubles created at home by intrusions from other relations. Mary is deeply committed to taking care of their shared family life, but she increasingly faces the tensions it creates for her between showing considerations for the others, even though "They don't show any considerations for me. None of them!" and their support for the changes she wants at home is ambivalent. Paul is away most of the time and at first knows how not to become too involved in family troubles while his increasing engagement in family life is mixed with doubts and the feeling that he can always withdraw again if it gets too much for him. The point is that due to such differences between their conducts of everyday life, they are only partly able to gather around a joint conduct of everyday family life. It must include their different personal conducts of everyday life in different ways and degrees. Their overlapping lives fit incompletely in a shared conduct of everyday family life, and they find it difficult to address the unsettled issues and reach joint arrangements of them. That is part of the reason why Mary takes so much over for some time. These difficulties are a matter of what is practicable for them, what is attractive and agreeable to them, and what it is fair to stand for in relation to each other and the future of their shared lives.

Considering Other Parts of Members' Lives

Everyday family life is divided into two parts: one in the morning and another later in the day and in the evening when members return from work, school, and other activities elsewhere. This social arrangement of rhythms of activities in the structure of social practice deeply constrains the shaping of a conduct of everyday family life and introduces issues to be resolved in order to accomplish it well. How to manage members' transitions out of and into the family is such an issue. The person moving through the transition may find ways of dealing with it such as using transportation time to disengage from the former place and read a magazine or a newspaper or in other ways hold him- or herself a bit apart from the others upon returning so as to gradually tune in on what is coming. The persons receiving homecoming members may find ways of doing so such as leaving him or her alone for a while, offering a refreshment, or asking how the day has been and striking up a conversation that eases the person well into their joint life. The ways of dealing with returns must also fit the conduct of everyday life of the receiving person and her concerns when the others return. In this family, Mary is alone to receive Angie when she returns from school. In session 11, Mary says: "She's rarely in a good spirit like today, happy, throwing her school bag into a corner and starting to talk." Ingrid: "How do you think Angie returns?" Mary: "A little sad and sometimes quite irritable. You definitely shouldn't happen to say 'Hi' in the wrong way, then. . . . But then I ignore her, and then it usually passes." Angie says she does not notice how she reacts when she returns but wants Mary to leave her alone for a while. She wants to be by herself for a while but not to care that she lets her mood hit down on her mother uncensored. For Mary, though, this is not acceptable. She spends most of her day at home taking care of the others, and her life depends on having a nice time with them at home. Mary: "She should not vent her bad mood on me. I've been home all day having a nice time, and then Angie returns from school. Donna might do the same." Mary finds it difficult not to be hurt by these reactions and definitely wants Angie to manage this transition better. But Mary is also uncertain how to understand and react to it. Angie might be cross at Mary for some reason, or she might be in a bad mood because of troubles in school, and then Mary would want to be overbearing and help her plus try to make her stop displacing troubles. But it is difficult for Mary to distinguish what is the matter so she cannot be entirely certain what to try to teach Angie about handling transitions.

In the conduct of everyday family life, there is no way around considering the other parts of the members' everyday lives. Family members must try to understand the parts of others' lives in which they do not participate and find ways to handle the uncertainty about what they do and do not understand. In session 11, Ingrid asks: "What do you as parents know about how Angie is when she is with others?" Mary: "I'm usually only told that they are well behaved, nice." Paul: "Exemplary." Mary: "And capable, precisely according to the book." Ingrid: "Because I recognize from many other families that it's at home that the problems . . ." Mary: "Yes, yes. It's absolutely not when they are out. In school they say that they attend to their things, are well-behaved and well brought up, do what they are told, and so on. That's the only thing I've been told." Being thus informed, Mary and Paul likely believe that whatever problems occur at home are somehow grounded in their lives at home. But Mary continues: "And then Angie returns telling me she is irritated because the kids are very noisy. But the teacher only knows what goes on in class, not in the breaks." Whom should Mary believe, then, especially when none of her sources cover everything she wants to know? The uncertainty goes so far that Mary and Paul are not sure whether some of their daughters' current troubles go back to being bullied in their old school two years ago.

Besides the uncertainties of understanding members' lives in other places, the family cannot control the impact of events in other places on its members nor keep these impacts away from their family life. They must be ready to readjust their conduct of family life in line with such external events. Because their influence on what happens in other places is limited, they easily have reasons to get worried. In the next session, session 12, after our meeting with Angie's teachers, Mary is now worried that Angie might be too quiet and passive: "I've been like that in school too. I also always sat in a corner. It was terrible, and then it makes me sad to hear when my own children – except Donna – often just sit there. Like her teacher said: when asked, she answers." Angie objects that the other children ridicule her if she raises her hand in class. So how may her parents care about this other part of her life?

Other concerns point in the opposite direction of uncertainties and worries. They appreciate the richness in each others' lives afforded by activities in other places. From their location in the family, they seek to leave room for them, support them, and join in creating such possibilities for richer lives and relations (Haavind 2002). Donna says appreciatively that Angie has exciting things to do, meaning things outside the home, and that her mother loves to hear what Donna is doing elsewhere, which brings them closer to each other. Paul and Mary often enjoy that Angie is doing things in other places. Mary sews a horse blanket for her riding, and Paul makes a box for her gear in the stable. But Angie insists the box must be finished here and now and gets cross because Paul did not make it immediately. Paul: "She does not consider whether it fits what I'm doing." Supporting their children in other places may still create troubles at home.

One thing family members can do at home when they cannot know directly what goes on in members' lives in other places is to rely on asking when they return how they have been doing today in school, at work, and so forth. In this way they show they care and strike up a conversation in which they pursue their care. They build family relations in which members care for each other, in other places too, by telling and commemorating, perhaps consulting each other and working over troubling issues afterwards at home. To many people, this is an important part of what family life should be: a haven to return to where people do care for each other and where they may work over everything – that is, as seen from the particular location and concerns of family life. At least it does not make sense to divide the care for other family members into parts and only care for their lives at home. Indeed, family care should be about "the whole person" and not about parts of their lives. In contrast, professional care, say for colleagues at work or for children in school and kindergarten, is divided and partial. Yet, how can family members pursue such care by talking when members such as Angie or Donna, do not want to talk about it? They want to keep their lives in other places to themselves, that is, separate from the family supervision, consultation, and judgment, which talking about it easily entails. Instead, Mary then watches how Angie is when she returns, but this irritates Angie who wants to be left to herself, and Angie's irritation bothers Mary.

Telecommunication is a means for family care when members are in different places as when telephone lines from workplaces get busy when children return from school (Aldous 1996, 8–9), children are asked to call home while on school excursions, or cell phones are used to care for children being out alone in late evenings. Still, an important part of caring for how family members are doing in other places must be to support their self-confidence because they will be in other places without the caring companionship of their family members, and because they want to have greater parts of their lives in other places to themselves. Their coparticipants in other places also often dislike or ridicule family, especially parental, supervision and intervention.

Because family life is only a part of its members' everyday lives, its links and separations from their activities in other places matter for how it may be conducted. Conducting it well involves striking a good balance between isolation and dispersal of the family. When we meet this family, it is quite isolated and has broken off some prior contacts in response to its growing troubles. Unlike many Danish families, the parents have no regular contacts in associations, clubs, evening schools, and the like aside from Paul's sports activities. Looking back at their troubles in the last session Paul says: "Many things may also be because we are quite isolated. We have nobody to share our worries with. I have no parents, and Mary has a mum she can't really talk to. . . . Nobody ever thinks about how we are." Mary: "No." Paul: "We've never had any close friends." Their neighborhood is not very inviting. In session 21, Mary says: "Our neighbors are real busybodies. They really are. You can barely walk across the floor before they – they are really nasty. And, of course, we are nervous that they are going to [file a complaint, OD]." The rules they set up for Donna being alone at home are marked by their consideration for these nasty neighbors who accused Donna of all sorts of things. Their kin also reacted against Donna when she "flipped out" a couple of years ago. She became unpopular, they will not take her to visit them, and she will not go. They side with their daughter against their kin and have withdrawn from them as a reaction. Distancing itself from its surroundings the family ties itself down in deeper isolation. They see no relatives and friends, and their children do not bring friends home because nothing exciting goes on in this isolated family. Instead, the children visit friends in their homes, except that the other families do not want to let Donna's gang in. As the children extend their activities in other places and the family is still not very good at gathering around a joint conduct of family life, the opposite of isolation threatens their family life, namely dispersal. It is difficult for them to gather at all, to make appointments, not to be interrupted by more exciting opportunities, and so forth. Scheduling therapy sessions also becomes more complicated.

Taking Care of Each Other at Home

Family members cannot take care of each other at home by considering only their shared life at home. It involves relating to each others' lives in other places too. Talking to each other, noticing how each other are, leaving each other be, and supporting each others' self-confidence are means of caring for each other in other places from at home. Parents take care of their children from at home by structuring their conduct of everyday life: Making them get out of bed, preparing breakfast for them, sending them to school in time, telling them when to return home, taking them places, scheduling meals and bedtimes, and so forth, gradually allowing them to take over more of their conduct of everyday life without ever leaving all responsibility to them. Doing this is crucial to what Paul and Mary mean by taking care of their children. When their children seem unwilling to accomplish the part the parents assume they should, Paul tends to put pressure on them while Mary tends to show consideration. Showing consideration is crucial to Mary's understanding of love and care and an expression of sympathy and pity for a troubled Angie. Mary then takes more things upon herself as the easiest way to "make things run smoothly." In general, parents are quite ready to take over and feel they want and should take care of things for their children when their children cannot on their own or their parents believe their children will not be able to because of their lack of abilities and understanding of what is at stake and what it takes to accomplish something. Parents then redefine their children's scopes by re-appropriating some of their parental authority and responsibilities. But by taking over, the parents may eventually do too much so that the children do not develop their abilities and self-confidence. In session 12, Ingrid asks: "Why do you think you got into doing many things for her?" Mary: "Yes, why? There are probably many reasons. It's probably the terrible thing built into you that you should do as much as possible, and unfortunately too much, right. Because when you do something, you don't think of that you might harm somebody by not letting them do it themselves." To conduct an everyday family life well, uncertainties about how best to care for each other and about the suitable delineation of individual chores and responsibilities must be addressed and negotiated. But "The others won't talk," Mary often complains, and conflicts between them persist about the conduct of their shared family life. These conflicts are about their care for each other, their distribution of chores and responsibilities, their ordering and timing of activities and presence in the family, and their organizing of joint and separate activities.

In order to succeed, the conduct of everyday family life must incorporate suitable ways of caring for each other, and family members must rely on each other to make it work. They must rely on each other too when they seek to move beyond troubles and conflicts and change everyday family arrangements. The significance of relying on each other is also evident when they do not quite do so, that is, when the daughters do not quite trust Paul and he does not trust them or Mary does not quite rely on Paul and her daughters to be willing to continue changing the aspects of their joint life she wants changed. Distrust then gets in the way of establishing and sustaining a suitable conduct of everyday family life. But even when they distrust each other, they need to rely on each other to some degree in order to get through the day at home. It is, of course, easier to understand another member's needs when she articulates and pursues them openly. As long as she does not, it is difficult for the others to understand her as a person and really rely on her, and when she begins to do so much more, the others change their understandings of her. Members may then more clearly consider each others' needs in finding their individual ways of participating in family life. When Mary complains that her children think only of themselves, this self-centeredness must also be seen on the background that Mary did not make them aware of her needs – which they do consider and support once Mary articulates and pursues them. Articulating and pursuing their needs increases their understanding of the interpersonal dimensions of their lives so that they may find each other and come to understandings with each other in new ways. The significance of needing each other and relying on each other is also evident in Donna's isolation in her room where the fact that they did not trust each other and could not talk with each other is important for all of them. What hurts about this situation is the trust they miss so that what they might want to share with each other is cut off. They may isolate themselves from each other in part because they are hurt by not being able to rely on each other and create a joint life, as when Donna isolates herself in her "small castle" or Paul withdraws to brood over their troubles. The need for each other and for relying on each other then creates a wall of disappointment and blame. Indeed, family members often need each other and feel they can rely on each other – more than on other people – for support in troubles in other places. But this is precisely what Donna could not do when her troubles invaded their family home. Later when she "found out in hospital" that she really needs them and cares for them, they were caring for her as being ill.

Furthermore, realizing that others need you and rely on you is important in creating and sustaining self-confidence. Donna's self-confidence is affected by realizing this in relation to her parents and to a friend in trouble. It has a similar effect on Angie to realize that a friend needs her.

The conduct of everyday family life encompasses issues of fairness concerning the distribution of obligations, considerations, and care for each other. They may be distributed in instrumental terms through struggles and negotiations between parties with diverse interests, or in recognition of overlapping and joint concerns. In this family, the distribution changed from fighting over whose turn it is to be considered into finding overlapping and joint concerns. But some issues of fairness are not resolved, for instance, about relieving the children from family obligations so that they may pursue their lives in other places without such constraints and about distributing and sharing responsibilities between the parents for conducting their everyday family life. There are also limits to family members' support and recognition of each other. While Paul recognizes that it is unfair that Donna and her friends have no place to be, he neither supports them in searching for a place or fighting to create one elsewhere nor wants them to hang out in their flat.

Being a "We" with Four Different Persons

That their family life is something they have in common is crucial to its meaningfulness (Taylor 1995b). Sharing it creates meanings and qualities they appreciate. They realize that they all appreciate these shared qualities in various ways and in this sense feel they belong to it. So they constitute a "we" that all members are particular parts of. They cultivate and pursue these qualities of "we-ness," and it would be a deep loss of meaning and a problem if these qualities corroded. Particular situations and experiences assist them in finding their "we" anew, in touching base and staying in touch, that is, in sustaining their orientations toward their family and defining what they share in their overlapping lives. The "we" of their family is marked by the general cultural understanding of family life, but is the particular "we" of their particular family, living thus together in this place, consisting of these members with these qualities and mutual relations. Still, members do not always attend to those common qualities, may take them for granted, and may even lose sight of them. The "we-ness" is carried by their family practice as its joint history and as re-produced and changed current qualities. It is articulated in shared family memories and stories which assist them in finding it again.

Others needing me may be the "we," my family needing me as is clearly the case for Mary and is Paul's reason to join the therapy sessions. Their family needs them in various ways, and they need their family in various ways. Still, they are not part of this "we" for the same reasons, and it does not have the same meaning to them. Their shared family life has different meanings to them, and they stress the meanings of different aspects. They even disagree on some meanings other members attribute to it. Just as the "we" of this family differs from the general cultural understanding of family life, individual members have different understandings of it, and being a part of it has different meanings to them. Indeed, it is important that they understand, recognize, and leave room for such differences between them in the way they conduct their shared family life. If they do not, it will create troubles and not work. Their conduct of everyday family life must combine sustaining important commonalities with recognizing important differences. Creating and sustaining strong bonds between them calls for leaving room for differences and conflicts between them over their joint life. Succeeding in interweaving shared, different, and conflicting personal concerns and conducts of everyday life in their joint conduct of everyday family life "makes it much nicer to be here," Mary says.

Members must develop a self-understanding about their part in their joint family life and about it as a part of their personal conduct of everyday life with a particular personal significance. They must configure and pursue their concerns and stances about their joint family life and their way of taking part in it. Angie feels under pressure always to be in a good spirit, mentally present and caring when she is at home but objects to it and adopts the stance that she should be entitled to be left alone sometimes when she has other things on her mind. Mary adopts the stance of being responsible in the last instance for their joint family life and in return wanting them to be pleased by it and to pay attention to her when they are at home because it is the key area of her everyday life. They develop different understandings of their family life, which are mediated by their different positions and concerns in relation to it and by the different significance of their joint family life in their personal conducts of everyday life. What is more, these different personal understandings are partial understandings of their family life. Their understandings are different and incomplete. They are aware of only some aspects, of which some are different ones, and they understand the same aspects differently too. The joint conduct of a family life comprises several partial understandings and modes of participation. Their understandings of each others' perspectives on their joint family life are also partial, that is, they do not reach complete understandings of each other. In addition, they are more or less confused or unsettled about how to understand their joint family life and their own participation in it, and they may be dissatisfied by it.

Intimate Troubles

The dark side to the significance of their joint family life, their care for each other and the intimacy of their relations with each other is that they are easily disappointed and hurt by each other. Thus, in the strong and complex conflict between Donna and her parents Donna is hurt, and Paul and Mary are disappointed and bitter. These feelings and the meaning of this conflict between them is saturated with their feelings of care and love for each other. That is why what her parents say can hit Donna really hard and why it matters so much to her that they are full of distrust as well as why she wants to get even with them and have their belief in her restored. But it is also why Paul and Mary are full of distrust and bitterness and yet do not turn their backs on her completely. In fact, their conflict is also driven by and aimed at a critique of their care for each other. But caring about each other makes them more vulnerable in conflicts with each other, and their intimate knowledge of each other makes them especially able to hurt and humiliate each other. This is the complex background for Mary's and Paul's feelings toward Donna and for Donna. They criticize the way the others take part in caring for each other, including for particular others. This may indeed change their feelings for each other. It may make them change their ties with each other, break up, go separate ways and move out, or regret it and severe the damages so that they may restore a worthwhile family life. Another dark side to the intimacy of their family relations is that they do not turn things in their minds before saying and doing things as they do toward strangers and friends. It is more acceptable to let one's mood loose on the others and treat each other worse than they allow themselves to treat other people or get away with treating even close friends. Paul and Mary mind very much when Angie does so in relation to them, but it is no problem to her. They are sometimes very rude to each other. While being rude is ordinarily seen as the opposite of being on close and intimate terms, these qualities are closely linked in family relations.

Family members deal with troubles in their everyday family life in different ways. When the sisters are in conflict with each other, they get mad and slap each other, which their parents try to avoid by keeping them apart, for instance, when their conducts of everyday life collide in the bathroom in the morning. Since Angie often stirs up troubles by getting cross, the others try to get around this by noticing how she is doing without asking her directly and by showing consideration for her when it happens so that these troubles do not escalate. In troubles between other family members, Angie soon withdraws to her room. When Angie or Donna are involved in troubles, they end up going to their rooms where Donna often broods over the troubles and after some time tries to get over it by pulling herself together. Having quarreled, especially Angie, Donna, and Paul often cannot get on good terms with each other again on the same day, but the next day things go on as if there had been no trouble. Perhaps they then consider what they say and do a bit more and watch more for signs of lingering troubles. First of all, though, the passing of the night gives them a chance to sleep on it and start on a fresh next day. In many instances troubles between them are dealt with in this way and, thus, seem to disappear with the passing of days. But in some instances Mary goes to Angie's or Donna's room to talk to them about it later "when they have calmed down." She does the same in relation to Paul who cannot talk about troubles either before they have passed. Mary thus helps them get over troubles and return their family life back to normal. She also does so because she believes they should deal with family troubles by talking about them, hoping that her doing so with them may in due time enable them to do it more directly. Furthermore, Mary finds it difficult to refrain from talking about troubles when the others are unwilling to: "If you adjust yourself and keep your mouth shut, it goes quite well. None of them want to talk about anything, and I can't stand that forever." Donna believes she should learn to but is not sure that she can, and Paul thinks he is not very good at it and never will be. He prefers to return to it later. Insisting on the need to talk about troubles is then a burden on Mary. This difference between them also has to do with their different responsibilities for the conduct of their joint family life. Mary holds on to most of the responsibility because she believes the others would not take care appropriately. Their different preferred ways of dealing with family troubles also have to do with the different meaning of this family life for them because it plays a different part in their personal conducts of everyday life.

Such differences between them often disturb their conduct of a joint family life, and they disagree over whether their different ways are appropriate parts of it. In this sense their conduct of a joint family life contains ruptures and conflicts and is a matter of disagreement. But some conflicts lead to changes in their conduct of everyday family life and are part in the unfolding of their trajectory of family life.

11.2. The Changing Family Trajectory

The trajectory of family life is a changing part of its members' changing life trajectories. It is brought about by members changing their conduct of their everyday family life and personal lives. There are limits to how my study can illuminate the family trajectory. My materials mainly illuminate the family trajectory as triggered by the children's life trajectories while I know less about reasons for changes in the family trajectory linked to the parents' life trajectories and the members' lives in other places. My study also follows this family for less than two years. But I am primarily interested in the personal and interpersonal aspects of the family trajectory, and the subjective horizon of this family's pursuit of its future trajectory is limited. Members do not look very far ahead at their future family trajectory, and they find it hard to imagine exactly how it will be. When comparing their family trajectory with other families, they do not take the other families as indications of how it will be for them. In fact, they have reservations about the trajectories of these other families, including the parents' families of origin, and are not certain that their family life will proceed like them, indeed, they hope not. Besides, their understanding of families further along in a similar trajectory is marked by how they understand their family life at the present point in its trajectory; therefore, it is different from how they will understand it if and when they reach a similar point and situation. Nonetheless, the trajectory of this family is tied to the social arrangements for personal life trajectories and family trajectories, and these ties will provoke them to change their family trajectory and lend all family trajectories some similarities. Since these arrangements are tightest and have shorter intervals for children than adults, the impact of institutional arrangements for children on their family trajectory stands out most clearly in my study. That said, events with no fixed timing in institutional trajectories play a substantial part in holding back and pushing forward, affecting and changing the direction of their family trajectory. So, just like the members of this family do not intend and plan their personal life trajectory as a whole, they do not intend and plan their family trajectory as a whole. The intentions they do have in pursuing a future family life are not directed at bringing about a certain family trajectory as a whole. These intentions are more limited and particular. Members do not set up their family trajectory as a project and plan to fulfill. They do have projects and plans for their family life, but they do not turn their family trajectory as a whole into a project and plan. They do not live their lives in order to realize a particular trajectory though they are involved in one that is emerging.

In family development theory the family trajectory is conceptualized as a set of regular normative stages, with associated transitions, in a family career, such as the coming together of couples, the birth of children, their eventual departure from home, and the parents' retirement from work (Aldous 1996; Klein and White 1996). These stages are not like the biologically based, universal stages Erikson (1965) posits for the individual life course. They are social stages with a regular normative sequence. Family development theory recognizes differences and variations in the timing, duration, and sequence of stages across families but focuses on regular normative patterns of stages in family careers. The theoretical emphasis on a common sequence may hence turn families who do not follow this normative career into mere variations thereof or into families who did not quite make it. Likewise, events may be seen as mere instantiations of stages and transitions. I recognize that regular patterns are apparent to some extent but stress that events with no fixed timing influence the realization and direction of the trajectory, opportunities shape it, and members' agency plays a substantial part in its determination and realization (Abbott 2001, 153–154). Furthermore, in line with a science of variables, family development theory conceptualizes other contexts – work, education, and so forth – as external influences impinging on family life, that is, as external stimuli. The externalization of other parts of members' lives turns the family trajectory into an entity in and of itself instead of a changing part in its members' changing conducts of life across contexts. The theory loses sight of the importance of how members conduct their lives across places for how they unfold their family trajectory as a part thereof. As members' engagements in other places change, and as the links between their family life and lives in other places change, they change their family life too. Their family trajectory is an outcome of how members conduct their lives together and separately at home and in other places.

From the standpoint of family development theory, family life develops when a family accomplishes the tasks associated with the stages and transitions of the family career (Aldous 1996). Development is just another name for normatively regular change. A family's dealings with these pinpointed tasks are seen as indications of development while other changes in how a family deals

with its ongoing family life recede into the background of relative insignif-
icance. The theory thereby loses sight of the important quality of development. Development occurs whenever persons (in this case persons assembled
in a family) increase their joint command over their life conditions (in this
case their family life) and increase their abilities for such a joint command
(Holzkamp 1983). With a broader perspective on the social practice of a family trajectory, changes of many kinds occur in the family situation, in different
directions, and with variable timings and durations. So the family practices
and the personal abilities it takes to sustain and increase a joint command
over family life vary and do not constitute a sequence of stable accumulations.
This complicates the pursuit of development. But it does not eliminate the
need to consider issues of development as issues of sustaining and increasing a
joint command over life circumstances. As an outcome of prior developments,
family members become able to understand and accomplish similar things in
similar situations, but their situation, concerns, and commitments change and
call for other practices and abilities. They do not lose their prior abilities,
but new changes may reduce their command over what now are relevant life
circumstances. Many variations, shifts, and changes occur in the activities and
relations of this family, and far from all are brought about by members as
realizations of their joint and individual command over their circumstances.
They are not stable scopes of possibilities brought about by an organized body
of subjects, but shifting, varying, and changing opportunities appearing and
disappearing beyond their control. This makes it complicated to give their
family life a definite direction and accomplish its trajectory in that direction.
A larger or smaller part of their family trajectory must be pursued by seizing
passing opportunities in due time. Members may even find it difficult and
not so important to distinguish between the pursuit of stable possibilities at
their joint command and the utilization of passing opportunities. But it would
be stretching it too far to believe that they just celebrate fluidity and flexibility. Authors emphasizing the occurrence of frequent changes in different
directions point to increasing discontinuities in lives across time, that is, in
the unfolding of personal trajectories and family trajectories. Whether they
are right in claiming that therefore "People feel the lack of sustained human
relations and durable purposes" (Sennett 1998, 98) is another matter, though.
They do not clearly document how stability and change matter in lives subject
to frequent changes and variations in contrast to lives marked by long-lasting
bonds, and this may, indeed, vary too. The significance of stability and change
even varies between persons at different points in their life trajectories.

In the pursuit of those changes that bring about their family trajectory,
members do not change everything at the same time. Change is partial, and
since the various parts of a family life are linked, further change will be limited
if they do not change other parts too. So they must re-focus and re-configure
their pursuits of changes, indeed, change their pursuit of change to be able to
continue changing. Thus, they must turn to changing other things than their
problems in order to be able to pursue stable changes of those problems. In

addition, some family activities, concerns, and stances have a longer duration than others, and members may want to hold on to them while changing other parts. While their family ties have qualities that are more long-term than most other ongoing relations, some aspects of these ties change faster than others. In other words, while some family matters are quite long-term, other family matters and events only matter for the time being. How particular parts of their family life or particular events matter depends on their links to other parts and events in their ongoing family trajectory. In the course of their family trajectory, members re-configure and re-define what now matters to them. Some aspects of their family life, thus, lose significance, perhaps to regain a similar or different significance at a later point in their trajectory. These fluctuating meanings and configurations depend on the changing links and separations between their family life and their lives in other places, which turn their current family life into a changing part of their changing life trajectories and re-define the meaning, future perspectives, and direction of their family trajectory.

Changing Understandings and Pursuits of a Family Trajectory

During my study, the members of this family increasingly make changes intended to promote their family trajectory and personal life trajectories. Thus, the parents change their care for their daughters to increasingly rely on the daughters' efforts in bringing about changes in their life trajectories together with others. In so doing, they change their family arrangements so that their family trajectory and the members' personal trajectories may proceed. Abbott calls such changes in a joint field of social practice "microtransformations" in the shape of an "internal metamorphosis" that changes "member properties" or a "microstructural change" that changes its "internal arrangements" in a way that "may affect its aggregate properties" (2001, 158). These changes in their family life are brought about because their family trajectory must unfold in such a way that it remains a suitable part of members' unfolding life trajectories across places. What is more, such changes in their family life are occasions for members to take a broader perspective on their family trajectory. They consider its prior course and possible future directions and, in this instance, change its direction. In doing so, they re-consider their family trajectory in light of the parents' family of origin and of the children gradually leaving their joint family. They consider their unfolding family trajectory as a changing shared part of personal life trajectories that are linked across generations through this family trajectory (Elder 1998; Moen and Erickson 1995).

In this sense, concerns to change their individual lives are linked with concerns to change their joint family life and their lives with others elsewhere. Change cannot be completely separate and individual. Sometimes it implies up-rooting yourself from joint practices, changing those joint roots – that is, the joint activities, relations, and ties that members enjoy and are troubled by. It may also be a joint change of their joint life and relations. After all, possible and meaningful changes depend on others changing, too. To do so well, they must understand their own and each others' current concerns. These different concerns may hold new features and features they have ignored or not quite understood. Changing their joint family trajectory hence involves changing their self-understandings and their understandings of the others so that they find themselves where they are now standing. It involves changing their stances on their joint family life and on their personal conduct of life and life trajectory. They are not always certain that they understand each others' concerns and changes, and it is not always certain which role they played even in changes they are proud of. Thus, Paul believes Angie begins to do things on her own because he changed how he takes care of her at home while Angie points to changes in other places as triggers. They may also be shaken and confused over the issues they seek to change and, therefore, have troubles finding what they stand for and finding each other in their pursuit of joint changes. As Paul puts it in interview 8, "In the beginning we each grappled with the problems on our own." They had not found each other, that is, developed a common understanding and come to understand differences between them in such a way that they may link and balance off their pursuits. Their new understandings must encompass the new demands they make on each other, their new feelings of entitlement and new relations of authority in their joint family life. The growing children will not continue to accept the old forms of authority and feel entitled to a larger say over their concerns and some family matters, while the parents do not quite see it that way. Because of the different meanings of their shared family life in their personal life trajectories, they do not attend to their everyday family life in the same way and are not equally committed to pursing their family trajectory. From the point of view of a by now peripheral person, Donna puts it like this in interview 10: "I really think it goes well at home, but I'm not so much at home." Not being much at home changes the meaning of family life for her. "We've got more to talk about when I'm not so much at home. I live my own life, and I like that a lot." During that winter, her parents do not go to the countryside, but "I'm not cross because they don't go. I think it's cozy they are at home when I return from work and so forth." This changes the meaning and perspectives of the parents' lives too. In interview 7 Mary says: "Neither Paul nor the children have been home, and then you are going to live quite a different life. . . . I fight more for it than I've ever done, precisely because the children are growing up. It isn't fair that I then have to sit here." The meaning of their joint family life and their perspectives on its future trajectory are changing. Talking about their family life over the summer in interview 8 Mary says: "Being alone in the countryside – what peace!" Donna: "It's also wonderful to be at home, you know." Angie: "Yes." Mary: "I would not like to be here in the weekends. It's so hot, and that air. In the countryside there are smells and birds. Oh, that's lovely. We have a wonderful time up there."

Indeed, members must change their conduct of everyday family life in ways suitable for sustaining a good joint family life. Failures in this respect play a large part in why family troubles get out of hand and family life stiffens. They will not succeed if they do not somehow manage to combine parts of their different perspectives and concerns in a common focus on their joint family life and re-define this common focus along with the changing trajectories of the family and its members. Especially Mary is fighting for this. Donna's understanding of her relation to her family is also changing, and, at first, she complains that her parents do not recognize this change. Later the parents do recognize that their children are growing so that their concerns about their joint family life now are different; they are better able to articulate what they mean, and it becomes easier to understand them. The children do not want to do the same things any longer, and they have to find new things to engage in jointly. The year before we met them, Donna suddenly did not even want to come along on a joint fall vacation to another country. Many new things happen to the children elsewhere, and other things fade into the background for a while or are dropped, first of all at home. Still, as Donna puts it: "And then my mother likes to hear what's happening. Then she comes into my room: 'What happened today, Donna?' That's fun." Her life in other places is worth telling and hearing about at home. If the family does not somehow manage to create an attractive place for unfolding what they are concerned about, they may direct themselves toward other places. Paul plunges into sports activities for awhile, among other things, for such reasons, and the children do not bring friends home because their isolated family life is boring so that it is more fun to go to their friends' homes. Donna and her gang only come to their flat because the other parents will not let them in. To create a rich joint family life, they must attend to what they may need each other and want each others' company for. This is crucial to Paul and Mary's re-orientations toward each other and their children. Compared to earlier, they are better able to pursue their personal concerns in ways that are not too crudely against the others. This is a matter of improved mutual understandings about their joint life. Though they always did as best they can, they are finding better ways to create room for everyone in the conduct of their joint family life and recognize the importance of other places in their personal life trajectories.

Changing Arrangement of Family Care

To sustain changes of their family trajectory, they must change their arrangements of family care. The resolution to the conflict about Donna being alone at home on weekends is marked by the developmental issue of there being no way around giving her another chance since she is getting older so that they need to reach new arrangements. Likewise, both children expand their activities and relations in other places, and the links with their lives in these places and the significance of these other parts of their lives change. For that reason, the family care for them has to reach beyond their home in other ways, at first to enable them to participate in these other places, later to support that participation in new ways. Of the parents, Paul engages most in caring for the children's participation in other places, while Mary focuses most on taking care of their lives at home, including how their lives at home are affected by their participation in other places. Not being present in these other places, the parents' care from home is marked by varying uncertainties about how their children are doing and what the parents need to care about. They have to change their care in the direction of fostering their children's self-confidence to do what they need and want without their parents. But the parents' uncertainties easily fill their care for their children at home with worries. As Mary puts it in session 8, "I don't know how Angie is doing in school, but I don't believe she's having a very nice time." To some extent, they must trust the teachers as professional caretakers in school to have an eye on her for them. But perhaps the teachers have too much else to take care of? From at home it is also difficult to find out whether and how their care affects their children's ongoing lives and changes. In addition, as the children move on in their trajectories, the parents must re-draw the lines between what they care for and what they leave to their children. They must withdraw from caring for some things and begin to care for other things. In this sense, the parents come to "take it much easier with the children" than they ever did. In the last interview, Mary says about her changing care for Angie: "And I've stopped fussing so much over her as I did. And this helps too. She makes up her own mind about things. She really does, and she's become good at it." Still, despite the fact that the parents take care of less for their children, uncertainties and worries over what to care for and what not to care for never completely disappear even though the reasons for caring and the arrangements of care across places change. The parents continue to keep an eye on how the daughters might be doing in other places noticing, for instance, that the children are easier to be around when things improve in other places so that the parents may take this as a good sign. But the children's situations frequently change, and so do their states of mind at home. The parents and children often fight over the changing arrangements of care and authority among them, for instance, when Donna or Angie want to decide something alone without regard for what their parents think or when Angie wants Mary to leave her alone when she returns from school. At stake is the children's insistence that their parents recognize they are engaged in other places apart from their family with other intimacies, which they want to themselves and their parents normally to stay clear of. Unlike their parents, they do not re-situate themselves into their family by telling about them when they return. But sometimes troubles make the children need to talk, or they enjoy telling their parents about exciting new things.

Along with changing their family care, members must change the arrangements of their conduct of everyday family life in the course of, and as a means for, their family trajectory. Many changes of family life call for rearrangements of this shared area of their personal conducts of everyday life, leaving new, suitable room for everyone. The existing arrangements incorporate memories of why they came to conduct their shared family life in this way, and they may have to find other ways to hold on to some past concerns or drop them. Instead, they must build new ways of arranging things and talking them over. Thus, they must find new joint arrangements that reconcile the fact that Donna no longer agrees to ask permission for as much as she did and may go around her parents in setting up things while they still want a decisive say over matters of their home. But new joint arrangements must be accomplished, and they sometimes fail in doing so and do not know what to do about it. Paul: "What the hell shall we do? I can't see any . . . That's why when she says 'I move out,' then I respond 'That's alright, then. Then try to see if it gets any better somewhere else.'" Ingrid: "Is it alright, then?" Paul: "Of course, it isn't. But it's almost the only way I can think of for her to try it out for herself." If they cannot accomplish necessary new joint arrangements, they cannot live together. Then, as Paul says, Donna must move out, or in other situations he wants to leave. But it may be difficult to negotiate new arrangements, and the others may be willing or unwilling to change their conduct of life and participation in family life accordingly or be pursuing changes in other, conflicting directions. They may then only be able to combine some aspects of their family life while others are left unresolved for the time being, such as the distribution of family chores and responsibilities. Finally, they must watch when it is time to change their arrangements again as their situation and conduct of life change. And they may neglect doing so, thus, creating new troubles as it happened when their situations changed over the last summer.

Learning and Getting It Right or Wrong

They must all learn to unfold their family trajectory in relation to a changing situation. In session 12, Ingrid says: "A new period is also beginning for you." Paul: "Yes, it certainly is. Now one suddenly has time to pursue one's own interests if one can find any of them. But one has to learn that." Learning it is brought about by doing, exploring, and re-considering, for instance, about Angie getting cross and being dissatisfied, which her parents come to understand in another way. In session 22, Mary says: "Angie's snarling and shifting moods are ordinary puberty problems." Paul: "We do not mind it so much as we did with Donna." In learning about it, they compare the trajectories of their two children and their own ways of dealing with and understanding them.

Some of this learning is not addressed in a direct, forward-reaching way. Rather, they learn in a backward way; as they run into troubles, they come to understand outcomes of ignored or neglected aspects and issues when these issues suddenly present themselves to them in a pressing manner as problems that are no longer easy to get around. They are then forced to re-consider what they did not attend to and may learn about the risks of ignoring and neglecting what needs to be taken care of. Thus, when the children were young, they arranged their family life and jobs so as to accommodate their children's needs and a life with small children. Hence Mary and Paul worked on different hours and were not much at home together, which in turn affected their spouse relationship and their practice of upbringing in ways they did not realize then. They gradually changed that arrangement, again primarily triggered by the children's trajectories. During our study, they changed it again, partly for other reasons. They come to understand it as part of the background for the troubles between parents and children and as causing dissatisfactions for the parents. This learning involves regretting and correcting prior practices and arrangements in light of later consequences, events, and demands. Other reasons for learning this stem from the institutional arrangements for children's trajectories, which make it necessary to learn it. Learning about many issues of family trajectories is triggered by the family's links to these institutional arrangements that secure a sociostructural impact on the learning of family trajectories. Learning to unfold family trajectories also incorporates learning about special issues such as troubles and symptoms. They must learn to deal with troubles and symptoms in ways that do not disrupt their everyday conduct of family life and get in the way of pursuing their joint family trajectory.

They must also find ways to combine what they learn so that a joint life may unfold rather than that they all pursue changes in diverse directions. But it may be difficult to change their arrangements together. Thus, the parents disagree over their arrangements of upbringing. In session 4, Mary says: "Earlier when I worked at night, Paul almost never interfered in the upbringing of the girls. And the problems were smaller. It was easier. But when Paul came into the picture and they grow older, then they say more and Paul and I are quite different. And then it becomes more impossible. We have very different points of view." Two sessions later she adds: "And then he steps forward saying 'It's not going to be like this.' And I think 'What on earth is that?' That's very hard to get used to, also for the children. Because mostly it is Paul they call 'bastard' and things like that." And another two sessions later: "I decided things alone. By God, that's not always fun, and it absolutely need not be right. So even if we disagree, we might perhaps turn it into a discussion. But Paul never wanted to discuss, not about the children either. And that's why I reacted when he begins to state his mind more towards the children. Actually, it is lovely. It can change my mind on some things now and then." Having had the responsibility and running things on her own, she must suddenly leave room for him, even let him in, watch him withdraw again and then pick up after him. Mary calls this "confusing."

In correcting and regretting their earlier practices and arrangements because they realize that they led to troubles, they are sometimes stunned and shocked. Talking in session 12 about Mary having done so much for Angie, Ingrid asks her: "Why do you think you got into doing many things for her?" Mary, stunned and shocked, with long pauses: "Yes, why? There are probably many reasons. . . . It's probably the terrible thing built into you that you should do as much as possible, and unfortunately too much, right. Because when you do things, you don't think that you might harm somebody by not letting them do it themselves."

The learning about life trajectories is obviously open-ended. A substantial part of it is also learning from what they do not want their family life to be.

The members of this family are often more certain what they want to get out of or rid of than what they want instead. Before they gradually find what they want instead, they then have to consider and explore different options for some time. Thus, this family knows of no clear positive model for their family life, only negative ones, or at least ones against which they have various significant reservations. Much of their learning from their troubles and problems also consists in becoming clearer about what they do not want.

Changing Commitments and Understandings with Each Other

Being stunned is an occasion to reconsider your understandings and stances about the trajectory your family life has taken. In support of his wife, Paul continues: "It also goes way back to your childhood because it wasn't too good for you. And then you thought it should be as good as possible for your children." Mary: "Yes, it's, it was, but, you know, it's awful. You know, what can I say?" Paul: "You said it many times." Mary: "Yes." Paul: "It's not going to be like that for them." Mary: "No, it's not going to be like that for them. All parents probably say so." Paul: "Well, yes, but it's going to be better for them, right." Mary: "Yes." Mary is changing her understanding of love and of how best to care for her children. She is still committed to loving them as best she can, among other things, because of her own trajectory. But she is realizing that the way she did it is not the best way. She needs to take care of them in a different way. However, in some respects she is not sure what the best way is and confused about it like she was about the best way to move on in her own trajectory. Paul and Angie here support Mary in various ways, even when it implies siding against each other.

The four members' commitments to their joint family life are different, and so is their reliance on each other to take care of its trajectory. The children are less committed to take care of their joint family trajectory and do not notice and mind many things their parents care about or are troubled by. When it comes to raising family issues and pursuing their family trajectory, primarily the parents must change things, make other demands, and keep pursuing them. If they do not, nothing may happen. And of the parents, the mother pursues the trajectory of their joint family life the most. Still, to some extent they must all rely on each other to take part in bringing about their joint family trajectory even if they recognize that their stances and commitments differ, and even if their reliance on each other may be shaken by family troubles. At times they are on guard toward each other and do not quite trust everybody to be ready to make new arrangements and stand behind them. Mary feels that it is up to her to take care of things, get talks about family issues started, and say that now is enough: "I am the one to make things move." She changes her life trajectory to fit her responsibilities and commitments for their joint family trajectory. Therefore, this joint family trajectory plays a special part in her life trajectory. Issues of fairness and recognition of differences are linked to all this, occupy them, and give rise to struggles between them. On the whole, they move slowly but with contradictions toward more shared responsibilities for their joint family trajectory. The teenage daughters change their commitments in their joint family trajectory. They begin to pursue a trajectory of their own over and above just throwing themselves into this and that. While they pay less attention to their joint family trajectory, they occasionally redefine their commitment to it. Donna finds out while in hospital that she needs her family, now and in the future. She is on the way into a world of youth activities apart from her family and school but wants to hold on to her family relations in the long run. Mary's commitments in their joint family trajectory are so much stronger that she is more dissatisfied with an improved family life. Nonetheless, it matters to all of them, to Donna too, that the others recognize their participation in their joint family life as satisfactory and appropriate. In session 19, she says that she tries to be nice to her parents also in order to "prove to myself that I can do something for my mum and dad so that they become happy." Their recognition is proof to her that she is playing the part she wants to play and feels she should play.

Coming to an understanding with each other about their individual parts in the trajectory of their joint family life is important to them – also when they cannot accomplish it. Thus, for some time Donna is "very disappointed" in their joint life, especially about her father, and because of the lack of understanding between them, she sometimes feels like moving out. Paul too now and then threatens to leave because of the lack of understanding between them about their joint family life. Donna withdraws as a reaction to this lack of understanding: "But then I live in my own small world, right. And then I've got my friends when I return from school. And then I have my own small room, right. And they are just there." She does not pay attention, indeed, "I simply don't listen to him" when he addresses issues between them. In this situation, they get on each others' nerves: "We should stop snarling so much at each other. We irritate each other in some way – all the time. But I don't know why. It's just something between us. We are both irritating, right." Therefore, "It will be difficult to begin to talk with each other again after so long time." Paul is of a similar opinion, accuses her of never listening to what he says and adds, "She's too self-willed, pig-headed." Because of the lack of understanding between them Paul agrees when Donna wants to move out. It is his reaction to her not listening to him and not keeping the joint arrangements they make. He wants to stop having to care about her, and then she must take care of herself, "try it herself, feel what it's like." They shut each other out and reduce their care for each other. Donna imagines doing so by moving entirely into the new, separate youth world opening up to her. Still, their joint family trajectory and future care for each other is at stake in their reactions to these controversies. When Paul gives up so much that he tells Donna she can leave, Mary says: "But I'm also afraid Donna will feel even more disregarded. As late as just before we came here she said she might as well go to hell because there was nothing but problems with her." So when are children to move out? When do they really want to move out? When have their parents really had enough?

And how is this related to caring for them, now and in the future, including having a joint future? Paul and Donna both want a joint future, and Paul is afraid it will be lost if she moves out now: "If she gets into such a place, then maybe we never see her again." They both realize they have to get on better terms with each other to be able to make new arrangements. Withdrawing and shutting each other out has made this more difficult. And yet they are afraid that any opening may be usurped by the other.

Changing Family Relationships

When we meet the family, the sisters often fight and slap each other and get irritated over getting in each other's separate ways. Donna would also rather be with her friends than take part in the sessions to help Angie, which suits Angie fine because she finds it difficult to be in the center when Donna is around. They only support each other when they are attacked en block by their parents. This sibling relationship has a history. But relationships must change to stay alive and develop rather than crumble as their personal and family trajectories unfold. The re-production of their relationship occurs through change and development. They need to realize this and care about it, at least to some extent. Indeed, what counts as close family relationships changes in their unfolding lives and family trajectories. Thus, the contents, qualities, and significance of the relationship between the sisters change into enjoying talking with each other about things that occupy them, joining overlapping networks of friends, going to parties together, talking about boys, having a job in the same place, and so forth. When Angie begins to do new things, Donna occasionally suggests that she would like to join her and appreciates that "She is not so cross, happier" because "She's got something to do." Indeed, they both enjoy having lots of things to do, and this is part of what joins them. Donna believes that they talk more now "because she has grown older." They also quarrel less. Donna says in interview 5, "We grow older. You can talk much better with her, in another way." For instance, they confide more in each other. They care about these changes in their relationship and do something to bring them about and sustain them, but they are also surprised by them. They find it hard to explain why they occur and even to describe them. They seem to change in parallel ways and then discover the new joint activities and qualities of their relationship that these parallel changes afford. In interview 8, Angie admits: "I cannot understand how we can be together for so long now." Donna seconds her.

The qualities and issues of the relationship between parents and children also change as their life and family trajectories unfold. Thus, Angie wants her parents to leave her alone more often, but she still wants them to understand her well in her changing separate life. She feels entitled to other things, pushes for their recognition thereof and gets cross, even provokes and pesters them anew if they do not. This gets Paul down sometimes. It affects the relationship between him and Mary too because Paul withdraws from her too when brooding over it. Even the relationship between the sisters is affected. While Donna recognizes that she was like this once herself, she now believes that her parents "are too nice to her when she flips out because I don't think she understands when you tell her." Ingrid: "Do you also think your mum and dad were too nice to you." Donna: "Yes, I think so." She found out that it is better to ask and talk things over instead of just pushing. Before she found out, she also "wanted to be contrary to them, see how far I could go." Meanwhile Donna realized that "I cannot be without my mum and dad." The parents too notice these changes in their relationship with their daughters. In interview 8, Paul says: "You notice in the girls that they've grown. They are more reasonable. I am very excited to see how Donna will be doing when she starts vocational school. What she gets out of it and what she can use it for afterwards." Their mutual relationship is filled with other concerns and qualities. To some extent their relationship is gaining qualities characteristic of a relationship between adults combined with a history of parent–child caring. There is a similar change at work in the ways in which they make arrangements with each other. They more often explicitly schedule and agree to them, looking for things the others might want to do too. They also recognize each others' needs to be engaged in different things separately, enjoying spending their time separately.

Parallel to these changes in the relationship between parents and children, the parents focus more on their spouse relationship and consider their family and life trajectories more in light of it. This is also enabled by their finding new ways of joining each other as parents, and troubles from their parent–child relationship may get in the way of unfolding their spouse relationship. Thus, to Mary it is like getting a problem more on top of the others when Paul says that he has had it because of the troubles with the daughters. It feels like a threat to their spouse relationship that he might leave. In fact, such an episode got Paul down because it disrupted a long period in which he and Mary had a really nice time together on their own. It hurts Mary that Paul lets this get in the way of their unfolding spouse relationship. At work she talks to other women having similar troubles with their teenage daughters, and she takes this much easier than she ever did. It affects her more "when Paul starts to say he's had it 'cause that's a strange solution." At the same time Mary and Paul have come closer to each other because they were able to join more in their parenting. In session 20, Mary says: "We've never agreed so much and talked so much about the children as while we've been going here." But they remain different in some respects. Thus, Mary feels she simply must go to sit at Donna's bedside in the hospital, which Paul would not do though Mary persuades him to come along for a visit a couple of times.

Intricacies of a Changing Family Trajectory

As their joint family trajectory unfolds, members must change in ways that depend on changing their participation in other places too. Not every change they might want in their family life is, therefore, possible. In a study of working mothers, Garey stresses that due to the links between the contexts of work and family life "Flexibility and variation are central characteristics of the lives of employed women over time" (1999, 165). Here flexibility and variations are not outcomes of large scopes for autonomous living. On the contrary, they are called for because of the personal constraints of combining two areas of life with diverse demands, rhythms and directions of change. According to Garey, working mothers sometimes drift along with extraneous events and let significant others make major life decisions for them (189). A considerable degree of variation is also possible within the structural arrangement of this family's conduct of everyday life. Still, members must be suitably open to variations in their everyday family life and to changes in their family trajectory. In session 15, the parents say that for some time they were used to doing things without Donna, and now she suddenly wants back in so that they must change the arrangement of their everyday family life. Though Donna wants to re-open their relationship, she is not welcomed back with open arms. Paul: "Yes, but then she must come and talk." Donna: "That's just difficult when you don't believe in me."

Because their family life is involved in the social arrangements of its members' life trajectories, it runs into problems if they do not move suitably along in their joint family trajectory, seize suitable opportunities to do so, and develop the necessary abilities and relationships. But even a forced change may lead to a new positive understanding of what you want, appreciate, and pursue. Some persons may pursue their life and family trajectories by seeking and seizing new opportunities and appreciating a life with shifts and variations. This is the case for the daughters who are not settled down in their family of origin. How hopeful or disappointed they all are for their future affects the ways in which they pursue their family trajectory. Paul is not so hopeful about the future, pays less attention to it, and pursues it less intensely within a narrower horizon, and this family as a whole does not gather much around the pursuit of a joint future. Some imagined futures then appear as unrealistic dreams causing regrets and complaints especially over other members whom they do not consider to be doing what they should to enable changes. At the beginning of this therapy, Angie's prior experiences have made her not believe much in being able to make a difference and conduct her life more fully. She does not show much hope but seems quite indifferent. At other times, necessary changes are simply not possible, only partly possible, or do not succeed, or they find out that a change came too late. Thus, Mary and Paul regret not having changed their relations to their children earlier. Some things they would now very much like to do with them are no longer possible because their children already moved on in their trajectories beyond prioritizing joint family activities. Nonetheless, on the whole, the members of this family increase their engagement in possible future relationships with each other and in the future trajectory of their joint family. This is also seen in the increase of a developmental understanding of each others' lives. Thus, they come to understand Angie's troubles as being grounded in her dependency and her need of a growing self-confidence.

In interview 7, Paul says: "She has been very dependent. She has been too weak. And when she gains more self-confidence, those problems may decrease." Mary: "When she is with others, she never makes her mark. She is very insecure." The parents come to understand their own troubles and concerns in a similar way and to insist on the pursuit and recognition of their joint and separate trajectories. Mary: "You sort of start to think more about your needs, and they accept it when you tell them. I've got a lot out of that." In contrast to earlier, doing so even feels quite okay, and it would be "unfair" to have to give it up. But while the daughters changed in a way that reaches into an unknown future, only in interview 8 at the end of their therapy does Paul talk about beginning to be able to think ahead: "But besides like Mary I think it is very nice to be alone. We've come so far that we begin to be able to think a bit more ahead and see that it is really very nice to mind ourselves."

As in individual life trajectories, the pace of the ongoing family trajectory varies. It is pursued with varying intensity, periodically in full focus and at other times discontinued for a while. On the way, the relevance and meaning of particular enduring circumstances and concerns vary and change, some lose their meaning and other new ones are added, thus, constituting a varying and changing constellation of particularly relevant and meaningful circumstances, events, and concerns (Abbott 2001, 170). In session 19, Donna says that things have gone really fast for her in the last couple of years. She was held back by troubles and is now jumping ahead, "sometimes a bit too fast." But now she would like to try to live on her own, not to get away from her parents, but "because I would like to. Not too far from home so that I could come home every day and hear what's up." As the pace of one member's trajectory changes, it affects the family as a whole. Things continue to move fast for Donna for some time, but nine months later in the final interview with her the meaning of her all-important move into vocational school has changed and her trajectory unfolds at a lower pace: "It can be hard sometimes to go to vocational school. It's a long day. I leave at seven and am home shortly after four. In the first two months it was great fun because it was something new. Now we must go through the same things every day. I don't even have time to come home on Monday and Friday before my jobs. On Saturday I work from seven to three." When things are moving fast, they often have occasion to reconsider their unfolding trajectory, to place their present life in a larger perspective of their past and possible futures, and to change the way in which they deal with the present to make it fit their pursuit of a re-considered future trajectory. When Donna considers leaving home, it makes her redefine her relationship to the others. She puts her family relationships in a different perspective. In session 19, she adds: "I just want my own. I have so too at home, but it's not the same way. I want to prove that I can take care of myself because I still don't think they really believe that. . . . I want us always to stick together when I've left home. It isn't going to be like not seeing your mum and dad because you are on bad terms with each other. I won't have it like that." Her new future perspective changes her concern for preserving her family relationships.

Understanding Transformations

Did this family trajectory pass a turning point during our study? To find out for certain, we must be able to define the new direction their trajectory has come to take (Abbott 2001, 245–250). But while important features of this direction are becoming clear, their family life has not yet fully settled into a changed direction. Mary and Paul are trying to resolve their discords over it. Disagreements and troubles and the burdens of taking care of those troubles have held them back, and only as they ease does their scope and energy to unfold a future family trajectory with other qualities increase. Only then have the parents "come so far that we begin to be able to think a bit more ahead," as Paul puts it. But their understandings and concerns about their joint family life and its future trajectory have certainly changed and will affect the course it will take because it changed which qualities of a joint family life they no longer find acceptable or appreciate and want to promote and cultivate. This change in understandings and concerns has a history too. As Abbott puts it, "a past of many depths shapes the present" (124). One layer of depth that stands out to Mary and Paul is the way in which a confrontation with their families of origin lies behind their pursuit of different qualities for their own family trajectory. They wanted a break with the kind of family life in their families of origin and set out to create something quite different. Individual persons may also create breaks with respect to other dimensions of their stances on their unfolding lives (Minz 1984). In session 12, Ingrid asks the parents in which respects their family life should be better for their children. Mary: "So much love as one can possibly . . . Or love, I never got that, and they surely do. I love them more than anything on earth, simply. And then I probably did too much for them." Ingrid: "Love means you would never refuse them, never. You've always got time." Mary: "Always time, yes. And I'm certain it pays off when they get older." Their turn to their family of origin and their own parents is done in a particular way by a particular family as a part of dealing with issues in the ongoing trajectory of their family. Meanwhile they have found out that this early impact on how they conduct their family life has led to something other than what they intended and that this contradiction between intentions and outcomes "is terrible." Bruner (1990, 133) points to a similar phenomenon in a case study of the narrative of the Goodhertz family where the parents pursued a family trajectory in which they are concerned about protecting their children from their own generation's experiences with poverty-related miseries. As a result of that, combined with the current circumstances of a family life in New York, a different contradiction in their family life emerged for their children. It is a contradiction between what is safe and dangerous, boring and exciting. In the family I analyze in this book, the parents each in their way change their minds on how to conduct their family life in a reaction against the unintended outcomes of their early commitments. In session 24, Mary says that not stating their minds toward their children has been a crucial part of the reasons for the problems that emerged and that, therefore, the two of them really are the problem. "There must always be peace, and that's what's wrong, simply. Everything must run smoothly. No problems. Don't talk about that. There aren't going to be any problems. We must always talk nicely and be nice to each other and all that. And that's not possible. I can't, nor can the others. . . . No problems, no anger, no nothing. It's always been like that. We created it ourselves, and when the children grew up, they started to protest against it and don't do things the way we want." So their children reacted against the way they did things as Mary and Paul reacted against the family life of their own childhoods. However, in a social practice such as family life deeply marked by long-term participations and commitments, changes are characterized by a combination of transformations and continuations. Mary: "I think it's got something to do with one's childhood. Because for both of us at home one didn't have problems even though my father always said they were there to solve. But you only talked about the sun, the wind, and the weather, and the same goes for Paul at home. And there were no emotions either." Ingrid: "Many were brought up like that." Mary: "Yes, but some continue. I've always tried not to, I think, but I've not been able to anyhow." In this statement Mary confronts her former stance of showing consideration and giving her children as much love as possible. She is shocked over what she sees as outcomes of her former practice and no longer fully understands what she did then. In this sense Mary certainly – and Paul too in a similar way – appreciates that she now sees their lives in a different perspective and that other things matter to her now than earlier. She even finds it difficult to understand her former reactions, concerns, and understandings, which the changes she has gone through have transformed into other reactions, concerns, and understandings. They are, therefore, not easily accessible to her any more. In trying to remember them, she may take recourse to their prior family arrangements seeking to recover the reasons why they arranged their joint family life in that way then. The transformations have limited their grasp on their earlier family life, just like they cannot quite imagine how their future family life will be, among other things, because they cannot quite imagine the transformations of their understandings and concerns which will take place between now and then.

12   Research in Social Practice

In this chapter I present an unconventional analysis of the craft of research in order to characterize how my project is to be understood and its outcomes evaluated. In section 12.1 I address aspects of the craft of research in my project. In so doing, I change the perspective of analysis from the clients in this case to the researcher in this project. But the fundamental standpoint of analysis remains the same since I consider research as a social practice based on the theoretical framework adopted throughout the book. In sections 12.2 and 12.3, I zoom in on the development of theoretical concepts and empirical outcomes that are closely related in a case analysis. These issues are taken up after the case analysis because I insist on the primacy of subject matter over method and theory over methodology (Holzkamp 1983, chapter 9). In view of the importance attributed to the generality of knowledge in conceptions of research, issues about conceptual and empirical generalization are central in these two sections. Especially in a book analyzing a single case, there is no way around addressing these issues in arguing for the validity of my outcomes. In section 12.4, I move beyond issues about the production of knowledge to issues about the uses of research outcomes in social practice. My decentered analysis of the uses of therapy sessions elsewhere and later suggests an understanding of the relations between the production of knowledge and the uses of research elsewhere and later, which differs from the ordinary understanding of the application of research findings. It raises a wealth of issues about the relations between researchers, professionals, and just plain folks in social practice, which make it impossible to hold on to an understanding of the craft of research as an activity that can be defined by looking only at the activities, procedures, and ideas of researchers.

12.1. Researching Persons in Social Practice

In working on projects, researchers gather experiences that emerge from participating in particular ways in particular social practices with particular relations to the activities and experiences of various others. In their analyses of these experiences, the claims researchers make result from their engagements in these practices. Researchers come to know by inquiring in social practices. All human beings come to know in this way, though the knowing of researchers is also affected by the training and cultivation of a research practice. Alcoff (1996, 218 ff) argues that the truth claims researchers advance are grounded in worldly, practical, historical, contextual local practices of knowing, in what she calls an immanent realism. Truth is immanent to a domain of human reality because it is a product of an interaction between knower and known. Hence, truth claims are indexical, that is, they point toward definite aspects of the world as their referential basis. This assures us of the grounding of our truth claims in particular, local practices. In that sense, the truth claims of this study refer indexically to my participation in particular, limited ways in the work of a unit of outpatient child psychiatry in Copenhagen. They are based on my participation as a cotherapist in the sessions of these particular cases, in meetings with my interviewer and cotherapists about the ongoing study of these cases, and in meetings in this unit about their work, my participation, and this project in relation to their work.

But truth claims have a more comprehensive practical grounding as well. "The knower is always already in the world, committed to a large array of beliefs, engaged in ongoing projects and practices," as Alcoff (221) puts it. My social practice as a researcher comprises other parts and commitments than my participation in the work in this unit. Again this is true for every human being. Like the clients in my project, I pursued particular issues and concerns across diverse contexts in working on the project. I decided to make the project when we launched a series of Theory–Practice–Conferences of critical psychology where it was presented and discussed several times. It was presented and discussed at meetings in the research group of the Center for Health–Humanity–Culture and at other research conferences. It has been deeply involved in my collaboration with Jean Lave throughout these years with numerous discussions and readings of each others' ongoing work. Publications about topics in the project arose from these occasions and networks and affected its development. Moreover, my social practice of research on the project was involved in my efforts in this unit and these sessions and in my practice at the university with teaching, reading, writing, supervising students, and so forth. My work on the project was a particular, intermittent part in my trajectory across times and places on and off work. As I moved into and out of these other practices and compared my understandings of the project with issues and understandings in them, I addressed my understandings and concerns from the project in particular ways. These other contextual concerns and issues affected which phenomena and issues I found particularly relevant to analyze in working on the project and how I linked them. Gradually issues and understandings came to stand out other than those established during my immediate participation in the unit and in these sessions. My diverse, positioned understandings and concerns triggered a process of comparing and linking that affected my development of a particular, complex understanding and framework. Thus, other engagements in other practices countered the emergence of core blindness in my understanding in this project and these sessions. Moving into other practices allowed me not to become fully engrossed in particular local configurations of experience and practice. It allowed me to develop a particular other, more comprehensively grounded understanding of what goes on in this unit and these cases. After all, I am neither a full-time clinician nor a full-time teacher of therapy, and this facilitated a different understanding of the social practice of therapy. My social practice of not being a full-time member of this unit and of moving across the diverse social practices of doing therapy, research, teaching, supervision, attending conferences, and so forth facilitated my understanding of the cross-contextual complexity in the social practice of therapy. It made me realize the significance of the – obvious but underrated – cross-contextual way in which therapy works. I wanted to focus on how sessions leave traces in clients' lives at home when I started the project, but I ended with a frame of analysis about contexts, their links and arrangements, people's participation in them and across them with different but linked concerns, and so forth. My chances for comparing with other, later projects based on a similar approach and carried out in various fields of social practice (see my introduction), fostered and solidified my framework. Discussing issues about my framework with colleagues and students in various places and beginning to write about it gradually assured me of it.

What I said earlier goes against what we might call an immediacy fixated (Holzkamp 1983) conception of the social practice of research. By this I mean a conception of research as grounded in the immediate procedures of doing research as an isolated activity – as research methods (and therapeutic methods) are generally presented in the literature. Not all aspects of a researcher's changing understanding and stances about a project are brought about while being immediately involved in it and dealing directly with these materials and their analysis. The re-search of a project advances by linking practices, understandings and concerns across contexts with diverse activities, coparticipants, issues, and purposes. Indeed, the conditions of possibility of the knowledge researchers produce are located in and across the practices of their trajectories of participation. In identifying what they take to be general aspects and outcomes of a project, researchers juxtapose local experiences from it with other local experiences in their trajectories.

But, of course, the social practice of a research project encompasses participants other than the researcher(s). It holds participants with diverse perspectives on its topic and conduct. How may researchers then relate to these diverse perspectives in their analysis of project materials? And how may they reconcile this diversity with what is ordinarily seen as the goal of research: the production of general findings? The predominant solution to this quandary lies in insisting that the perspective of the researcher simply is the general perspective, and that the outcome of his analysis, hence, is general. All other perspectives are excluded from the analysis, and the researcher's perspective is then more easily taken as the general standpoint on the subject matter (Smith 1990). In addition to a professional-centeredness and a professional monopoly of interpretation, we here see a researcher-centeredness and a researcher monopoly of interpretation. In less extreme solutions to the quandary, the perspectives of others, especially nonexpert others such as clients and other just plain folks, are re-interpreted and subsumed to the privileged perspective of the researcher (or another professional such as a therapist). At the opposite end of the spectrum, we find what amounts to a liberalist standpoint of analysis. A social practice is analyzed in such a way that a multitude of autonomous perspectives are presented side by side. For instance, Papadopoulos and Byng-Hall (1997) and Reimers and Treacher (1995) aim their studies of user-friendly family therapy at presenting multiple voices. However, doing so turns research into a babble of voices. It merely takes the existence of multiple personal perspectives into account but not their mediation through the different positions of these participants in social practice. Using my theoretical framework, we may consider how these multiple perspectives are mediated through these participants' particular positions with particular scopes and partial participations in the social practice in question. This includes considering the impact of their particular, position-mediated relations with other participants on their participation and on the first-person perspective of their experiences, which incorporate "my" relation to the experiences of others, to "their" relation to "my" experiences, and to the relationship between "us." It also includes considering a present situation and context as a part of evolving participant trajectories and of participants' pursuits of concerns and stances through their trajectories. Personal dimensions of meaning become comprehensible in this way. As I see it, the clients in this book basically understand their joint life and their own and each others' experiences in this way, and therapists may understand client experiences and their experiences as therapists inside and outside sessions in this way too.

The framework I presented analyzes multiple perspectives, voices, and relations as particular parts in structures of social practice. Differences and similarities between participant experiences may then be seen as being grounded in their linked participation in particular structures of social practice. The framework provides a basis for understanding and linking the competing claims of their diverse perspectives as grounded in their diverse, linked participations in structures of social practice (Dreier 2005). It is not just a framework based on an individual perspective or on relations between persons; rather it is based on an understanding of persons as participants in structures of social practice with a situated understanding of personal perspectives as particular and partial relations to structures of ongoing social practice. The framework also lets us comprehend that and how structural arrangements of social practices and personal trajectories infuse participants' understandings. It even lets us see impacts thereof on personal modes of participation and understanding that clients, other plain folks, and therapists do not notice and reinterpret as being due to particular individual properties and differences (Dreier 1987; 1988a). An example is the bracketing of the significance of the therapeutic arrangement of seclusion, which I take to be so pervasive that I chose it as the starting point of my case analysis.

Following Holzkamp (1996, 87–95), I call an analysis that reflects its basis in multiple perspectives a "metasubjective understanding." But my approach differs from Holzkamp's conception of metasubjectivity. According to him, a metasubjective understanding is reached by reflecting on what goes on within the immediate situation of the research encounter and its mediation through the overall societal structure. His notion does not encompass the significance of various structural arrangements of local social practices, such as the impacts of the framing of the immediate research situation or therapeutic encounter. In taking the practical grounds of subjectivity and intersubjectivity as given within the boundaries of the immediate encounter, he overlooks the significance of the participants' diverse trajectories of participation in structures of social practice. His search for the structural mediations of immediate experiences hence remains underdetermined and becomes a matter of mental representation more than of ongoing practices. Regardless of how we were to comprehend an overall societal structure (and its mediation) in the first place, this conception does not explicitly point us toward analyzing the structural arrangements of particular, local social practices, personal relations, modes of participation, and trajectories. It cannot guide our analysis of the significance of such structural arrangements for persons. Nor can we analyze in any precise and concrete manner how overall structural aspects and personal experiences are mediated without a theorizing of structural arrangements of local social practices, personal trajectories, and modes of participation in them. Smith (1987; 1990) suggests another way of dealing with the quandary of the multiple perspectives, interpretations, and narratives that come with insisting on a nonexclusionary study of persons in everyday social practices. She proposes to consider them in their relation to the existing relations of ruling. But, again, linking particular personal perspectives to existing power structures does not replace an analysis of the significance of the structural arrangements of particular social practices for personal experiences, relations, modes of participation, trajectories, and other aspects of the psychological study of persons in social practice.

Research in line with a conception as mine is not directed at comprehending persons and things as if they were isolated entities but at comprehending how they are linked and hang together in structurally arranged social practices. Holzkamp (1988) characterizes knowledge in psychology as "*Widerspruchs- und Zusammenhangswissen*": knowledge about contradictions and hanging together. Likewise, Schatzki (1996; 2001; 2002) speaks of knowledge about the hanging together of social practice or its nexus or simply its *Zusammenhang*. Every link of a nexus is, of course, not equally important, and the purpose of a particular study is not to define how everything hangs together, that is, to depict a totality. Its purpose is to analyze the particular hanging together of a particular social practice and to define which links in that social practice are especially important in comprehending the topic of the study. An analysis is always limited to what are judged to be the relevant links in a particular study of a particular practice.

All persons develop particular understandings of themselves and the social practices they participate in that highlight particular links as important and set aside other aspects as unimportant. But participants in a joint social practice must somehow link their diverse understandings with each other about how things hang together, which links matter, and how things therefore may be done. Participants may succeed in linking their understandings more or less completely and for longer or shorter stretches of time. Researchers may focus on determining the relations between the diverse perspectives of various participants by analyzing the practical, position-mediated links between them in a structure of social practice. Their analysis may then contribute to the self-understandings of the involved persons as particular, located participants in this practice and to the exchange of perspectives and understanding between them. Their work may guide persons in finding themselves and each other where they are located in particular relations in particular contexts in their unfolding trajectories in structures of social practice. It may clarify the, more or less problematic, hanging together of their lives in a shared practice and the possible effects of re-producing or changing this practice on their shared and individual lives. Such a contribution from research is nonexclusionary. Just plain folks and other experts, such as therapists and educators, may engage in similar endeavors. In their work, researchers develop concepts, theories, and empirical findings as analytic means for this endeavor.

But the concrete nexuses that we study and in which people live their lives hold commonalties as well as differences. Therefore, research cannot disregard the comprehension of differences. It must ground commonalties as well as differences in a social practice and comprehend them as aspects thereof. This allows participants to understand that there is a common ground in the structure of their social practice for commonalties as well as differences between their scopes, understandings, and concerns. What participants have in common, or the differences between them, may, of course, matter more or less to them, but it is never just the differences or the commonalties that matter. Participants join in practices, which, besides shared meanings, matter differently to them so that they take part in different ways. Indeed, they may recognize differences between their participations, understandings, and concerns as reasonable and legitimate parts of their shared social practice. They may recognize the coexistence and intersection of commonalties and differences as being due to the many-sidedness and richness of social practices with diverse positions and trajectories. In fact, participants may also join each other in a shared social practice because it affects them differently. They may appreciate and want to preserve some of these differences and to overcome others. Finally, they may realize that they can affect differences and commonalties between them by changing their participation and the arrangements and structure of their social practice.

How may an analysis be critical when it considers a social practice so much from within and includes participants' understandings? First, it may be critical by identifying the significance of other aspects, links, limitations, and possibilities than the participants realized. Second, it may be critical by offering a more comprehensive analysis than participants' particular perspectives and, thus, place their current understanding and participation in a different light.

Third, it may be critical by showing how participants are affected by commonalities and differences in a social practice and how this may be changed by altering their social practice, its arrangements, and their participation in it. Fourth, it may be critical by showing that some participants adopt stances on their participation that contribute to preserve differences standing in the way of a more equal and joint social practice. But it is not critical by articulating merely one subjugated voice – such as the voice of the client in therapy. In my study, the clients are not analyzed as one client voice but as persons relating to other persons in their positioned participations in relations to others in structures of social practice. Fifth, analyzing how persons' understandings and participation emerge from particular positioned relations with others in particular structures of social practice may be a further source of critique of the ways in which those persons currently understand themselves and take part. Because it takes multiple parties – in a particular realization of their commonalities and differences – to re-produce and change a social practice, understanding their links in a structure is necessary for changing this social practice. In fact, though this study focuses on clients, it is highly relevant for therapists, holds critical implications for their understanding and conduct of therapy, and may encourage them to explore other ways of conducting therapy together with their clients. Sixth, an analysis may be critical because it reflects the local and wider social and historical grounds for the practice studied and, thus, the local and historical character of its issues and possibilities. Seventh, it may be critical because it reflects the significance of particular arrangements and trajectories and their links to wider social structures and relations of ruling. Eighth, it may hold a critique of particular theoretical understandings of a social practice, of professional expertise, and of its relations between experts and plain folks. Thus, my study is motivated by my disbelief in the professional-centered, knowledge-based paradigm of research on therapy and other professional practices as derived from a set of techniques that stem from a stock (or several competing stocks) of well-bounded knowledge. It shows important aspects and dynamics of the social practice of therapy, which the general findings from that research cannot capture.

By working on a project, a researcher's focus and understanding develop. Though my design, my conduct of the project, and the foci of my analyses are affected by my background understanding and general agenda, my framework and agenda are not fixed. They change, among other things, provoked by my conduct of the project. I launched this project as a study of the workings of therapy. As in some other studies of a professional practice, I reach further into the everyday practices of ordinary people in order to improve our understanding of how professional practices relate to and affect people's everyday lives. So I approach everyday practice from the standpoint of professional practice and with a view to what matters especially in relation to professional practice. Though I do not adopt an altogether professional-centered view, it is certainly a special view on everyday practice that emphasizes particular links between everyday practice and professional practice, while other aspects of everyday practice go unnoticed. What is more, the study makes me realize that we need to know much more about everyday life and to understand it in another way than professional-centered approaches (Lave unpublished manuscript). It shows that, as we extend our research into the everyday, we must move through a critique of prevalent paradigms of research to develop other ones that reach across contexts. This is in line with Holzkamp's (1995) critique of the unworldliness of experimental and therapeutic research in psychology. In a closely related move, Lave (1988, 4) shows how her research on "everyday math practices" called on her to critique functionalist notions of "math" to be found identically everywhere and gradually unfold a series of different kinds of observations and experiments while probing which ones proved most fruitful in promoting her research agenda of a situated understanding of everyday math practices. This implied not presupposing or arranging a situation in which she might delineate and study "school math." Instead, she studied the everyday practice of "just plain folks" to locate relevant activities of calculation for closer study (47). Likewise, my present project is merely a step on the way toward more suitable and comprehensive designs for studying personal trajectories in structures of social practice more fully and deeply.

12.2. Conceptual Dimensions and Outcomes of the Project

My project is exploratory and theory generating. The materials were not sifted through a pre-given, fixed theoretical framework and used to test certain hypotheses derived from it. Instead, the project led to changes in the framework and in the understanding of the materials, which affected each other. On the way, a changed theoretical framework evolved, and my understanding of what these materials may tell us changed so that they gained a different relevance as a result of my analyses. The conceptual developments during the project deeply affected my analysis of therapy in social practice. Indeed, they ended up [sic] defining the framing and starting point [sic] of my analysis in chapter 4. They also deeply affected my analytic approach to the study of other social practices.

Analyzing my materials with my theoretical framework led to many surprises and struggles, which proved analytically very fruitful. They forced me to pay close attention anew to particular episodes and to the clients' statements and the concepts they used in particular situations and contexts. They also made me revise and expand my understanding of the case and my theoretical framework. Thus, the clients' confusion when asked about changes and their not noticing changes forced me to re-consider my preconception of change. It made me add concepts about variations and shifts and consider the changing meaning and pursuit of change. Their statements about having to think more about things first triggered me to re-conceptualize the pursuits of change. Their use of concepts as self-confidence and pulling myself together made me elaborate my analysis. And the list goes on. So the clients' descriptions and commonsense concepts challenged me to re-consider and develop my conceptual framework. They also challenged me to reflect how the position as a therapeutic agent of change affects understandings of clients.

The theoretical framework in this book rests on a conception of knowledge as the analytic determination of nexuses. The knowledge created is about nexuses and about persons as parts of nexuses. A psychological phenomenon such as anxiety is thus analyzed by grasping what it is linked to for a particular person in the social practice in which this person participates. A theory holds a set of concepts that refer to the various general aspects of its subject matter – in my theory to general aspects of persons in structures of social practice. Its concepts are linked into a theoretical order, and it may function as a framework precisely because its concepts are ordered in relation to each other – though a theory may still be incomplete and its order incompletely determined as the theoretical framework in this book. The general, theoretical links between the concepts in my framework were laid out in the presentation of the theory. The place of a concept in the theoretical order, that is, its particular links to other concepts in the framework, define its theoretical status relative to other concepts in the theory. It also defines the background presuppositions of a particular concept. Since concepts in a theory gain a particular meaning by being linked to other concepts in it, my understanding of a concept differs from how the same term is understood in other theoretical frameworks. Thus, the concept of personal life trajectory differs from other conceptual understandings of life trajectory (such as Elder 1998; Giddens 1991) and life history. The conceptual understanding of self-confidence also differs from other commonsensical and theoretical understandings thereof.

Besides being an ordered understanding of its subject matter, a theory is a general grasp of the aspects and links of its subject matter. The links between the concepts in a theory capture what are claimed to be general links between the aspects of social practice these concepts refer to. As seen in the general presuppositions of the concepts I modified and added due to my case analysis, the conceptual outcomes of my work on this material are claimed to hold for much else than just this case – though, of course, not necessarily in the same manner.

Generalization plays a key role in conceptions about the aim of research. Sometimes it is even claimed that it is the name of the game and that there is nothing more to it. But controversies over pieces of research often turn on issues of generalization. Generalization is often conceived of in diverse ways, and various conceptions thereof are confounded in discussions so that confusion arises. Therefore, I must briefly consider some issues about generalization. What is more, the conception of generalization in my framework is not well-known, often misunderstood, and may stand out more clearly by contrasting it with taken for granted, mainstream notions of generalization.

Mainstream research on persons and social life is framed as a study of variables. A researcher isolates these variables for study and reasons about them afterward in his interpretation of the data to make sense of them and make them "reasonable" (Holzkamp 1987; 1994). The psychology of variables studies classified variables, that is, classes of phenomena – such as cognition, emotion, anxiety, the unconscious – rather than concrete phenomena. These classes are abstracted – that is, isolated – from whatever they are linked to in concrete personal social practice, and the researcher works out abstract relations between them. As a result, classes of variables are judged to cause other classes of variables. Calhoun argues about this paradigm in mainstream sociology: "While causal reasoning may be applied to discrete events, it is more commonly used in social science to refer to classes of phenomena, treated as internally equivalent, that influence other classes of similarly equivalent phenomena" (1995, 4). Abbott adds that "action and contingency disappear into the magician's hat of variable-based causality where they hide during the analysis, only to be reproduced with a flourish in the article's closing paragraphs" (2001, 98). In other words, the abstraction discards particular personal and contextual aspects and links. The resulting conception is decontextualized (Dreier 1993a), impersonal and extralocal (Smith 1990), that is, removed from the concrete unfolding of everyday life. This creates a disciplinary universe marked by abstraction and hypostatization, which fits the institutional character of its involvements and fosters an institutional epistemology. It produces a researcher-centeredness in the disciplinary discourse by not allowing the concrete experiences, understandings, and reasons of others to be asserted. Researchers assert a monopoly of interpretation over their research subjects by replacing concrete persons and social practices with classes of variables.

Mainstream psychology searches general causes for general effects and conceives of such general, causal links as abstract, general mechanisms consisting in relations between abstract, general variables. The same abstract variables and mechanisms are claimed to lie behind the same general effects irrespective of when and where and whose behavior we study. In this sense, the variables, the mechanisms, and their causal impacts are fixed. Such a conception claims that general knowledge holds identically everywhere and for everyone. We should find it everywhere, and everybody is subjected to it. It should be trivial and unproblematic to transfer from the research situation, where it was constructed, into other situations and to apply it there. Direct transfer and identical application of general knowledge should be the name of the game. This conception of general knowledge frames the mainstream conception of skills and learning. Lave (1988; unpublished manuscript) targets this conception in her critique of the learning of cognitive skills and their transfer across contexts as an identical basis of situated cognitive accomplishments. I target it too in a similar critique of learning as the transfer of general session insights and as the basis of client accomplishments and activities elsewhere and later (Dreier 1999a; 2001; 2003). The interest in only what is judged to be general turns the general into an abstraction and presents it as an entity isolated from its concrete embeddedness with particular and singular aspects and with cultural and personal understandings. It reveals a poverty of abstract, general theory that must remain relatively culturally insensitive, contextually insensitive, and personally insensitive. Confounding an abstract generality with a concrete, contextual, or personal phenomenon amounts to reductionism and essentialism concerning the complexity and peculiarity of concrete phenomena and persons. The abstraction of generalities complicates our grasp of comprehensive, dynamic, concrete links.

In variable-based studies, the person ceases to be recognized as an agent and is reduced to an arena in which causal variables operate. Causal mechanisms between variables are construed as doing whatever happens rather than as tools persons draw on in situated ways to realize their accomplishments (Harré 1997). Personal agency and understanding are thus ignored, that is, suppressed and de-legitimated. Concrete persons are subsumed to an abstract representational order, and when persons voice situated experiences against it, they fall to the ground as beside the point of the abstract discourse (Mehan 1984; 1993; Smith 1990). Such disciplinary paradigms are instances of a science of control in contrast to a science of the subject (Holzkamp 1983). Abstract and fixed, that is, reified representations of everyday practices and persons confront concrete persons as a foreign power and an alienated expression of their own powers. In attempting to understand and make the best of these representations in their everyday lives, persons must retract the abstractions, that is, take back into their particular situation what was removed from all particular situations and, in so doing, re-combine the abstractions with other particular aspects of the present situation to re-construe its peculiar order. The discourses of abstract representation with their tenets of direct transfer and identical application are not of much help in accomplishing this.

The abstract conception of generalization implies a "contempt for description" which Abbott holds to be a "central reason for sociology's disappearance from the public mind" (2001, 121). Neither description nor particulars but only generalizations are claimed to count as scientific findings. This claim is especially directed against qualitative studies (for responses from qualitative research, see, e.g., Andenæs 1999; Cherry 1995; Haavind 1999; Kvale 1996; Markard 1991; Silverman 2001). In accounts of findings from a project, one would then have to separate what is claimed to be general from the rest and present it as the only scientific finding. Leaving room for description and particulars in relation to general aspects, on the other hand, is an argument for a different conception of generalization and conceptual analysis. I shall return to this after introducing a second major strand of arguments in characterizing the conceptual analysis and outcomes in my project.

A theory about social practice and persons must reflect that they exist in activity. They are re-produced and changed through activity and must, therefore, be studied in activity. The aspects and links of social practice are not fixed but dynamic, and we learn about their dynamics by studying their re-production and change. That is why social practices and persons hold "temporal effects of many sizes, . . . a past of many depths" (Abbott 2001, 124). The strength, pace, and meaning of particular aspects of social practices and persons are also changed in practice by participants. My materials are full of instances of these phenomena. An example of a longstanding temporal effect is seen in the importance to the parents of creating a family life that is different from their families of origin by being deeply marked by their love for their children. At the same time, what this implies changes toward caring for the unfolding of increasingly important parts of their children's lives elsewhere so that their family life must be redefined. An example of a passing aspect is the emerging, and for some time prevalent, significance of being cross, which soon changes again and recedes into the background. These are instances of response shifts in which persons cease attending to certain aspects and emphasize other aspects instead or re-define the meaning of particular aspects and the links between them. Changes in the strength and meaning of particular aspects are seen in their evolving personal stances and in Angie's anxiety and self-confidence. Such changes in particular aspects, and in the importance of various links between them, are crucial to personal change processes in life trajectories and to what therapy is meant to promote. Hence, we need a theoretical framework that – instead of defining fixed and isolated general mechanisms – allows us to comprehend nexuses and, above that, how these nexuses are brought about and change. It should allow us to comprehend what it is that changes the parents' practice of care, what makes the concern with being cross come to the fore and recede again, what makes the parents' personal stances evolve, what brings about and changes Angie's anxiety and self-confidence, and so forth. Accordingly, our concepts focus on characterizing persons by their potentials and abilities (Holzkamp 1983; or, as Harré 1997 puts it, their powers) in relation to their possibilities as participants in social practice, rather than by fixed personal properties that let us understand them as always basically the same.

The prevalent analysis of change in mainstream psychology claims that a set of unchanged causal variables lies behind the production of change. Once constituted, the same general causal variables or mechanisms retain the same basic causal status and impact even if individuals change and these variables and mechanisms cause those changes. The causal variables and mechanisms are claimed to be unaffected by the changes they produce. Thus, personality variables, such as traits (cf. the critique by Quackenbush 2001) are claimed to cause personality changes but remain unaffected by them. This leads to the paradoxical consequence that personality changes do not affect the key personality variables so that one must consider individual changes to be rather impersonal and claim that really no change of personality occurs, or only a superficial one of little theoretical import. The basic personality pattern is fixed and does not change. It is general and abstract.

My conception, on the other hand, is a general framework about a complex and changing nexus. A theory meant to capture linked aspects in a changing social practice must combine generality with change. It must aim at comprehending a changing composition and dynamics of social and personal practices and how aspects emerge and change with changing links between them. Even general aspects and links emerge and change in changing nexuses. Furthermore, the various exemplars of changing nexuses, which such a theory is meant to capture, are not identical. So, it is a general framework for comprehending peculiar and changing nexuses. In analyzing concrete contexts, situations, trajectories, and persons, we encounter peculiar orders of general, particular, and singular aspects, a "peculiar logic of the peculiar subject matter" (Sève 1972). Consequently, the concrete significance of general aspects and links may differ and vary. This mode of understanding the logic of concrete subject matters is dialectics as the study of concrete nexuses. There is a vast literature on this. In his notes on reading Hegel, Lenin nicely summarizes key characteristics of dialectics:

> Let us begin with the most simple, the most ordinary, the most widespread, and so forth, with an arbitrary statement: the leaves on the tree are green; Iwan is a human being; Shutschka is a dog, and the like. Already here is (as Hegel brilliantly noticed) dialectics: the singular is general. . . . Hence the opposites (the singular is contrary to the general) are identical: the singular only exists in the connection that leads to the general. The general only exists in the singular, by virtue of the singular. Every singular is (in one way or the other) general. Every general is (a part or an aspect or the essence of) the singular. Every general only approximately includes all singular objects. Every singular is incompletely incorporated in the general, and so forth. Every singular is connected with another kind of singular (things, phenomena, processes) through thousands of transitions, and so forth. (Lenin 1971:340; translation OD)

In other words, we cannot take for granted that the concrete place and significance of general aspects are the same everywhere. Their place and significance vary and change and must be identified anew in concrete instances. Their links to other aspects referred to by other concepts also vary and change and must be identified anew. The concrete qualities of the aspects that general concepts refer to may, therefore, vary and change and must be identified anew. These variations between particular nexuses of a similar kind have multiple sources. Nonetheless, general concepts are claims about what is generally present and crucial. They are necessary assumptions incorporating our prior general knowledge that may open our understanding of the "peculiar logic of peculiar subject matters" if we bear in mind what I just wrote about the varying place, links, significances, and qualities of general aspects. But a general framework does not fit particular concrete contexts, situations, trajectories, and persons equally because they differ, vary and change.

It follows that we must distinguish between a general conceptual order and the peculiar practical and personal orders of particular instances. If we want to get particular instances right, we must not conflate them with a theory's general conceptual order. That would lead to a researcher-centered analysis. Many concepts in my framework are meant to capture the creation and change of particular personal orders. They focus on the fact that persons re-evaluate, change, and re-combine the aspects and links they attend to and address in their trajectories in structures of social practice highlighting persons as taking into consideration or ignoring, configuring and understanding, composing and pursuing, learning and adopting stances, anticipating and bringing about. A dialectical view on concepts allows us to analyze particular social and personal practices without claiming that their configurations and dynamics are identical. In developing a theory, we identify general links between its concepts to clarify it as an analytic tool for comprehending concrete practices. But it would be a mistake to try to find precisely the general conceptual order of a theory in every instance we study. Theoretical concepts are not just applied directly onto materials as if they predefine their structure, dynamics and meaning as identical with the general structure, dynamics and meaning in the conceptual order of the theory. Approaches to theorizing, which do not distinguish between concepts and practices, such as many discourse theories, are at a loss here. They must mistake the general, conceptual order of their theory as the structure to be found everywhere in practice, and then go on finding just that every time everywhere. A researcher-centered analysis comes out of not distinguishing between discourses as general concepts that researchers are experts on, on the one hand, and social practices, on the other hand, so that discursive distinctions and links between discourse elements come to play the role of divisions and links in social practice.

In my analysis of practices and persons, I recognize the particular place, significance, and qualities of a concept in relation to other aspects of a situation, context, trajectory, or person so that I may conclude that what this concept refers to has a special significance in this situation, context, or trajectory or for this person. Particular instances of what a concept refers to are not identical. They have common aspects and links but are different in other respects. They resemble each other rather than being identical (Medina 2003; Wittgenstein 1953, sections 66 and 67). These resemblances emerge from the complex and dynamic qualities and links of the phenomena my concepts refer to. For instance, anxiety in general reflects a person's feeling that her grip on her situation is uncertain, threatened, or about to be lost (Osterkamp 1975; 1976; 1991). This general quality and dynamics of anxiety informs and guides my analysis of concrete instances. But in particular situations and persons, particular aspects and links are added that create peculiar qualities and dynamics of anxieties. Thus, Angie's anxieties vary across contexts and change over time. What these anxieties then mean to her and what she may do to handle them affect the qualities and dynamics of her anxieties. Likewise, there are general links and dynamics behind the formation and change of self-confidence. But Angie's changing feelings of self-confidence are also marked by the particular links and dynamics of her life trajectory. Her self-confidence has similar as well as different qualities and links compared to, say, the self-confidence of persons involved in elite sports or various competitive relations. Peculiar personal qualities and dynamics of self-confidence thereby emerge.

My analyses are also guided by considering the understandings and concepts of the persons I study. These personal understandings reflect the peculiar personal order of their participation in social practice and incorporate concepts from commonsensical, cultural understandings and forms of life. Thus, Angie's concept of self-confidence reflects a peculiar personal dynamics and order of her participation in social practice in relation to the folk psychology of cultural forms of self-understanding. So does Donna's concept of pulling herself together. My analyses thereof depend on their statements to capture the phenomenological qualities and order of their self-understandings. But I add other aspects and dynamics that they do not mention. Guided by my framework, I consider how they link and change these self-understandings along with their changing participation in their trajectories of participation in social practice. But while their self-confidence and pulling themselves together clearly are affected by their changing participation, their personal concepts do not make these practical links and changes explicit. I therefore reach a different conception of these concepts than they articulate, that is, a critical re-interpretation of their self-understandings. This re-interpretation is a critique of a personalized understanding that severs their personal functioning from its grounding in particular aspects and dynamics of their social practices so that it appears as if abstract, internal mechanisms cause their feelings and behaviors.

In spite of elaborations during the study, my conceptual framework still grasps the case I analyzed incompletely. A theoretical framework is, of course, always incomplete in the sense that it only comprises the general aspects and links of its subject matter. Concrete descriptions of practices are always richer than general conceptions. But my definition of the conceptual aspects, links, and order of the theoretical framework is also incomplete with gray zones, uncovered terrain, and so forth. A degree of analytic uncertainty and doubts about the outcomes of the preceding analyses therefore remains. Since I analyze changing practices and persons, I also face questions of when something is a variant of a given order or a changed order. Qualitative changes in existing orders – in the course of a therapy or in wider historical terms – call for revisions of the analysis. Keeping up with changing practices, may require modifying the general order of a theory.

Concepts do not hold ready-made answers to our quest for understanding a particular subject matter. In the analysis of empirical materials, concepts direct our attention toward the possible existence, place, links, and quality of certain aspects of our subject matter. Since their concrete place, links, and quality are as yet undefined, concepts cannot provide ready-made answers to our analytic queries. They guide us by suggesting particular questions about our materials (Calhoun 1995, 7; Holzkamp 1983): Is the aspect which this concept refers to present? Where is it located in the present configuration? How is it linked to which other parts of it? Which role does it play in this social practice? How are we to characterize its particular qualities and dynamics? There are many other questions. Concepts guide our observations and ground our questions. What is more, because concepts are general, they suggest, say, that we look for personal concerns, but they do not tell us which personal concerns we may find, their particular qualities, what they are linked to, or how they are pursued. Theoretical concepts serve as analytic means for our comprehension of social practices and persons. By using them, we may reach new understandings of concrete social practices and persons, but we may also come to introduce new concepts in order to improve our analytic means of understanding concrete practices and persons.

12.3. Empirical Dimensions and Outcomes of the Project

In mainstream research it is assumed that empirical and theoretical generalizations are created separately. Empirical studies are conceived as vehicles for reaching general, empirical findings and theory as a preexisting, fixed theory being tested by means of new data or applied to make sense of them. But in studies such as mine, the interplay between conceptual and empirical analyses brings about the conceptual and empirical outcomes. The frame of analysis is developed by exploring what it takes to analyze these materials so that coherent sense can be made of them in important ways. On the way, several analytic takes on the materials are explored. But only the one that developed my analyses further is presented in writing the book.

The empirical outcomes of a project such as mine are multidimensional. They are about this particular case; the practice of therapy; the practice of family therapy; family life and family trajectories; structural arrangements and trajectories of participation; persons as participants in social practice; and personal life trajectories and other phenomena and issues of personhood. That makes it complicated to summarize the outcomes. Moreover, the generality of outcomes from projects such as mine is subject to debate. Still, even materials from a single case contain general empirical aspects, and its analysis is based on empirical generalizations. Many statements in my analysis presuppose widespread empirical generalities and are claimed to hold for a much wider range of (personal) social practice than this case. Indeed, materials from all empirical studies – not just case studies – are necessarily particular materials stemming from the particular times and places when they were gathered. So, all empirical studies of general issues involve references beyond their materials. In my study, I refer to widespread generalities and consider a single case in relation to typical contexts, arrangements, and trajectories. The concrete contexts I study are particular exemplars of types of social contexts such as therapy sessions, family homes, and schools. So, my analysis of the case presupposes a generalization of types of contexts, arrangements, and trajectories. While I recognize that the concrete exemplars are not identical with these types, the typifications guide my analysis of them. My recognition of similar arrangements, links, aspects, and trajectories in other social practices also strongly affects the direction in which the analysis of these materials developed and testifies to the generality of its issues and outcomes. In short, my references to generalities lend credibility to the case analysis (Silverman 2001, chapter 8), support its claims, and serve as a critique of other studies of the practice of therapy which neglect their significance.

Contrary to this, some cultural psychologists separate generality and particularity by juxtaposing human universality – as seen in cognitive mechanisms – and particularity. They argue that cultural psychology should be concerned with studying the "likely connection between particular events" (Benson 2001:51, following Bruner 1990). This restricts cultural psychology to the study of particularities. But severing general features from concrete practices presupposes that generalities are abstract entities rather than general aspects varyingly linked with particular aspects in concrete practices. A disinterest in generality also shines through when Benson argues for the significance of location and place in a cultural psychology but is strangely vague about the types of places he may address. After all, our comprehension of concrete places can only be anchored in structures of social practice if we recognize the existence of types of places.

By referring to empirical generalities in particular statements, I make it clear which claims to wider validity they hold. I include significances of arrangements, links, and aspects of social practice with a high degree of empirical generality such as the structural separation of particular kinds of social contexts with particular associated purposes; the fact that particular social practices (such as therapy) are meant to work across places; the arrangement of separate and secluded occasions (sessions) with experts (who are strangers to you) for that purpose; the fact that such occasions (sessions) merely are particular limited parts of people's (clients') lives across places; the fact that persons live their lives, face troubles, change, learn, and develop in trajectories of participation in such structures of social practice; and so forth. In evaluating the empirical generality of my case analysis, the wide frequency of these and other arrangements and aspects in social practice must be recognized.

However, the main empirical outcome of an analysis such as mine lies in the comprehension of concrete and changing nexuses. I seek knowledge about links between phenomena and events and how they are re-produced, vary, and change in changing nexuses. My outcome is not a matter of identifying a variable, phenomenon, or event as an isolated generality. The prevailing conception of empirical generalization concentrates on assessing the distribution and frequency of a particular cause, phenomenon, and event couched in statements about "always when x then y" (Holzkamp 1983, chapter 9). Such an empirical generalization calls for other materials and methods than in my study where I am not directly concerned with documenting and predicting such frequencies but with identifying nexuses in social practice and characterizing their changing dynamics. Furthermore, when I identify general aspects in nexuses, I argue that their impacts vary in concrete instances depending on their particular place and particular links to particular other aspects in those instances.

The empirical outcome of a study such as mine can in fact never merely consist in generalities. If outcomes must be general in order to count as outcomes, studies such as mine may even seem to lead to no real, pure findings, and knowledge about particular nexuses in concrete instances which such studies offer may be rejected as knowledge not worth gathering. Behind this rejection lurks the assumption of generalities as isolated and abstract generalities, that is, a conception of generality that differs from and cannot be applied as a measure for studies aimed at gaining knowledge about nexuses in which general, particular, and singular aspects cannot be separated and which are changing nexuses of such aspects. Knowledge about concrete nexuses is a genuine kind of knowledge, different from knowledge about isolated generalities. A study may deliver a genuine contribution to knowledge irrespective of how general the comprehended nexus is.

Particular instances of social practice may be characterized by similar qualities, links, and dynamics. They are similar and not identical since practices with the same general aspects also hold different aspects and links in particular patterns. Particular instances are not characterized by an identical nexus, and we need to identify the place, links and impact of a general aspect in this instance by raising it as a question rather than taking it for granted as a pre-given answer. We must study how instances are composed. Likewise, the general aspects we claim to hold beyond a particular case do not necessarily hold elsewhere in an identical manner with identical links and dynamics. How they hold in other instances must be studied too. Claims to typicality and generality are not claims to identity between all exemplars of a type of practice.

In his later philosophy, Wittgenstein underscores that instances of things, persons, situations, contexts, practices, or whatever are not strictly identical but show "a complicated network of overlapping and criss-crossing similarities" and differences (Wittgenstein 1953, section 66). Even those we categorize as the same are similar in some respects and different in other respects. As Medina puts it,

> we treat all kinds of different things as the same although they are not strictly identical in any respect; that is, in our categorizations different things are treated as instances of the same category even though there is no aspect (or set of aspects) that they all have in common: many different kinds of activities are called games and many different kinds of artifacts are called chairs; and we can always add new items to the list of things that fall under these concepts (we can always invent new kinds of game and produce new kinds of chairs). (2003, 660)

Thus, particular families are not mere instances of a general essence of family life lurking behind their surface but show "family resemblances" (Wittgenstein 1953, section 67; see Toulmin 1996, 214). Indeed, according to Wittgenstein, concepts are like families. Their members resemble one another in many different ways: some may have similar hair; others, similar noses; others may share particular ways of talking or similar laughter. Families are composed of heterogeneous elements exhibiting some similarities, but there is no fixed set of necessary and sufficient conditions that determines membership. Medina adds that

> the analogy between families and concepts underscores change: a family is a living unit whose members come and go; and, similarly, what is covered by a concept is subject to change and must be left open. Moreover, even when the extension of the concept does not change, even when the membership in the family remains the same, the relations among the members of the family (as well as their relations with other families) change as differences become visible and family ties are relaxed. (2003, 661–662)

A degree of uncertainty and disagreement remains when we determine the links between general, particular, and singular aspects in concrete instances. The degree of typicality of single cases and the precision of our knowledge about their nexus is then marked by some uncertainty. Moreover, while I may ground claims to generality in my case analysis, I cannot certify this generality empirically. This uncertainty is complicated by the fact that therapy takes place behind closed doors and that accounts of therapy are unreliable descriptions and understandings of what took place and how they work (Dreier 1983; 1993b). I cannot even certify the generality of this case by detailing what we did because I cannot know precisely what goes on in other cases. This difficulty is grounded in the current state of affairs in the social practice of therapy. Because of it, a crucial part of the judgment about the fit and generality of my claims is up to readers who are therapists and family members. Add to this that therapy is conducted in diverse agencies, settings, and arrangements and marked by diverse and competing traditions. This makes it difficult to document to what degree the analysis in this book holds – and whether it holds equally – for all practices of therapy. Indeed, due to this uncertainty, the concrete conduct of therapy is held in the grip of personal, local, and traditional preferences (Dreier 1998b). Yet, since I analyze therapy as a social practice, I focus on features shared by any and all practice of therapy, although their significance and the ways in which they are played out differ in different settings and schools of therapy.

My emphasis on the existence and significance of variation is an outcome of the case analysis, which goes against assumptions about the uniformity, and in that sense generality, of concrete practice. Variations occur because partic-ipant activities are grounded in a complex range of possibilities and concerns that must be realized selectively. Variation matters to all participants, it has contextually different ranges and significances, and its meaning differs across their life trajectories. By contrast, variations are uninteresting to mainstream research, which construes uniformity and repetitiveness – as a kind of overgen-eralization (Wortham 2006, 275) – in their analysis of ongoing practices. The experimental study of variables considers variations broadly taken as a distur-bance to be ruled out as a symptom of the lack of control over the experimental research situation where only the dependent variable is allowed to vary. Varia-tion is thus highly restricted and controlled. Some researchers grant a limited role to variation. As mentioned in chapter 6, Valsiner (1984) distinguishes between the typological and variational epistemological frameworks in psy-chology where changeability is essential in the latter. He claims that variability within a context is not essential but, nonetheless, generated by the system of person–environment relationships. This is in line with my claims that a par-ticular range of variability is characteristic of particular contextual scopes and arrangements and, hence, changes as social practices change. But, in contrast to Valsiner, I emphasize the often major personal significance of variation in ongoing personal social practices and of arrangements leaving room for varied modes of participation. I also argue that we must not lose sight of variations by subsuming them under empirical generalizations and the general conceptual order of our theories. Variability as well as changeability are typical features of ongoing, personal social practices and should be studied as such.

The elucidation of the multicontextuality of the social practice of therapy and the everyday lives and changes of persons in social practice is a further outcome of my project. It counters oversimplified conceptions of persons, family life, and therapy and speaks against regarding the personal relations between those practices as a transfer of abstract generalizations and in favor of a situated conception of generalization. A multicontextual study emphasizes the composed and variable nature of personal activity and understanding in social practice. Taking account of the multicontextuality of people's lives is also methodologically important in considering mainstream ways of doing research and developing other ones. Research in psychology and related disciplines is typically done in one delimited situation/context so that the multicontextual character of social practice and subjectivity is lost. Holzkamp (1995, 828) calls it the "birth error of psychology" to separate a pure experimental or thera-peutic reality from an everyday reality of less scientific dignity resulting in an "intentional blindness towards experimental subjects' and patients'/clients' everyday conduct of life, both as a fact and as something to conceptualize scien-tifically." Moreover, the contexts studied are typically ones in which experts – researchers or professionals – are in charge and more easily exert a monopoly of interpretation. At the same time, since researchers and professionals do not study their subjects and clients in other contexts of their ordinary lives, they remain blind to the fact that their subjects and clients retain a corresponding monopoly of interpretation over their own affairs and reactions in those other places, which subverts expert claims about them.

Determining the scope of possibilities for participants in their social prac-tice is a crucial aim for my analyses. Following Holzkamp (1987; 1993; see also Markard 1991), the psychological analysis of the scope of possibilities, which conditions and events in social practice afford persons, is called an anal-ysis of the meaning of those possibilities. An empirical analysis of persons in social practice also comprises how participants realize those possibilities. It involves an analysis of participant activities in relation to those possibilities and of participant reasons to realize particular possibilities rather than others or to refrain from realizing particular possibilities. This approach acknowl-edges the significance of activity – in my study, what the clients, the therapists, and others really did – for what turns out to be the outcome. So an empirical analysis of persons in social practice incorporates the analysis of participant activities and of the outcomes as outcomes of participant activities. Moreover, the realization of possibilities may include the changing of possibilities. I do not just identify a scope of possibilities or compare scopes of possibilities for different persons or at different times or places. I analyze how persons change their possibilities and react to changes in them which just happen or which they brought about. In accordance with the purpose of therapy, change processes are at the center of my analysis. Issues about the generality of my findings are, therefore, not just issues about the generality of given scopes but about the generality of the other scopes that the participants bring about in their personal social practices.

But the realization of scopes of possibilities is always selective and, hence, varied and diverse. Even realizations of a similar scope of possibilities depend on similar participant abilities too, and participants may act upon differences between these similar situations rather than their similarities. This reduces the likelihood of similar outcomes even from similar starting points. In short, I study things that are done in a particular way and might have been done otherwise. This underscores not simply being interested in how widespread and, in that sense, empirically general an outcome is, say, to which extent this case and its course of changes are representative of family therapy casework. Rather, I claim that something similar to what occurred in this case may be done by means of similar modes of participation in similar structures of social practice with similar problems. In other words, I do not generalize about the distribution and frequency of particular states of affairs but about the possibilities and dynamics of changes in social practices.

Besides similar possibilities and abilities, participants must have similar reasons to change if outcomes are to become similar. After all, participants will not change in similar ways just because their researchers are keen to document generalities. We cannot expect them always to follow scrupulously in the footsteps of others even in similar situations. What is more, studying possibilities and their realization is not merely a matter of how widespread they are but of how widespread they may become. It is a matter of identifying possibilities for their generalization in practice. Realizing them in diverse or generalizing ways is up to the readers of such an analysis, to people, to future practice. We may compare instances and learn from those comparisons, but if generalizations are about possibilities in the world, they must, first of all, be generalized in practice. Possibilities become general by being realized in general in practice (see discussion that follows and Andenæs 1999; Dreier 1998c). The current distribution of scopes of possibilities, of course, matters. But when we are interested in finding new scopes of possibilities and learning about the dynamics and scopes for changing present nexuses, finding just one new instance of what is possible may be crucial (Haug 1981) and point the way for future changes.

All the same, I pointed to general aspects in the possibilities and dynamics of changes in this case. Thus, changes linked to therapy must be pursued across contexts in relation to the structural arrangement of a sequence of secluded sessions allowing particular possibilities. They are marked by clients who are subjected to intended change efforts from their therapists and who feel supervised by their therapists and obliged to change and, hence, by the dynamics of clients pulling themselves together. Change processes are affected by the occurrence and timing of events elsewhere and by the points the clients have reached in their life trajectories. Still, such general aspects have peculiar impacts in individual cases and may be realized in various ways. They interact with other particular aspects of concrete changes, and their impacts change in the course of changes. An analysis of a changing practice must hence grasp changes in its composition and dynamics. The links between aspects and their qualities and significances change, some general and particular aspects appear and disappear, finite events and pursuits occur and end, and participant responses to similar situations change. Participants' concerns, understandings, stances, and abilities change too. In addition, elements in complex practices change at different rates, which affect their composition and dynamics. In short, the course of complex changes is marked by various increasing or decreasing similarities. Complex changes often lead to new similarities and new differences in new constellations of social and personal practices.

A case analysis offers an opportunity to learn about the changeability of personal social practices regardless of how general, peculiar, or varied they are. Change does not follow a general course. There are different courses and kinds of change. The courses and composition of change differ between parents and children who seize them from particular positions, contexts, and compositions in their conducts of everyday life and life trajectories. While Angie begins changing in events and relations with her friends elsewhere, linking her pursuits from there with sessions and her life at home, Mary's pursuits of changes center on her life at home and are primarily triggered by her attempts to resolve current family troubles. The primary location, the cross-contextual composition, the reasons, and the dynamics and pursuits of their changes differ. In addition, some changes are minor ones, not easily noticeable and difficult to discern from ongoing variations. Many changes do not lead to changes in the structural arrangements of the social practices in which persons participate. Among them are minor changes in current arrangements and in participants' participation, concerns, and understandings. In short, a general concept of change must encompass the fact that practices of change also change.

In my analysis of change, I deal with changing links between phenomena and events and how they are re-produced, vary, and change in changing nexuses. My primary interest is not the sheer occurrence of a phenomenon or an event, but its identification in nexuses and the dynamics of those nexuses, and I do not seek to document and predict the frequency and probability of the occurrence of phenomena or events. I identify links between places in structures of social practice and persons moving around in them with more or less clear and changing understandings thereof, agreeing or disagreeing with particular arrangements and practices while having or not having made up their minds about them with particular consequences for themselves, their practice, and their changes. I define problems in the same way by determining what they are linked to, the dynamics of their practical grounds, place, and meaning. I reconstruct changes in problems from confused troubles toward problems identified and located in their practice. And I analyze the varying and changing salience and meaning of particular troubles in their ongoing lives.

In sum, I study changes in nexuses as well as changes of nexuses. However, since I analyze the social practice of therapy, I recognize that I am to be dealing with not only a changing practice but also with a practice intended to bring about changes. Change is in focus and on the agenda in many ways. This general aspect of the social practice I study affects the qualities, meaning, and dynamics of the course of changes.

12.4. Uses of Research in Social Practice

Research outcomes are defined and published in the hope that they will be used elsewhere and later. A general theory may be used to analyze particular, concrete nexuses. In doing so, persons pick up the general, analytic proposals of a theory, perhaps consider and argue about it, and use its concepts as analytic tools to guide their understanding of themselves, each other, and their shared and separate social practices. The outcomes of my empirical analyses make certain possibilities visible and comprehensible and their realization imaginable and perhaps believable. They identify possibilities analytically and thereby offer "possibilities for thinking" (Dreier 1993b). My empirical outcomes consist in analytic claims about possibilities not yet generalized in practice. These analytic claims only become general in practice by being realized in general in practice. Readers, therapists, clients, just plain folks may adopt these analytic possibilities as their standpoint in directing their participation and pursuits of change in practice. Their judgments, situations, and activities are involved in the practical generalization of the analytic generalizations I propose, which, until then, remain hypothetical, virtual, and potential. The proof of their generalizability in practice is up to all of us. General analytic claims only become general in practice by being realized in general in practice.

But the mainstream conception of research is aimed at the production of knowledge, while bracketing its use or seeing it as taking place in practices external to research. Conceptions of empirical generalization mostly bracket its use or see it as a direct application outside the boundaries of research. Hence, generalization is normally taken merely to be about the production of knowledge and not the generalization of the social practices concerned.

Generalization is the name of the game in the field of research broadly taken where researchers compete with each other over the claimed generality of their findings – in abstraction from their use by others. In higher education, general knowledge is transmitted and acquired. Individual students are to internalize it and, thus, come to represent, transfer, and apply it in their activities as scholars (Dreier 2001; 2003; Lave unpublished manuscript). They are to become bearers of generalities, and their positions in the rating scales of student assessments reflect how well they acquire this general knowledge and come to represent it. Still, even researchers use knowledge selectively, reinterpret and modify it, and so forth – not unlike professionals and just plain folks. Generalization is also intertwined with other issues for researchers such as struggles over what counts as knowledge in a discipline or field. And it is less obvious that generalization is the name of the game in the use of research findings.

Mainstream research claims that the generality of findings defines their usefulness. General findings are useful because of their generality, whereas findings about particularities or about the "the peculiar logic of the peculiar subject matter" are of limited and doubtful use. The tight coupling between generality and usefulness rests on a conception of use as the transfer of general knowledge to a, more or less limited, set of situations across places with the same general features followed by their direct application in these situations. This is the model of knowledge seen in the model of learning as the transmission, internalization, transfer and application of general knowledge (Lave unpublished manuscript; Dreier 2001; 2003). It implies that a project only matters if it produces directly transferable and applicable results, that is, generalizations that hold identically and can be implemented identically across diverse contexts and for diverse participants. Strictly speaking, such findings are of no use in different situations, scopes, practices, therapies, personal troubles, trajectories, and what have you – unless these differences can be neutralized and bracketed so that a direct and identical application may take place. If this conception is to guarantee the usefulness of general knowledge, the world must consist in situations based on and driven by the same general properties.

When a belief in the generality of knowledge is combined with the externalization of use from the re-production sites of knowledge, concepts like transfer and application must generate the link to situations of use and instruct the proper use elsewhere. But, as argued in this book, this model rests on a particular structural arrangement of the re-production of knowledge and its relations to use and of the relations between sites of expertise and ordinary practices. Here direct application of general knowledge via transfer is the name of the game for the use of knowledge. Direct application presupposes a scientific knowledge that maintains its generality in the practices where it is to be used. Analytic and practical generalizations may be confounded precisely because of the belief that, across places, the world consists in and is structured by the same basic generalities represented in the body of knowledge of research. If the world were like that, we need not study uses in other places systematically. They can be derived directly from the body of general knowledge. However, the concepts of transfer and application of knowledge neither capture well what is involved in using insights from therapy sessions nor the uses of research outcomes. Direct application presupposes a docile following of expert knowledge where users aim at "getting it right" by complying with general knowledge. This view on application is researcher-centered rather than user-centered, and this conception of general knowledge grants knowledge a normalizing function. It makes researchers continue competing over their analytic generalizations with an uneasy feeling that their outcomes are not really used as intended, as hoped, or as they should.

But many research outcomes are not a fixed and final knowledge to be transported around the world. They are an incomplete and open-ended knowledge involved in transformations within and beyond the practice of research. Believing that the outcomes of a research project are complete and fixed when it ends or in the written account is a too retrospective point of view involved in the abstraction of research practice to be modeled elsewhere and later. Thus, when knowledge produced in sessions is picked up and included in other practices with other scopes, concerns, and coparticipants, it is re-interpreted, negotiated, modified, and changed. We have also seen that knowledge is not just used after the knowledge production is completed. On the contrary, there is interplay between the production and use of knowledge throughout the therapy, and it involves the designated users as well as the designated producers. Production and use can neither be separated in terms of times, places, or agents. Knowledge is produced, not the least by clients moving into and out of the designated sites of production and application. Using knowledge is a key factor in producing it in a structural arrangement that calls for participant trajectories into and out of the designated sites of production and use. Studying this turns into practice research, which sees the knowledge produced as being involved in changes in social practice.

Likewise, whether the outcomes of my project hold in practice afterwards is a matter of whether, how, and to what extent they are used. To hold as outcomes about practice, they must be realized in practice. This study works in practice if people pick it up accordingly elsewhere. In that respect, it is no different from other studies or interventions, regardless of the immodesty of their claims. Because its outcomes are about activities and presuppose activity to be brought about, re-produced, and generalized in the future, to what degree they will hold is up to what people do with them in social practice beyond its time and place. The generalization of its outcomes in practice is a matter of practices elsewhere and later – as are uses that modify and change its outcomes. Indeed, general outcomes may be particularized, and particular outcomes may be generalized. As outcomes of a research project, they are but analytic proposals to be realized and generalized in practice. If ever they are to become generalized in practice, others must pick these analytic proposals up in other practices with similar scopes, arrangements, issues, concerns, and participants.

The standpoint of critical psychology on generalization of practice in practice is directed at the generalization in practice of people's scopes of possibilities (Holzkamp 1983, chapter 9), implying a generalization of their access to general resources and an equal share in the joint command over relevant affairs. It is also directed at the generalization of personal abilities to take part in this. We may then ask how people may join in extending shared scopes of possibilities and, more specifically, creating joint possibilities for using the analytic resources of research for such purposes. But reading a book is done individually, or, if it is done in groups, they are often not those groups of coparticipants in the social practices where readers may want to use its analytic proposals. If individual readers find issues worth pursuing, they face the challenge of finding ways to interest their coparticipants in joint pursuits. This is a complex personal and social process during which what gets used may be filtered and modified in various ways (Dreier 1989). Joining around a generalization in practice also presupposes (the bringing about of) a particular social situation with similar participant concerns in using the analytic proposals of a research project in the practice in question. In a broader perspective, it presupposes the bringing about of a sufficient measure of political unity of joining around such a common pursuit. This is far from always the case and cannot always be brought about, and that cautions us to take a broader view on the uses of research outcomes than as general means for the generalization of practice.

The expanding practice of research increasingly offers outcomes with competing and contradictory knowledge claims to potential users in other practices. This has made various addressees and the general public more wary of simply taking over and applying a specific knowledge claim. Since all competing and contradictory knowledge claims cannot be general, the general attitude toward knowledge has changed in the direction of seeing research outcomes as particular knowledge proposals (Dreier 1998c). This complicates what is presumed to be a simple and direct knowledge transfer.

Furthermore, knowledge from research is used in multiple and diverse ways by multiple others such as clients, therapists, families, school teachers, students, and researchers. Instead of one general use of research outcomes, there are many particular and selective uses. Depending on their local situations, understandings, and concerns, readers will realize the analyses in this book in particular and selective ways. And in using these outcomes they will be modified and developed further to become usable in situated practices and remain relevant and adequate (Dreier 1999a; 1999c; 2001; 2003). The usability of outcomes involves much more than a simple and direct transfer and application elsewhere. It involves much the same complex processes as in relation to pieces of advice and insights in sessions. Regardless of what was accomplished in sessions, it must be pursued through chains of action across different and similar places and linked to whatever else goes on and matters in these places, to their different and similar scopes, to the different and similar concerns and stakes of varying constellations of participants, and to the fights and mutual understandings between the varying participants about how to include and use them. In practice as well as analytically, users must understand and realize outcomes in situated ways. So, outcomes will be pursued in other ways than first understood when they were gained in the context of research or therapy. They will be subject to further learning elsewhere and later, and users will often come to their own understandings of them and draw their own conclusions.

Concrete uses then hold mixes of general and particular, similar and different aspects of the research outcomes, which reflect their situated inseparability and constellations in particular places, and their association with particular meanings and concerns. As argued earlier, the significance of research is not restricted to its generalizations. Whether a finding is general or not may not even be decisive for making some use of an analyzed link or nexus. Nor must what participants find important to analyze and change in their particular context correspond to a general aspect in the research outcomes. They may want to pursue a particular aspect of the outcomes. On top of that, there are often conflicts over the optional uses of research outcomes. Indeed, the outcomes may become a subject or a means of conflict that would have to be overcome in order to make room for a generalizing use.

In expanding our understanding of the usability of research outcomes beyond the claimed generalizations, we must take the occurrence of different uses and the use of differences one step further. Potential users may also learn from differences between the social practice analyzed in a project and their own social practice. In some respects, they may want to make their practice more similar to the researched practice, but they may not want to do so in other respects. On the contrary, they may get a clearer understanding of how they want their practice to be or become different in certain respects. They may want to do things differently and include and modify aspects of the outcomes selectively in such a way that they preserve differences. While theories of learning focus on generalization, to the point of believing in instituting identical practices, persons do not just learn from discovering or wanting to increase similarities but also from recognizing differences (Dreier 1999a; 1999c; 2001; 2003). Comparing with outcomes from another practice may lead to new understandings and proposals for what to do in practices that are both similar to and different from it – or even its opposites in some respects. Thus, persons may learn about conducting or using therapy from a different way of conducting or using it while insisting on not wanting to do it in that way. They may rather want to do it in a different way that becomes clearer by contrasting it with particular aspects of how it was done and, perhaps, selectively including and modifying some aspects thereof in their practice. Persons may also learn from the analysis of a particular scope and process of change compared with their other concerns for change in, perhaps, other directions in the face of other scopes in other practices. Much learning from historical research has this character to it. Due to such learning, persons may now come to realize what they want and do not want their practice to be and become. A conception of learning insisting one-sidedly that the situation of learning and situations of use have to be or become identical oversimplifies and abstracts the situations involved to incorporating basically the same generality. It then conceptualizes the links between the situations of learning and use as a matter of direct transfer and application of a fixed outcome from the learning situation. Differences and similarities between situations are, of course, not only a matter of comparing their present states but also their scopes of possibilities for change and the diverse modes of realizing diverse change processes that diverse participants may select in practice.

We can now see that the production and use of knowledge in the social practice of research must be understood by means of a conception of learning and knowledge similar to the one used for participants in other fields of social practice. This opens a wider perspective on the study of the social practice of research and various fields of professional expertise, and it places the prevalent conception of generalization in a different perspective. Indeed, the dimensions and issues of use explode and relativize the issue of generalization as presented in the research literature. But it does not call into question the assumption that an analysis must contain generalizations in order to be to a suitable means for generalizing social practices.

References

Abbott, Andrew. 2001. *Time Matters: On Theory and Method*. Chicago: University of Chicago Press.

Alcoff, Linda. 1996. *Real Knowing: New Versions of the Coherence Theory*. Ithaca, NY: Cornell University Press.

Aldous, Joan. 1996. *Family Careers: Rethinking the Developmental Perspective*. London: Sage.

Andenæs, Agnes. 1999. Generalisering: Om ringvirkninger og gjenbruk av resultater fra en kvalitativ undersøkelse. In Hanne Haavind, red. *Kjønn og fortolkende metode. Metodiske muligheter i kvalitativ forskning*. Oslo: Gyldendal Norsk Forlag, 287–320.

Asay, Ted R., and Michael J. Lambert. 1999. The Empirical Case for the Common Factors in Therapy: Quantitative Findings. In Hubble, Duncan, and Miller, eds., 23–55.

Bandura, Albert. 1999. Social Cognitive Theory of Personality. In Lawrence A. Pervin and Oliver P. John, eds. *Handbook of Personality: Theory and Research, Second Edition*. New York: The Guilford Press, 154–196.

Barham, Peter, and Robert Hayward. 1991. *From the Mental Patient to the Person*. London: Routledge.

Barlösius, Eva. 1997. *Naturgemäße Lebensführung. Zur Geschichte der Lebensreform um die Jahrhundertwende*. Frankfurt am Main: Campus Verlag.

Behringer, Louise. 1998. *Lebensführung als Identitätsarbeit. Der Mensch im Chaos des modernen Alltags*. Frankfurt am Main: Campus Verlag.

Bellah, Robert N., Richard Madsen, William M. Sullivan, Ann Swidler, and Steven M. Tipton. 1996. *Habits of the Heart: Individualism and Commitment in American Life*. Berkeley: University of California Press.

Bennett, Michael. 2005. *The Purpose of Counselling and Psychotherapy*. Houndmills: Palgrave Macmillan.

Benson, Ciarán. 2001. *The Cultural Psychology of Self: Place, Morality and Art in Human Worlds*. London: Routledge.

Bergin, Allen E., and Sol. L. Garfield. 1994. Overview, Trends and Future Issues. In Allen E. Bergin and Sol L. Garfield, eds., *Handbook of Psychotherapy and Behavior Change*. New York: Wiley, 821–830.

Bohart, Arthur C., and Karen Tallman. 1999. *How Clients Make Therapy Work: The Process of Active Self-Healing*. Washington, DC: American Psychological Association.

Borg, Tove. 2002. Livsførelse i hverdagen under rehabilitering. Et socialpsykologisk studie. AUC: Ph.d.-afhandling. Århus: Center for Sundhed, Menneske, Kultur.

315

Bourdieu, Pierre, and Loïc J. D. Wacquant. 1992. *An Invitation to Reflexive Sociology*. Chicago: University of Chicago Press.

Breckenridge, Carol A., and Candice Vogler, eds. 2001. The Critical Limits of Embodiment: Reflections on Disability Criticism. *Public Culture* 13:35.

Bruner, Jerome. 1990. *Acts of Meaning*. Cambridge, MA: Harvard University Press.

Bruner, Jerome. 1996. *The Culture of Education*. Cambridge; MA: Harvard University Press.

Calhoun, Craig. 1995. *Critical Social Theory: Culture, History and the Challenge of Difference*. Oxford: Blackwell.

Cherry, Frances. 1995. *The 'Stubborn' Particulars of Social Psychology: Essays on the Research Process*. New York: Routledge.

Christensen, Lone Rahbek. 1987. *Hver vore veje*. København: Museum Tusculanum.

Crossley, Nick. 1996. *Intersubjectivity: The Fabric of Social Becoming*. London: Sage.

Curtis, Rebecca, C., and George Stricker, eds. 1991. *How People Change: Inside and Outside of Therapy*. New York: Plenum Press.

Daly, Kerry J. 1996. *Families & Time: Keeping Pace in a Hurried Culture*. London: Sage.

De Léon, David. 2006. The Cognitive Biographies of Things. In Alan Costall and Ole Dreier, eds., *Doing Things with Things: The Design and Use of Everyday Objects*. Aldershot: Ashgate, 113–130.

Derrida, Jacques. 1982. *Margins of Philosophy*. Chicago: University of Chicago Press.

DeVries, Marten V. 1997. Recontextualizing Psychiatry: Toward Ecologically Valid Mental Health Research. *Transcultural Psychiatry* 34:85–218.

Donovan, Jenny L., and D. R. Blake. 1992. Patient Non-compliance: Deviance or Reasoned Decision Making. *Social Science and Medicine* 34:507–513.

Dreier, Ole. 1979. Die Bedeutung der Hausarbeit für die weibliche Psyche. In Dorothee Roer, Hrsg., *Persönlichkeitstheoretische Aspekte von Frauenarbeit und – Arbeitslosigkeit*. Köln: Pahl-Rugenstein, 31–46. Danish edition: Husarbejdets betydning for den kvindelige psyke. *Udkast* 1980 8:347–368.

Dreier, Ole. 1980. *Familiäres Sein und familiäres Bewußtsein. Therapeutische Analyse einer Arbeiterfamilie. Texte zur Kritischen Psychologie Bd. 11*. Frankfurt am Main: Campus Verlag. Revised edition of Ole Dreier. 1977. Familieværen og bevidsthed. En analyse af en familie i behandling. København: Dansk Psykologisk Forlag.

Dreier, Ole. 1983. Tagungsbericht. *Forum Kritische Psychologie* 12:184–188.

Dreier, Ole. 1984. Probleme der Entwicklung psychotherapeutischer Arbeit. In: Karl-Heinz Braun and Gerd Gekeler, Hrsg., *Objektive und subjektive Widersprüche in der Sozialarbeit/Sozialpädagogik*. Marburg: VA&G, 137–150.

Dreier, Ole. 1987. Zur Funktionsbestimmung von Supervision in der therapeutischen Arbeit. Ein Erfahrungsbericht. In Wolfgang Maiers and Morus Markard, Hrsg., *Kritische Psychologie als Subjektwissenschaft. Klaus Holzkamp zum 60. Geburtstag*. Frankfurt am Main: Campus Verlag, 44–56.

Dreier, Ole. 1988a. Denkweisen über Therapie. *Forum Kritische Psychologie* 22:42–67.

Dreier, Ole. 1988b. Zur Sozialpsychologie der Therapie von Übergewichtigen. Bemerkungen zum Aufsatz von Haisch & Haisch. *Zeitschrift für Sozialpsychologie* 19:287–296.

Dreier, Ole. 1989. Fortbildung im psychosozialen Bereich als Einheit von Forschung und Praxis. *Forum Kritische Psychologie* 24:48–84.

Dreier, Ole. 1991. Client Needs and Interests in Psychotherapy. In Charles Tolman and Wolfgang Maiers, eds., *Critical Psychology – Contributions to an Historical Science of the Subject*. Cambridge: Cambridge University Press, 196–211.

Dreier, Ole. 1993a. Re-searching Psychotherapeutic Activity. In Seth Chaiklin and Jean Lave, eds., *Understanding Practice: Perspectives in Activity and Context*. Cambridge: Cambridge University Press, 104–124.

Dreier, Ole. 1993b. *Psykosocial behandling: En teori om et praksisområde*. København: Dansk psykologisk Forlag. Second edition 2002.

Dreier, Ole. 1994. Personal Locations and Perspectives: Psychological Aspects of Social Practice. In Niels Engelsted et al., eds. *Psychological Yearbook*. Copenhagen: University of Copenhagen, 1, 63–90.

Dreier, Ole. 1996. Ændring af professionel praksis på sundhedsområdet gennem praksisforskning. In Uffe Juul Jensen, Jens Quesel, and Peter Fuur Andersen, red. *Forskelle og forandring. Bidrag til en humanistisk sundhedsforskning*. Aarhus: Philosophia, 113–140.

Dreier, Ole. 1997. Subjectivity and the Practice of Psychotherapy. In Charles Tolman, Fran Cherry, Ian Lubek, and Rene van Hezewijk, eds., *Recent Trends in Theoretical Psychology*. York: Captus Press, 55–61.

Dreier, Ole. 1998a. Client Perspectives and Uses of Psychotherapy. *The European Journal of Psychotherapy, Counseling & Health* 1:295–310.

Dreier, Ole. 1998b. Terapeutisk kompetence i en problematisk praksis. *Psyke & Logos* 19: 618–642.

Dreier, Ole. 1998c. Tradition og fornyelse i dansk psykologi. *Nordiske Udkast* 26: 23–38.

Dreier, Ole. 1999a. Læring som ændring af personlig deltagelse i sociale kontekster. In Klaus Nielsen and Steinar Kvale, red., *Mesterlære – Læring som social praksis*. Copenhagen: Hans Reitzels Forlag, 76–99.

Dreier, Ole. 1999b. Personal Trajectories of Participation Across Contexts of Social Practice. *Outlines* 1:5–32.

Dreier, Ole. 1999c. Uddannelse og læring i praksis. In Anders Siig Andersen, Kim Pedersen, and Karin Svejgaard, red., *På sporet af praksis*. Copenhagen: The Danish Ministry of Education Press, 42–58.

Dreier, Ole. 2000. Psychotherapy in Clients' Trajectories Across Contexts. In Cheryl Mattingly and Linda Garro, eds., *Narratives and the Cultural Construction of Illness and Healing*. Berkeley: University of California Press, 237–258.

Dreier, Ole. 2001. Virksomhed – læring – deltagelse. *Nordiske Udkast* 29:39–58.

Dreier, Ole. 2003. Learning in Personal Trajectories of Participation. In Niamh Stephenson, Lorraine H. Radtke, René J. Jorna, and Henderikus J. Stam, eds., *Theoretical Psychology: Critical Contributions*. Concord, Canada: Captus University Publications, 20–29.

Dreier, Ole. 2005. The Social Practice of Psychotherapy: Theory – Structure – Critique. In Aydan Gülerce, Arnd Hofmeister, Irmingard Staeuble, Guy Saunders, and John Kay, eds., *Contemporary Theorizing in Psychology: Global Perspectives*. Concord, Canada: Captus Press, 162–170.

Dreier, Ole, Margaret Kleinmanns, Monika Konitzer-Feddersen, Hans-Peter Michels, and Anneli Raitola. 1988. Die Bedeutung institutioneller Bedingungen psychologischer Praxis am Beispiel der Therapie. In Joseph Dehler and Konstanze Wetzel, Hrsg., *Zum Verhältnis von Theorie und Praxis in der Psychologie*. Marburg: VA&G, 81–112.

Duffy, Ann, and Norene Pupo. 1992. *Part-Time Paradox: Connecting Gender, Work, and Family*. Toronto: McClelland and Stewart.

Eckert, Penny. 1989. *Jocks & Burnouts: Social Categories and Identity in the High School*. New York: Teachers College, Columbia University.

Elder, Glenn H. 1998. The Life Course as Developmental Theory. *Child Development* 69:1–12.

Eliasson, Rosemari, and Pär Nygren. 1983. *Närstudier af psykoterapi: Psykiatrisk Verksamhet Bd. 2*. Stockholm: Prisma.

Engeström, Yrjö, Ritva Engeström, and Tarja Vähäahu. 1999. When the Center Does Not Hold: The Importance of Knotworking. In Seth Chaiklin, Mariane Hedegaard, and Uffe Juul Jensen, eds., *Activity Theory and Social Practice*. Aarhus: Aarhus University Press, 345–374.

Erikson, Erik H. 1965. *Childhood and Society*. Hammondsworth: Penguin Books.

Estroff, Sue E. 1985. *Making It Crazy: An Ethnography of Psychiatric Clients in an American Community*. Berkeley: University of California Press.

Fleeson, William. 2004. Moving Personality beyond the Person-Situation Debate. *Current Directions in Psychological Science* 13:2, 83–87.

Forchhammer, Hysse. 2006. The Woman Who Used Her Walking Stick as a Telephone: The Use of Utilities in Praxis. In Alan Costall and Ole Dreier, eds., *Doing Things with Things: The Design and Use of Everyday Objects*. Aldershot: Ashgate, 131–146.

Foucault, Michel. 1997. Subjectivity and Truth. In Paul Rabinow, ed., *Michel Foucault. The Essential Works 1. Ethics*. London: Penguin Books, 93–106.

Fraser, Nancy. 1997. From Redistribution to Recognition? Dilemmas of Justice in a "Postsocialist" Age. In Nancy Fraser, *Justice Interruptus. Critical Reflections on the "Postsocialist" Condition*. New York: Routledge, 11–40.

Freud, Sigmund. 1975. *Schriften zur Behandlungstechnik. Sigmund Freud Studienausgabe, Egänzungsband*. Frankfurt am Main: Fischer Verlag.

Funder, David C. 2001. Personality. *Annual Review of Psychology* 52:197–221.

Gardner, Michael E. 2000. *Critiques of Everyday Life*. London: Routledge.

Garey, Ann. 1999. *Weaving Work and Motherhood*. Philadelphia: Temple University Press.

Gergen, Kenneth J. 1995. Singular, Socialized and Relational Selves. In Ian Lubek et al., eds., *Trends and Issues in Theoretical Psychology*. New York: Springer, 25–32.

Gergen, Kenneth J. 1997. Theory under Threat: Social Construction and Identity Politics. In Charles Tolman, Fran Cherry, Ian Lubek, and Rene van Hezewijk, eds., *Recent Trends in Theoretical Psychology*. York: Captus Press, 13–23.

Giddens, Anthony. 1991. *Modernity and Self-Identity: Self and Society in the Late Modern Age*. Stanford, CA: Stanford University Press.

Gordon, Colin 1980. Afterword. In Colin Gordon, ed., *Michel Foucault: Power/Knowledge*. Brighton: Harvester, 229–259.

Greenberg, Leslie. 1999. Ideal Psychotherapy Research: A Study of Significant Change Processes. *Journal of Clinical Psychology* 55:1467–1480.

Griffiths, Morwenna. 1995. *Feminisms and the Self: The Web of Identity*. London: Routledge.

Haavind, Hanne. 1999. På jakt etter kjønnede betydninger. In Hanne Haavind, red., *Kjønn og fortolkende metode. Metodiske muligheter i kvalitativ forskning*. Oslo: Gyldendal Norsk Forlag, 7–59.

Haavind, Hanne. 2002. Contesting and Recognizing Historical Changes and Selves in Development. Unpublished manuscript. Department of Psychology, University of Oslo.

Habermas, Jürgen. 1987. *The Theory of Communicative Action, Vol. 2: System and Lifeworld*. Cambridge: Polity Press.

Haisch, Jochen, and I. Haisch. 1988. Zur Effektivitätssteigerung verhaltenstherapeutischer Gewichtreduktions-Programme durch sozialpsychologisches Wissen: Entwicklung und Prüfung attributionstheoretischer Maßnahmen bei Übergewichtigen. *Zeitschrift für Sozialpsychologie* 19:275–286.

Hanks, William F. 1996. *Language and Communicative Practices*. Boulder, CO: Westview Press.

Harper, David J. 1996. Deconstructing 'Paranoia': Towards a Discursive Understanding of Apparently Unwarranted Suspicion. *Theory & Psychology* 6:423–448.

Harré, Rom. 1997. *The Singular Self: Introduction into the Psychology of Personhood*. London: Sage.

Harré, Rom, and Grant Gillett. 1997. *The Discursive Mind*. London: Sage.

Haug, Frigga. 1976. *Erziehung und gesellschaftliche Produktion: Kritik des Rollenspiels*. Frankfurt am Main: Campus Verlag.

Haug, Frigga. 1981. Dialektisk teori og empirisk metodik. *Udkast* 9:8–26.

Hogg, Christine. 1999. *Patients, Power & Politics: From Patients to Citizens*. London: Sage.

Højholt, Charlotte. 1993. *Brugerperspektiver: forældres, læreres og psykologers erfaringer med psykosocialt arbejde*. København: Dansk psykologisk Forlag.

Højholt, Charlotte. 1999. Child Development in Trajectories of Social Practice. In Wolfgang Maiers, Betty Bayer, Barbara Duarte Esgalhado, René Jorna, and Ernst Schraube, eds., *Challenges to Theoretical Psychology*. York: Captus Press, 278–285.

Højholt, Charlotte. 2000. Børns udvikling og deltagelse: en teoretisk udfordring. *Nordiske Udkast* 28:43–59.

Højholt, Charlotte. 2001. *Samarbejde i børns udvikling. Deltagere i social praksis*. København: Gyldendals Forlag.

Holland, Dorothy, and Jean Lave. 2000. History in Person: An Introduction. In Dorothy Holland and Jean Lave, eds., *History in Person: Enduring Struggles, Contentious Practice, Intimate Identities*. Santa Fe: School of American Research Press, 3–33.

Holland, Dorothy, William Lachicotte Jr., Debra Skinner, and Carole Cain. 1998. *Identity and Agency in Cultural Worlds*. Cambridge, MA: Harvard University Press.

Holzkamp, Klaus. 1977. Kann es im Rahmen der marxistischen Theorie eine kritische Psychologie geben? In Karl-Heinz Braun and Klaus Holzkamp, Hrsg., *Kritische Psychologie*, Bd. 1. Köln: Pahl-Rugenstein Verlag, 46–74. Reprinted in: Klaus Holzkamp. 1978. *Gesellschaftlichkeit des Individuums. Aufsätze 1974–1977*. Köln: Pahl-Rugenstein Verlag, 202–230.

Holzkamp, Klaus. 1983. *Grundlegung der Psychologie*. Frankfurt am Main: Campus Verlag.

Holzkamp, Klaus. 1985. "Persönlichkeit" – Zur Funktionskritik eines Begriffs. In T. Hermann and E.-D. Lantermann, Hrsg., *Persönlichkeitspsychologie: Ein Handbuch in Schlüsselbegriffen*. München: Urban & Schwarzenberg, 92–101. Reprinted in: *Forum Kritische Psychologie* 22, 1988, 123–132.

Holzkamp, Klaus. 1987. Die Verkennung von Handlungsbegründungen als empirische Zusammenhangsannahmen in sozialpsychologischen Theorien: Methodologische

Fehlorientierung infolge von Begriffsverwirrung. *Forum Kritische Psychologie* 19:23–58.

Holzkamp, Klaus. 1988. Praxis: Funktionskritik eines Begriffs. In Joseph Dehler and Konstanze Wetzel, Hrsg., *Zum Verhältnis von Theorie und Praxis in der Psychologie*. Marburg: VA&G, 15–48.

Holzkamp, Klaus. 1993. *Lernen. Subjektwissenschaftliche Grundlegung*. Frankfurt am Main: Campus Verlag.

Holzkamp, Klaus. 1994. Am Problem vorbei. Zusammenhangsblindheit der Variablenpsychologie. *Forum Kritische Psychologie* 28:5–19.

Holzkamp, Klaus. 1995. Alltägliche Lebensführung als subjektwissenschaftliches Grundkonzept. *Das Argument* 37:817–846. Danish translation: Daglig livsførelse som subjektvidenskabeligt grundkoncept. *Nordiske Udkast* 1998 26:3–31.

Holzkamp, Klaus. 1996. Manuskripte zum Arbeitsprojekt 'Lebensführung.' *Forum Kritische Psychologie* 36:7–112.

Hook, Derek. 2003. Analogues of Power: Reading Psychotherapy through the Sovereignty-Discipline-Government Complex. *Theory & Psychology* 13:605–628.

Hougaard, Esben. 1996. Psykoterapeutisk procesforskning. In: *Individualism and Commitment in American Life*. Berkeley: University of California Press.

Hougaard, Esben. 2004. *Psykoterapi: Teori og forskning*. 2. udgave. København: Dansk Psykologisk Forlag.

Howe, David. 1990. *The Consumers' View of Family Therapy*. Aldershot: Gover Publishing Co.

Howe, David. 1993. *On Being a Client: Understanding the Process of Counseling and Psychotherapy*. London: Sage.

Hubble, Mark A., Barry L. Duncan, and Scott D. Miller, eds. 1999. *The Heart and Soul of Change: What Works in Therapy?* Washington, DC: American Psychological Association.

Huniche, Lotte. 2002. "Huntington's Disease in Everyday Life." PhD dissertation, Department of Psychology, University of Copenhagen.

Huniche, Lotte. 2003. Learning from the Voiceless. *New Genetics and Society* 22:257–269

Hutchins, Ed. 1993. Learning to Navigate. In Seth Chaiklin and Jean Lave, eds., *Understanding Practice: Perspectives on Activity in Context*. Cambridge: Cambridge University Press, 35–63.

Hutchins, Ed. 1995. *Cognition in the Wild*. Cambridge, MA: MIT Press.

Jefferson, Andrew M. 2004. Confronted by Practice: Towards a Critical Psychology of Prison Practice in Nigeria. PhD thesis, Department of Psychology, University of Copenhagen.

Jensen, Uffe Juul. 1987. *Practice and Progress: A Theory for the Modern Health-care System*. London: Blackwell.

Jurczyk, Karin, and Maria S. Rerrich. 1993. Einführung. Alltägliche Lebensführung: der Ort wo 'alles zusammenkommt.' In Karin Jurczyk and Maria S. Rerrich, Hrsg., *Die Arbeit des Alltags: Beiträge zu einer Soziologie der alltäglichen Lebensführung*. Freiburg: Lambertus Verlag, 11–45.

Klein, David M., and James M. White. 1996. *Family Theories: An Introduction*. London: Sage.

Kleinman, Arthur. 1988. *The Illness Narratives Benson, Ciarán. 2001. The Cultural Psychology of Self: Place, Morality and Art in Human Worlds*. London: Routledge.

Kvale, Steinar. 1996. *InterViews. An Introduction to Qualitative Research Interviewing.* London: Sage.

Lambert, Michael, J. 1992. Psychotherapy Outcome Reserch: Implications for Integrative and Eclectic Therapists. In J. C. Norcross and M. R. Goldfried, eds., *Handbook of Psychotherapy Integration.* New York: Basic Books, 94–129.

Lamiell, James T. 2003. *Beyond Individual and Group Differences: Human Individuality, Scientific Psychology, and William Stern's Critical Personalism.* London: Sage.

Langan, Celeste. 2001. Mobility Disability. In Carol A. Breckenridge and Candice Vogler, eds., The Critical Limits of Embodiment: Reflections on Disability Criticism. *Public Culture 13*, 35:459–484.

Lave, Jean. 1988. *Cognition in Practice: Mind, Mathematics and Culture in Everyday Life.* New York: Cambridge University Press.

Lave, Jean. 1992. Word Problems. In P. Light and G. Butterworth, eds., *Context and Cognition: Ways of Learning and Knowing.* New York: Harvester/Wheatsheaf.

Lave, Jean. 1993. The Practice of Learning. In Seth Chaiklin and Jean Lave, eds., *Understanding Practice: Perspectives in Activity and Context.* New York: Cambridge University Press, 3–32.

Lave, Jean. 1996. Teaching as Learning in Practice. *Mind, Culture, and Activity* 3:149–164.

Lave, Jean. 1997. On Learning. *Forum Kritische Psychologie* 38:120–135.

Lave, Jean. Unpublished manuscript. Changing Practice. Social and Cultural Studies in Education. Graduate School of Education. University of California at Berkeley.

Lave, Jean, and Etienne Wenger. 1991. *Situated Learning: Legitimate Peripheral Participation.* Cambridge: Cambridge University Press.

Lee, Benjamin, and Dilip P. Gaonkar, eds. 2002. New Imaginaries. *Public Culture 14*, 1.

Lenin, Vladimir, Iljitch. 1971. *Gesammelte Werke. Band 38.* Berlin: Dietz Verlag.

Leont'ev, Aleksej Nikolajev. 1978. The Problem of Activity in Psychology. In A. N. Leont'ev, ed., *Activity, Consciousness and Personality.* Englewood Cliffs, NJ: Prentice Hall.

Leont'ev, Aleksej Nikolajev. 1979. *Problems of the Development of the Mind.* Moscow: Progress Publishers.

Lewis, Dan A., Stephanie Riger, Helen Rosenberg, Hendrik Wagenaar, Arthur J. Lurigio, and Susan Reed. 1991. *Worlds of the Mentally Ill: How Deinstitutionalization Works in the City.* Carbondale and Edwardsville: Southern Illinois University Press.

Liggett, Helen, and David C. Perry. 1995. Spatial Practices: An Introduction. In Helen Liggett and David C. Perry, eds. *Spatial Practices.* London: Sage, 1–12.

Maiers, Wolfgang. 1996. Historicity of the Subject: Subjectivity of Life History. In Charles Tolman, Fran Cherry, René van Hezewijk and Ian Lubek, eds., *Problems of Theoretical Psychology.* York: Captus Press, 62–72.

Maluccio, Anthony N. 1979. *Learning from Clients: Interpersonal Helping as Viewed by Clients and Social Workers.* London: Free Press.

Mammen, Jens. 1983. *Den menneskelige sans: Et essay om psykologiens genstandsområde.* København: Dansk psykologisk Forlag.

Mangini, Michele. 2000. Character and Well-being. *Philosophy and Social Criticism* 26:79–98.

Markard, Morus. 1991. *Methodik subjektwissenschaftlicher Forschung. Jenseits des Streits um quantitative und qualitative Methoden.* Berlin: Argument Verlag.

Markard, Morus, and Klaus Holzkamp. 1989. Praxis-Portrait. *Forum Kritische Psychologie* 23:5–49.

Marx, Karl. 1995. *The Eighteenth Brumaire of Louis Napoleon*. Marx/Engels Internet Archive.

Mattingly, Cheryl. 1998. *Healing Dramas and Clinical Plots*. New York: Cambridge University Press.

McAdams, Dan P. 1996. Personality, Modernity and the Storied Self: A Contemporary Framework for Studying Persons. *Psychological Inquiry* 7:295–321.

McLeod, John. 1990. The Client's Experience of Counseling and Psychotherapy: A Review of the Research Literature. In D. Mearns and W. Dryden, eds., *Experiences of Counseling in Action*. London: Sage, 1–19.

McLeod, John. 1997. *Narrative and Psychotherapy*. London: Sage.

Medina, José. 2003. Identity trouble: Disidentification and the Problem of Difference. *Philosophy & Social Criticism* 29:657–682.

Mehan, Hugh. 1984. Institutional Decision-making. In Barbara Rogoff and Jean Lave, eds., *Everyday Cognition: Its Development in Social Context*. Cambridge, MA: Harvard University Press, 41–66.

Mehan, Hugh. 1993. The Construction of an LD Student: A Case Study in the Politics of Representation. In Seth Chaiklin and Jean Lave, eds., *Understanding Practice. Perspectives in Activity and Context*. Cambridge: Cambridge University Press, 241–268.

Middleton, David. 2003. *History Matters*. The Faculty of Humanities Lecture. The University of Copenhagen, March 28, 2003.

Miller, Peter, and Nikolas Rose. 1994. On Therapeutic Authority. *History of the Human Sciences* 7:29–64.

Miller, Scott D., Barry L. Duncan, and Mark A. Hubble. 1997. *Escape from Babel: Toward a Unifying Language for Psychotherapy Practice*. New York: W. W. Norton & Co.

Minz, Gabi. 1984. Opdragede som opdragere: Om venstrefløjens særlige interesse for Alice Miller. *Udkast* 12:239–258.

Mischel, Walter, and Yuichi Shoda. 1999. Integrating Dispositions and Processing Dynamics within a Unified Theory of Personality. In Lawrence A. Pervin and Oliver P. John, eds., *Handbook of Personality: Theory and Research, Second Edition*. New York: The Guilford Press, 197–218.

Moen, Phyllis and Mary A. Erickson. 1995. Linked Lives: A Transgenerational Approach to Resilience. In Phyllis Moen, Glen H. Elder, and Kurt Lüscher, eds., *Examining Lives in Context: Perspectives on the Ecology of Human Development*. Washington, DC: American Psychological Association, 169–210.

Mørck, Line Lerche. 2006. *Grænsefællesskaber: Læring og overskridelses af marginalisering*. Frederiksberg: Roskilde Universitetsforlag.

Neufeldt, Victoria, and David B. Guralnik, eds. 1997. *Webster's New World College Dictionary, Third Edition*. New York: Macmillan.

Nissen, Morten. 1994. Brugerindflydelse og handlesammenhænge i psykosocialt arbejde. PhD thesis, Department of Psychology, University of Copenhagen.

Osterkamp, Ute. 1975. *Grundlagen der psychologischen Motivationsforschung 1*. Frankfurt am Main: Campus Verlag.

Osterkamp, Ute. 1976. *Grundlagen der psychologischen Motivationsforschung 2: Die Besonderheit menschlicher Bedürfnisse – Problematik und Erkenntnisgehalt der Psychoanalyse*. Frankfurt am Main: Campus Verlag.

Osterkamp, Ute. 1991. Emotion, Cognition and Action Potence. In Charles Tolman and Wolfgang Maiers, eds., *Critical Psychology: Contributions to an Historical Science of the Subject*. Cambridge: Cambridge University Press, 102–133.

Osterkamp, Ute. 2000. Lebensführung als subjektwissenschaftliche Problematik. *Forum Kritische Psychologie* 43:4–35. Danish translation: Livsførelse som subjektv-idenskabeligt grundproblem. *Nordiske Udkast* 28:5–28.

Osterkamp, Ute. 2003. On the political dimension of 'private' behaviour and the subjective dimension of political actions. *European Journal of Psychotherapy, Counselling & Health* 6:67–70.

Papadopoulos, Renos K., and John Byng-Hall, eds. 1997. *Multiple Voices: Narrative in Systemic Family Psychotherapy*. Tavistock Clinic Series. London: Duckworth.

Polkinghorne, Donald. E. 1988. *Narrative Knowing and the Human Sciences*. Albany: New York State University Press.

Potter, John, and Margaret Wetherell. 1992. *Discursive Psychology*. London: Sage.

Prior, Lindsay. 1993. *The Social Organization of Mental Illness*. London: Sage.

Quackenbush, Steven. 2001. Trait Stability as a Noncontingent Truth: A Pre-empirical Critique of McCrae and Costa's Stability Thesis. *Theory & Psychology* 11:818–836.

Reimers, Sigurd, and Andy Treacher. 1995. *Introducing User-friendly Family Therapy*. London: Routledge.

Rennie, David L. 1990. Toward a Representation of the Client's Experience of the Psychotherapy Hour. In G. Lietaer, J. Rombauts, and R. van Balen, eds., *Client-Centered and Experiential Therapy in the Nineties*. Leuven, Belgium: Leuven University Press, 155–172.

Rennie, David L. 1994a. Clients' Deference in Psychotherapy. *Journal of Counseling Psychology* 41:427–437.

Rennie, David L. 1994b. Storytelling in Psychotherapy: The Client's Subjective Experience. *Psychotherapy* 31:234–243.

Reuterlov, Hakan, Torbjorn Lofgren, Karin Nordstrom, Ann Ternstrom, and Scott D. Miller. 2000. What Is Better? A Preliminary Investigation of Between-Session Change. *Journal of Systemic Therapies* 19:115–119.

Ricoeur, Paul 1992. *Oneself as Another*. Chicago: University of Chicago Press.

Roberson, Mildred. H. B. 1992. The Meaning of Compliance: Patient Perspectives. *Qualitative Health Research* 2:7–26.

Rogers, Tim B. 2003. Applying Spatial Critique to Theory in Psychology: Toward a Useful Third Space. In Niamh Stephenson, Lorraine II. Radtke, René J. Jorna, and Henderikus J. Stam, eds., *Theoretical Psychology: Critical Contributions*. Concord, Canada: Captus University Publications, 105–114.

Rose, Nikolas. 1996a. Psychiatry as a Political Science: Advanced Liberalism and the Administration of Risk. *History of the Human Sciences* 9:2–23.

Rose, Nikolas. 1996b. *Inventing Our Selves: Psychology, Power, and Personhood*. Cambridge: Cambridge University Press.

Rowan, John, and Mick Cooper. (Eds.). *The Plural Self: Multiplicity in Everyday Life*. London: Sage.

Sands, Anna. 2000. *Falling for Therapy: Psychotherapy from a Client's Point of View*. London: Macmillan Press.

Schatzki, Theodore R. 1996. *Social Practices: A Wittgensteinian Approach to Human Activity and the Social*. Cambridge: Cambridge University Press.

Schatzki, Theodore R. 2001. Practice Mind-ed Orders. In Th. R. Schatzki, K. Knorr Cetina, and E. V. Savigni, eds., *The Practice Turn in Contemporary Theory*. New York: Routledge, 42–56.

Schatzki, Theodore R. 2002. *The Site of the Social: A Philosophical Account of the Constitution of Social Life and Change*. University Park: Pennsylvania State University Press.

Schön, Donald. A. 1983. *The Reflective Practitioner: How Professionals Think in Action*. New York: The Free Press.

Searle, John. 1995. *The Construction of Social Reality*. New York: The Free Press.

Seidel, Rainer. 1976. *Denken. Psychologische Analyse der Entstehung und Lösung von Problemen*. Texte zur Kritischen Psychologie Bd. 6. Frankfurt am Main: Campus Verlag.

Sennett, Richard. 1998. *The Corrosion of Character: The Personal Consequences of Work in the New Capitalism*. New York: W. W. Norton & Company.

Sève, Lucien. 1972. *Marxismus und Theorie der Persönlichkeit*. Frankfurt am Main: Verlag Marxistische Blätter. Danish edition: København: Rhodos 1978.

Shoda, Yuchi, and Scott Leetiernan. 2002. What Remains Invariant: Finding Order within a Person's Thoughts, Feelings and Behaviors across Situations. In Daniel Cervone and Walter Mischel, eds., *Advances in Personality Science*. New York: Guilford Press, 241–270.

Shotter, John. 1997. Wittgenstein in Practice: From the Way of Theory to a Social Poetics. In Charles Tolman, Fran Cherry, Ian Lubek, and René van Hezewijk, eds., *Recent Trends in Theoretical Psychology*. York: Captus Press, 3–12.

Siegfried, Jurg, ed. 1995. *Therapeutic and Everyday Discourse as Behavior Change: Towards a Micro-analysis in Psychotherapy Process Research*. Norwood, NJ: Ablex Publishing Co.

Silverman, David. 2001. *Interpreting Qualitative Data: Methods for Analysing Talk, Text and Interaction*. London: Sage.

Sloan, Tod. 1996. *Life Choices: Understanding Dilemmas and Decisions*. Boulder, CO and London: Westview Press.

Smith, Dorothy E. 1987. *The Everyday World as Problematic*. Boston: Northeastern University Press.

Smith, Dorothy E. 1990. *The Conceptual Practices of Power: A Feminist Sociology of Knowledge*. Toronto: University of Toronto Press.

Smith, Dorothy E. 2005. *Institutional Ethnography: A Sociology for People*. Lanham, MA: AltaMira Press.

Smith, John L. 2000. *The Psychology of Action*. London: Macmillan Press.

Sørensen, Estrid. 2005. *STS Goes to School: Spatial Imaginaries of Technology, Knowledge and Presence*. PhD Thesis, Department of Psychology, University of Copenhagen.

Stack, Carol. 1999. *Call to Home*. New York: The Free Press.

Strauss, Anselm L. 1993. *Continual Permutations of Action*. New York: Aldine de Gruyter.

Strauss, Anselm, and Juliet Corbin. 1988. *Shaping a New Health Care System*. San Francisco: Jossey Bass.

Sveen, Karen. 2000. *Klassereise: Et livshistorisk essay*. Oslo: Forlaget Oktober.

Tallman, Karen, and Arthur C. Bohart. 1999. The Client as a Common Factor: Clients as Self-Healers. In Mark A. Hubble, Barry Duncan, and Scott C. Miller, eds., *The Heart and Soul of Change: What Works in Therapy?* Washington, DC: American Psychological Association, 91–131.

Taylor, Charles. 1985a. The Concept of the Person. In Michael Carrithers, Steven Collins, and Steven Lukes, eds., *The Category of the Person: Anthropology, Philosophy, History*. Cambridge: Cambridge University Press, 257–281. Reprinted in Charles Taylor. 1985. *Human Agency and Language: Philosophical Papers 1*. Cambridge: Cambridge University Press, 97–114.

Taylor, Charles. 1985b. *Sources of the Self: The Origins of Modern Identity*. Cambridge: Cambridge University Press.

Taylor, Charles. 1991. *The Ethics of Authenticity*. Cambridge, MA: Harvard University Press.

Taylor, Charles. 1995a. To Follow a Rule. In Charles Taylor, *Philosophical Arguments*. Cambridge, MA: Harvard University Press, 165–180.

Taylor, Charles 1995b. Irreducibly Social Goods. In Charles Taylor, *Philosophical Arguments*. Cambridge, MA: Harvard University Press, 127–145.

Tolman, Charles. 1994. *Psychology, Society, and Subjectivity: An Introduction to German Critical Psychology*. London: Routledge.

Tolman, Charles, and Wolfgang Maiers, eds. 1991. *Critical Psychology: Towards an Historical Science of the Subject*. Cambridge: Cambridge University Press.

Tompkins, Michael A. 2004. *Using Homework in Psychotherapy: Strategies, Guidelines, and Forms*. New York: The Guilford Press.

Toulmin, Stephen. 1996. Concluding Methodological Reflections: Elitism, and Democracy among the Sciences. In Stephen Toulmin and Björn Gustafsen, eds., *Beyond Theory: Changing Organizations through Participation*. Amsterdam: John Benjamins Publishing Co., 203–225.

Urry, John. 2000. *Sociology beyond Societies: Mobilities for the Twenty-First Century*. London: Routledge.

Valsiner, Jaan. 1984. Two Alternative Epistemological Frameworks in Psychology: The Typological and Variational Modes of Thinking. *The Journal of Mind and Behavior* 5:449–470.

Valverde, Mariana 2002. Experience and Truth Telling: Intoxicated Autobiography and Ethical Subjectivity. *Outlines* 4:3–18.

Wallerstein, Robert S. 1986. *Forty-Two Lives in Treatment: A Study of Psychoanalysis and Psychotherapy*. New York: The Guilford Press.

Wallin, Annika. 2003. Explaining everyday problem solving. PhD Dissertation. Lund University Cognitive Studies.

Weber, Max. 1952. *The Protestant Ethic and the Spirit of Capitalism*. New York: Scribner.

Wittgenstein, Ludwig. 1953. *Philosophical Investigations, Third Edition*. New York: Macmillan.

Wortham, Stanton. 2006. *Learning Identity: The Joint Emergence of Social Identification and Academic Learning*. Cambridge: Cambridge University Press.

Yalom, Irwin I., and Ginny Elkin. 1974. *Every Day Gets a Little Closer: A Twice Told Therapy*. New York: Basic Books.

Author Index

Abbott, Andrew, 24, 25, 131, 271, 273, 284,
  285, 296, 297
Alcoff, Linda, 77, 288
Aldous, Joan, 264, 271
Andenæs, Agnes, 297, 307
Asay, Ted, 14

Bandura, Albert, 133, 136, 188
Barham, Peter, 9, 19
Barlösius, Eva, 189
Behringer, Louise, 188
Bellah, Robert, 203
Bennett, Michael, 93
Benson, Ciarán, 29, 188, 303
Bergin, Allen, 11, 79
Bohart, Arthur, 4, 10, 12, 15, 17, 18, 19, 95
Bourdieu, Pierre, 107
Breckenridge, Carol, 33
Bruner, Jerome, 29, 260, 285, 303

Calhoun, Craig, 22, 40, 44, 104, 108, 296,
  301
Cherry, Fran, 297
Christensen, Lone, 237, 255
Crossley, Nick, 22, 98
Curtis, Rebecca, 15

Daly, Kerry, 257
de Léon, David, 25
DeVries, Marten, 18
Donovan, Jenny, 14
Dreier, Ole, 6, 7, 11, 12, 15, 23, 29, 36, 38, 39,
  42, 44, 83, 110, 134, 185, 230, 305, 313
Duffy, Ann, 237

Eckert, Penny, 45, 213
Elder, Glen, 191, 192, 237, 273, 295
Eliasson, Rosemari, 10, 13
Engeström, Yrjö, 131
Erikson, Erik, 271
Estroff, Sue, 20

Fleeson, William, 188
Foucault, Michel, 58
Fraser, Nancy, 124
Freud, Sigmund, 14
Funder, David, 16

Gardner, Michael, 26
Garey, Ann, 101, 227, 232, 236, 237, 240,
  283
Gergen, Kenneth, 31
Giddens, Anthony, 27, 38, 185, 195, 196,
  295
Gordon, Colin, 4
Greenberg, Leslie, 6, 9
Griffiths, Morwenna, 40, 197

Haavind, Hanne, 263, 297
Habermas, Jürgen, 23
Haisch, Jochen, 136
Hanks, William, 107
Harper, David, 76
Harré, Rom, 29, 33, 76, 297, 298
Haug, Frigga, 19, 307
Hogg, Christine, 11, 14
Højholt, Charlotte, 53, 155, 195, 256
Holland, Dorothy, 24, 25, 260
Holzkamp, Klaus, 22, 23, 25, 28, 30, 34, 105,
  106, 133, 149, 182, 185, 201, 291, 294, 306,
  311
Hook, Derek, 28, 58
Hougaard, Esben, 3, 6, 7
Howe, David, 9, 11
Hubble, Mark, 18
Hutchins, Ed, 132

Jensen, Uffe, 4, 64, 175
Jurczyk, Karin, 182

Klein, David, 271
Kleinman, Arthur, 9, 174, 175
Kvale, Steinar, 49, 297

327

Subject Index

The Learning in Doing series was founded in 1987 by Roy Pea and John Seely Brown.